The New Political Islam

THE NEW POLITICAL ISLAM

HUMAN RIGHTS, DEMOCRACY, AND JUSTICE

Emmanuel Karagiannis

PENN

University of Pennsylvania Press
Philadelphia

A volume in the Haney Foundation Series, established in 1961 with the generous support of Dr. John Louis Haney.

Published by
University of Pennsylvania Press
Philadelphia, Pennsylvania 19104-4112
www.upenn.edu/pennpress

Printed in the United States of America
on acid-free paper
10 9 8 7 6 5 4 3 2 1

Library of Congress Cataloging-in-Publication Data

Names: Karagiannis, Emmanuel, author.
Title: The new political Islam : human rights, democracy, and justice / Emmanuel Karagiannis.
Other titles: Haney Foundation series.
Description: 1st edition. | Philadelphia : University of Pennsylvania Press, [2018] | Series: Haney Foundation series | Includes bibliographical references and index.
Identifiers: LCCN 2017036430 | ISBN 978-0-8122-4972-9 (hardcover : alk. paper)
Subjects: LCSH: Islam and politics—History—21st century. | Muslim converts—Political activity—Europe. | Muslims—Political activity—Europe. | Sunnities—Political activity—Middle East. | Shiites—Political activity—Middle East. | Islamic fundamentalism—21st century. | Human rights advocacy—Religious aspects—Islam. | Democracy—Religious aspects—Islam. | Justice—Religious aspects—Islam. | Terrorism—Religious aspects—Islam.
Classification: LCC BP173.7.K3655 2017 | DDC 320.55/7—dc23.
LC record available at https://lccn.loc.gov/2017036430

*In memory of Alexandros Petersen
and Konstandinos Erik Scurfield*

Contents

Preface

The rise of political Islam has attracted great public, government, and academic attention in the West. It is fair to say that Islamism has been largely viewed by many with dismay and fear due to its perceived anachronistic and totalitarian nature. In an era of globalization, the blurring of politics and religion seems antimodern and irrational. In 2012, Farhad Khosrokhavar, a prominent scholar of the Islamic world, observed confidently that "the age of Islamism is over, not as an ideology or a credo among minority groups, but as a motto that could convince the people of its feasibility."[1] Yet Islamism in its various forms has reached almost every Muslim community in the world and Islamist groups are still on the march.

The term *political Islam* in itself is contested by both academics and Islamists. Some critics say that it is a redundant term because the distinction between political and nonpolitical domains of social life is not relevant anymore; the modern state has significantly expanded its functions to influence every aspect of organized life.[2] For many Islamists, the term is problematic because Islam is inherently political; thus *din* (religion) and *dawla* (state) depend on each other. But such views tend to ignore the diversity that exists within the Muslim faith. In particular, Sufism and its mystical beliefs constitute an important part of Islam that is often despised by those who favor the politicization of the faith.[3] This is not to say that Sufism is apolitical; actually, Sufi orders have been involved indirectly in politics (e.g., the Gülen movement in Turkey). Sufism is rather nonpolitical in the sense of avoiding political interpretations of Islamic concepts, rituals, and practices.[4]

Therefore, it is essential to distinguish ontologically the religion from its political expression. So what is political Islam and what is Islamism? The two terms are often treated as synonymous. Nazih Ayobi defines political Islam as "the doctrine and/or movement which contends that Islam possesses a theory of politics and the state."[5] Guilain Denoeux describes political Islam or Islamism as "a form of instrumentalization of Islam by individuals, groups and organizations that pursue political objectives."[6] Finally, Frederic Volpi argues that Islamism "refers to the political dynamics generated by the activities of those people who believe that Islam as a body of faith has something crucial to say about how society should be organized."[7]

This book will maintain the use of the term *political Islam* to describe *a global social movement that seeks to mobilize Muslims into activities that have political ramifications.* It is a diverse and nonhierarchical collectivity of different actors who share some ideas and perceptions. Accordingly, Islamism refers to *the ideology and practices of parties, groups, and prominent individuals that claim that Islam must regulate every aspect of public and private life.* It is a fluid and unsystematic set of beliefs and practices that is open to change and adaptation in accordance with local conditions. Due to its broad character, "Islamism should not be linked exclusively with political violence and militancy."[8]

Political Islam has expanded on all continents, but its internationalization is politically and culturally localized.[9] It is a movement of movements that revolve around the interplay between the global and the local. The interconnectivity of societies has contributed to the spread of Islamism but at a great cost: different versions of this ideology have emerged based on specificities.

In today's world, however, it is necessary to move beyond the global-local dichotomy because there is growing overlap between them. Paul Lubeck has observed that "the new global infrastructure integrates the disparate members of the global *umma* by encouraging Muslims to communicate, study, travel to fulfill the diverse Muslim obligations."[10] The umma now consists of Muslim communities that interpret political and social realities in their own distinct ways. In this context, Islamist parties and groups have adopted universal political and social norms bypassing the nation-state. Political Islam is the embodiment of a synthesis between global ideas and local applications. Indeed, it is a social movement that must be studied from a new angle.

Political Islam's Manifestations of Glocalization

Islam is projected to be the religion of one-third of the world's population by 2050, reaching parity with Christianity around 2070.[11] The content of

Islam is determined by the relationship between universality and particularity. It is a religion of 1.7 billion people worldwide and professes a single message about submitting to God and worshipping him alone. Yet it is practiced differently in many countries and communities. In fact, Islam is divided both horizontally and vertically. The Sunni-Shia divide has raged since the death of Prophet Muhammad in 632, generating dissimilar theological beliefs, rituals, and traditions. In addition, each of the two denominations contains schools of jurisprudence (*madhahib*) that offer different methodologies of setting Islamic rules and regulations.[12] Ethnic and cultural elements have also significantly diversified the Muslim faith. It has been suggested that one of the reasons why Islam has come to be a global religion is its ability to become local.[13] Many scholars have recorded how Islamic tenets have been blended with native practices and customs. As a result, there is an Ethiopian Islam, a Kazakh Islam, a Thai Islam, and so on.[14] To put it simply, Islam is as highly varied as any major religion.

Similarly, political expressions of the Muslim faith are vastly divergent because they accommodate local circumstances. Islamist parties and groups have utilized a variety of political methods to achieve their aims, ranging from engaging in peaceful activism to participating in the electoral process to using violence and coercion. Political Islam does not exist as a single and homogeneous movement because it constantly incorporates new political realities, different identities, and dynamic cultural influences. Although its extraordinary dynamism is connected to the globalization processes, political Islam has become more fragmented in recent years.

This glocalization of political Islam and, subsequently, of Islamism has accelerated during the post-9/11 era for a variety of reasons that I discuss later. The term *glocalization* was put forward during the 1990s by Ronald Robertson to describe the relationship between the global and the local. I return to the history of the term in the Introduction. The book attempts to link the concept of glocalization with the framing theory that derives from the social movement paradigm. Islamists of different varieties have consciously syncretized religion, culture, and politics by using certain schemata of interpretation. The book's central claim is that *there is a new political Islam consisting of activists, politicians, and militants who have acted as glocalizers by transferring global ideas and norms to local Muslim communities.* This categorization of Islamists is based on their preferred method of engagement with Muslim communities. It does not necessarily describe the ideological content of their action, which can be anything from reformism to fundamentalism.

To begin with, Islamist activists have increasingly used human rights language to question the socioeconomic and political status of Muslims living in the West and elsewhere. More specifically, they have employed the master frame of human rights to explain and criticize the marginalization and targeting of fellow Muslims. Religious freedom and respect for Islam are themes that have been at the core of Islamist activism. Simultaneously, some of them advocate the establishment of an Islamic state as the ultimate defender of Muslim rights. With the use of this master frame, they can gain ethical legitimacy over their opponents and undertake a moral obligation to help fellow Muslims.

For instance, Hizb ut-Tahrir, an international Islamist group with neo-caliphate aspirations, has often used the language of human rights to criticize Western governments for their policies vis-à-vis Muslim communities. In September 2013, the group accused Belgian authorities of violating the Universal Declaration of Human Rights and the Declaration of Principles on Tolerance because they launched an antiradicalization initiative. It supported the view that "Muslims . . . are not entitled to the rights of thought and expression to maintain their cultural identity and uniqueness, as well as their difference in behavior and appearance as regarded obligatory for them in their religion."[15] The use of this master frame could allow Hizb ut-Tahrir to become more mainstream and acceptable to Muslims and non-Muslims alike.

While every situation is unique, the human rights master frame can bridge and connect Muslims in different locales and communities because concerns over rights and freedoms are a source of social stress and political upheaval. Therefore, it has been observed that the need to respect individual rights and civil liberties has featured highly on Islamist agendas.[16] The instrumentalization of human rights by Islamist activists is a development that indicates the exposure of political Islam to broader ideational frameworks. Islamist activists function as agents of glocalization since they seek to apply a human rights framework to local contexts.

In addition, the universal idea of democracy can be found, perhaps unexpectedly, in many Islamist discourses. It is true that the standard view of many Islamists is that the parliament is not supposed to legislate like the Sharia; this is a privilege left to God. Nevertheless, Islamist parties and organizations have accepted elections as the only method of coming to power in their countries. As a consequence, there are Islamists who have embraced the master frame of democracy, which emphasizes political equality and majority rule, while offering to them important political legitimacy.

In Egypt, for example, the overthrow of President Hosni Mubarak led to the first democratic election in the history of the country. Despite its long history of clandestine existence, the Muslim Brotherhood-affiliated Freedom and Justice Party formed a government in 2012, supporting political reforms in Egypt. After the outbreak of protests against President Mohamed Morsi, the Freedom and Justice Party declared its intention to "safeguard ballot-box legitimacy, defend the principles of democratic process, and affirm that the people's choice for president and MPs are red lines."[17] Following the military coup of July 3, 2013, the Brotherhood stated that "the restoration of the democratic process certainly means respecting the will of the Egyptian people as expressed in all the elections which the whole world affirmed were free and fair."[18] The arrested president of Egypt, Mohamed Morsi, was even portrayed as "an icon for democracy."[19] Hence one of the world's most important Islamist organizations borrowed and utilized the global idea of democracy during different phases of its engagement in Egyptian politics.

The political participation of Islamist parties has given rise to a new form of Islamism, the Islamo-democracy, which employs Islam as a force of democratization. It does not deny the importance of particular political and cultural elements and traditions. In fact, it aims at combining communal realities with Islamic tenets and beliefs. Islamo-democracy is a new trend that has changed the nature of political competition in some Muslim-majority countries.

Finally, Sunni and Shia militants have exploited the concept of justice to deliver their belligerent messages locally. The justice master frame is a powerful cognitive schema that resonates well with different Islamic tenets and traditions. Islamist militants have tapped into certain moral and ethical principles to utilize the virtue of justice for the purpose of mobilizing support. They tend to stress equality among Muslims, although they largely follow sectarian policies. In this way, militants claim a responsibility to protect Muslim communities in order to justify actions against their opponents.

For example, Hizb'allah has built its narratives around the idea of justice. The Lebanese group has defended the view that justice can only be achieved by pursuing *muqawama* (resistance) against Israel and other countries or movements.[20] Moreover, General-Secretary Sayyed Hassan

Nasrallah holds the view that "peace based on injustice and violation of rights cannot be a true peace and will immediately collapse"; consequently, peace and stability in Lebanon or any other place in the world is conditioned on achieving justice.[21] The group has assumed a responsibility to protect those who suffer from injustice; thus, on the thirteenth anniversary of the Resistance and Liberation Day commemorating the Israeli withdrawal from South Lebanon, Nasrallah stated that "we in the Islamic resistance will continue to assume our responsibility. . . . I say to the people that trust the Resistance and bet on it: your Resistance will stay with you defending you!"[22] In other words, the group has utilized the justice master frame to achieve its goals inside and outside Lebanon.

The theme of justice can appeal to wide Muslim audiences because it has a religious base. Islam proclaims justice to be a God-given virtue and of supreme significance. Muslims must live under a just system. It is not a coincidence that both Sunni and Shia groups have relentlessly pursued justice-seeking and justice-making aspirations. In spite of their sectarian differences, Islamist militants of all sorts have declared their intention to restore justice against evildoers who persecute Muslim communities.

The book explores several case studies of individuals, groups, and parties that function as Islamist agents of glocalization. These cases represent the new political Islam that is on the rise. Each one has its own significance in size, popularity, or influence. European convert-activists have become increasingly important as (often uninvited) interlocutors between authorities and Muslim communities; Hizb ut-Tahrir has led the way in international Islamist activism due to its ability to initiate actions in different locations worldwide; Turkey's Justice and Development Party, Egypt's Muslim Brotherhood, and Tunisia's al-Nahda are mass political parties and organizations that have participated in the political system advocating the convergence of Islamic and certain democratic values; nonviolent Salafi groups, like al-Nour and the Reform Front in Egypt and Tunisia respectively, have entered the electoral process, breaking a long-standing taboo against political participation; Hizb'allah and the Mahdi Army are the two most powerful Shia militant groups in the Middle East; and finally, al-Nusra and the Islamic State of Iraq and Syria have made international media headlines for their violence and fanaticism.

Methodologically speaking, the book is largely based on a qualitative analysis of discourses deriving from statements, speeches, and interviews, as well as materials produced by Islamists. In addition, I obtained data from online videos and social media in order to understand the dynamics of the new political Islam. Finally, the book draws on the existing literature on social movements, globalization, and political Islam.

Structure of the Book

The Introduction describes the phenomenon of glocalization, which includes constant interactions between the global and the local. Given the multidimensional nature of globalization, I argue that the concept of glocalization is more suitable for describing the particularization of universal ideas, discourses, and practices. The chapter describes the transformation of political Islam into a global social movement with many local components. The glocalization of Islamism has been achieved by three types of agents: the activists, the politicians, and the militants. With the help of master frames, the new Islamists have transferred global ideas about human rights, democracy, and justice to local audiences.

Part I comprises an introduction and Chapters 1 and 2. The part introduction briefly discusses the origins of human rights and explains the content of the human rights master frame. It also describes the growing tendency of Islamist activists to utilize human rights discourses in order to promote their political goals.

Chapter 1 analyzes the activism of European converts to Islam who have attempted to promote Islamist agendas in their countries. It first describes the experience of conversion for Europeans who have embraced Islam. The chapter focuses on organizations run by converts and prominent convert-activists that have propagated a hybrid Islamism. While these Islamists have different backgrounds, orientations, and goals, they have all utilized the master frame of human rights to gain support and transmit their messages to their communities.

Chapter 2 examines Hizb ut-Tahrir, known for its international activism. The chapter first describes its ideology and strategy, then analyzes Hizb ut-Tahrir's activities in Western countries, South and Southeast Asia, the former Soviet Union and China, and the greater Middle East. Due to its global presence, the group has to take into account different political and cultural settings. Finally, the chapter assesses how Hizb ut-Tahrir has functioned as an agent of glocalization by adopting the master frame of human rights and adjusting it to local needs.

Part II consists of an introduction and Chapters 3 and 4. The part introduction describes the evolution of democracy and the content of the
democracy master frame. Then it discusses briefly the relationship between
Islam and democracy from the viewpoint of Islamic thinkers.

Chapter 3 is dedicated to Islamist parties that have entered the democratic process and come to power through elections. They have espoused a
new version of Islamism that combines pluralism with Islamic values,
namely the Islamo-democracy. The chapter focuses on three parties that
represent this political trend: Turkey's Justice and Development Party,
Egypt's Muslim Brotherhood, and Tunisia's al-Nahda. While they have different origins and perspectives, these Islamist parties have recognized
democracy as the preferred political system. I argue that they have utilized
the master frame of democracy to mobilize support and gain legitimacy.

Chapter 4 analyzes electoral Salafism in Egypt and Tunisia. Newly established Salafi parties tend to have ultraconservative views on social issues,
but they have denounced the use of violence. They have chosen to campaign through the parliaments and within the constitutions. The al-Nour
party in Egypt and the Reform Front in Tunisia have advocated the implementation of Sharia by democratic means. The chapter first describes the
characteristics of electoral Salafism in North Africa, then explains how and
why Salafis have applied the democracy master frame to their local
environment.

Part III comprises an introduction and Chapters 5 and 6. The part
introduction focuses on the concept of justice as developed by religion and
philosophy. Also, it discusses the substance of the justice master frame and
the Islamist perspective on justice.

Chapter 5 examines Shia militancy in Lebanon, Syria, and Iraq. The
chapter concentrates on Hizb'allah and the Mahdi Army, which are the two
largest groups fighting against Sunni militants in the Middle East. It examines their history, evolvement, and strategy. Both have portrayed themselves
as defenders of Shia power. I argue that their understanding of justice
derives from Shia history and theology. Finally, the chapter analyzes how
the two groups have acted as agents of glocalization by adopting the master
frame of justice.

Chapter 6 analyzes the militancy of Sunni groups in Syria and Iraq.
It describes the origins and evolvement of al-Nusra and ISIS, which have
attempted to overthrown Shia-dominated regimes in the Middle East. Both
groups are part of the Jihadi-Salafi movement. The chapter examines their

effort to establish a polity where justice will prevail; this can be achieved only with the implementation of Sharia (as they interpret it). Sunni militants have functioned as glocalizers of Islamism because they have utilized the master frame of justice to achieve their local goals.

The Conclusion briefly discusses the emerging relationship between the West and the new Islamists. It offers some thoughts as well about a more constructive approach to the rise of the new glocalized political Islam.

Note on Transliteration and Spelling

The book includes texts originally published in Arabic, French, German, Greek, and Turkish. I have tried to limit the use of diacritics and adopt the most common English spellings of Arabic names and terms. Non-English words have been italicized on first use, apart from the most commonly used terms such as Quran and Sharia. When Islamic terms are included in a quotation, I have provided the translation in brackets. I have used Maulana Muhammad Ali's English translation of the Quran[23] and Richard Netton's *A Popular Dictionary of Islam*.[24]

Introduction

I went to the West and saw Islam, but no Muslims; I got
back to the East and saw Muslims, but not Islam.

Muhammad Abduh (1849–1905)

Political Islam has often been viewed as static and monolithic. However, it
has changed significantly since the time of Ayatollah Khomeini's triumph
in Iran in the late 1970s and the mujahidin resistance in Afghanistan in the
1980s. Although political Islam first appeared in the greater Middle East, it
has now spread across the world.[1] From Europe to Southeast Asia and from
Russia to sub-Saharan Africa, Islamist parties and groups are on the rise.

This is a *new* political Islam that is global in scope and increasingly local
in action. Some Islamists favor activism, some others participate in the
democratic process, and fewer even advocate violence. The diversity of
approaches derives from different realities and orientations. They all share
the ideology of Islamism that advocates a greater public role for Islam; yet
it is not a well-defined set of ideas but rather holds very different meaning
for different groups of people.

The wide geographical spread of political Islam has challenged conventional understandings of globalization, which often privilege the global over
the local. In a context of worldwide economic and social changes, local
manifestations of Islamism are becoming more prevalent and diverse. The
new political Islam is a complex and dynamic social movement that has a
dialectical relationship with globalization.

From Globalization to Glocalization

Despite more than twenty years of research, scholars still debate what globalization is.[2] There are many definitions that emphasize the economic

dimension of the phenomenon. Thus, globalization is defined as "greater international mobility of investment, capital and production, accompanied by a significant increase in international trade."[3] Moreover, globalization can be understood as an economic form of transnationalism, namely the connectivity across state borders that could include immigrants, social movements, and capitalism.[4] Although many analysts identify economic globalization with late modernity, the world did experience another such period between the late nineteenth century and the early twentieth century.[5] It was a time of massive immigration from the Old Continent to the New World, the rapid development of the socialist movement, and the increased flow of trade among developed economies. A second phase of globalization started in the 1960s with growing commercial and financial transactions; this phase intensified with the dissolution of the Soviet Union and the liberalization of markets in the early 1990s. Nevertheless, some scholars have disputed the existence of globalization, arguing that what really exists is regionalization, namely the formation of trading blocs that compete against each other.[6]

But globalization cannot be understood as an economic phenomenon alone because it has affected in other ways the lives of millions of people around the world.[7] Anthony Giddens asserted that "globalization can be defined as the intensification of worldwide social relations which link distant localities in such a way that local happenings are shaped by events occurring many miles away and vice versa."[8] This sociopolitical globalization has been facilitated by increased international travel, more efficient telecommunications, and the widespread use of English. It is not a neutral process; Alex Inkele has argued that globalization "involves the movement of national populations away from diverse indigenous cultural patterns towards the adoption of attitudes, values and modes of daily behavior that constitute the elements of a more or less common world culture."[9]

If Inkele is right, then globalization can be perceived by many as a process of homogenization of culture and practices that undermines their own ontological security.[10] Moreover, globalization possibly threatens human security since there is evidence that it significantly increases fatalities from ethnic conflicts.[11] But the conflictual nature of globalization cannot be taken for granted in the world of Islam. Actually, it seems that new interactions and convergences between the global and the local have been absorbed into the social and cultural fabric of Muslim communities, thereby giving birth to a new political Islam.

The concept of glocalization can best describe the global-local nexus of political Islam. It originates from the Japanese word *dochakuka*, which refers to the agricultural principle of adapting farming techniques to local conditions.[12] In the early 1990s, Japanese corporate executives started using the word to describe the customization of a global product for a local market. For example, the McDonald's Corporation has promoted products that have a local flavor so that they become more attractive to certain markets. Ronald Robertson introduced glocalization into the broader arena of social sciences.[13] The term was then adopted by sociologists and communication scholars in order to explain how the process of globalization has been embraced by local communities.[14] In the words of Barry Wellman, "glocalization is a neologism meaning the combination of intense local and extensive global interaction."[15] Moreover, as Fruma Zachs wrote, "glocalization refers to the ways in which social actors construct meanings and identities within a sociological context of globalization."[16] According to Wayne Gabardi, glocalization "represent[s] a shift from a more territorialized learning process bound up with the nation-state society to one more fluid and translocal."[17] But the concept of glocalization is not without its critics. For instance, William Thornton argued that glocalization "amounts to an inoculation against further resistance" since it "serves capitalist globalization by naturalizing it."[18]

Nevertheless, glocalization will serve as a theoretical tool of analysis for the new political Islam that has emerged in recent years. This book partly draws on Ronald Robertson's glocalization thesis, which emphasizes culture and variation along the global-local axis. More specifically, Robertson examined the cultural experiences that have been produced by the interaction between the global and the local. He criticized the widespread view that the former is proactive, whereas the latter is reactive. Globalization is bringing new opportunities along with threats. In effect, he argued that there are attempts in contemporary life to combine homogeneity with heterogeneity and universalism with particularism.[19] The increasing interconnectedness of people, places, and activities has created a world where localized geographical space coexists with globalized virtual space. Furthermore, the late American sociologist Charles Tilly argued that people respond to opportunities and threats generated by globalization by employing bottom-up networks, namely social movements, to create new relations with centers of powers.[20]

Against this background, political Islam has borrowed ideas and practices from the global marketplace and has attempted to implement them locally. Indeed, many Islamists now think globally and act locally. Robertson has pointed to the pivotal role of the nation-state in providing an "official" interpretation of global ideas and practices, and then initiating a process of importation and hybridization.[21] It is true that the sovereign state still commands significant authority and legitimacy. However, it does not have exclusive control anymore over such processes. The rapid emergence of nonstate and semistate actors has changed fundamentally the sociopolitical landscape, especially in the Muslim world where borders are usually artificial and disputed. Therefore, it is more accurate to claim that different actors are shaping, sometimes together and sometimes separately, the process of adoption and interpretation of ideas and practices that have traveled across the world.

The Three Phases of Political Islam

From the late nineteenth century to the interwar period, a whole generation of Islamic thinkers across the Muslim world discussed and considered the relationship between din (religion) and dawla (state). Sayyid Jamal al-Din al-Afghani (1838–1897), the father of Islamic modernism, condemned Western imperialism, criticized the class of *ulama* (Islamic scholars), and advocated pan-Islamic unity.[22] One of his disciples was the grand mufti of Egypt Muhammad Abduh (1849–1905), who initiated reforms in administration and education. The Egyptian scholar argued that "there is no religion without a state and no state without authority and no authority without strength and no strength without wealth."[23] Rashid Rida (1865–1935), a Syrian-born author and activist who lived and worked in Egypt, built upon the ideas of al-Afghani and Abduh. In his famous book *The Caliphate, or the Supreme Imanate* (1923), he advocated a reconceptualization of the institution of caliphate that would take into account the existence of modern states. He envisioned a caliph with religious and spiritual authority who would preside over Muslim states and Muslim communities under foreign rule in a kind of confederation.[24] One year after the abolishment of the caliphate by Kemal Ataturk, the Egyptian religious judge Ali Abd al-Raziq (1888–1966) asserted in his book *Islam and the Principles of Governance* (1925) that there was no religious obligation to re-establish the caliphate; in fact, Muslims could establish any form of government as long as it serves their interests.[25]

In this intellectual context, the ideology of Islamism came into being in a Middle East dominated by colonial powers. It is widely accepted that political Islam is a modern social movement that was born with the establishment of the Muslim Brotherhood (al-Ikhwan al-Muslimun) in British-controlled Egypt in 1928. Hasan al-Banna (1906–1949), the founder of the Brotherhood, envisioned a grassroots organization that would Islamize the Egyptian society that had been exposed to the forces of westernization.

Although foreign supporters established branches of the Brotherhood in their home countries, the parent organization showed little interest in international affairs. Despite al-Banna's pan-Islamic rhetoric, the Ikhwan remained largely an organization with national aims and ambitions.[26] As a result, the Egyptian authorities viewed the group with suspicion; President Gamal Abdul Nasser attempted to crush the Muslim Brothers, while his successor Anwar Sadat tried to marginalize them politically.[27] However, the 1967 defeat in the Arab-Israeli war undermined pan-Arabism and paved the way later for the reemergence of the Brotherhood in Egyptian politics.

The Brotherhood's branches in neighboring countries performed differently, depending on their relationship with the ruling elites. The organization was systematically targeted by the Baathist regime in Syria, while it formed a tactical alliance with Jordan's Hashemite royal family against nationalists and communists.[28] Interestingly, the Muslim Brotherhood utilized different political methods in different situations: the mother organization used activism and violence, the Syrian branch participated in parliamentary elections but then resorted to violence, and the Jordanian branch engaged almost exclusively in activism. By the mid to late 1970s, the Ikhwan and its satellites were one way or another under tight control; therefore, Islamism had not made serious inroads in the region.

Two important developments on the periphery of the Arab world resulted in the revival of Islamism in the late 1970s: the Iranian Revolution and the Soviet invasion of Afghanistan. The overthrow of the shah of Iran by a coalition of nationalists, leftists, and Islamists led to the creation of the Islamic Republic of Iran in April 1979.[29] Ayatollah Khomeini came to dominate the postrevolutionary Iranian political scene, establishing the system of *vilayat al-faqih* (the guardianship of the jurist).[30] The newly born Islamic Republic was to be governed by a high-ranking Shia cleric who must act as the supreme leader of the government. Despite its doctrine of exporting the revolution, Iran remained inward looking and parochial. The Khomeini regime's nationalist tendencies, along with the eight-year war against neighboring Iraq, can possibly explain the chronic isolation of Iran from the Arab world.

The Soviet invasion of Afghanistan in December 1979 unleashed an unprecedented wave of Islamist militancy. Arab fighters were recruited by Islamist charities and organizations based in Pakistan and other Muslim-majority countries. Consequently, thousands of young volunteers poured into the border areas between Afghanistan and Pakistan to join the mujahidin movement against the Red Army and its communist allies in Kabul. The story of the Soviet-Afghan War and the Arab volunteers in Afghanistan has been well documented; Osama bin Laden and his mentor, Abdullah Azzam, became famous for their struggle against the Soviet Union.[31] Yet the military contribution of the Arab volunteers has been overestimated; the mujahidin insurgency remained a localized ethnonationalist conflict.[32]

The decade of the 1980s witnessed also the spread of Islamism in the Levant. In Lebanon, the Shia group Hizb'allah fought against the Israeli Defense Forces, which had invaded the country in 1982 to chase Palestinian guerrillas. While Hizb'allah adhered to Khomeni's pan-Islamic ideology, its main aim was to liberate the occupied Lebanese territories and establish an Islamic republic in the country.[33] The founding of Hamas in the Gaza Strip in 1987, during the first Intifada, reconfirmed the localized nature of political Islam.[34] The group started as an offshoot of the Muslim Brotherhood in the Occupied Territories. Hamas criticized the Palestinian Liberation Organization and other Palestinian groups for being too moderate in their approach toward Israel; therefore, it became the first group to advocate the establishment of an Islamic state in the historic Palestine.

The Muslim Brotherhood, the Iranian Islamists, the Afghan mujahidin, Hizb'allah, and Hamas confined themselves within national boundaries. The nation-state was the unit of identification in spite of their pan-Islamic discourse, which was more for domestic consumption or to attract foreign support than anything else. Thus, Islam was utilized as a mobilization structure by religious leaders to promote political aims in a certain geographical area. They used different methods ranging from engaging in activism to participating in the electoral process to using violence. In every case, the early political Islam was *localist* in its approach. These Islamists largely aimed at liberating a country—from a dictator or foreign rule—and then establishing an Islamic state. Thus, the first generation can be described as *Islamist nationalists*.[35]

The emergence of al-Qaeda in the late 1980s was a development that changed the nature of political Islam. Al-Qaeda decided to target the so-called far enemy, namely the United States and other Western countries, rather than fighting local adversaries. The main unit of identification for the second generation of Islamists was the totality of believers, the umma. Instead of confronting local opponents, al-Qaeda claimed that there was an open-ended religious conflict between the umma and non-Muslims.[36] Thus, it made frequent reference to conflicts in the Middle East, South Asia, the North Caucasus, and the Balkans, portraying Muslims as the victims of infidel discrimination and aggression. In reality, al-Qaeda constructed a new transnational identity to promote its utopian vision of an Islamist take-over of the world. This new post-territorial identity aimed at creating a *Homus Islamicus* who would live and die by the Quran and the Kalashnikov. This new man would have allegiance to the umma and not his country of origin.

Osama bin Laden attempted to revolutionize political Islam, trying to compel even his Afghan hosts, the Taliban, to adopt a globalized scale of engagement.[37] The rise of al-Qaeda coincided with the intensification of globalization in the early 1990s. Indeed, the group embraced some of its achievements (e.g., advanced communication technology, freer movement of people) to grow stronger. Its strategy and approach was *globalist*, since it perceived itself as a vanguard of chosen fighters who would defeat the umma's enemies and establish a global caliphate. Al-Qaeda reached its zenith with the September 11, 2001, attacks in New York and Washington.

In addition to al-Qaeda, a handful of other Islamist groups adopted a globalized scale of engagement. One of them was Hizb ut-Tahrir al Islami (the Islamic Liberation Party—hereafter Hizb ut-Tahrir). Although it has shared the vision of a global caliphate, the group has denounced the use of violence as a legitimate means to gain power. Hizb ut-Tahrir has expanded geographically, opening branches in many different countries.

In his book *Globalized Islam*, published in 2004, Olivier Roy asserted that political Islam could be divided into two subgroups: Islamists and neo-fundamentalists. He argued that a schism has emerged between mainstream Islamist groups like Hizb'allah and Hamas, which call for the establishment of an Islamic state on the national Lebanese and Palestinian soil respectively, and neofundamentalist groups like al-Qaeda and Hizb ut-Tahrir that seek to establish a caliphate, not embedded in any particular society or territory.[38] This change of focus on the part of neofundamentalists is not hard to understand. Madawi al-Rasheed has argued that "the unity of the *umma*, its humiliation and its expected rejuvenation are portrayed as transnational themes mobilizing Muslims regardless of their cultural background."[39]

The question is what stands behind this new division. Roy noted that "Islamic neofundamentalism is not a simple reaction against westernization but a product and an agent of the complex forces of globalization."[40] Frederic Volpi observed that "although Islamism was from its very beginning an aspiring global movement due to the universalistic character of Islam as a religion, it is the process of compression of space and time characteristic of the late twentieth century globalization that empowered contemporary Islamism."[41] Furthermore, Peter Mandaville argued that "global sociocultural transformations are giving rise to new forms of transnational politics," in which the nation-state plays a decreasing role; political identities (including the Islamic one) are now defined by multiple political spaces.[42] To sum up, the rise of this globalized political Islam has been viewed as the consequence of worldwide changes. The argument goes that advances in information and communication technology, faster transportation of people, and growing interactions between Muslim communities gave rise to a new Islamism. Therefore, the second generation can be described as *Islamist globalists*.

But how globalized is political Islam actually? It is true that certain issues, like the Bosnian war of the 1990s, have functioned as unifying themes for this diverse social movement.[43] The outburst of anti-Islamic propaganda has also occasionally brought together Islamists of varied orientations and backgrounds. Another indication of political Islam's globalism is the emergence of transnational Islamist networks that usually include Islamic charities, nongovernmental organizations (NGOs), legal and clandestine groups, Muslim religious leaders and preachers, and individual followers.[44] Some of them have been involved in mobilizing Muslim volunteers to fight in the Kashmiri insurgency from 1989 onward,[45] the Algerian civil war from 1992 to 1998,[46] and the Russian-Chechen wars during 1994–1996 and 1999–2001.[47]

Yet globalization has not produced more homogeneity within political Islam; if anything, Islamists are more divided and polarized than ever. The current antagonism, for instance, between the Muslim Brotherhood and the Salafis in Egypt,[48] the Justice and Development Party or AKP and the Gülen movement in Turkey,[49] and al-Qaeda and the Islamic State of Iraq and Syria (ISIS)[50] indicate the fragmentation of political Islam into localized entities that struggle for political and ideological supremacy. Apart from dealing with the political considerations of the moment, these Islamist parties and groups have attempted to position themselves physically, mentally, and socially. French Marxist philosopher Henri Lefebvre identified three dimensions of space: the perceived space (*l'espace perçu*) that has a physical form; the conceived space (*l'espace conçu*) that is a mental construct where ideological, political, and cultural conflicts take place; and the lived space (*l'espace vécu*) inhabited and used by cultural producers (e.g., artists, intellectuals) who shape the other two dimensions.[51] Islamists compete with each other in all dimensions: they seek physical space to consolidate their activities; they defend and promote their interests, ideas, and norms in the mental space; and they define and maintain, with the help of religious leaders, interpretations of reality in social space.

The scale of space is another important aspect of the analysis about political Islam because its ideology has a global assertion that can be applied only locally. The global and the local are not only locations but also processes. Therefore, all Muslim spaces under conditions of globalization are hybrids of integration and differentiation.[52] This means that Muslim polities and entities absorb and interpret external influences and universal norms for the purpose of adapting them to their own environment.

Despite all this, some authors have claimed that Islam is the antithesis of globalization because it opposes modernity.[53] Yet, as discussed earlier, political Islam itself is a product of modernity since it grew as a movement during the twentieth century. Indeed, the relationship between Islam and modernity goes deeper and is more fundamental. Immanuel Kant was probably the first to notice an affinity between modernity and cosmopolitanism.[54] Islam has arguably shaped modernity through its inherent cosmopolitanism; the latter is demonstrated by the annual pilgrimage to Mecca and other sacred places in Saudi Arabia, the transnational Sufi orders, and missionary and educational activities that include international traveling experiences.[55] More specifically, thousands of people travel every year to pursue Islamic higher education and many Muslim scholars visit foreign countries to acquire knowledge. Indeed, the Muslim faith has encouraged the believer to travel for religious purposes. The Islamic term *rihla* refers to a journey that is made for the purpose of seeking the divine truth. The umma is a world of constant interactions and communications. Therefore, Islam in general and the social movement of political Islam in particular

| Islamic cosmopolitanism | Modernity | Globalization |

Figure 1. The relationship between Islamic cosmopolitanism,
modernity, and globalization

can accommodate and join the globalization process, which is a period of "high modernity."[56] The inductive relationship between Islamic cosmopolitanism, modernity, and globalization is represented in Figure 1.

Not surprisingly, the ideology of Islamism in its various forms has entailed a global message about the establishment of a true Muslim society in accordance with the will of God. However, its application has not been an easy task given that Muslim constituencies have their own understanding of what a proper Islamic society ought to look like. Despite their global reach, Islamists of all sorts have to adjust to different political and cultural settings surrounding Muslim communities. In other words, the globality of the umma is disputed by the specificity of its local components, which often have territorial boundaries and ethnic identifications.

Therefore, it can be argued that between the first generation of Islamist nationalists and the second generation of Islamist globalists stands now a new generation of Islamists, who have blurred the lines between global influences and local constraints. The Islamist activism on behalf of distant others, the resurgence of a localist neocaliphatism, the rise of Islamo-democrats who blend Islamic values with democracy, the emergence of electoral Salafis who seek a change from within the system, and the sectarianization of Islamist militancy have indicated the development of a new political Islam that is characterized by high heterogeneity and adaptability. Due to its distinctive character, the new political Islam is the epitome of glocalization. Its adherents are far less ambitious than their globalist predecessors who did not achieve their grandiose aims. However, the new Islamists are not against globalization per se; in fact, they have taken advantage of global processes to achieve their local aims. Their version of Islamism is usually exclusive and divisive in its approach. The totality of Muslims is not anymore the unit of identification. Instead, they have focused on Muslim communities within and beyond national borders. Amitai Etzioni defines community as "first, a web of affect-laden relationships among a group of individuals, relationships that often crisscross and

Table 1. The three phases of political Islam

	Scale of engagement	Unit of identification	Main adversary
First generation of Islamists	Localized	The nation-state	National governments and foreign powers
Second generation of Islamists	Globalized	The global umma	The West
Third generation of Islamists	Glocalized	The community	Western governments, secularists, other Islamic denominations

reinforce one another (as opposed to one-on-one or chain-like individual relationships); and second, a measure of commitment to a set of shared values, norms, and meanings, and a shared history and identity—in short, a particular culture."[57]

Therefore, the third generation can be described as Islamist communitarians. Their imagined community is composed of pious Muslims, whose loyalty and identity is determined by their adherence to a particular version of Islamic authenticity.[58] The list of adversaries now includes Western governments, Arab regimes, secularists, and other denominations. It is an all-out confrontation against those who are perceived deviant or hostile. It should be noted that this new category includes groups that initially were classified as Islamist nationalist (e.g., Hizb'allah) or Islamist globalist (Hizb ut-Tahrir). The three phases of political Islam are outlined in Table 1.

The Forces of Glocalization

The emergence of the third generation is largely the result of important international developments that have taken place in the last ten to fifteen years. To begin with, the 9/11 events and the U.S. War on Terror not only raised tensions with Muslims around the world but also resulted in the strengthening of a pan-Islamic sense of solidarity. The U.S. president

George W. Bush once stated that "this crusade, this war on terrorism is going to take a while."[59] Whether it was intentional or unintentional, the use of the word *crusade* evoked feelings of anger and frustration in the Muslim world. The invasion of Iraq in 2003 proved in the eyes of many Muslims the existence of a hidden agenda to confront and humiliate Islam. In fact, Pew Research Center surveys have indicated that most Muslims in the greater Middle East and South Asia clearly believe that the West has followed an anti-Muslim strategy by invading Muslim-majority countries.[60] Consequently, relations between the West and Muslims during the years of George W. Bush's presidency reached a nadir. More importantly, U.S. interventionist policies unintentionally triggered a demand for pan-Islamic unity. For example, a 2006 survey conducted by the University of Maryland found that 74 percent of Pakistanis, 71 percent of Moroccans, and 67 percent of Egyptians supported the idea of establishing a global caliphate.[61]

That being said, the Muslim world is hardly united and monolithic. Muslims do not share a single overriding identity. Every Muslim society has its own history and problems that determine its path. Therefore, this new pan-Islamism does not always mean statehood; it rather underscores the need to formulate proper Islamic responses to transnational challenges as an alternative to Western ones. In effect, the Muslim world tries to address new challenges perceived as threatening and disruptive. Yet, realistically speaking, this can be achieved only if there is local awareness and management of global issues. In an era of global ecological crises, for example, Islamists have been able to formulate policy responses for the preservation and protection of the environment. Therefore, Islamist groups like Hizb'allah, the Muslim Brotherhood and Hizb ut-Tahrir have paid growing attention to climate change, pollution, and water management.[62] Since they favor local solutions to global challenges, these communitarians represent a new generation of Islamists.

Another important factor facilitating the glocalization of political Islam has been the massive use of the Internet and the new media by millions of Muslims in the Middle East and elsewhere. In this way, they have been able to avoid state censorship and receive information about developments in other parts of the world. As a result, local events like the attempted burning of copies of Quran by a Protestant pastor in south Florida in July 2010 have attracted the attention of millions and poisoned relations between Muslims and Western governments.[63] The speed of information delivery is so fast that time and space have been relativized. In this smaller world, the differences between Muslims and non-Muslims appear larger. The interaction and intermingling of Muslims and Westerners have reinforced each other's identities and perceptions of the self and the other.[64] The increased awareness of differences can fuel antagonism or facilitate ideational transfers. Interestingly, these two outcomes sometimes happen at the same time: Islamists criticize Western societies and embrace ideas that are cherished by the latter. This contradiction reflects the duality of globalization, where homogenization and heterogenization co-occur and shape each other.

In addition, social media like Facebook and Twitter have provided new opportunities for Islamists to propagate their messages and recruit members and sympathizers locally and globally. The use of social media has reduced the distance between producer and consumer.[65] For instance, ISIS has been a pioneer organization in using Twitter to communicate with sympathizers around the world.[66] The speed and flow of information have created a conceived space that is beyond the control of states. It is a new virtual battleground where the umma and the individual could unite to fight against the perceived adversaries. Simultaneously, different Islamists compete for the hearts and minds of the pious Muslims in the lived space. This environment of virtual competition did not exist in the first few years after 2000; it is largely the result of the social media revolution since the mid-decade.[67]

Finally, there is a reverse trend from global to local that has strengthened ethnoreligious loyalties. During the mid-1990s, Benjamin Barber's *Jihad vs. McWorld* discussed the retribalization of societies as a reaction to globalization.[68] It can be argued that the rise of the new political Islam is just one of the consequences of this development. Since globalization is eroding state power and authority, people are becoming conscious of their own long-suppressed particularities. Robert Kaplan has observed that "loose and shadowy organisms such as Islamic terrorist organizations suggest why borders will mean increasingly little and sedimentary layers of tribalistic identity and control will mean more."[69] Tariq Ramadan has argued that "globalization contains the paradox that at the same time that it causes the old traditional points of reference to disappear, it reawakens passionate affirmations of identity that often verge on withdrawal and self-exclusion."[70] Indeed, the new Islamism has been instigated by the ongoing fragmentation of Muslim identity under conditions of globalization. This development has benefited those who favor confrontation over compromise because narrower identities tend to be exclusive.

The Arab Spring revolutions in North Africa and the Middle East have accelerated this trend toward sociopolitical localism. While Tunisia and Egypt have remained territorially intact, Libya, Syria, and Iraq do not exist anymore as unitary states. Instead, they have disintegrated into fiefdoms and quasi-independent regions. The outbreak of civil wars and insurgencies, the use of proxy armies by external powers, and the emergence of ISIS as a quasi-state possibly indicate the breakdown of the entire post-World War I regional order. This process of disintegration is leading to the formation of new identities that are reinforced by conflicts over Islamic authenticity.

Under these conditions, new glocalized dynamics can be identified. Many Muslims are now mobilized to demand equality, representation, and justice in their communities. Islamists are obliged to address this neolocalism in order to survive politically and remain relevant. However, Islamists would look out of touch with reality if they do not engage with the forces of globalization as well. For this reason, the new Islamists have attempted to reach out to local constituencies by redefining global ideas and practices. In effect, the new generation of Islamists has promoted the particularization of Islamism. It is a cognitive process facilitated by the construction and transmission of master frames that include widely accepted ideas and norms.

Conceptualizing the Glocalization of Political Islam

Since the early years of this century, a growing number of scholars have applied social movement theory to explain the emergence of Islamist movements in the Arab and Muslim world.[71] They have argued that it is possible to analyze political Islam by using the same concepts that have been employed in other cases. Mario Diani defined social movements as "networks of informal interactions between a plurality of individuals, groups or associations, engaged in a political or cultural conflict, on the basis of a shared collective identity."[72] Social movement theory incorporates various dimensions of collective action, including structural factors, mobilization of resources, responses to political opportunities, and framing.[73] Therefore, it treats political Islam as a social movement that is not fundamentally different from movements like the radical Left of the 1960s, the environmental movement of the 1970s, and the antinuclear movement of the

1980s. Bringing some elements of social movement theory to bear on political Islam offers the potential to better explain its emergence and development. In fact, it is an alternative to explanations that present political Islam as a monolithic and expansionist movement.

The globalization literature has also examined the question of political Islam. Samuel Huntington's *Clash of Civilizations* addressed the cultural and religious reorganization of world politics in the era of globalization. He predicted a perpetual conflict between the West and Islam.[74] Peter Mandaville's *Islam and Politics* focused on the complex interactions between globalization and Islam that "could lead many Muslims toward reactionary forms of Islamism."[75] Abdulaziz Sachedina argued that "the declining sovereignty of Muslim states and their increasing inability to regulate economic and cultural exchanges are the two main issues that bring Muslims together to challenge globalization."[76] Again, political Islam is understood as incompatible with worldwide integration. Yet other scholars tend to view Islam as more harmonious with globalization because Muslims and the West have long been interconnected through international trade and other economic activities.[77]

This book attempts to identify and explain the processes and factors leading to different fusions of the global and the local within political Islam. For this reason, it follows an integrated approach combining elements from the globalization debate and the social movement literature that emphasizes framing. In effect, it provides a theoretical understanding of the new Islamism that privileges ideas, identity, and culture.

The starting point is to understand how global transformation affects local realities in the Muslim world. According to Robertson, glocalization explains how the symbiosis between the global and local differs according to particular cultural circumstances.[78] George Ritzer defines glocalization as "the interpenetration of the global and the local resulting in unique outcomes in different geographic areas."[79] In the era of globalization, Muslim polities and communities are open to outside pressures and influences. It follows that a social movement like political Islam cannot remain intact under such conditions; Islamists have to take into account both global developments and local perspectives. As a result, they follow different approaches and methods depending on the political and social circumstances.

The goal of restoring the historic caliphate is indicative of political Islam's glocalization. Many Islamist parties and groups have shared the vision of a worldwide Muslim state, but without solving the problem of method and territoriality. The Palestinian-led Hizb ut-Tahrir has made the caliphate the centerpiece of its ideology but has not specified its future location. It has tried to achieve this goal through international activism. In contrast, the Pakistani group of Jamaat-e-Islami has argued that the caliphate can first be established in Pakistan. For this purpose, it has participated in general and local elections. Finally, ISIS has declared the establishment of a caliphate in Syria and Iraq, and has launched a military campaign to expand its territory.

The glocalization of Islamism means that in reality there are many political Islams. In 2005, the International Crisis Group divided Sunni Islamism into three groups: the political, consisting of parties like the Muslim Brotherhood and Turkey's Justice and Development Party that aim at gaining power at the national level; the missionary, which has two main components, the Tablighi movement and the Salafis; and the jihadi, which has three subgroups: antiregime, irredentist, and global.[80] Yet this typology is outdated for three reasons: first, Salafi parties have participated in the electoral process although they have very different characteristics from those included in the first group; second, there are political parties whose main focus is global activism rather than gaining power at the national level through elections (e.g., Hizb ut-Tahrir); and third, there is a new type of jihadi groups that can be best described as sectarian (e.g., ISIS, Mahdi Army). Hakan Yavuz provided a more comprehensive typology of political Islam that includes both Sunni and Shia groups; he categorized them as society oriented or state oriented and legitimate or illegitimate.[81] However, this typology follows a dichotomous logic that ignores the importance of external dynamics and the complexities of political Islam that can be both legitimate and illegitimate.

This book proposes a new (perhaps simpler) framework of analysis. I argue that the new political Islam is represented by three agents of glocalization: the *activists*, the *politicians*, and the *militants*. These glocalizers initiate the process of adoption and adaptation of global ideas, norms, and practices across time and space.[82] Therefore, the book offers a new categorization of Islamists based on the nature of their involvement in public life. Although some groups have had multiple engagements, their core mission has remained essentially the same. For instance, both Hizb'allah and Hizb ut-Tahrir have participated in parliamentary elections; yet the former remains a militant group, while the latter is involved almost exclusively in activism.

The Activists

Some analysts have used the term *Islamic activism* to describe the mobilization of Muslims around political and religious issues. Quintan Wiktorowicz has described Islamic activism as "the mobilization of contention to support Muslim causes."[83] The International Crisis Group equals Islamic activism with "the active assertion and promotion of beliefs, prescriptions, laws, or policies that are held to be Islamic in character."[84] Joshua Hendrick has defined it as "the political and social mobilization of actors who deploy a specifically Islamic discourse to express their aspirations for social change."[85] In this book, the term *Islamist activism* is used to describe *any systematic effort to mobilize human and other resources for the purpose of promoting an Islam-based agenda by nonviolent means.* It should be noted that the word *Islamist* implies an ideologized process of coordination to achieve political aims.

Islamist activism outside the Muslim world first appeared in the late 1980s, when the Salman Rushdie Affair erupted in Great Britain. Thousands of Muslims protested against the British author and burned copies of his book *The Satanic Verses*. Since the 9/11 events, Islamist activism has become more sophisticated; Muslim activists are better organized and more mobile. They have taken a stance on many pan-Islamic issues (e.g., the Prophet Muhammad cartoons controversy) and have made their presence felt in many countries. They tend to rely on the Internet for the propagation of their messages.

Interestingly, some of them are of convert origin. Being familiar with the political culture and system of government of their own countries, they feel confident in defending Islamist agendas. They have acted alone or on behalf of Islamist groups. European convert-activists are not the only ones who mobilize for Islam-related issues. Hizb ut-Tahrir has pioneered Islamist activism in Europe and internationally. The group has refused to use violence as a tool of political change; instead, it has favored the widespread dissemination of leaflets and party literature in universities, mosques, and other public areas for the purpose of re-Islamizing the society. It has also extensively used the Internet and the new media to propagate its radical, by Western standards, messages.

However, the days when Islamist activism was manifested in violent demonstrations and flag burning have long gone. The new generation of Islamist activists is more likely to call attention to Islamophobia and human rights violations of Muslim citizens in the West and elsewhere. This change of discourse has been the result of new global trends. According to Samuel Moyn, human rights in their current form can be traced back to President Jimmy Carter's years in office when they were used as a foreign policy tool against the Soviet Union and its allies.[86] Since then, human rights have preoccupied public discourses on ethnicity, religion and integration.

In this context, Islamist activism has increasingly adopted the political language of human rights to make local claims and confront opponents. For this purpose, a number of prominent individuals and groups have promoted Islamist agendas that focus on the collective rights of Muslim populations. Thus, they have constantly amended human rights discourses to reach out to communities and propagate their messages in accordance with their local needs.

The Politicians

Islamism has long been synonymous with extremism and antimodernity. Francis Fukuyama wrote one month after the tragic events of 9/11 that "there does seem to be something about Islam, or at least the fundamentalist versions of Islam that have been dominant in recent years, that makes Muslim societies particularly resistant to modernity."[87] What Fukuyama did not foresee was that one part of political Islam would eventually absorb the so-called liberal idea, namely the combination of representative democracy and market economics.[88] As a result, Islamist parties have joined the democratic mainstream and have come to power through the ballot box. They have participated in Islamist politics, which can be understood as *the pre-electoral, electoral, and postelectoral struggle and maneuvering for the support of Muslim causes and the Islamization of society.*

In Turkey, most Islamists have accepted the secular nature of the state. Despite its inclination to authoritarianism, the Islamist-leaning AKP has recognized the electoral process as the most important mechanism of modern democracy. Indeed, elections could provide crucial legitimacy to a party like it that seeks to promote a new political agenda. The AKP has managed to integrate the post-Cold War global democratic imperative into Turkish Islamism. In this way, a new version of Islamism has come into being, the Islamo-democracy that promotes Islam as a force of democratization and progress. The Arab Spring revolutions of 2010–2011 reinforced the drive toward Islamo-democracy. The largely peaceful demonstrations proved the unstoppable power of the people against autocratic regimes. With the help of social media networks and the Internet, citizens were able to mobilize and protest. Islamist groups failed initially to comprehend the new dynamics of democratization.[89] Yet they quickly managed to grasp the momentum and increase their popularity. Consequently, Islamist parties came to power through elections.

The Islamo-democrats operate within the bounds of the constitution and tend to avoid a winner-takes-all approach. In practice, this often means that they are willing to raise only symbolic, but not politically important, issues like the wearing of the hijab (headscarf). In this way, they could appeal to large fractions of the population. They usually avoid controversial issues (e.g., legalization of polygamy) and seek to build strong alliances with other political forces that do not object to the growing religiosity of the population (e.g., nationalists). They follow an agenda drafted on the basis of compromise and consensus, even if not always wholeheartedly.

Furthermore, the electoral process has gained widespread recognition as an expression of people's desires even by those who have traditionally denounced democracy as a man-made political system. Salafi parties have been established in Egypt and Tunisia in order to participate in the post-Arab Spring political systems. In effect, some Salafis now see elections as a way to advance their faith-based agenda aiming at the establishment of an Islamic state ruled by Sharia. Despite having a globalist outlook, Salafis have increasingly discussed local issues of concern such as the status of the economy, education, and health.

The symbiotic relationship between democracy and new political Islam should come as no surprise. Since the end of the Cold War in the late 1980s, there has been a wave of democratization across the world. In the early 1990s, Olivier Roy observed the "failure of political Islam" to offer a viable alternative to Western democracy.[90] Yet there is a new generation of Islamist leaders who work within the political system to achieve change. Thus, the global trend of democratization has been fused with local Islamist agendas.

The Militants

The post-Cold War era has witnessed the outbreak of many Islamist-inspired insurgencies. The problem is not new, but it has now become more of an intra-Muslim affair. In recent years, Sunni and Shia militants have used excessive violence to overthrow or support sectarian regimes, while annihilating hostile communities.

For the purpose of this study, Islamist militancy is defined as *the aggressive and often violent pursuit of a cause associated with Islam in opposition to other parties.* Contemporary militants have become more focused on the achievement of local objectives, rather than global ones that have proved to be unattainable and unrealistic. After all, the ongoing franchising of al-Qaeda has demonstrated that all politics—even Islamist—is local, not global. The localization of Islamist militancy means that control over territory is a necessary step to accomplish this mission. But the achievement of statehood is rarely a peaceful process. The change of territorial or political status quo is often resisted by fellow Muslims of different political orientation or sectarian affiliation. Islamist militancy is not only more localized but also more factional.

On the one hand, Shia groups have taken up arms for the protection of friendly regimes and the empowerment of Shia communities. After the U.S. invasion of Iraq and the demolition of the Baathist state, Shia militant groups like the Mahdi Army were formed to defend Shia rights against the new Sunni opposition. In Lebanon, Hizb'allah has often claimed to be a nonsectarian resistance group fighting for the independence and sovereignty of Lebanon. Yet the Shia group has now targeted its opponents in Syria on the basis of religious affiliation.

On the other hand, Sunni extremists have engaged in a war against Shia-dominated regimes in Syria and Iraq. They have accused Shia Muslims of being heretics who have distorted the Muslim faith and have conspired against Sunnis. The sectarianization of Islamist militancy means that there is a new political goal: Sunni militants have carried out ethnic cleansing against Shia populations, seeking to establish a Sunni-only state.

Militant Islamists have fought not only for power but also for recognition. This new form of Islamist militancy is linked to identity politics as much as power politics. In spite of globalist tendencies, they have adhered to a localist vision of an idealized communal life restricted to members of a specific denomination. Thus, sectarian affiliation is becoming the prime criterion for acceptance and participation in the society. This fragmentation of the Muslim identity is not, of course, a unique development. In fact, the leadership of the Muslim world has historically been contested by numerous religious-political groups claiming to represent true Islam.

Interestingly, both Sunni and Shia militants have used discourses that emphasize the need for justice because their community has been targeted by evildoers. While Islam preaches about *general* justice applicable to all humans, militant Islamists have focused more on *reciprocal* justice. This form of justice can rationalize political violence against opponents and excuse collateral damage killings. It is based on a dichotomous logic that dictates certain responses to out-group members. It follows that, from a sectarian viewpoint, this justice entails the recognition of identity based on a notion of moral superiority.

Islamist Agents of Glocalization and Master Frames

The existence of glocalization alone does not explain the rise of the new political Islam. The missing link is a process of social construction that links the global with the local through cognitive schemata that are known as frames.[91] I argue throughout that the glocalization of political Islam entails a framing process, defined as "the conscious strategic efforts by groups of people to form shared understandings of the world and of themselves that legitimate and motivate collective action."[92]

Framing theory has explored how social movements construct and disseminate messages to gather support. It derives from new social movement theory, which stresses culture as a key issue in understanding collective action.[93] According to Erving Goffman, a frame is an interpretive schema through which information is encountered and processed.[94] In effect, it constitutes a form of discourse that draws on shared meanings.[95]

Social movements have used frames to communicate key messages to the public in order to mobilize supporters. Therefore, there are three different categories of frames: diagnostic frames that focus on the problem, prognostic frames that offer a desirable solution, and motivational frames that encourage potential participants to join a social movement.[96] Islamists have typically utilized Quranic concepts to construct powerful frames. For instance, Sayyid Qutb's interpretation of *jahiliyya* (i.e., the pre-Islamic period) has served as a diagnostic frame, identifying the lack of Sharia as the main problem in contemporary Muslim communities. The Ikhwan's famous slogan "Islam is the solution" (*al-Islam huwa al-hal*) represents a prognostic frame that offers a solution to Muslims' problems. Finally, Islamist mobilization is framed as a religious duty in order to provide potential sympathizers with a powerful incentive; for example, Hizb ut-Tahrir has claimed that its members constitute "an *umma* within the *umma*," a group of people that has a special mission in life that would be rewarded in the afterlife.[97]

Successful frames often resonate with a master frame, which is a set of meanings that enjoys even broader popular resonance.[98] According to Pamela Oliver and Hank Johnston, "movement participants draw upon master frames to portray their perceived injustice in ways that fit the tenor of the times and thus parallels other movements."[99] Therefore, master frames tend to be as generic as possible; only then can they be used by many aggrieved groups.[100] Johnston has argued that "master frames can be thought of as a general formula for solving problems related to the opposition movement: what collective actions are appropriate, who might be acceptable allies, what demands can be voiced, which ones are better left unvoiced, and how to interpret the responses of the regime."[101] Only a handful of master frames have been identified that are shared by multiple social movements, including the environmental justice frame,[102] the hegemonic frame,[103] the nationalism master frame,[104] the anti-imperialism frame,[105] and the anti-Americanism frame.[106]

David Snow and Robert Benford argued that master frames can be either restricted (i.e., theme focused) or elaborated (i.e., broad and detailed).[107] Social movements adopt those master frames that resonate with the culture and situation of potential sympathizers. Master frames are usually transmitted through the media, conversations, speeches, slogans, and visual representations (e.g., photos).[108] Therefore, the concept of master frames places more emphasis on strategies than on value orientations of social movements.[109]

I argue that glocalization is realized when a master frame is reappropriated into a local context and then experiences a transformation through specific political and cultural circumstances. More specifically, Islamist glocalizers have utilized master frames to facilitate local adaption and adoption of global ideas. Thus they hope to gain more legitimacy in an era when time and space have been compressed by communication and other technological advancements. The new Islamists have largely utilized three master frames based on themes that have significant appeal to Muslims.

The master frame of human rights was first used by African American activists in the United States in the early postwar period.[110] It was also endorsed by Third World movements for national independence in the 1960s and 1970s. Social and sexual minorities adopted it during the 1990s and the first decade of this century. Islamist activists in Europe and elsewhere have increasingly depended on this master frame to justify actions and promote aims. They have portrayed Muslims as victims of discrimination and racism who deserve demonstrations of solidarity. It is not a coincidence that there is an evolving debate within Islamist circles regarding the essence of human rights in Islam; indeed, there have been attempts to provide a codification of these rights (e.g., the Cairo Declaration of Human Rights in Islam).

The master frame of democracy has been utilized by many groups and parties around the world. According to Thomas Olesen, the dominance of the democracy master frame is connected to the end of the Cold War.[111] In particular, the anticommunist revolutions of 1989 in east Europe appropriated the democracy master frame.[112] Islamo-democrats like the AKP, the Muslim Brotherhood, and al-Nahda have capitalized on the popularity of this master frame to achieve legitimacy against their domestic opponents. It is a powerful means of overcoming concerns about their political agendas.

The master frame of justice has been particularly popular among insurgent and terrorist groups; indeed, its application is almost a necessary part of a successful violent mobilization. For instance, the Irish Republican Army employed this master frame to gain support from a disillusioned community.[113] Within the Islamic context, the master frame can evoke sympathy and stir feelings of anger and revenge since it often draws on historical narratives and Muslim traditions. As ironic as it may seem, both Sunni and Shia militant groups have used this master frame to justify their campaigns of terror against their opponents. Hence Shia militants in Syria fight to achieve justice for the suffering of their ancestors against Sunni militants, who believe in the just cause of saving Islam from the heretics.

The master frames that have been adopted by Islamist glocalizers are represented in Figure 2. Although the three master frames and their components can sometimes overlap with each other, they draw from distinct global ideas and originate from different traditions of normative thought. Thus, it is necessary to examine how various Islamists have utilized them to mobilize supporters and remain relevant.

Conclusion

Globalization is a modern phenomenon that elicits the transformation of space and time under conditions of multidimensional interdependence. It includes constant interactions between the global and the local. Therefore,

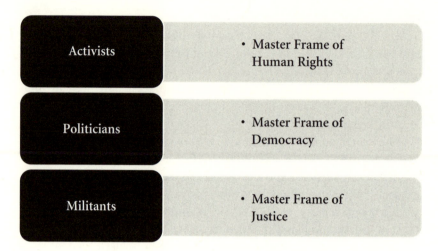

Figure 2. Islamist glocalizers and master frames

globalization is simultaneously a top-down and bottom-up process of ideational and cultural change. Given the multifaceted nature of globalization, one can argue that the concept of glocalization is more suitable for describing the particularization of universal ideas, discourses and practices.

Political Islam can be understood as a global social movement with many local components. It has gone through three different phases: the Islamist nationalism of early adherents who focused on the nation-state, the Islamist globalism of the second generation that addressed the universality of the umma and the Islamist communitarianism that acknowledges local diversity while maintaining a global awareness. The glocalization of political Islam has been achieved by three types of agents: the activists, the politicians, and the militants. These glocalizers have their own preferred political method and understanding of Islamism. Consequently, they seek to apply different versions of Islamism that in reality constitute fusions of global ideas and local politics and culture.

This glocal convergence has been possible due to the use of framing. The master frames of human rights, democracy, and justice have been utilized by the new Islamists to gain legitimacy and mobilize support among diverse Muslim constituencies. They can elicit emotions and convey messages for the purpose of community empowerment and recognition. The new political Islam is a global movement of synthesis and antithesis that constantly adopts and adapts to processes and ideas locally.

PART I

___

Islamist Activism and the Master Frame of Human Rights

Modern human rights emanated from the Age of Enlightenment. The English Bill of Rights (1689), the U.S. Declaration of Independence (1776), and the French Declaration of the Rights of Man and of the Citizen (1789) included provisions for the protection of human rights. The cause of human rights was advanced further after the first half of the twentieth century because the two world wars resulted in massive casualties. The Universal Declaration of Human Rights (UDHR), adopted by the United Nations General Assembly in 1948, is generally considered to be the founding document of the international human rights regime. It was designed to have the maximum recognition and acceptance. Therefore, the document understandably did not have any religious connotations and references.

Despite the signing of the UDHR, the international community did not immediately prioritize the protection and advancement of human rights. The decolonization of Africa and Asia began in the early postwar years. As a result, gross violations of human rights by the colonial powers took place in Algeria, Vietnam, Cyprus and elsewhere. Moreover, the Cold War between the West and the East sidelined concerns about the protection of human rights. In 1973, however, the U.S. Congress declared the promotion of human rights as a principal goal of U.S. foreign policy, while stating its intention to impose sanctions on those countries that violate them systematically.[1] At the same time, NGOs with a human-rights agenda gained more recognition. In 1977, for instance, the New York-based Amnesty International was awarded the Nobel Peace Prize for its work in the field.[2]

The Muslim world was not absent from this process. Despite its general character, the UDHR was not well received by all Muslim-majority countries. Saudi Arabia abstained from the vote in the General Assembly claiming that the Declaration reflected Western culture.[3] Moreover, Riyadh objected to Article 18 (which states that everyone has the right to change religion) because Sharia considers conversion to another faith as apostasy punishable by death.[4] Saudi skepticism regarding the compatibility of the UDHR with Islam was not an isolated attitude. During the thirty-sixth session of the UN General Assembly in 1981, the Iranian ambassador stated that the UDHR was based on an interpretation of the Judeo-Christian tradition; Iran could not implement it since it had already adopted Sharia as the law of the land.[5]

But Islam has its own history with human rights. *Risalat al-Huquq* (Treatise of Rights) was probably the first document outlining basic human rights. It was written by Zayn al-Abidin (659–713), son of Imam Hussein and great-grandson of Prophet Muhammad. *Risalat al-Huquq* consists of different sections which include the rights of subjects (e.g., wife, slave), relatives (e.g., parents, child), and others (e.g., those under protection of Islam).[6] In the modern era, two declarations confirmed Islam's close relationship with human rights: the Universal Islamic Declaration of Human Rights and the Cairo Declaration on Human Rights in Islam. The former was issued by the Islamic Council, a nongovernmental organization in 1981, whereas the latter was adopted by member states of the Organization of the Islamic Conference in 1990. While they share many elements, they give emphasis to different areas: the Universal Islamic Declaration focuses on political freedoms and the Cairo Declaration expresses security concerns.[7] Nevertheless, the Pakistani scholar Muhammad Khalid Masud has argued that Western scholars "dislike the use of religious language by Muslims because they believe that human rights are secular."[8]

Individual Muslim states have also attempted to provide an Islamic perspective on the issue, if only to shield themselves from international criticism of their human rights record. In 2007, for instance, the Egyptian Ministry of Education published a textbook for elementary students who take Islamic religious classes; it claimed that the Quran was "the first international document in all history proclaiming human rights, more than fourteen centuries ago."[9] These rights, sanctioned by the Quran, include the freedom of opinion and the right to conduct business and own property.[10]

The relationship between Islam and human rights is a topic of paramount importance for the image of the faith. The Iranian philosopher Abdolkarim Soroush has observed that Islamic thinkers, for many years, almost ignored the debate about human rights because "the language of religion and religious law is the language of duties, not rights. . . . They concentrate more on what God expects from them than what they themselves desire; they look among their duties to find their rights, not vice versa."[11] However, this is not entirely true. Abu A'la Maududi, one of the most influential Muslim political philosophers in the twentieth century, provided a perspective on human rights based on the Quran and the Sunnah. In his opinion, "since in Islam human rights have been conferred by God, no legislative assembly in the world, or any government on earth has the right or authority to make any amendment or change in the rights conferred by God."[12] His list of Islamic human rights incorporated not only the widely accepted rights to life, freedom, and equality but also the right to protest against tyranny, the protection of honor, and the right to avoid sin.[13]

The Saudi Islamic scholar Abd Wahhab Abd Aziz al-Shishani has offered a more conservative approach, claiming that there are two categories of rights: those for God and those for humans.[14] The rights of God contain acts of worship and rituals and the provisions of Sharia for the protection of life, property, reason, and family. Consequently, al-Shishani asserted that these rights cannot be abolished or amended. The rights of humans include freedom to worship, freedom of belief, and equality. Yet these human rights are not absolute, but are subject to certain restrictions. For example, freedom of belief cannot extend to allowing Muslims to change their religion.[15]

Finally, the Turkish Sufi leader Fethullah Gülen, who has been living in self-exile in the United States, has argued that Islam recognizes certain human rights like freedom of expression, the right to marry and have children, and the right to own property.[16] In this way, the Turkish thinker has tried to bridge the gap between the Western liberal tradition and the Quranic interpretation of human rights. Gülen's choice of rights is carefully made to ensure a convergence of understandings about them. Hence he could demonstrate that Islam is not antithetical to the Enlightenment's emphasis on reason and progress.

*   *   *

The end of the Cold War and the fall of communism in the late 1980s were a catalyst for the revival of the debate over human rights. The post-Cold War era has been characterized by freer movement of people, advancements in communication technology, increased capital flows and, more importantly, the increased transmission of ideas and knowledge. Justin Gest argued that globalization has enabled minority groups to express and follow their individual preferences in the face of dissenting majorities, but it is the global human rights regime that has made it possible.[17] Besides, Yasemin Soysal pointed out that individuals do not draw their rights from citizenship alone; their rights are now defined at the transnational level as "human rights."[18] Consequently, the master frame of human rights has come to dominate public and intellectual debates about the status of ethnic and religious minorities, gender relations, and the treatment of immigrants.

Due to its wide acceptance, the master frame is subject to constant modification. Indeed, the master frame of human rights is so broad that it is possible for many different social actors to use it for their purposes. In Latin America, many movements "interpreted and framed their grievances through the master frame of human rights that provided them with language and concepts that resonated with the lived experiences of their members."[19] In South Korea, feminists have used the frame to eradicate violence against women.[20] Also, it has been utilized by activists to promote the rights of LGBT persons in Europe, the United States, and elsewhere.[21] Most recently, pro-Kremlin separatists in eastern Ukraine have utilized the master frame to gain support among the local population and make counterclaims about Russian expansionism.[22] In spite of its noble aim, the logic of this master frame is clearly dichotomous and builds oppositions, such as good versus evil, modern versus medieval, dignity versus depravity, civilization versus barbarity. As a result, it can easily provoke emotion and incite inspiration. It is a powerful ideational tool to address a target audience and mobilize support.

This master frame consists of three main components. First, there is a generic framework of rights and freedoms that is theoretically applicable everywhere, irrespective of country or government. This framework includes the first generation of civil and political rights and the second generation of social, economic and cultural ones.[23] In other words, this component includes both negative and positive rights. The former *negatively* protect the individual from abuses because it calls for inaction; for example, the state cannot revoke the right to life, liberty and security, freedom of religion, and freedom of speech. The latter *positively* protect the individual because they require the state to intervene in their support; for example, the right to food, health and housing, the right to education, and the right to benefits of science and culture. The wide range of rights included in this component means that the master frame of human rights has a tremendous flexibility and adaptability in its functioning.

Second, it contains and gives ethical legitimacy to those who pursue an agenda that privileges the protection of human dignity and autonomy. This legitimacy derives from religious teachings, as well as the reasoning of the Enlightenment. Both religious and secular scholars have emphasized the sanctity of human rights. The boundaries of ethical legitimacy are not well defined, but must resonate with the moral reasonableness of a community. Under certain conditions, this component could increase the chances of a successful mobilization. For example, Martin Luther King Jr. was aware of the importance of ethical legitimacy for his effort to mobilize the African American community.[24] In March 1981, Irish Republican prisoner Bobby Sands went on hunger strike to protest against the British government's decision to abolish the special category status for members of paramilitary groups in Northern Ireland; his struggle for political prisoners' rights, followed by his death, lent unprecedented ethical legitimacy to the Irish republican cause.[25]

Third, it claims a moral obligation to help human beings when they suffer and need support. This component draws from a long tradition of humanitarianism that all major religions and cultures share. For instance, the Quran states that Muslims have the religious duty to protect each other's rights because "we have created you from a male and female, and made you into peoples and tribes, so that you might come to know each other" (49:13). Here the obligation to help human beings is a moral rather than legal request. It implies a sense of shared destiny, at least among members of the same community. Thus, it can justify interventionist action at various levels; for instance, activists would feel obliged to take direct action to prevent or stop violations of human rights. The promotion of a moral obligation to help fellow human beings is probably still the most efficient way of mobilizing individuals into action. The master frame of human rights is described in Figure 3.

Not surprisingly, many activists have used human rights to defend and promote Islamist agendas. They have presented their demands as a matter of protecting fundamental rights and freedoms. This communicative strategy can provide them with an ethical legitimacy over their adversaries while

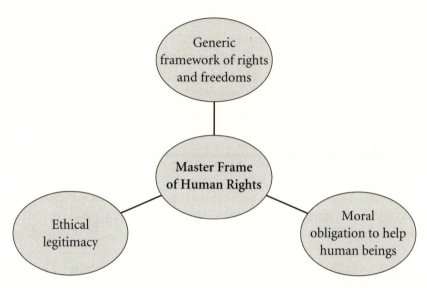

Figure 3. Components of the master frame of human rights

justifying a moral obligation to act unilaterally. In this way, these activists operate as agents of glocalization because they seek to apply the master frame of human rights to local environments.

Within the European context, the European Court of Human Rights has tried several high-profile cases of Muslims whose human rights were allegedly violated. In the famous *Dahlab v. Switzerland* case (2001), the court examined the ban of the Islamic headscarf (hijab). The Swiss convert Lucia Dahlab was a primary school teacher who was fired from her job because she wore a headscarf. She subsequently decided to appeal to the European Court. The court considered "the impact that a powerful external symbol such as the wearing of a headscarf may have on the freedom of conscience and religion of very young children."[26] Therefore, it came to the conclusion that it is "difficult to reconcile the wearing of an Islamic headscarf with the message of tolerance, respect for others and, above all, equality and non-discrimination." The European Court confirmed its pro-secular approach in the cases of *Sahin v. Turkey* (2004) and *Dogru v. France* (2008). Despite these rulings, Islamist activists have managed to stir a debate about tolerance, secularism, and the treatment of Muslims in Western societies.

In recent years, there have also been a growing number of European Muslims who have appealed to the justice system of their own country to defend their rights. In 2006, for example, the United Kingdom's House of Lords ruled in the *R (Begum) v. Governors of Denbigh High School* case that a person's right to manifest a religious belief, namely wearing a headscarf, could be interfered with under certain circumstances.[27] In September 2013, a German federal court ruled against the exemption of a Muslim girl from mixed-gender swimming classes in a high school in Frankfurt; instead, it recognized the right to wear the Islamic bathing suit (*burqini*).[28] These cases were taken to the court by individual Muslims who did not necessarily adhere to an Islamist agenda; yet their cases quickly gained publicity because of the politicized issues involved.

Against this background, various initiatives have been taken to address Islamophobia and mistreatment of Muslims. The Measuring Anti-Muslim Attacks project was launched by British Muslims, human rights activists and concerned citizens in 2012. It aims at the documentation of anti-Muslim incidents across the United Kingdom. It has received funding from a variety of sources, including the British government. Although the project has focused exclusively on reporting incidents, its very existence points to a wider trend of utilizing human rights to address issues relating to the Muslim faith. In neighboring France, the Association for the Defense of Human Rights—Collective Against Islamophobia (Association de défense des droits de l'Homme—Le Collectif contre l'Islamophobie en France) was established in 2003 to protect Muslims from bigotry and Islamophobia. Yet the organization has been accused of promoting Muslim visibility and exploiting human rights for its own interests.[29]

The debate over human rights is a double-edged sword for Islamist activists. Kate Zebiri has argued that the "dominance of human rights discourse offers hope to dispossessed Muslims but can also give rise to the construction of Islam as politically repressive and intolerant, as well as oppressive of women and minorities."[30] Indeed, there is growing criticism of Muslim countries for the treatment of the female population. For instance, many Western NGOs have criticized the Saudi regime for its ban on female driving.[31] Also, Western organizations and media have expressed concern about the discrimination faced by religious minorities (e.g., Ahmadiyya and Bahá'ís) and the persecution of LGBT people in the Muslim world.[32] In fact, the protection of human rights in Muslim-majority countries is a constant source of friction between the West and the Muslim world.

However, Islamist groups have increasingly used this master frame to achieve political aims at a time when the language of human rights has dominated public discourses especially in liberal democracies. Islamist activists have adopted a pro-human-rights approach seeking to reveal what they see as the West's hypocrisy and double standards, while gaining more legitimacy and support for their actions. In effect, they have learned from the experiences of Western activists who have benefited politically by framing their struggle in terms of human rights. The European convert-activists and Hizb ut-Tahrir are two examples of glocalizers who have utilized the master frame of human rights to promote Islamist agendas.

Chapter 1

The Activism of European Converts

What if Islamophobia continues to increase? What if I am
threatened with death as in the deportation of the Jews?
What should I do if I am deported because of the niqab?
                                        Nora Illi, June 25, 2011

Islam has grown demographically in most European countries due to the influx of immigrants and refugees from Muslim-majority countries. Additionally, thousands of Europeans, who belong to majority ethnicities, have converted to the Muslim faith. In total, there are probably around 200,000–350,000 converts, making up 1.5 to 2.5 percent of the European Union's Muslim population.[1] Most of them grew up in modern and secular societies so naturally they adjust Islam to match their needs. Despite public perception to the contrary, they usually consider religion a private matter.[2] Indeed, many European converts follow Sufism, which tends to be more inclusive and spiritual than other forms of Islam.[3] Therefore, they usually balance Islamic beliefs with a modern lifestyle. Moreover, many of them have developed hybrid identities that combine local cultural elements with their new faith.[4]

However, there are growing signs of politicization among European converts since the 9/11 events. Several prominent Islamist activists in Germany, Greece, Great Britain, the Netherlands, Switzerland, and even Russia are native Europeans. These converts have taken a public stance on many issues that have agitated Europe's Muslim communities like the Prophet Muhammad cartoons controversy during 2005 and 2006. In fact, a new class of activists of convert origin has come into existence in some European countries. Their activism is Islamist-oriented in nature because it has a political rationale and political implications. For example, the demand for the banning of certain cartoons violates the freedom of expression that lies at the heart of modern Western democracy; therefore, it implies a conscious rejection of liberal values in the name of religious supremacy. Likewise, requests for gender segregation in public places (e.g., universities) relate to fundamental rights and freedoms. Convert-activists think and act *politically*.

The subject of religious conversion has been discussed by many scholars since the 1960s.[5] John Lofland and Rodney Stark defined conversion as a process by which "a person gives up one perspective or ordered view of the world for another."[6] For the purpose of this analysis, a convert is one who has changed membership from one religious group to become Muslim. While there are no reliable statistics on previous religious affiliation, it seems that most Europeans were Christians before converting to Islam.

There is an extensive literature on European converts, including those who have been involved in jihadi activities.[7] But these analyses have not considered the role of European converts as activists who pursue Islam-based agendas in their respective countries. Interestingly, these convert-activists have increasingly used the language of human rights and anti-Islamophobia to reach out to their own communities and beyond. In effect, they have acted as glocalizers of Islamism by applying the global idea of human rights to local environments.

This chapter first describes Islamic conversion in Europe, focusing on three different waves. Although each individual may have his or her reasons to embrace Islam, it is still possible to identify general trends. It will then examine organizations run by converts and prominent convert-activists that have been increasingly visible in their efforts to promote and defend Islamist causes. While activists have different backgrounds, orientations and goals, they have all utilized the master frame of human rights. More specifically, they have used its three main components—generic framework of rights and liberties, ethical legitimacy and moral responsibility—to mobilize support and gain influence in European societies. Thus, they have developed and adhere to a glocalized version of Islamism.

The History of Islamic Conversions in Europe

The conversion of native Europeans to Islam is hardly a new development. The first wave of conversions occurred in England in the late nineteenth century. Following a journey to Morocco in 1887, William Quilliam, a well-known lawyer from Liverpool, converted to Islam and upon his return to England he became a preacher.[8] Quilliam established the Liverpool Mosque and the Muslim Institute and he soon attracted a number of converts. He criticized British involvement in Sudan, urging Muslim soldiers from British India to refrain from attacking Sudanese Muslims. Finally, Quilliam left Great Britain and was reported to have gone to the Ottoman Empire in 1908.[9] This first generation of converts was usually middle- or upper-class citizens who turned to Islam as an alternative to Christianity. The Muslim faith represented for them, at the time of the British Empire, an exotic other.

The second wave of conversions took place in west European countries from the late 1960s till the late 1980s and was the result of two important developments: post-World War II Muslim immigration and the rise of protest movements. The first generation of Muslim immigrants remained rather isolated from the rest of society. Consequently, mixed marriages with native Europeans were not common during the 1950s and most of the 1960s. However, the second and third generations of Europe's Muslims have increasingly married outside their religious group. In France, for instance, the intermarriage rate has been very high: half of Muslim men marry non-Muslim women and one-fourth of Muslim women marry non-Muslim men.[10] Although circumstances differ from country to country, many non-Muslim partners typically convert to Islam to get their in-laws' approval; for example, many British women changed their religion in order to marry a Muslim man.[11]

Additionally, individuals involved in hippie and other counterculture movements embraced Sufism as a spiritual alternative because it calls for self-exploration. Thus, Sufi Islam can be appealing to those who rejected the Christian faith for being too materialistic. The growing secularization of European societies has also contributed to the development of a new religious market composed of disenfranchised individuals who have been looking for guidance and salvation.[12]

Following the collapse of communism in the late 1980s, there has been a third wave of conversions. In the post-Cold War era, Islam has come to be seen as a religion of rebels. Olivier Roy has drawn attention to "protest conversion," which can be divided into four categories: the politicized rebels who admire the anti-imperialistic rhetoric of political Islam, the religious nomads who convert to Islam after experimenting with other faiths, individuals with a criminal record who find refuge in Islam, and members of minority groups (e.g., blacks and people of mixed race) who are attracted to Islam because of its cross-racial appeal.[13] Interestingly, some famous converts are former Marxists including prominent French philosopher Roger Garaudy and the imprisoned terrorist Carlos the Jackal. This should not come as a surprise. Islam and Marxism prioritize group goals over individual interests and claim to be universal.

Moreover, a growing number of conversions are connected to the realities of modern urban life in some western European countries. Many young people have embraced Islam to improve their chances of social acceptance in predominantly Muslim neighborhoods. According to Gilles Kepel, "in poor districts [of Paris and other major French cities], it has become a reverse integration."[14] In reality, disillusioned youngsters have felt peer pressure to convert to a religion that would open new social opportunities for them. In the French context, this new religious affiliation is an inseparable part of the youth subculture that includes Muslim hip-hop music, anti-establishment comedy, the "quenelle" gesture created by comedian and activist Dieudonnè (known for his anti-Semitic views), and graffiti art.[15]

Besides these general trends, there are individual reasons for each person to convert to Islam. It is common for many new Muslims to mention an event that changed their lives forever and eventually led to their conversion. For instance, a conversion is sometimes a break from the troubled past. Samantha Lewthwaite, the widow of 7/7 London suicide bomber Germaine Lindsay and herself fugitive, could be an example of this category of converts; she turned to Islam after her parents' divorce.[16]

Conversion to Islam is usually a life-changing experience. The new adherents adopt a Muslim name in order to prove their allegiance to their new faith. They are also keen to demonstrate to their friends and relatives their commitment to the Islamic way of life. Therefore, they very often quit drinking alcohol and change their eating habits. Conversion to Islam is not always acceptable to parents and other family members. Many converts, particularly women, have mentioned the difficult time they had with parents and siblings when they announced to them their decision to embrace Islam.[17]

On the other hand, the conversion creates new relationships and bonds for them. Despite the reluctance of many born Muslims to accept these newcomers, converts could become members of communities and gain fresh social and professional opportunities. They could travel for pilgrimage or go abroad to study, they could socialize with Muslims from different parts of society or foreign countries and benefit from this interaction, and they could receive social support in dealing with isolation and marginalization. The joining of groups and networks of Muslims would certainly reinforce their own newly acquired identity.

Converts as Islamist Activists

The postwar growth of Muslim communities in several European countries has created new challenges and dilemmas for policymakers and societies. The process of integration of Muslim populations has often proved to be contentious with (at best) mixed results. Western European countries have adopted two models of integration: multiculturalism and assimilationism.[18] The former has promoted the coexistence of the dominant national identity with other cultures, while the latter has imposed westernization on ethnic minorities for the purpose of assimilating them into the majority culture. Great Britain, the Netherlands, and Belgium have endorsed the multiculturalist model, whereas France has applied the assimilationist one. However, both models have largely failed for a variety of reasons. As a result, it is fair to say that the majority of European Muslims feel marginalized and underrepresented.

While the first generation of Muslim immigrants avoided confronting authorities, the second and third generations have not hesitated to campaign for Islam-related issues. Indeed, Islamist activism in Europe has been on the rise in the last thirty years. The Salman Rushdie affair in the late 1980s was the first major incident of Islamist activism in Europe; the publication of the *Satanic Verses* brought about unprecedented mobilization of young Muslims who protested against the British author and what they saw as his blasphemous book on the life of Prophet Muhammad. The Leicester-based Islamic Foundation, which had focused on *da'wa* (preaching of Islam) activities, took a leading role in the protests against Rushdie's *Satanic Verses*.[19] The 1991 Gulf War and the Palestinian Intifada kept the interest of British Muslims alive and the level of Islamist activism high.

During the 1990s, Islamist and Islamist-leaning NGOs and civil society organizations started to carry out advocacy activities. The London-based NGO Islamic Human Rights Commission was established in 1997 to defend Muslims in Great Britain and elsewhere. According to its website, its aspiration "derives from the Qur'anic injunctions that command believers to rise up in defence of the oppressed."[20] However, the commission has been accused by its critics of being a "Khomeinist group" because it has staged the annual Ayatollah Khomeini-inspired al-Quds day parade in London.[21] Also, the commission has organized annually the controversial awards of Islamophobia to draw attention to the continued mistreatment of many Muslims in the West.

The 9/11 events and the terrorist attacks in Madrid and London fundamentally changed public views on internal security, Muslim immigration, and Islam in general. The subsequent tensions between Muslims and non-Muslims gave a new momentum to Islamist activism. But this time, it was not only Muslim-born individuals who were mobilized for the purpose of promoting Islam-based agendas, but European converts as well. The latter usually feel more confident than Muslims of immigrant origin to criticize government policies and pursue political goals. The born Muslims often have mixed feelings toward converts: some are skeptical of them, while others view them as mediators between authorities and the Muslim community because they are part of two worlds. The next sections provide a brief description of organizations run by converts and then an account of individual convert-activists.

Organizations Run by Converts

There are only a small number of Islamist and Islamist-leaning groups and organizations in Europe run and controlled by converts. However, their existence clearly indicates the gradual Europeanization of Islam; it is not anymore solely the religion of immigrants but has grown roots in the continent's societies.

The Salafi-oriented Islamic Party of Britain was established at the time of the Rushdie affair in September 1989. The party was dissolved in 2003 because it never managed to gain much support from Muslims in constituencies where it stood. In the November 1990 by-election, for example, held in the constituency of Bradford North, an area with a large Muslim population, the party won only 2.2 percent of the votes (800 votes).[22] In reality, the huge majority of British Muslims, who are of South Asian origin, could not identify with a party run mostly by white converts. The party was founded and led by David Musa Pidcock (president), who is English, and

Sahib Mustaqim Bleher (general-secretary), who is German. Another reason for its limited electoral appeal was probably its hard-core ideology. The party argued that "Islam is the solution to the world's problems. No other religion, way of life or culture can possibly succeed, because only truth can satisfy the soul of humankind, and only the guidance, laws, and concepts taught to us by God are capable of achieving just balance."[23] In other words, the Islamic Party of Britain believed in the superiority of Islam and advocated the imposition of Sharia, which automatically limited its appeal among secular British Muslims.

The Association of British Muslims (AOBM) was established in 1974 and claims to represent the interests of British converts. It is a Sufi-oriented organization. The AOBM has promoted a British Islam, arguing that local traditions are "compatible with Islam."[24] In effect, the association has supported the Anglicization of Islam, which is often viewed as a religion of ethnic minorities. The AOBM is a rather apolitical organization that advocates integration and avoids controversial issues. It has focused on public activities such as conferences, public lectures, and community and charitable services. Some of its members were involved in the humanitarian missions in the western Balkans in the early to mid-1990s; for instance, Neil (Ibrahim) Golightly, a thirty-four-year-old convert from Glasgow, was killed while trying to bring food and supplies to besieged Sarajevo in August 1995.[25]

The Salafi-leaning Finnish Islamic Party (Suomen islamilainen puolue) was established in 2007 by Finnish converts Abdullah Tammi and Abdullah Rintala. Its membership is unknown but estimated to be only a few hundred. The party, which has limited influence among Finland's sixty thousand Muslims, supports a ban on alcohol sales and gender segregation for Muslims.[26] It has also favored Finland's withdrawal from the European Union. The party has increasingly taken a stand on pan-Islamic issues (e.g., the U.S. invasion of Iraq). Due to Tammi's past as a KGB agent, the party has also followed a pro-Russian line.[27] For example, it has been highly critical of Estonia for its "apartheid policies" under which the "educational system discriminates against Russian-speakers."[28]

Spain's Islamic Association (Junta Islamica) is open to all Muslims, but its leadership consists mainly of Spanish converts. The group has sparked some controversy in regard to the al-Andalus issue.[29] For several years, Junta Islamica has unsuccessfully petitioned both the local church authorities and the Vatican to open the former Great Mosque of Cordoba, the symbol of Muslim Spain for centuries, to Muslims. The repatriation of Moriscos is another issue raised by the group. Following the Reconquista of Andalusia in 1492, the remaining Muslim population converted to Christianity under the threat of exile and came to be known as Moriscos. One hundred years later, however, the Spanish throne expelled them to North Africa. The persecution of Muslims by Christian medieval armies and the loss of Spain have often been mentioned by Islamists as a proof of Western intolerance. Therefore, several Islamist groups, including al-Qaeda, have openly called for the reconquest of al-Andalus. At the beginning, the issue was taken lightly; yet following the Madrid bombings in March 2004, the Junta Islamica's interest in al-Andalus has only reinforced suspicion among conservative segments of the society that Spanish converts have a secret agenda to re-Islamize Spain. But Junta Islamica is only part of a larger network of organizations run by Spanish converts; for instance, Liberación Andaluza (Andalusian Liberation) has advocated the repatriation of Moriscos, the establishment of Arabic as one of the official languages of Andalusia, and eventually the creation of an independent Andalusian state.[30]

In the Netherlands, there have been two political parties run, mainly or partly, by Dutch converts. The Party of Islam Democrats (Islam Democraten) was established in The Hague in 2005. It has participated in local elections calling for an "end to discrimination against Muslims."[31] One of its most well known members is Armoud van Doorn, a former senior member of the Far Right Dutch Freedom Party of Geert Wilders who converted to Islam. The Dutch Muslim Party (Nederlandse Moslim Partij) was established by two Dutch converts, Henny Kreeft and Jacques Visser, in 2007. The party sought to defend Islam and Muslims from unfounded attacks and promoted Islamic values in the Netherlands; in fact, the Dutch Muslim Party was founded as a reaction to the rise of anti-Muslim populism expressed by the Far Right politician Geert Wilders. It participated in several local elections but failed to win any seats. Finally, despite its moderate tone, the party did not attract a substantial following and was dissolved in 2012.[32]

The Association of Muslims in Greece (Enosi Mousoulmanon Elladas—hereafter AMG) was established in 2003 to "defend the Muslims' rights in several fields."[33] The current president, Naim el-Ghandour, is a naturalized Greek citizen of Egyptian origin with pro-Muslim Brotherhood sympathies, but AMG is run mostly by Greek converts. The country's Muslim population is estimated at around 700,000–800,000 people, including the large

Albanian immigrant community whose members tend to be secular and excluding the indigenous, largely Turkish-speaking, Muslim minority of northeastern Greece.[34] Despite constituting only a small percentage of the Muslim community in Greece, the AMG's converts have been vocal and active in their efforts to promote an Islamist agenda. At the beginning, the AMG focused on symbolic issues such as the construction of a mosque and a Muslim cemetery in Athens, where the majority of the Muslim population currently resides. Following the wars in Lebanon and Gaza in 2006 and 2008 respectively, however, the AMG has increasingly taken part in protests and sit-ins against the United States and Israel. The group also protested against the release of the controversial *Innocence of Muslims* short film in 2012.

The National Organization of Russian Muslims (Natsional'naya organizatsiya russkikh musul'man) was established by Russian converts in June 2004. The organization has viewed Islam as "a path to the rebirth of the Russian nation" and as "a means to the world-wide liberation of the oppressed."[35] It has been eager to promote the creation of a Russian Islam that could fill the spiritual vacuum left by the declining influence of the Russian Orthodox Church. Vadim Sidorov, the chairman of NORM, is a member of the Murabitun World Movement, which advocates the peaceful restoration of the caliphate. In December 2011, Sidorov drafted the Islamic Civic Charter, which calls for the elimination of "lists of prohibited literature and the practice of banning literature" and the replacement of the "current law on political parties to allow such groups to be formed on regional, religious and ethnic grounds."[36] More importantly, the Islamic Charter demanded "the political resolution of the Caucasus problem [i.e., the Islamist insurgency in Chechnya and Dagestan] by means of broad dialogue with social forces and the participation of authoritative mediators."[37] Sidorov has apparently joined forces with a new Muslim-dominated movement, Intersoyuz.[38]

To sum up, these organizations have different orientations and goals. The Islamic Party of Britain and the Finnish Islamic Party can be classified as Salafi; the AOBM and Spain's Islamic Association are Sufi-oriented; the AMG has been partly influenced by the Muslim Brotherhood; and the National Organization of Russian Muslims is a sui generis organization. However, they all represent a new class of activists of convert origin who promote Islam-related agendas in their home country. In effect, they have endorsed localized versions of Islamism (apart from the AOBM) that combine pan-Islamic issues and concerns with their communal issues. Yet they

Table 2. Organizations run by converts

	Country	Orientation	Status
Association of British Muslims	United Kingdom	Sufi	Active
Islamic Party of Britain	United Kingdom	Salafi	Dissolved
Finnish Islamic Party	Finland	Salafi	Active
Islamic Association	Spain	Sufi	Active
Dutch Muslim Party	The Netherlands	Mainstream	Dissolved
Party of Islam Democrats	The Netherlands	Mainstream	Active
Association of Muslims in Greece	Greece	Muslim Brotherhood-leaning	Active
National Organization of Russian Muslims	Russia	Caliphate	Active

have managed to attract media and public attention because they have used a human rights discourse to defend their cause. Table 2 summarizes the main features of organizations run by converts.

Individual Convert-Activists

In addition to those who have joined or have formed groups, there are individual converts who have become involved in Islamist activism. They usually enjoy the status of celebrity in their respective Muslim community, since they are largely seen as proactive, brave, and selfless. These convert-activists are often at the center of public campaigns that support faith-based demands and aspirations.

Yvonne Ridley, a British journalist who converted to Islam two years after being freed from Taliban captivity in October 2001, is one of the most well known Islamist activists in Europe. In June 2004, Ridley ran as a candidate in European Parliament elections for the Respect coalition party. The party had been established by former Labour MP George Galloway together with the Socialist Workers Party, the Revolutionary Communist Party of

Britain, and prominent members of the Muslim Association of Britain and the Muslim Council of Britain. The party manifesto condemns "Islamophobia and the demonization of Muslim communities."[39] Ridley herself has turned into a controversial figure, referring to Shamil Basayev as a rebel leader who "led an admirable fight to bring independence to Chechnya"[40] and defending Abu Musab al-Zarqawi for his 2005 Amman bombings in Jordan.[41] In March 2009, Ridley cofounded with Galloway the pro-Hamas charity Viva Palestina. She has been a very active blogger commenting on Islam-related issues.

Pierre Vogel (a.k.a. Abu Hamza) is another famous Islamist activist. He was born in Germany and converted to Islam at the age of twenty-three while he was a professional boxer. After studying under a scholarship for two years in Mecca, Vogel returned to Germany and started preaching Salafism.[42] Vogel has used the new media to reach out to a younger audience of Muslims. In December 2009, the Swiss authorities banned him from attending a demonstration against the minaret ban in Bern. He has claimed that membership in the umma takes priority over nationality.[43] Due to his anti-integration messages, Vogel has been monitored by the German security services, which worry about radicalism among the country's large Muslim community.[44]

Abdul-Jabbar van de Ven is a leading Salafi activist in the Netherlands. He converted from Catholicism to Islam at the age of fourteen. He studied in Amman and Medina before returning to the Netherlands. He has preached Islam in the Salafi-oriented al-Fourqaan Mosque in Eindhoven, which has been linked to jihadi groups. Like Pierre Vogel, Van de Ven has used the Internet to approach young Muslims. He has also been known for his controversial statements regarding the assassination of Theo van Gogh, a film director.[45] Van de Ven was also implicated in the case of Jason Walters, a radical Dutch-American convert, who was a member of the notorious Hofstad group that killed the Dutch director.[46]

Abdurraheem Green is a British-Polish Salafi-oriented preacher who converted from Catholicism to Islam at the age of twenty-six. He runs the charity organization Islamic Education and Research Academy, which has been accused of promoting anti-Semitism and homophobia.[47] Indeed, Green himself has not hidden its belligerent views on Jews and gays.[48] Yet he has increasingly used the Internet to deliver messages to Western Muslims.

Denis Mamadou Cuspert (a.k.a. Abou Malleq) was a rap singer turned Islamist activist. He converted to Islam after meeting Pierre Vogel in

2009. Following his conversion, he started propagating Islamist messages. His songs praised Osama bin Laden and jihadi warriors. Cuspert served as a role model for Muslim teenagers of immigrant origin who struggle to cope with social exclusion and racism. Indeed, Cuspert was accused of inspiring Arid Uka, a Kosovo Albanian, who killed two American airmen at the Frankfurt airport in March 2011. Although he denied any direct connection with Uka, Cuspert did not hesitate to argue that "the brother hasn't killed civilians. . . . [Uka] has killed soldiers who had been on their way to kill Muslims."[49] Finally, Cuspert became a jihadi fighter himself sometime during 2013; first he went to Egypt to join members of Millatu Ibrahim, a banned German Salafi group, and from there he ended up joining ISIS in Syria.[50] In October 2015, he was killed by a U.S. airstrike near ar-Raqqa.[51]

Nicolas Blancho converted to Islam at the age of sixteen. He is the founder of the Islamic Central Council of Switzerland (Islamischer Zentralrat Schweiz), a controversial Salafi-oriented organization that has taken a confrontational stance on many issues; for instance, Blancho provoked a public outcry when he refused to condemn the stoning of adulterous women in Afghanistan.[52] According to Markus Seiler, director of the Swiss Federal Intelligence Service, the Islamic Central Council has espoused an ideological, not violent, extremism.[53]

The twenty-seven-year-old Nora Illi, the director of women's affairs at the council, is probably Switzerland's most famous *niqab* (i.e., face veil) wearer. She converted to Islam at the age of nineteen. Illi has gained the status of a celebrity who is reported on and sought after by the Swiss media. As a teenager, she was involved in demonstrations for Palestine where she met her future husband, Qassim Illi, a fellow Swiss convert.[54] Qassim Illi became known for his pro-Hamas statements, endorsing suicide attacks against Israeli citizens.[55]

Finally, Hamza Andreas Tzortzis is a British-born convert of Greek origin who is known as a self-declared intellectual activist. He converted to Islam at the age of twenty-two.[56] He has been accused of being close to Hizb ut-Tahrir and of promoting its pan-Islamic cause in public forums and on university campuses.[57] Tzortzis has blamed liberal values and Western individualism for social ills and problems. Therefore, he has claimed that "Islam provides that framework for moral motivation and accountability."[58] Tzortzis has been keen to emphasize the cultural heterogeneity within Islam because his audience is highly diverse.

Table 3. Prominent convert-activists

	Nationality	Background	Orientation
Nicolas Blancho	Swiss	Leftist	Salafi
Denis Mamadou Cuspert	German	Unknown	Jihadi-Salafi
Abdurraheem Green	British-Polish	Unknown	Salafi
Nora Illi	Swiss	Leftist	Salafi
Yvonne Ridley	British	Leftist	Pro-Hamas
Hamza Andreas Tzortzis	British	Apolitical	Pro-Hizb ut-Tahrir
Abdul-Jabbar van de Ven	Dutch	Apolitical	Salafi
Pierre Vogel	German	Apolitical	Salafi

All these convert-activists have gained publicity for their inflammatory rhetoric and criticism toward Western governments. No matter why they converted to Islam, they now act with defiance and self-assertiveness, sometimes on the borderline of the law. But Islamist activists of convert origin do not constitute a coherent group. They have different political backgrounds and religious orientations. Ridley, Blancho, and Illi are former leftists, whereas Vogel and Cuspert have no significant political history. While Vogel, Cuspert, Illi, and Van de Ven advocate Salafism, Ridley, Tzortzis, and Green consider themselves just Muslims. Although they all feel part of the umma, convert-activists have to address a local audience that cares about specific issues and problems.

The convert-activists are usually self-taught, mobile, and technologically savvy. Some of them, especially the males, had a form of religious training in a Middle Eastern country. Therefore, they can preach in mosques and religious centers. In contrast, the females lack religious knowledge and usually focus on highly symbolic issues like the wearing of the hijab or niqab and the banning of minarets. Yet all of them have been exposed to debates about human rights and their contemporary meaning. Table 3 summarizes the main features of prominent convert-activists.

Convert-Activists Between the Global and the Local

The September 11 events aggravated the already strained relations between the West and the Muslim world. The fact that the perpetrators of the terrorist attacks were Muslims, who had traveled to the United States from European cities, brought the Continent's Islamic communities into the spotlight.[59] The homegrown Madrid and London bombings on March 11, 2004 and July 7, 2005, respectively, only confirmed in the eyes of some people the untrustworthiness of European Muslims.

The targeting of Western civilians by jihadis has provoked a media near hysteria in regard to Islam. There are so many examples of statements and writings that have unjustifiably attacked Muslims that it is almost impossible to compile a relevant anthology. However, a few of them attracted much attention due to the celebrated personality of the commentator or the outrageousness of the statement. In October 2006, Joan Smith of the British newspaper the *Independent* declared that "I can't think of a more dramatic visual symbol of oppression, the inescapable fact being that the vast majority of the women who cover their hair, faces and bodies do so because they have no choice."[60] In December 2014, a French TV commentator, Eric Zemmour, argued that "this situation of a people inside a people, of Muslims inside French people, will lead us to civil war. . . . Millions of people live here in France and refuse to live in the French manner"; therefore, he did not exclude the possibility of deporting five million Muslims from the country.[61]

To make matters worse, there are a growing number of Far Right and populist political parties that have openly endorsed racist and xenophobic views against Muslims.[62] France's National Front (Front National), the Alternative for Germany (Alternative für Deutschland), Greece's Golden Dawn (Chrysi Avgi), and Italy's League of the North (Lega Nord) have constantly scapegoated Muslims. They have contributed to what Jocelyne Cesari called the "securitization of Islam in Europe" by influencing the policymaking process on relevant issues (e.g., immigration laws, antiterror policies).[63]

Media bias and the rise of Far Right parties have stirred up a climate of Islamophobia that has alarmed Muslim communities. The term *Islamophobia* was defined by the Council of Europe as "the fear of or prejudiced viewpoint towards Islam, Muslims and matters pertaining to them. . . . Islamophobia is a violation of human rights and a threat to social cohesion."[64] In 2005, a European survey results showed that "many Muslims have experienced verbal assaults in public transportation means and other public places. Muslim women who wear the headscarf and Muslim men who travel with women dressed this way are particularly frequent targets of offensive comments."[65] According to a 2006 survey of the Pew Research Center, 51 percent of Germany's Muslims, 42 percent of Great Britain's Muslims, 39 percent of France's Muslims and 31 percent of Spain's Muslims believe that native Europeans are hostile to Muslims, while 19 percent of German Muslims, 28 percent of British Muslims, 37 percent of French Muslims and 25 percent of Spanish Muslims had a bad personal experience.[66]

Since they are a minority within a minority, converts have been particularly vulnerable to Islamophobia and racism. A study published by the NGO Faith Matters found that during 2001–2010, of the stories reported about converts by British media, 62 percent related to terrorism. In other words, converts were stereotypically identified by the media as a security threat to the British society.[67] The study also surveyed 122 British converts; 47 percent of them claimed that most British people are hostile to Islam.[68] Moreover, 84 percent of the respondents believed that they could act as a bridge between the Muslim community and the rest of British society.[69] These surveys indicate that Muslims in general and converts in particular have been targeted on the basis of their religious affiliation. They are often viewed as an outgroup that cannot be trusted because it is the fifth column of an expanding religion seeking to infiltrate European societies.

Indeed, Islamist activists of convert origin have often attributed their traumatic personal experiences to Islamophobia. It is these experiences that, partly at least, motivated them to take a public stance on Islam-related issues. Yvonne Ridley proclaimed that "when I converted to Islam and began wearing a headscarf, the repercussions were enormous. . . . I instantly became a second-class citizen. I knew I'd hear from the odd Islamophobe, but I didn't expect so much open hostility from strangers."[70] Although she may have exaggerated what actually happened, the description of her experience seems believable given the post-9/11 climate.

Ridley does not seem to be the only activist who has been a victim of Islamophobic attitudes. Abdul-Jabbar van de Ven claimed to have a similar experience in the Netherlands. In late November 2004, during an interview with a TV channel, the Dutch convert said that "It is impossible to describe what I've experienced in recent years. The atmosphere is totally intolerant. The AIVD [i.e., the Dutch Secret Service] follows me, looks at my email, and listens to my phone. . . . Even worse is what you get in the form of threatening letters and emails and phone calls. . . . And just because I am Muslim. . . . I'm sure that I will eventually leave the Netherlands and go somewhere where I can normally [practice] my faith. . . . More and more Muslims, even Dutch, [leave] because [they] will not be treated as equal."[71]

Here Abdul-Jabbar described an atmosphere of intimidation and fear that threatened basic rights and freedoms. The interview took place a few weeks after the assassination of the film director Theo van Gogh by a Dutch-Moroccan on November 2, 2004. According to the European Monitoring Centre on Racism and Xenophobia, there were 106 violent attacks against Muslim targets during November 2–30, 2004, in the country.[72] Given the prevailing Islamophobia in the Netherlands, his claim cannot be easily dismissed. His words not only revealed a deep sense of frustration with the Dutch authorities, but also an implicit call for Muslims to migrate to another (presumably Muslim) country in order to freely practice their religion.[73] Other convert-activists have also depicted a very negative picture of Muslims' place in European societies. Following the Swiss authorities' decision to refuse him entry to the country, Pierre Vogel argued that "the smear campaign against us is spreading throughout Europe more and more, and that is obvious. I am afraid that, in the future, [Muslims] will be slaughtered. We face a very dark future."[74]

At first glance, one may be tempted to doubt these accounts. But the 9/11 events and the subsequent terrorist attacks on European soil have further isolated many Muslim communities that have been suffering ever since from a siege mentality. After all, as opposed to some other religious groups, Muslim citizens tend to be more publicly visible and thus exposed to discrimination and abuse.

Against this background, convert-activists have adopted the human rights master frame for the purpose of spreading their messages and gathering support. The generic framework of rights and freedoms that comes with the master frame is very useful for their purposes. It allows them to define their demands as part of the wider debate on human rights; thus, they can gain more acceptance and recognition. Islamophobia has been identified as the prime cause of these violations; according to this logic, the fear of Islam has led to intolerance and hate against Muslims. Consequently, they can easily find political allies that are concerned about the growing influence of the Far Right in European politics and the rebirth of intolerance on the continent. Hence the master frame can bridge the gap between conservative Islamists and liberal or left-wing citizens.

There are quite a few examples of convert-activists using this component of the human rights master frame. Nicolas Blancho once stated that

"Switzerland's Muslims should enjoy the same respect and the same rights as all other groups" and he raised the case of female Muslim teachers who "if they wear headscarf, they have almost no chance of finding a job."[75] Yvonne Ridley has also drawn attention to discrimination against Muslims. In June 2014, for example, she criticized the British magazine the *Spectator* for its cover depicting a schoolboy carrying a copy of the Quran in the left hand and a massive sword in the right. She compared it to a cartoon published by the German newspaper *Süddeutsche Zeitung* depicting a caricature of Mark Zuckerberg, the founder of Facebook who is an American Jew, as an octopus controlling the world.[76] In essence, Ridley portrayed the stigmatization of British Muslims as the new anti-Semitism.

The Swiss convert-activist Qassim Illi has compared Islamophobia to anti-Semitism as well. Following the 2009 referendum to ban minarets in Switzerland, he argued that "the hatred against Islam seems structurally comparable only with the anti-Semitism ideology. . . . Although each group [of voters] probably originally had its own motives for the yes vote . . . they share a common dislike of Islam."[77] During an interview, Nora Illi wondered, "what if Islamophobia continues to increase? What if I am threatened with death as in the deportation of the Jews? What should I do if I am deported because of the *niqab*?"[78] Vogel has also warned of a "Holocaust against Muslims" in Europe.[79] The frequent reference to anti-Semitism is not a coincidence; any mentioning of it is bound to get attention from many Europeans.

However, convert-activists do not share the same perception of rights and freedoms. According to Abdurraheem Green, the Universal Declaration of Human Rights is a document that serves only the interests of the West. More specifically, he has argued that "Westerners have written in their charter of Human Rights . . . that one of the rights of the human being is to choose their religion. . . . This charter of the human right is in direct opposition to what Allah has revealed."[80] Hamza Andreas Tzortzis has also rejected the standard Western understanding of human rights. Instead, he has attempted to offer an Islamic alternative. For instance, he once said that "we as Muslims reject the idea of freedom of speech, and even of freedom."[81] He has also provided an analysis of how human rights are framed in the context of Islamic military jurisprudence. From his point of view, "defensive jihad is to push the occupiers out and has nothing to do with terrorism; in reality, it is a basic human right."[82] Moreover, he claims that "mass murder, ethnic cleansing, sectarianism, intolerance, killing journalists, kidnapping and other evils are the very opposite of the compassionate and merciful behavior that is the hallmark of a true Islamic state."[83] Thus, the logic goes, Islam has prescribed different rights than the West.

In any case, the use of this frame gives the convert-activists an ethical legitimacy that resonates well with European social and legal norms. As a result, their struggle to defend "Muslim rights" does not seem unique or extraordinary; it is part of a larger movement for human rights and equality that deserves acknowledgment. Like other discriminated communities, Muslims need to be defended by committed individuals who have devoted their efforts to this noble cause. It is possible that some convert-activists may suffer from a guilt complex vis-à-vis their new community because they used to be part of the non-Muslim majority. Consequently, their involvement is often characterized by passion and determination.

More importantly, this ethical legitimacy could function as a mobilizing structure for grassroots campaigns. Certain social groups like intellectuals and professionals are more likely to participate in an effort to protect the human rights of Muslims, however they are defined, than outright political actions. Therefore, the universality of human rights is mainstreaming Islamist activism and the participation in it. At the same time, however, this sense of ethical legitimacy could discourage the inclusion of Muslims in European societies because it creates psychological borders between them and the rest of the society. Also, it can be used as a political weapon against European governments indicating their failures to protect the civil liberties and freedoms of Muslim citizens. In this case, ethical legitimacy could become ethical supremacy over the perceived adversaries.

Finally, the human rights master frame comes with a moral obligation to help Muslims. Pierre Vogel has explained the theological rationale for the moral obligation to defend human rights. While claiming that "the doctrine of human rights has become a means to spread Western moral imperialism," he admits that "the words of the Quran and the [Hadith] contain rights and responsibilities."[84] Therefore, Vogel argued that "every person has a right to . . . shelter and security, and if their God-granted rights are denied to some people it is the responsibility of other people, to render these rights."[85] Likewise, Abdurraheem Green has argued that "the right of the human being is to be pressurized to follow the true religion that they should be living in an environment where they are encouraged or even forced to remain upon the truth that will take them to paradise and keep them away from the hellfire."[86]

These convert-activists largely perceive themselves as a vanguard that practices "jihad by tongue" (*jihad bil lisan*); this form of jihad involves educating Muslims and non-Muslims about Islam and to strive with one's tongue to support good and fight wrong. In practice, this is done through speeches, debates and other public activities. The Islamic Central Council of Switzerland has, for example, declared that "Phobias against minorities are a problem of the majority society and require efforts to curb them at all levels of public life. . . . The Muslims are themselves under an obligation to correct today's widespread misrepresentation of Islam through increased participation in public discourse. The Islamic Central Council adheres to the motto: 'public creates confidence' [*Öffentlichkeit schafft Vertrauen*]."[87]

Interestingly, Islamophobia and the growing number of anti-Muslim attacks have made converts more conscious of the problems facing the global umma. For instance, Yvonne Ridley has been a vocal supporter of Palestinian human rights. In mid-July 2014, she published a short article in her blog *Analysis and Opinion* about the Israeli-Hamas war in Gaza. She quoted Bishop Desmond Tutu, the "tireless fighter for equality, justice and peace" regarding the duty to fight injustice. Her article concluded by an open call to support Palestinians; in her words, "you do not have to be a Muslim to support Palestine—just human."[88]

Most recently, the Russian occupation of Crimea during 2014 has raised awareness among convert-activists about the rights of the local Muslim community and has prompted calls for intervention. For example, the Finnish Islamic Party has declared that "[human] rights of Islamic Tatars in Crimea should be secured! . . . The Islamic Tatars should get again the Islamic Tatar Khanate, which was in Crimea before the year 1783 when Russia took over Crimea. An Islamic state would be the best solution in the Crimean crisis!"[89] Again, Islamist demands are presented as human rights issues that are needed to be addressed accordingly. The proposed Islamic state would be the ultimate guarantor of human rights for Muslims.

Overall, it can be argued that the Islamist activism of European converts has increasingly relied on the master frame of human rights. They have tried to utilize it because its universal acceptance strengthens their case against adversaries. It is a very powerful tool for those convert-activists who have denounced violence and seek to promote Islamist agendas both at home and abroad. Due to their particularization of human rights, they have functioned as Islamist agents of glocalization.

Conclusion

Despite being negatively presented in the media and elsewhere, Islam has won thousands of new followers in many European countries. Native Europeans are attracted to Islam for a variety of reasons, ranging from personal traumatic experiences to political curiosity and rebellion. No matter why they embraced Islam, the majority of European converts have fully participated in social and economic life since they consider religion a private matter.

However, this is not the case with all of them. Being confident and with a sense of mission, some converts have been turned into activists supporting Muslim rights and often propagating Islamist messages. While these converts come from diverse backgrounds, they share a deep sense of personal commitment to the defense of Islam from the perceived adversaries. For this purpose, they have utilized the master frame of human rights. Islamist activists have used the language of human rights to criticize the West for the treatment of its Muslim citizens.

They have adhered to a generic framework of rights and freedoms that can be applicable to local Muslim communities. Consequently, they have framed many issues as human rights violations in order to promote a localized version of Islamism. They have focused on rising Islamophobia and the violations of individual liberties without abandoning their Islamist cause. The universality of human rights provides convert-activists with ethical legitimacy. It is a powerful tool justifying Islamist claims and interventions. As a result, it could increase the chances of a successful mobilization because it gives a sense of rightfulness and meaningfulness; the protection of Muslim rights is a noble cause worth supporting. Furthermore, the human rights master frame brings a moral obligation to defend fellow Muslims from discrimination and abuse. Thus, Islamist activism is portrayed as a legitimate response to injustice.

The activists of convert origin are situated between two worlds: the umma and the local Muslim community. On the one hand, they defend the rights of Muslims in distant places like Palestine and Crimea. They are moved by other Muslims' suffering and feel obliged to demonstrate their solidarity. On the other hand, they function as political entrepreneurs in European societies that often have prejudices against Islam. With the help of the human rights master frame, this dual activism is making European converts representatives of glocalized Islamism.

Chapter 2

The Activism of Hizb ut-Tahrir

Muslims living in the West have only one option when
faced with insults against their beloved Prophet—and that
is to speak out. . . . We continue to speak out
loudly—despite the mockery and hatred.

Abdul Wahid, January 8, 2015

Islamist activism has been accelerated by the emergence of groups that have
global goals but local membership. One of the most internationalized
Islamist groups is Hizb ut-Tahrir al-Islami (the Islamic Liberation Party—
hereafter Hizb ut-Tahrir), which was founded in 1953 by the Palestinian
Islamic scholar Taqiuddin an-Nabhani. His life trajectory was turbulent as
he lived in several countries, where he went through a variety of experiences.

The founding leader of Hizb ut-Tahrir studied at the prestigious al-
Azhar University and the Dar al-Ulum College in Cairo.[1] Although he was
trained to work as a high school teacher, Nabhani eventually joined the
Islamic court system in the British-mandated Palestine as a legal assistant.
The 1948 Arab-Israeli War forced him to leave his homeland and to find
refuge in neighboring Syria. He shortly left for Jordan to take up the position
of Sharia judge in the Court of Appeal and then join the Islamic College
in Amman. Nabhani moved to Syria in 1953 and from there he went
to Lebanon.

In the early 1950s, Nabhani developed his vision about the revival of
the Muslim world. He viewed the establishment of the state of Israel in
1948 as a proof of Arab decay. From his point of view, the umma could be
saved only by a Leninist-type vanguard party that would radically change

the society. Being a politically active Palestinian who had lived in several Arab countries, Nabhani understood the importance of transnational action. He developed an identity that combined cosmopolitanism, religious piety, and pan-Islamism.

On November 17, 1952, he applied to the Jordanian Ministry of Interior to register Hizb ut-Tahrir as a political party. Its name Islamic Liberation Party stressed the goal of setting Muslim countries free from colonial influence and control. According to Nabhani, "Hizb ut-Tahrir stands against colonialism in all its forms and aims to liberate the umma from the colonialist intellectual leadership and to remove its cultural, political, military and economical influence from the Islamic lands."[2] Thus he envisioned a party that would fight for a new political and cultural order in the Muslim world.

Nabhani was unable to register Hizb ut-Tahrir as a legal party in Jordan because it rejected Arab nationalism and the institution of monarchy, and promoted pan-Islamism.[3] To make matters worse, the Jordanian authorities issued a decree banning Hizb ut-Tahrir and arrested its leadership, holding the leaders for two weeks in March 1953.[4] The antagonism and mutual distrust between Palestinians and native Jordanians probably played a role in this decision. The ban and the subsequent arrests had a deep impact on the party leadership, which became even more secretive and suspicious of outsiders. In spite of its clandestine status, Hizb ut-Tahrir started to propagate its ideology in the country. The party gradually established cells and attracted some following among devout Muslims in neighboring Arab countries.

Nabhani died in Beirut on December 20, 1977. He was replaced by Abdul Qadeem Zaloom, a founding member and a fellow Palestinian who was also trained as a teacher in Egypt. The new leader was credited with the expansion of the group outside the Middle East. When the latter died in April 2003, he was succeeded by Ata Abu Rashta, an Egyptian-educated civil engineer of Palestinian origin and former party spokesman in Jordan. As of this writing, Rashta is the international leader of Hizb ut-Tahrir.

This chapter analyzes the ideology and strategy of Hizb ut-Tahrir and describes its activities in Western countries, South and Southeast Asia, the former Soviet Union and China, and the greater Middle East. I argue that Hizb ut-Tahrir has adopted a global agenda resonating with local constituencies. Indeed, the group has functioned as an Islamist agent of glocalization by embracing the master frame of human rights and applying it locally.

Party Ideology and Strategy

Hizb ut-Tahrir has developed an ideological framework that emphasizes Muslim political unity, superiority of Islam over all other religions and civilizations, and confrontation with the West. More importantly, the party strongly believes that it is on a sacred mission from Allah to save the umma. This belief is based on a hadith, narrated by Muhammad al-Bukhari, that "foretold that a distinct band of people, a Party bonded around the *Aqeedah* (belief) of Islam, standing firm against the tyrants, not deviating from the *Deen* (religion) of Islam . . . will suffer the afflictions, trials and tribulations against the tyrants, but will stick to the *Deen* of Islam and will be victorious and establish the order of Allah and his *Deen* upon the Earth."[5] Hence the implication of this is that Hizb ut-Tahrir is involved in a cosmic struggle between good and evil. It represents a community of chosen individuals who are determined to fulfil their God-given duty.

Hizb ut-Tahrir has claimed that the abolishment of the caliphate by Kemal Ataturk in Turkey in 1924 meant the end of Muslim unity and the beginning of Muslim decline. The caliph was not as powerful as he used to be due to the fragmentation of the Ottoman Empire; yet he was still symbolically the leader of the entire Muslim world. Moreover, Sunnis believed that only he could declare jihad against the umma's enemies. Since the caliphate was the only institution protecting the umma, it follows that its re-establishment is the only solution for the revival of the Muslim world.

Therefore, the party favors a radical political change through the annihilation of all Muslim-majority states and the restoration of the caliphate. For this purpose, it has adopted a three-stage program of action that allegedly resembles the Prophet Muhammad's path toward establishing the first Islamic state in Medina:

First stage: Recruitment of members.
Second stage: Islamization of society through activism.
Third stage: Establishment of an Islamic state and spread of Islam.[6]

From Hizb ut-Tahrir's point of view, the umma has been divided into many weak and nominally independent states that are controlled by Western powers. The party has argued that nationalism is a Western ideology and the territorial borders of Arab and Muslim states are an artificial creation. According to the party ideologues, "Islam rejects the concept of nation-states. This idea did not emanate from Islam rather it was concocted by the West and implemented in the Christian kingdoms. . . . This was then conveyed to the Muslims once we had lost the very entity which united us: the *Khilafah* [i.e., caliphate]."[7] Since the party rejects the concept of the modern nation-state, it has divided the world into provinces (*vilayate*); a province can coincide with a nation-state or a particular region within a state. Accordingly, each branch of Hizb ut-Tahrir corresponds to a separate vilayate. In effect, every vilayate forms a Muslim community with each own peculiarities and issues.

Hizb ut-Tahrir has criticized Sudan, Iran, and Saudi Arabia for claiming to be Islamic states because they do not fulfill all criteria. The party has argued that "for a land to be considered an Islamic State, every single article of the country's constitution, every rule and law, must emanate from the Sharia."[8] Hizb ut-Tahrir has claimed that Sharia is not the sole source of these countries' legislation. It has also denounced the declaration of a caliphate by ISIS because it did not follow the proper methodology for doing that and the security situation is too precarious.[9] Therefore, it wants to re-establish the Islamic state that existed in the seventh century under the Prophet Muhammad and his first four successors, namely the Rightly Guided Caliphate (Khilafat-e-Rashida). The Islamic system of government must be based on four principles:

- Sovereignty is of Sharia and not of the umma.
- Authority is of the umma because the appointment of a caliph is its God-given right and the caliph governs the umma on its behalf.
- The appointment of a caliph is an obligation on all Muslims. There must be only one caliph in the Islamic State.
- The caliph alone has the right to adopt and enforce laws and legislation.[10]

Hizb ut-Tahrir has denounced the use of violence as a tool for political change. The group is clear in its call for existing regimes in the Muslim world to be overthrown peacefully and replaced by the caliphate. Hizb ut-Tahrir experimented with elections during the 1950s, only to come to the conclusion that authorities would never allow the party to compete fairly. Consequently, the group has turned to political activism to achieve its main goal.

Hizb ut-Tahrir was organized by Nabhani to function as a vanguard party of highly trained and committed agitators; yet he envisioned its transformation into a mass party. The former are dominated by a charismatic leader and recruit selectively, whereas the latter have usually collective leadership and aim at massive recruitment. While both types of parties seek to have an impact beyond their membership, they have different perspectives on social order. Vanguard parties tend to view societies not only as hierarchically structured but also as immature; as a result, they prefer wooing elites. In contrast, mass parties believe in the power of masses and seek to build grassroots support.

The party has a selective recruitment policy. Indeed, it may take up to two years to become a full member. Hizb ut-Tahrir has targeted university students, professionals, and businessmen in order to gain influence in certain segments of society. Members of the party have distributed leaflets and books in universities, mosques, and shopping centers. Also, the group has increasingly used the Internet and other new media to spread its ideology. It has built websites in many different languages (e.g., Arabic, Turkish, Russian, French, German, Urdu).

Notwithstanding the efforts to present itself as postethnic and pan-Islamic, Hizb ut-Tahrir remains an Arab-dominated group favoring the Arabization of the umma. For example, article 8 of the constitution that Nabhani wrote for the future Islamic state declares the Arabic language as official.[11] However, its rank-and-file membership consists of many nationalities, including Westerners who converted to Islam. Although Hizb ut-Tahrir does not seek to recruit exclusively from Sunni Muslims, it is obvious that the party is not attractive to Shia Muslims or members of Muslim sects (e.g., Ahmadiyya, Druze).

The group seeks societal transformation through collective acceptance of its ideology, but there is likely to be a need to use some kind of pressure to overthrow hostile regimes. Imran Waheed, senior member of the British branch, wrote an article published by the *Khilafah Magazine* in July 2002, in which he revealed how the group has envisioned stage 3: "A day will come when the Muslims will take revenge against all those who participated in their oppression. . . . Hizb ut-Tahrir does not use weapons or resort to violence, nor uses any physical means in its call . . . [but] do not expect, that these rulers and their regimes will collapse all by themselves. On the contrary, patient believers are required to shake these regimes and uproot them."[12] Such a wording implies that tyrannical rulers could be overthrown by acts of civil disobedience such as massive protests. This nonviolent, but highly confrontational, strategy of activism resembles the one used by Ayatollah Khomeini to bring down the shah in Iran.

The International Activism of Hizb ut-Tahrir

In the first three decades of its existence, Hizb ut-Tahrir remained essentially a Middle Eastern group. From the 1980s onward, Hizb ut-Tahrir has managed to establish a presence in several Western countries that have sizable Muslim communities. It has targeted both Muslims of immigrant origin and converts to Islam. Since the mid-1990s, the group has also become active in the post-Soviet republics and China.

Most of the group's literature and communiqués are published by the British branch and its websites are run from Great Britain. While London serves as the logistic center for party activities, its international leader and many senior officials reside in the Middle East. Nevertheless, Hizb ut-Tahrir is banned in most regional countries because it seeks to overthrow the existing regimes. The party is legal only in Lebanon, the Palestinian Territories, Tunisia, Sudan and Yemen. Outside the Middle East, Hizb ut-Tahrir has freely operated in Western countries, apart from Germany. Additionally, it has a legal status in Afghanistan, Malaysia and Indonesia.

Europe, the United States, and Australia

The first cell of Hizb ut-Tahrir outside the Middle East was established in Great Britain during the early 1980s.[13] Under the charismatic leadership of Syrian-born Omar Bakri Muhammad, the group rapidly increased its activities. It became known to the wider public due to its protests against Salman Rushdie and his book *Satanic Verses*. The British branch gradually expanded its membership to include professionals and university students. Moreover, it adopted a more global and less UK-focused approach. In the early to mid-1990s, according to former senior member Ed Husain, party activists narrated tales of "pregnant women being raped by Serbs, who then cut their unborn babies from their wombs. . . . Hizb organized meetings and demonstrations across the UK on the theme of Muslim slaughter in Bosnia."[14] The suffering of Bosnian Muslims energized large segments of the British Muslim population. This was only the beginning of a greater strategy of internationalization.

In the early 2000s, Hizb ut-Tahrir Britain launched a campaign against the Karimov regime, accusing Uzbek security services of torturing and killing members of the party. On July 3, 2002, hundreds of British members queued outside the Uzbek Embassy in London to apply for a visa to visit the country.[15] The Uzbek diplomats, who were taken by surprise, refused to accept the protesters. In February 2006, the party organized a protest outside the embassy of Denmark over the satirical cartoons of the Prophet Muhammad published in a Danish newspaper.[16] In February 2010, female members demonstrated outside the French Embassy against the banning of the face veil (niqab).[17] Hizb ut-Tahrir also staged a protest against a U.S.-made, anti-Islam movie outside the U.S. Embassy in London in September 2012.[18] Overall, the British branch has been very active in bringing attention to pan-Islamic issues.

Hizb ut-Tahrir's activities in other European countries have included protests, sit-ins, and petitions. To start with, the group held a demonstration outside the Uzbek Embassy in Brussels during Islam Karimov's visit to the European Union and NATO in January 2011, which was apparently the first open manifestation of Hizb ut-Tahrir in Belgium.[19] In March 2013, Hizb ut-Tahrir held a conference about the restoration of the caliphate in the Netherlands.[20] The Danish branch has also organized high-profile events. It has succeeded in forming relationships with the broader Muslim community; in 2006, the group co-organized with local representatives of the Muslim Brotherhood and imams from Danish mosques a panel debate about the Jyllands-Posten Muhammad cartoons controversy.[21] Interestingly, Hizb ut-Tahrir Denmark has contributed innovative ideas in new fields of party activity such as environmental protection. In 2009, for instance, it published a pamphlet titled *The Environmental Problem: Its Causes and Islam's Solution.*[22]

Hizb ut-Tahrir developed a presence in the United States sometime during the 1990s. The first cells were probably established in Southern California's Orange County, where a large number of Arab Americans live.[23] Now its headquarters are located in Chicago. The U.S. branch organized a conference in 2009 to address issues of major concern for Muslims living in the West such as Islamophobia and intolerance. It has also held events on the crisis of world capitalism and the future of democracy. The group has avoided controversial topics, such as the role of the pro-Israel lobby in the formation of U.S. Middle East policy. The American branch has mostly relied upon the Internet to recruit members and attract sympathizers.

In addition, Hizb ut-Tahrir has established a strong presence in Australia, largely recruiting from the local Arab community. Therefore, the group organized a conference in September 2012 that largely focused on the Arab Spring revolutions. The local branch has been increasingly critical of Australia's role as a middle-sized power in the Pacific and its close defense links to the United States.[24] The Australian authorities have discussed the possibility of banning the group for inciting violence, but this has not taken place yet. As elsewhere, the local branch has used the Internet to spread its propaganda.

South and Southeast Asia

South Asia is an important region for Hizb ut-Tahrir because it is home to hundreds of millions of Muslims. President Pervez Musharraf banned the party in Pakistan in 2004 and, as a result, it went underground. In May 2011, a brigadier of the Pakistani armed forces was arrested for his alleged links to the group.[25] Moreover, the local branch suffered a major blow in March 2012 when nineteen members, including a few university professors, were arrested by police in Lahore.[26] Nevertheless, the group has been able to utilize social networks based on kinship and friendship ties.

In Bangladesh, the group was banned in October 2009. In December 2011, Hizb ut-Tahrir was accused of involvement in a failed coup attempt against the Bangladeshi government.[27] Despite state repression, the group has continued to recruit members from the middle and upper echelons of Bangladeshi society. Hizb ut-Tahrir even organized a rally in Dhaka in December 2012.[28]

The U.S. invasion of Afghanistan and the fall of the Taliban regime allowed Hizb ut-Tahrir to enter the Afghan political system. The newly established Afghan branch organized a conference on corruption in April 2012.[29] Nonetheless, the party has remained marginal in the war-torn country. Although most Afghans are familiar with the tenets of Islamism, they tend to support indigenous parties that have established patron-client relationships in the country.

Additionally, Hizb ut-Tahrir has established branches in Southeast Asia's two main Muslim countries. In Malaysia, the group has been able to attract support from students and intellectuals. The female members have been particularly active in organizing events and demonstrations.[30] The local branch has taken advantage of the rivalry between the country's two main Islamist parties: the United Malays National Organization and the Pan-Malaysian Islamic Party. Thus, it has presented itself as a pan-Islamic group above party politics.

In Indonesia, Hizb ut-Tahrir has systematically attempted to increase its popularity because the country has the largest Muslim population in the world.[31] In August 2007, its annual conference was attended by about eighty thousand people.[32] As in Malaysia, the women's section of the local branch has played an increasingly important role in party activities; for example, female members held a rally in Sarabaya, Indonesia's second-largest city, to celebrate International Women's Day on March 8, 2015. In spite of the group's patriarchal mentality, female members of Hizb ut-Tahrir have become more vocal and assertive.

Russia, Ukraine, and China

Hizb ut-Tahrir has made significant inroads in Muslim-populated areas of the Russian Federation. The first cells were established in Tatarstan and Bashkortostan in the mid- to late 1990s. Initially, the Russian branch was perceived by authorities as being too small to present any kind of serious threat. However, it has recruited enough committed members to generate momentum for its growth in Tatarstan and Bashkortostan.

In November 2012, eighteen members were arrested in Moscow, although the group claimed that the actual number of its arrested members was much higher.[33] Therefore, the Palestinian branch organized a protest at the Russian Representative Office in Ramallah, as did the Indonesian branch outside the Russian Embassy in Jakarta.[34] By late 2014, a few hundred Muslims of Tatar and Bashkir origin were convicted by Russian courts for membership in Hizb-ut-Tahrir. The group apparently lacks a sizable presence in Chechnya, although the autonomous republic has been a fertile soil for the growth of political Islam. Yet it has increased its activities in neighboring Dagestan, which has suffered from terrorist incidents in the last two decades; its nonviolent approach apparently appeals to devout Muslims who reject terrorism.[35]

In recent years, Hizb ut-Tahrir has established a presence in Ukraine as well. The group has targeted the Crimean Tatars, a Turkic ethnic group numbering approximately 230,000 people.[36] In August 2007, the Ukrainian branch of Hizb ut-Tahrir organized a conference titled "Islam: Yesterday, Today and Tomorrow" in Simferopol; event speakers called upon the 600 participants to "carry the message of Islam to the Ukrainian nation."[37] After the annexation of the Crimea by Russia in March 2014, the group has been banned by the local authorities.

Hizb ut-Tahrir has reportedly extended its influence into China's Xinjiang Autonomous Region populated by Uighurs, a Turkic Muslim group. Government repression and anti-Muslim policies have increased the appeal of Hizb ut-Tahrir. As a result, Chinese authorities have arrested members of the group in the region.[38] Such actions have provoked a response from other branches of Hizb ut-Tahrir. On March 14, 2015, the Australian branch organized a protest outside the Chinese consulate in Sydney.[39]

Central Asia

Following the disintegration of the Soviet Union, Hizb ut-Tahrir became active in Central Asia.[40] Uzbekistan became the hub of party activities in Central Asia during the 1990s. After the assassination attempt on President Karimov in February 1999, which the Uzbek regime blamed on Islamist militants, arrests of Hizb ut-Tahrir's members increased dramatically. Currently, several thousand members serve sentences in Uzbek prisons.[41] As a result, the group has been forced to scale down its activities in the country. Yet Uzbek members have received moral support from Hizb ut-Tahrir branches throughout the world. In May 2015, for instance, British members commemorated outside the Uzbek Embassy in London the tenth anniversary of the Andijan massacre.[42]

In Kyrgyzstan, the group has enjoyed more freedom than in neighboring countries. Kyrgyz authorities have banned Hizb ut-Tahrir, but they have not relentlessly persecuted its members. Also, it appears that some mosques have been utilized by the group as a recruitment base. In October 2012, for instance, an imam was detained by law-enforcement authorities in Jalal-Abad Province for allegedly being a member of the group.[43] In the last few years, Hizb ut-Tahrir has made inroads in southern Kyrgyzstan, which has suffered from ethnic tensions.[44] In May 2014, the Kyrgyz branch published a leaflet titled "Uzbek Intelligence Roams Kyrgyzstan Looking to Kill Muslims," claiming that there is a political battle between "those who are working to apply the principle of Islam through the establishment of the

Khilafah . . . and the advocates of nationalism adopted by the Uzbek security forces, and the advocates of democracy . . . led by the West."[45] Hence the local branch has blamed nationalism for the growing tensions between the Kyrgyz majority and the Uzbek minority, and has promoted pan-Islamism as a solution to the country's problematic ethnic relations.

The party has also been active in Kazakhstan, including the heavily Russian-populated northern provinces and big cities such as Almaty and Astana. The local branch has condemned the endemic corruption of Kazakh authorities abetted by the oil and gas industry. The Nazarbayev regime has responded to the rise of Hizb ut-Tahrir with a mixture of security measures, propaganda campaigns against the group, and economic concessions to areas that have strong pro-Hizb ut-Tahrir sentiments (e.g., Shymkent).

Finally, Hizb ut-Tahrir has expanded its activities in Tajikistan, which hosted, until recently, the only legal Islamist party in the region. The Islamic Revival Party of Tajikistan (IRPT), led by Muhiddin Kabiri, has embraced the democratic process and representative politics. The Tajik branch of Hizb ut-Tahrir fiercely accused the IRPT of collaborating with the Rahmon regime because it joined the political process after the 1992–1997 civil war.[46] Yet the IRPT was banned by the Tajik authorities in September 2015. Besides its attacks on its competitor, Hizb ut-Tahrir's propaganda in the country has focused on the government's corruption and the emigration of Tajik men to Russia.[47]

The Middle East and North Africa

The Middle East was originally Hizb ut-Tahrir's main area of operation, but heavy state repression forced the group to internationalize its activities. Currently, there are some indications that the group leadership has shifted its focus to the Middle East again. The Arab Spring revolutions of 2010–2012 provided a new momentum to political Islam. Hizb ut-Tahrir did not play any role during the events, but it has offered a post-Arab Spring political program that some pious Muslims could find attractive.

More than anything else, the ongoing Syrian crisis has attracted Hizb ut-Tahrir's attention. The group staged a protest in the Syrian city of Aleppo on November 9, 2012.[48] In April 2013, female members organized a press conference in Amman, Jordan, to discuss the situation in Syria, especially in regard to women and children.[49] In August of the same year, the Jordanian branch issued a news release with the names of mosques where members and sympathizers would gather to protest against the Assad regime.[50]

Hizb ut-Tahrir has portrayed President Bashar al-Assad as a Western agent who was appointed as a ruler by the United States. In October 2013, Hizb ut-Tahrir Britain published an article online about post-Assad Syria in which it advised the Islamist opposition to follow four steps: first, to eliminate all American presence and influence in the country; second, to put to trial members of the Syrian regime and to prohibit members of the pro-Western Syrian National Council from returning to the country; third, to develop weapons of mass destruction for the purpose of deterrence; and finally, to initiate a process of reunification of the Muslim world.[51] In January 2014, the international leader of Hizb ut-Tahrir, Ata Abu Rashta, gave a speech in an opposition-held area of Syria in which he blamed the Assad regime, the United States, and secularist dissidents for Syria's misfortunes. He asserted that "On the one hand, the crimes of the tyrant Bashar, which did not spare the humans or even the trees and rocks; whilst on the other, the continuous meetings in Istanbul, Cairo and Paris, in order to form an interim government to arrange a republican, secular, civil democratic system . . . in order to continue the American influence in the noble Al-Sham [i.e., Syria]. . . . However, these wicked people forget that Al-Sham is the Fortress of Islam, the Abode of Islam."[52]

Apart from Syria and Jordan, the group has increasingly operated in the Palestinian Territories. The local branch has become more vocal in recent years, taking advantage of its Palestinian origins and the area wide network of sympathizers.[53] Interestingly, the Israeli authorities have tolerated the existence of Hizb ut-Tahrir because it has denounced political violence. The Oslo Agreement and the establishment of a semiautonomous Palestinian entity has created new political space for the party, particularly in the West Bank. Thus, it has gained more supporters at the expense of other groups like Hamas and Fatah that have failed to improve the lives of Palestinians.

In addition to Arab countries, Hizb ut-Tahrir has viewed Turkey as a key country for two reasons. First, Istanbul was the seat of the caliph for almost five hundred years. The abolishment of the caliphate in 1924 has been an event memorialized by Hizb ut-Tahrir. Second, Turkey has a large Muslim population with links to Muslims in the Balkans, the Caucasus, and Central Asia. During the 1990s, Kemalist governments espoused a militant secularism; as a result, they banned the group and arrested its members for anticonstitutional activities. Yet the rise to power of the Justice and Development Party has not led to a decline in state repression against Hizb ut-Tahrir. Both the Kemalist and the Islamist-leaning AKP governments have viewed the party as a foe for different reasons: the former have accused the group of being Arab and having an agenda to Islamize the Turkish state and society; the latter has perceived it as a competitor for the hearts and minds of pious Muslims.

Although the local branch is still banned, it has tried hard to preserve a support base in the country. Therefore, it has maintained a number of websites for Turkish-speaking members and sympathizers. Hizb ut-Tahrir has criticized the AKP for compromising its principles in order to stay in power. In particular, the group has targeted Tayyip Erdoğan as a politician who failed to achieve the establishment of a true Islamist government in Turkey. Party ideologues have claimed that "it is the so-called 'White Turks' [i.e., Kemalist elite] in Turkey who have the real power, while Erdoğan can only make deals and try to limit their influence a little."[54] Furthermore, Hizb ut-Tahrir has argued that the AKP-promoted Turkish model "ought-not to be understood as an alternative to secularism, but rather a far more benign and insidious manifestation of secularism that incorporates Islamic values into its discourse by virtue of Islam being part of Turkey's national identity."[55] In this way, the group has accused the AKP of exploiting Islam to foster Turkish nationalism.

Hizb ut-Tahrir has also established branches in other regional countries in recent years. In Yemen, the group has attempted to play a role in post-Saleh politics. During 2013–2014, Hizb ut-Tahrir launched public awareness campaigns for the re-establishment of the caliphate.[56] Nevertheless, the current war in the country between the Shia Houthi movement and Saudi-led forces has politically marginalized the group.[57] Although it once had a strong presence, Hizb ut-Tahrir is now a very small political force in Iraq.[58] Its pan-Islamic rhetoric is obviously not appealing to a society divided on the basis of sectarian affiliation.

Hizb ut-Tahrir Between the Global and the Local

The group is keen to emphasize its ideological coherence and consistency. Since the early 1950s, it has advocated the establishment of a caliphate to unite all Muslims into a single state. Hizb ut-Tahrir's tenets and worldview are largely based on the writings of its founder. Internal discipline and obedience to the central leadership are necessary conditions for such an international group to maintain its cohesion. Therefore, there is a range of disciplinary measures for members who disobey the orders of the all-party leader, including expulsion.

However, Hizb ut-Tahrir has operated in very different national settings. The group is now active in more than forty countries, ranging from the United States to Indonesia and from South Africa to Denmark. Hizb ut-Tahrir can freely convey its messages and engage in polemic debates in Western countries. In contrast, its branches in most Muslim countries have typically faced severe repression that restricts their activities. As a result, significant differences can be found in Hizb ut-Tahrir's political strategy at the national level. Hizb ut-Tahrir in Uzbekistan and Pakistan aims at spreading its ideas to the society while remaining underground. The group takes advantage of the relatively relaxed political atmosphere to launch public relations campaigns in Indonesia and Malaysia, whereas it is still building its cadres in Afghanistan and Yemen.

The internationalization of Hizb ut-Tahrir has created new dilemmas and challenges for its leadership. While the group has to remain attached to the tenets of Nabhani's ideology, it needs also to address the concerns and problems of its different constituencies. Being active in many countries means that the group must adopt a cognitive schema that can transmit a global message to local audiences. It must resonate with different cultures and political environments. For this purpose, the group has utilized the master frame of human rights. It is the most suitable vehicle of communication bridging Hizb ut-Tahrir's globalist ideology with local concerns about discrimination and abuses.

In the mid-1990s, Hizb ut-Tahrir denounced human rights because "the origin of these rights is the Capitalist ideology's view of the nature of man, the relationship between the individual and the group, the reality of society, and the function of the state."[59] At that time, the group perceived human rights as a Western creation. However, the terrorist attacks in New York and Washington in 2001 dramatically increased the visibility of Muslims. Such a change was bound to have serious implications for the everyday life of millions of Muslims in the West. In the immediate post-9/11 period, Muslim citizens were monitored by authorities, physical and verbal attacks against Muslims were on the rise, and the media constantly identified Islam as a national security threat. In other words, Muslim communities suddenly became part of a larger conflict between the West and Islamist militants that was set on a global stage.

In this context, Hizb ut-Tahrir has endorsed the master frame of human rights to spread its ideas and gain influence locally. Since the master frame provides a generic framework of rights and freedoms, the group can choose what is useful and discard the rest. In fact, the group has mostly focused on individual freedoms vis-à-vis the state and women's Islamic rights that have come to the forefront in recent years. Thus, Hizb ut-Tahrir has ignored those rights and freedoms that contradict its ideology and do not serve its goals (e.g., right to self-determination).

To begin with, the British branch has increasingly discussed the growing Islamophobia that is gripping the country. In the words of a pro-Hizb ut-Tahrir commentator, "in regards to the Muslim community this discrimination is further driven by draconian anti-terror policies which stifle intellectual and political debate and place every man, woman and child in relative fear of their future in this country."[60] The party has denounced the targeting of British Muslims by far right groups, the media, and, to lesser degree, mainstream politicians. As a result, it has been able to attract sympathizers and supporters from among the country's Muslims.

The American branch has also paid attention to Islamophobia in the post-9/11 United States. Following the guilty verdict of the so-called Irvine 11, a group of Muslim students who protested against Israeli ambassador Michael Oren when he visited the University of California, Irvine, campus in February 2010, the group claimed that "one can sense Islamophobia has played a role in this verdict."[61] While criticizing the U.S. interventionist policy in the greater Middle East, Hizb ut-Tahrir America has at the same time stressed the human rights abuses committed against Muslims inside and outside the country. The local branch has claimed that "one of the key arguments for invading Iraq and Afghanistan was to set these countries up as models of democracy to be imitated across the Muslim lands. . . . [A] decade later the [United States] has abandoned such values through Guantanamo Bay, Belmarsh, Abu Ghraib, Bagram, the Patriot Act, anti-terrorism legislation of all guises, stop and search, internment, torture, sexual humiliation, executive ordered arrests, detention without trial, rendition of suspects to despotic regimes, brutal interrogations and illegal and imperialistic wars."[62]

Hizb ut-Tahrir's logic is simple but powerful: the West, principally the United States, has cynically used its pro-democracy rhetoric to violate and abuse the human rights of Muslim communities. By referring to well-known cases of torture in U.S. detention facilities, the group is able to employ the master frame of human rights. Through this method, its struggle appears more legitimate within the American context. Thus, the party can not only gain support but also protect itself from legal action.

Additionally, other branches in Western countries have expressed their concern about Islamophobia and abuses of human rights. In Denmark, Hizb ut-Tahrir has claimed that "the Danish politicians bear a huge share of responsibility for the rise in Islamophobia and hateful rhetoric that has become quite common in Denmark. Today Muslims are experiencing increasingly, not only on social media but also at congested places and in broad daylight, verbal and physical assault."[63] Hence the group implicitly criticized the far-right Danish People's Party and other political forces for their Islamophobic rhetoric that has led to the targeting of the Muslim community.[64] Again, a local branch of Hizb ut-Tahrir has utilized the language of human rights to denigrate its political opponents and gain more legitimacy and acceptance.

In Australia, Hizb ut-Tahrir has been under scrutiny because of its high-profile activities and events.[65] Given that a growing number of Australian Muslims have traveled to the Middle East to join jihadi groups, authorities have been concerned about the radicalization of the country's Muslim population.[66] The local branch has constantly refused to condemn not only ISIS's atrocities but also those who leave Australia to fight in Syria and Iraq.[67] Interestingly, it has attempted to twist the debate from jihadi terrorism to what it sees as the Australian government's racist approach to Muslims: "The notion that Muslims who go to Syria will become 'radicalised' and be a security threat when they return . . . is based in the all-too-familiar Islamophobic Orientalist narrative that sees Muslims as sub-human, somehow less civilized, unable to control themselves and hence needing the intervention of the civilized white man. Why are the same concerns about radicalization and national security not raised in relation to other Australian citizens training and fighting in the armies of foreign allies?"[68]

Here Hizb ut-Tahrir evokes the history of racism against Muslims. Its response implies that Western countries, including Australia, have suffered from a white man's burden syndrome toward the Muslim world. Hizb ut-Tahrir's argumentation is based on a widely accepted criticism of the West's Orientalist legacy in the Middle East; its message is that Muslim populations have not been treated humanely by Westerners. Such a powerful statement, which links Western interventionist policies to the human rights and dignity of Muslims, can easily resonate with some Australian Muslims who have Middle Eastern origin. In addition, the group aims at a wider audience that has viewed Australian foreign policy critically and has raised concerns about Islamophobia and racial profiling. In effect, the local branch has utilized the master frame of human rights to defend its ambiguous position on Australian jihadi fighters in Syria and Iraq, while reaching out to both Muslims and non-Muslims.

The Australian branch's agenda includes domestic human rights issues too. In mid-October 2014, the women's section of Hizb ut-Tahrir Australia criticized growing public hostility over the wearing of niqab or hijab; a statement claimed that "Muslims cannot rely on a weak meta-ethics to protect our 'rights'; rather, we should call for our rights through Islam and highlight the inherent flaws and contradictions of liberal secularism. We should demonstrate that the niqab is not just about 'wearing what we want', but part of a comprehensive Islamic social system that protects women, families and hence leads to a cohesive and safe society, free from the trappings that are created by a society based on liberal 'freedoms.'"[69]

The master frame of human rights has been increasingly utilized by branches of Hizb ut-Tahrir in non-Western countries as well. In Indonesia, the local branch confronted French diplomats over the publication of the Prophet Muhammad cartoons by *Charlie Hebdo* by challenging French arguments about freedom of expression. More specifically, Hizb ut-Tahrir's representatives accused the French government of "banning Muslim women from wearing burka" and persecuting individuals for "questioning the Holocaust."[70] But Hizb ut-Tahrir Indonesia did not only aim at contributing to international protests against what was viewed as blasphemy against the Prophet Muhammad. The global duty of defending the Prophet has to be combined with local political goals. The post-Suharto process of reconciliation has shed light on past violations of human rights committed by the army and paramilitary groups.[71] As a result, Indonesian society has been more aware of and sensitive to human rights issues.[72] In this context, the branch of Hizb ut-Tahrir has utilized the master frame of human rights to pursue a global agenda that has local applications.

In addition, the use of human rights master frame gives ethical legitimacy to Hizb ut-Tahrir. Thus, the group has portrayed its actions as well intended and showing concern for the dignity of Muslim communities. This is a very important component of the human rights master frame because it can allow Hizb ut-Tahrir to compete against other Islamist groups at the local level and simultaneously find allies outside the world of political Islam. Many people have the utmost respect for those who have altruistic beliefs and behavior. With the help of the human rights master frame, the party can remake its public image and prosper politically.

For instance, the Malaysian branch has drawn from this component to convey its messages to the country's Muslim population. Following the release of a U.S. Senate report on the CIA Detention and Interrogation Program in December 2014, Hizb ut-Tahrir Malaysia accused the United States of "saying that they are the defenders and upholders of human rights and are the guardians of international law, where in actual fact they are the real offenders."[73] More importantly, it claimed that Malaysian police "cooperated with CIA despite the fact that CIA is known to be untrustworthy, and [the Malaysian police] knows the inhumane character of CIA, and it knows how brutal and barbaric CIA is, especially against Muslims."[74] In this case, the appeal to human rights serves slightly different goals. The group aims at undermining Malaysia's relationship with the United States by portraying the country's leadership as guilty of violating the human rights of fellow Muslims for the sake of helping what it views as a U.S.-led war on Islam. Thus, it could increase its popularity among pious Muslims who have been critical of the cooperation between Kuala Lumpur and Washington. At the same time, the use of this master frame can connect the local branch's activities with a global agenda against torture and other cruel punishment.

Hizb ut-Tahrir Britain has grabbed every opportunity to criticize state-sanctioned narratives and discourses. The terrorist attack against the *Charlie Hebdo* magazine in Paris in January 2015 provoked new tensions between European governments and Muslim communities. The group has criticized the position of many European leaders regarding the freedom of expression. In the words of senior member of Hizb ut-Tahrir Abdul Wahid: "The freedom to insult the sacred symbols of Islam has become a tool to bully and persecute a minority community. . . . In this context an ultimatum has been served to Muslims . . . that it is not enough to say that [a] Muslim in a non-Muslim country under a covenant should not be a vigilante, killing people in broad daylight. . . . Rather, what is expected of a Muslim in Europe today is that you bow down before the god of free speech until you accept that every Prophet can be insulted. . . . That is an unacceptable expectation by those who attack Islam. Muslims living in the West have only one option when faced with insults against their beloved Prophet—and that is to speak out. . . . We continue to speak out loudly–despite the mockery and hatred."[75]

Wahid has based his criticism against European governments on a valid argument: Muslim communities are always expected to apologize and reaffirm their loyalty to the state. There has been a widespread suspicion of Muslim citizens, who are largely viewed by some politicians and media as untrustworthy and fanatical. Consequently, Muslim citizens must constantly condemn those co-religionists who use violence against civilians. What Wahid fails to mention is the general rise of intolerance against ethnic and religious minorities on the Continent. European Muslims are not the only religious community that has faced pressure and intimidation. In fact, most European societies are still susceptible to anti-Semitism.[76] Like Muslims, Europe's Jews have frequently been asked by certain politicians and media to condemn Israeli actions against Palestinian civilians.[77]

The use of the human rights master frame provides Hizb ut-Tahrir with the moral obligation to support fellow Muslims. This component has allowed the group to launch initiatives for the support of those Muslim communities deemed to be under threat. Hizb ut-Tahrir has used this component, among other things, to call for the protection of its members in Crimea from pro-Kremlin forces. Since the local branch became illegal after the Russian annexation of Crimea in late March 2014, it is the international leadership that has taken up the task to defend Crimean Muslims in general and Hizb ut-Tahrir's members in particular. In mid-May 2014, Osman Bakhach, who is the head of the Central Media Office, warned that "[Russian forces] are preparing to massacre the local Muslims. . . . Regardless of the international conflict that occurs in Ukraine between Europe, Russia, and America, Muslims are the first victims of Russian occupation of Crimea."[78] Therefore, he suggested that only the establishment of the caliphate could protect them from Russian aggression. The speed of events took the Ukrainian branch by surprise, but the group is likely to increase its activities stressing human rights violations against the Muslim population in Crimea.

The group has also focused on the treatment of Muslims in other conflict zones. More specifically, Hizb ut-Tahrir has launched a global campaign titled "Who Will Support the Muslims of Central Africa?" in order to increase awareness. According to the Women's Section of the Central Media Office of Hizb ut-Tahrir, "since 1st of February 2014, a diabolical and systematic campaign of genocide has been unleashed upon the helpless

Muslims of the region. . . . Female and minor members of the Muslim [community] . . . have been the target of unspeakable acts of barbarity. . . . Only with the re-establishment of the Khilafah . . . Muslims can be saved from bloodshed and systematic abuse."[79] Their tragic story confirms the claim that the human rights of Muslims are systematically abused by non-Muslims and this can stop only if the caliphate is restored. Hizb ut-Tahrir's narrative is simple and self-explanatory. Likewise, the group has campaigned against the persecution of the Rohingya Muslims in Burma. One of its statements argued that "the massacre of the Rohingya has exposed the hypocrisy of international bodies like the UN, human rights organizations and the global media. . . . Some have described them as the most persecuted minority in the world, yet the lack of prominence given to their cause show exactly how politicized humanitarian and human rights campaigning bodies are."[80]

Following the 9/11 events and the subsequent wave of Islamophobia in the West, the group has clearly changed its rhetoric. The endorsement of human rights has raised awareness and have offered crucial legitimacy to Hizb ut-Tahrir. Different branches have remarkably applied the same master frame, which is a testament to its strategic value and utility. They have adjusted it to the needs of the local community which is the unit of identification. Hence Hizb ut-Tahrir has exploited human rights as an ideological weapon against its perceived adversaries and their supposed hypocrisy.

Conclusion

Hizb ut-Tahrir is probably the most geographically far-reaching Islamist group. It has established a presence in many countries on different continents. While the group has tirelessly supported the utopian goal of re-establishing the caliphate, it has denounced the use of violence as a method of political change. Instead, it has advocated nonviolent political activism. However, Hizb ut-Tahrir has faced the challenge of transmitting messages across different political and cultural environments.

For this purpose, it has embraced the human rights master frame that carries a simple and straightforward message: there is a massive violation of human rights of Muslims throughout the world and its root cause is Islamophobia and anti-Muslim hatred. This master frame can easily be accepted by many communities and individuals. In particular, such rhetoric can evoke strong emotions from Western Muslims who are accustomed to the language of human rights. Consequently, they could identify more easily with a group that advocates Muslim rights. Hizb ut-Tahrir has portrayed itself as the sole defender of Muslims who have been targeted unfairly by Western countries and their allies on the basis of their religious affiliation.

It has promoted a global vision of the Muslim world, while focusing on the particular problems and issues that each community faces. Hizb ut-Tahrir has functioned as an agent of glocalization that adapts the universal master frame of human rights to local contexts. This cognitive schema can enable dissemination of a powerful message to different constituencies for the purpose of mobilizing support. In this way, it can connect many different situations together by offering the following solution: only the creation of an all-powerful Islamic state could defend Muslims from discrimination and abuse.

For more than a half century, the group has managed to grow and survive. Despite its confrontational messages, Hizb ut-Tahrir has maintained a nonviolent approach that serves as a reminder of the heterogeneity that exists within the new political Islam. The group does not constitute a security threat, although it has been subject to a securitization process in the Muslim world and elsewhere.

PART II

Islamist Politics and
the Master Frame of Democracy

Democracy is the most popular political system that has constantly spread across the world since the beginning of the twentieth century. Yet the first democracy was born in the ancient Greek city of Athens in the fifth century BC. It was based on a system of direct participation whereby citizens voted directly for legislation and executive action. The Roman Republic (509 BC–27 BC) was the first representative democracy, since its citizens were allowed to vote only indirectly. Modern democracy has its roots in three important documents: Magna Carta (1215), which limited the power of the English monarch; the U.S. Constitution (1787), which created a House of Representatives whose members were to be elected by the people; and the French Declaration of the Rights of Man and of the Citizen (1789), which established universal male suffrage.

According to Samuel Huntington, modern democratization took place in three waves. The first wave began in the early nineteenth century and lasted until the 1920s (e.g., United States, Great Britain, France). The second wave commenced after the defeat of the Axis and lasted until the early 1960s, when many European colonies gained their independence (e.g., India) and autocracies became democracies (e.g., Japan). The end of the Cold War unleashed a new wave of demands for political representation and rights. But Huntington argued that the establishment of liberal democracies in eastern Europe in the late 1980s was only part of the third wave of democratization that had started in southern Europe in the mid-1970s with Greece and Portugal.[1] Furthermore, some analysts have claimed that the Arab Spring revolutions constitute the fourth wave of democratization.[2]

The undeniable ideological prominence of democracy has been reinforced by globalization processes and their impact on national politics. The compression of time and space has led to the gradual homogenization of norms and procedures. With the exception of a few absolute monarchies (e.g., Saudi Arabia, Brunei), all countries claim to be democracies. Yet they have different understandings of democratic values and procedures. According to Robert Dahl, every democracy must have five criteria: effective participation (all citizens must be able to participate in policy debates), voting equality (every vote must be counted equally), enlightened understanding (every citizen must have the opportunity to learn about alternative policies), control of the agenda (all citizens must enjoy the opportunity to contribute to the political agenda), and inclusion of adults (all permanent residents have equal political rights).[3] Dahl's five criteria are the cornerstones of an ideal democracy. In reality, every society has come up with its own version of democracy. For example, the Kremlin has developed the doctrine of sovereign democracy (*suveryennaya demokratiya*) that refers to a top-down enforcement of political unity and conformity at the expense of pluralism and representation.[4] Likewise, the Chinese communist regime has advocated its own version of democracy (*minzhu*) as a means to promote order and stability.[5]

Nevertheless, Thomas Olesen has argued that "democracy, while entailing certain contentious potentials, is also closely tied to the interests of the dominant states and classes in the post-Cold War period."[6] It is certainly true that the United States and many European countries have aggressively promoted democracy as the only political system that guarantees equality, freedom, and justice. The impact of this policy has been intensified by the increased economic and financial transactions among nations that have stimulated ideational influences and cultural transfers. The dominance of democracy is reflected in efforts to evaluate and measure its spread across the world. The British Foreign and Commonwealth Office and the Council of the European Union have published annual reports on human rights and democratization. Western media have also covered extensively democratization issues. The weekly newspaper the *Economist* has even produced an annual Democracy Index categorizing 165 states into four groups: full democracies, flawed democracies, hybrid regimes, and authoritarian regimes.[7]

The truth is that democracy has multiplied across the world. Paul Hirst is right when he argues that "representative democracy is such a powerful tool of legitimation of the actions of government" that no mainstream politician will question it.[8] Indeed, democracy has proved to be a highly attractive and desirable political system capable of combining rule of law with majority rule.

The Muslim world has experimented with democracy for more than a century. The Ottoman Empire initiated some democratic reforms in the last quarter of the nineteenth century. The constitution of 1876 established a system of constitutional monarchy that lasted only two years before the restoration of absolute monarchy by Sultan Abdul Hamid II. Following the Young Turk Revolution in 1908, the sultan was forced to restore the 1876 constitution and re-establish the Ottoman parliament.[9] The next country experimenting with democracy was Azerbaijan. The Republic of Azerbaijan was established in May 1918 and became the first Muslim country to extend suffrage to women; members of the parliament were elected on the basis of proportional representation and special seats were reserved for ethnic minorities.[10]

The Muslim world went through a second phase of democratization after the end of the Second World War. Syria became an independent republic in 1946 and had its first parliamentary elections one year later; Turkey held its first legislative elections in 1950; Indonesia's first parliamentary elections took place in 1955 alongside those of neighboring Malaysia. Despite the organization of elections, democracy failed to develop strong roots in the Muslim world, which suffered from authoritarianism and repression.

Since the early years of this century, however, more and more Islamic groups and parties have joined the democratic process. The Muslim Brotherhood participated in the 2000 parliamentary elections in Egypt. The Palestinian Islamist group Hamas participated in the 2005 municipal elections and the 2006 legislative elections. Graham E. Fuller supports the view that "the majority of Islamist movements have long since reached the conclusion that democratization is the best overall vehicle by which to present their agenda to the public and to gain political influence and thereby eventually to come to power."[11] With the outbreak of the Arab Spring revolutions, this political trend has only been accelerating.

*   *   *

Democracy is not only a popular political system but also a powerful master frame. The prominence of the democracy master frame is the result of two factors. First, the end of the Cold War and the collapse of communism have strengthened the appeal of democracy in every part of the world. Second, international travel and the use of social media have made many people better informed about the benefits of democracy. Authoritarian leaderships have usually been blamed for systemic corruption and nepotism. In contrast, Western democracies are perceived as a land of opportunity.

It is hardly a surprise that many movements and groups have used the master frame of democracy to mobilize support and wage their political struggle. Rita Noonan observed that the democracy master frame was used by female activists against the Pinochet dictatorship in Chile in the 1980s.[12] During the mid-1990s, the revolutionary movement of Zapatistas managed to frame its uprising for the rights of the indigenous population in the Mexican state of Chiapas as part of a global drive for democratization.[13] The master frame of democracy was used by disability groups during protests in Egypt in 2010 and 2011 to promote equality among citizens.[14] It has also been utilized by dissidents facing authoritarian regimes in countries such as China, Myanmar, and Syria. Due to its widespread application, it is subject to localized interpretations. In other words, it has a high degree of flexibility and variability in accordance with particular political and cultural conditions.

The democracy master frame consists of three main components. First, it includes the principle of political equality, which can be summarized as one person, one vote. In a proper democratic system, the whole adult population can participate in free, fair, and periodic elections. This is a sensitive issue for some Muslim-majority countries, where the right of women to vote and run for public office either is not fully recognized (e.g., Saudi Arabia) or is disputed (e.g., post-Taliban Afghanistan). The acquisition of citizenship is often the prerequisite for equal political rights. Actually, some authoritarian regimes have refused citizenship to politically marginalized groups, such as members of ethnic minorities and foreign-born long-term residents. For example, the Assad regime has denied citizenship to thousands of Syrian Kurds, as have the Myanmar authorities with members of the Rohingya Muslim minority.

Second, the master frame contains the concept of majority rule whereby the decision making is carried out by those who received most votes. Without majority rule, democracy ceases to exist because a minority would dictate its will to the rest of society. This has been a particularly attractive component for post-war self-determination movements that represented

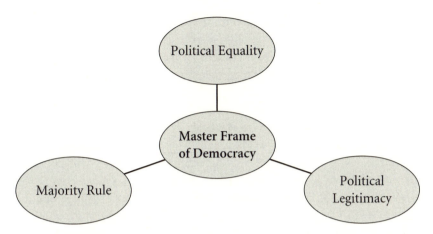

Figure 4. Components of the master frame of democracy

large ethnic groups (e.g., India 1940s, Cyprus 1950s, Algeria 1960s, Bangladesh 1970s, South Africa 1980s, Kosovo 1990s). The logic of this component is straightforward: the numerical strength of a majority can delegitimize any effort to establish a minority rule.

There, the master frame offers the value of political legitimacy that gives a normative advantage to those who claim to have the consent of the people. No modern political leader can afford to ignore the will of the majority. Thus, parties and movements that accept democracy, which privileges the many rather than the few, can gain more political legitimacy than antisystem parties (e.g., neo-Nazi parties, the radical Left). This is why even authoritarian regimes have organized elections and referendums to demonstrate, domestically and internationally, their alleged democratic nature. For example, Bashar al-Assad won his third term as president of Syria with 88.7 percent of the vote in June 2014.[15] The democracy master frame is described in Figure 4.

There is a long debate about the compatibility of Islam with democracy. It has been argued that *shura* (collective consultation) is the Islamic equivalent of democracy. There are two verses in the Quran referring to consultation: "And those who respond to their Lord and keep up prayer, and whose affairs are [decided] by counsel among themselves" (42:38) and "So pardon them and ask protection for them, and consult them in (important) matters" (3:158). Sadek Jawad Sulaiman, a former Omani ambassador to the

United States, has offered an interesting comparison between shura and democracy, arguing that "they both assume that majority judgment tends to be more comprehensive and accurate than minority judgment. . . . [Both] proceed from the core idea that all people are equal in rights and responsibilities . . . and they forbid privileges claimed on the basis of tribal lineage or social prestige."[16]

Many Islamic thinkers have elaborated on the relationship between Islam and democracy. Abu A'la Maududi, founder of the Pakistani Islamist group Jamaat-e-Islami, advocated the establishment of a theodemocracy that would be ruled by the entire Islamic community, not the class of the ulama. In his book *Islamic Law and Constitution*, Maududi argued that the theodemocracy is "in essence and fundamentals the antithesis of . . . Western secular democracy" because sovereignty belongs to God.[17] Since humanity is the vicegerent of God on earth, theodemocracy must be bound by Sharia. Maududi's ideas about theodemocracy later influenced the Taliban movement that established the Islamic Emirate of Afghanistan in 1996.

Yusuf al-Qaradawi, the Qatar-based intellectual leader of the Muslim Brotherhood, has also advocated a particular type of democracy. In his words, "the Islamic Movement and the Islamic Awakening have never flourished or borne fruit unless in an atmosphere of democracy and freedom."[18] Yet al-Qaradawi has not advocated a Western-type democracy for Muslim societies because "democracy is contrary to Islam [which] insists on the fact that Allah alone has the right of legislation while democracy means that the public has the right of legislation."[19] Instead, he has defended shura because "it is a pillar of ruling and governing in Islam. So, all decisions that are made by the state should be through *shura*."[20] But the Egyptian scholar leaves no room for any resemblance between shura and modern democracy; in the former, Muslims always have to take into account the Quran and the Sunnah, while in the latter, parliaments are usually restricted by constitutional provisions. Shura is open only to scholars and experts, whereas parliaments are open to anyone who has been elected by the voters.

Nevertheless, al-Qaradawi has asked Muslims to participate in elections, since "there is no harm in participating in the common house (Parliament) if the intention behind that is to back the truth and the right and to express refusal to the wrong and the evil."[21] Consequently, he has claimed that a parliament run by Muslims "would not be expected to pass a legislation that contradicts Islam and its incontestable principles and conclusive rules."[22] Moreover, he has suggested a constitutional provision stating all legislation must be compatible with Sharia.[23] Indeed, some Muslim-majority countries have incorporated such a provision in their constitutions. For instance, Article 1 of the Qatari constitution states that "Qatar is an independent sovereign Arab State. Its religion is Islam and Sharia law shall be a main source of its legislations. Its political system is democratic."[24] Likewise, the Egyptian constitution of 2014 contains a similar article declaring that "Islam is the religion of the State. . . . The principles of Islamic Sharia are the main source of legislation."[25]

Another Islamic scholar who has extensively discussed the relationship between Islam and democracy is Fethullah Gülen. His thoughts have influenced many Muslims who seek to accommodate the Muslim faith with Western modernity. He claimed that Islam upholds certain fundamental principles:

1. Power lies in truth.
2. Justice and the rule of law are indispensable.
3. Freedom of belief and rights to life, personal property, reproduction, and health (both mental and physical) have to be respected.
4. The privacy and immunity of individual life must be preserved.
5. No one can be convicted of a crime without evidence, or accused and punished for someone else's crime.
6. An advisory system of administration is needed.[26]

Irrespective of their alleged Islamic origin, these six principles have largely defined the modern Western state and its legal order. Thus, by enunciating them, Gülen has sought to prove the compatibility of Islam with modernity. Moreover, he has argued that "Islam recommends a government based on a social contract. During the rule of the first four caliphs (632 AD-661 AD) in particular, the fundamental principles of government mentioned above—including free elections—were fully observed."[27]

In particular, Gülen chose to stress the concept of shura as the Islamic foundation of democracy because "it is a method, a process of government, and way of life for Muslims."[28] His approach to the relationship between Islam and democracy seems extremely liberal. While it is true that the Muslim faith emphasizes justice and encourages freedom of thought, it also ascribes sovereignty to God. Yet Gülen probably feels the need to overemphasize Islam's democratic elements at a time of growing tensions between secularists and Islamists in Turkey and elsewhere.

Islamists have been increasingly keen to employ the democracy master frame locally in order to mobilize people and support their particularistic cause. With the help of this master frame, they can gain enough political legitimacy to seek policy changes. Since democracy means the power of the many over the few, Islamists can pursue majority rule through elections. But participation in elections does not always mean full acceptance of liberal values and norms. Islamists have often modified the concept of democracy to fit the local political and cultural context. In this way, they connect a global agenda of democratization with their own realities and goals. There are two examples of Islamists acting as glocalizers with the help of the democracy master frame: the Islamo-democrats and the electoral Salafis.

Chapter 3

The Politics of Islamo-Democracy in Turkey, Egypt, and Tunisia

We [the Muslim Brothers] aim to remove all forms of injustice, tyranny, autocracy and dictatorship, and we call for the implementation of a democratic multiparty all-inclusive political system that excludes no one. . . . There can be no question that genuine democracy must prevail.

Mohamed Morsi, February 9, 2011

Islamists first participated in elections after the end of the Second World War when the decolonization process led to establishment of new Muslim-majority states. Faced with regime repression and censorship, Islamist parties repeatedly resorted to low-profile campaigning seeking political legitimacy and influence. Nevertheless, participation in elections often came at a heavy cost: they were crippled by arrests of their members and confiscation of their assets. Still, there are several examples of Islamist parties participating in postwar elections.

Pakistan's Jamaat-e-Islami was established by Abul Ala Maududi in Lahore in 1941. The party participated in the first direct elections held in the newly established Pakistan for the provincial assembly of Punjab in March 1951.[1] It also participated in the parliamentary elections from 1970 to 2013, but performed poorly. The party has advocated the establishment of an Islamic state in Pakistan, ruled by Sharia, and has strongly opposed the West. According to its constitution, "for the desired reform and revolution, [the party] shall use democratic and constitutional means."[2] Yet its founder was known for his antidemocracy views. For example, he once stated that "I tell you my fellow Muslims, frankly: Democracy is in contradiction with your belief. . . . There can be no reconciliation between Islam and democracy, not even in minor issues."[3] Therefore, it can be argued that the party only tactically accepts democracy.

The Syrian branch of the Muslim Brotherhood was established sometime in the mid-1940s by Sunni Syrians who had studied in Cairo.[4] It managed to develop grassroots support and participated in parliamentary elections from 1947 to 1961. Some of its prominent members were even invited to join a coalition government in December 1949.[5] The Baathist coup of March 1963 forced the Muslim Brotherhood to go underground and later to launch a campaign of terror against the Hafez al-Assad regime.[6] For many years, it remained a clandestine organization with limited influence. Since the outbreak of the civil war in 2011, the branch of the Muslim Brotherhood has resurfaced as part of the Sunni opposition fighting against the Syrian regime.

Hizb ut-Tahrir has also occasionally participated in elections, although it has viciously rejected democracy as a Western political system that works against Islam.[7] In fact, its founder himself ran unsuccessfully for the Jordanian parliament in 1951 before the party was formally established. Despite being banned by the authorities, Hizb ut-Tahrir participated in the parliamentary elections of 1954 and 1956 but its candidates ran as independents.[8] Nonetheless, the party has opposed democracy because "the parliament does not legislate, rather the government proposes the laws and the parliament passes them. . . . Consequently, democracy is a fanciful idea, impossible to implement, is based on lies and misinterpretation and leads the people astray."[9] The party has not participated in any elections since then.

There is no doubt that the rise of electoral politics in the postwar Middle East and South Asia forced some Islamists to seek public approval of their ideas. The unit of identification was the postcolonial nation-state. But they held an ambiguous position regarding democracy. Notwithstanding their electoral participation, these Islamists largely viewed elections as a means to an end. They perceived democracy as 'un-Islamic' because it has not been sanctioned by Sharia.

In contrast to them, there is now a new generation of Islamists who have endorsed democracy and have viewed elections as a necessary, and even Islamic-compliant, process to gain power and implement their programs.[10] As Olivier Roy pointed out, "the only way for Islamists to maintain their legitimacy is through elections."[11] They have advocated a new version of Islamism, the Islamo-democracy, which blends Islam with some democratic elements. Their unit of identification is a particular community of Muslims defined by piety and religiousness. Three parties stand as the most significant in this regard: Turkey's Justice and Development Party (Adalet ve Kalkinma Partisi—AKP), Egypt's Muslim Brotherhood (al-Ikhwan al-Muslimun), and Tunisia's Renaissance Movement (Haraka al-Nahda).

This chapter describes briefly the rise of Islamo-democracy, then discusses the political dominance of the AKP in Turkey. Also, it covers the participation of the Muslim Brotherhood in the Egyptian political system and the emergence of al-Nahda in neighboring Tunisia. Finally, it analyzes how Islamo-democrats have utilized the master frame of democracy to mobilize support and gain legitimacy.

The Rise of Islamo-Democracy

The end of the Cold War and the collapse of communism gave new momentum to the spread of democracy globally. The Western paradigm of political and economic governance emerged triumphant and strong. In the early 1990s, Gudrun Krammer rightly observed that "a growing number of Muslims, including a good many Islamist activists, have called for pluralist democracy, or at least for some of its basic elements: the rule of law and the protection of human rights, political participation, government control and accountability."[12] One can argue that this development was almost an inevitable outcome of the cataclysmic events that took place after the fall of the Berlin Wall in 1989. The Muslim world had been contested by the two superpowers and the victory of the West over the Soviet Union sent shock waves through the greater Middle East.

Turkey, with its long tradition of westernization, was the first Muslim-majority country to experiment with the blending of Islam and democracy. The AKP has adopted a pro-democracy discourse and has justified its policies accordingly. Indeed, the rise of the AKP in Turkey in the first decade of this century signaled the birth of the Islamo-democracy, whereby electoral pluralism coexists with Islamic values. It is a version of Islamism based on consensual politics. While the success of the AKP can be explained by local political circumstances, the rise of Islamo-democracy is coincident with changes and events that occurred in that first decade, and I analyze it later in greater depth.

Almost a decade after the first electoral victory of the Islamist-leaning AKP in Turkey, the seeds of Islamo-democracy were planted in other Muslim countries. The Arab Spring revolutions have been hailed by many Western analysts as the Arab 1989 that could lead to the democratic trans-formation of the Arab World.[13] While it is still debatable what the causes were that produced the change, the overthrow of secularly minded Arab leaders created a political vacuum that has been filled by Islamists.[14] They played a minor role in the protests against Ben Ali in Tunisia and Hosni Mubarak in Egypt, but Islamists finally managed to come to power through democratic elections.[15] Notwithstanding some predictions, Iranian-style Islamist takeovers have not occurred yet.[16] Instead, a democratic version of Islamism has emerged in the greater Middle East.

The Unprecedented Success of the AKP

The father of modern Turkish Islamism was Necmettin Erbakan. He estab-lished the Welfare Party (Refah Partisi) in 1983 after the military returned power to civilian control. The party participated in the 1991 parliamentary election and received 16.9 percent of the vote and 62 seats.[17] In 1994, it won the local elections nationwide and gained control of Ankara and Istanbul municipalities. Tagip Erdoğan became the mayor of Istanbul. One year later, the Welfare Party scored 21.4 percent in the parliamentary elections and gained 158 seats in the Turkish parliament.[18] It formed a coalition government with the right-wing Correct Path Party led by Tansu Çiller.

On February 28, 1997, the Turkish military forced Erbakan to resign as prime minister in what came to be known as the postmodern coup; Turkish armed forces announced that his government did not enjoy the trust of the army anymore. The forced resignation of Erbakan revealed, once again, the extraordinary influence of the Turkish army in the country's political sys-tem. The Welfare Party was banned by the Constitutional Court in 1998 for violating the separation of religion and state. It was succeeded by the Virtue Party (Fazilet Partisi) in December 1998, which was also banned by the Constitutional Court in June 2001 for the same reason.

The AKP was established in August 2001 by Tagip Erdoğan and former members of the Islamist-oriented Virtue Party. On November 3, 2002, the newly formed party won 34.3 percent of the votes in the parliamentary elections; consequently, it gained the majority of seats and formed the first single-party government since 1987.[19] The first term of the AKP government was by all accounts very successful and productive. The new government initiated important reforms that set the pace for the transformation of the economy. The private sector prospered and exports increased significantly. The driving force behind the Turkish economic miracle has been the so-called Anatolian Tigers, namely the small to medium-sized export-oriented businesses based on family networks in Anatolia. According to Ömer Taşpinar, the economic reforms of Turgut Özal during the 1980s had already given new momentum to the stagnated Turkish economy.[20] Consequently, a class of entrepreneurial Muslim bourgeoisie was created that started seeking political emancipation. These businessmen have owned companies that are based in cities located in central Turkey.[21] They represent a kind of Islamic Calvinism that urges devout Muslims to work hard while abiding by Muslim values.[22] The AKP has recruited heavily from this new class of Muslim businessmen.

The solidification of democracy and the economic growth dramatically changed the image of Turkey. As a result, it gained the status of a candidate country for European Union membership in 2004, which was a longtime aim. The AKP won the parliamentary elections of July 2007 by increasing its share of votes to 46.6 percent.[23] The outstanding victory of the AKP was largely the result of its successful economic policies. The party was able to expand its support base and reached middle-class and professional Turks from urban centers. In 2008, Turkey became a member of the Group of Twenty major economies. In the same year, however, the country's Constitutional Court considered a ban of the AKP on the grounds that the party was antisecular. Finally, Turkey's top judges decided to uphold the legal status of the AKP by only one vote.

During the 2011 parliamentary elections, the AKP again won the majority of votes and seats in the parliament; it gained 49.8 percent of the votes and 327 seats.[24] This time Erdoğan took the opportunity to settle scores with the old Kemalist elite. Among other things, the AKP government utilized the EU accession process to undermine the power of the Turkish military.[25] In particular, the outbreak of the Ergenekon scandal discredited the army and the intelligence services, which had plotted to overthrow the country's leadership.[26]

Erdoğan managed to win the first-ever direct presidential elections in August 2014; he won 52 percent of the vote while his opponent, Ekmeleddin Ihsanoglu, received only 38 percent.[27] The Turkish leader has called for the establishment of a new republic in which executive power would be transferred from the prime minister to the president. In spite of its political dominance, the parliamentary elections of June 2015 were a setback for the AKP leadership since the party won only 40.87 percent of the votes and lost its parliamentary majority.[28] This proved to be a temporary problem for the AKP leaders. A new parliamentary election was held in November 2015. The AKP received 49.50 percent and formed a new government under Ahmet Davutoğlu.[29]

The success story of the AKP remains a puzzle to many analysts. The AKP has won more elections than any other political party in the history of the Turkish Republic. The AKP has portrayed itself as a party that sincerely cares about the well-being of all Turks. Therefore, it has provided extensive social services and welfare programs.[30] Moreover, the party has underscored the importance of conservative values, largely based on Islam, to gain a moral advantage over its competitors. [31] It is not a coincidence that Erdoğan invoked God's name when the AKP came under criticism for its policies.[32] The party's Islamic credentials can provide a shield against allegations of corruption and abuse of power. The AKP government has taken credit for Turkey's booming economy while engaging in culture wars over largely symbolic issues, such as the consumption of alcohol by the youth[33] and the wearing of veil in public.[34] More important, the AKP has managed to confront the militant secularism of the Kemalist elite.

The AKP has not been alone in this effort. Turkish Islamic orders have mobilized the faithful for the purpose of supporting the ruling party.[35] Their political patronage has been achieved, among other things, through NGOs and civil society organizations. Nevertheless, these religious networks have maintained their political autonomy and have even clashed with the AKP. During 2013–2015, the AKP government, and Erdoğan personally, had a public row with Gülen and his followers in Turkey, accusing them of establishing a "parallel state" by infiltrating key ministries, the police, and the judiciary.[36] Following the military coup of July 15, 2016, during which 265 people were killed, the Turkish government arrested tens of thousands of Gülen's supporters for their alleged participation in it.[37] Ankara has also asked for the extradition of the U.S.-based cleric because he allegedly masterminded the coup attempt against President Erdoğan.[38]

The party has not only gained political power, it has also achieved ideological hegemony. For this reason, it has promoted a new notion of nationalism that emphasizes Muslim identity as the defining element of

Turkishness. According to Senem Aslan, "the ideal Turk should have a moral character informed by Sunni Islamic values. [Islamists] criticize Kemalist nationalists for being elitist and imitative, forcing people to change their authentic selves in the name of westernization."[39] Thus, the AKP portrays itself as a force of democratization that represents the majority of the population against a tiny minority of nongenuine Turks. In reality, the party has addressed a particular community that shares common values and beliefs; they are the devout Sunni Muslims who were largely marginalized by the Kemalist regime. A study conducted during 2008–2009 found that voters of AKP tend to endorse Islamism more than those supporting other parties.[40] Another study conducted in 2003 showed that Turks belonging to the Shia sect of Alevis did not vote for the AKP in the general elections of 2002 but for the secular Republican People's Party (Cumhuriyet Halk Partisi).[41]

The issue of ethnicity is not regarded as being as significant as religious affiliation and devotion. In fact, the AKP has espoused a form of Turkish-sponsored pan-Islamism that has at its center the Palestinian issue. During a speech at Cairo University on November 17, 2012, Erdoğan asserted that "just as Mecca, Medina, Cairo, Alexandria, Beirut, Damascus, Diyarbakir, Istanbul, Ankara are each other's brothers, so, let the world know and understand that Ramallah, Nablus, Jericho, Rafah and Jerusalem are these cities' brothers and our brothers. Each drop of blood spilled in these cities is the same blood that flows in our veins. . . . Each tear is our own tear."[42]

His emotional words indicated a deep personal commitment to supporting the Palestinian cause. While the choice of Diyarbakir may have looked odd, it was meant to reach out to Turkish Kurds, who consider the city their unofficial capital. Almost a month later Erdoğan revealed that his government had entered into secret negotiation with the jailed leader of the Kurdistan Workers' Party Abdullah Ocalan.[43] He also sketched the borders of a future Palestinian state that would include the West Bank and the Gaza Strip, as well as the highly contested city of Jerusalem. Yet the Palestinian issue is just the means to the end of gaining influence in other Muslim communities; it is not a coincidence that Erdoğan mentioned only cities and not states.

Furthermore, the AKP has attempted to export its own model for governance in North Africa.[44] In 2012, for example, Erdoğan visited post-Arab Spring Egypt, Libya, and Tunisia to promote the AKP model. Although his offer was perceived by some as interference in the domestic affairs of these countries, the Turkish leader remained popular among the Arab public.[45] He has developed a reputation of an honest and straightforward politician who supports Muslim causes. In this post-9/11 era, the defense of Islam from its critics can be a rallying cry for those who believe that the West has an anti-Muslim agenda.

Currently, the AKP has a large majority of seats in the parliament and the country's top political positions are held by its leaders. One can only speculate about how long the AKP will remain the dominant party in the country. It could easily become the Turkish equivalent of the Liberal Democratic Party in Japan, the African National Congress in South Africa, or People's Action Party in Singapore. The real challenge will come when Erdoğan and other senior officials retire from political life; the second generation of AKP leaders would have to keep the party popular and relevant enough to maintain its dominant position in Turkish politics.

The Transformation and Fall of the Muslim Brotherhood

The Muslim Brotherhood is the world's first Islamist organization, established by Hasan al-Banna in 1928.[46] The founder of the Ikhwan was a primary school teacher and preacher in the town of Ismaliya. The Muslim Brothers grew rapidly in the 1930s and 1940s, building cadres in many Egyptian towns and rural areas. Al-Banna criticized not only the British government for its interference in Egyptian affairs but also the nationalist Wafd Party for its pro-secular stance. Indeed, the Muslim Brotherhood is credited with the formation of a new ideology that claimed to have answers based on the Quran and the Sunnah of the Prophet. The message of the Ikhwan was simple: "Allah is our objective, the Prophet is our leader, the Quran is our Constitution, and Dying in the way of Allah is our highest hope."[47] The Brotherhood relocated its headquarters to the capital Cairo in 1932 in order to increase its appeal.

During the Second World War, its relationship with the pro-British Egyptian authorities became confrontational due to the Brotherhood's sympathies with Nazi Germany. The party leadership established the Secret Apparatus (al-jihaz al-sirri), a paramilitary wing, to prepare a revolt against the British army and its local allies.[48] Following the end of the war, the Muslim Brothers challenged the Egyptian political establishment and its foreign patrons. The Arab-Israeli War of 1948 led to civil disturbances in Egypt; as a result, thousands of Muslim Brothers were imprisoned and tortured.[49] Hasan al-Banna himself was assassinated by pro-government gunmen on February 12, 1949.

The 1952 Free Officers Revolution was initially supported by the Brotherhood, since it abolished the monarchy, which was largely viewed as a British-controlled institution. But relations between the new regime and the Brotherhood gradually deteriorated because the new president, Gamal Abdul Nasser, did not want to share power with the organization. Therefore, he banned the Brotherhood and strove to eradicate its presence. His successors also repressed the Ikhwan because its grassroots activism was perceived as a threatening force. However, at certain periods of time, the Brotherhood was allowed to maintain a visible presence in the society. For instance, the Ikhwan published the magazine *Da'wa* during the years of Anwar Sadat's presidency.

Due to its problematic relationship with the Egyptian authorities, the Muslim Brotherhood has always maintained a strict policy of recruitment for security reasons. Potential members are identified by senior operatives before they go through five different levels: *muhib* (follower), *muayyad* (supporter), *muntasib* (affiliated), *muntazim* (organizer), and *ach'amal* (working brother).[50] Additionally, the Brotherhood has established a large number of NGOs and has run hospitals and schools. These Ikhwan-controlled entities have served as a recruitment pool for party members.

During the first decade of this century, the Muslim Brotherhood went through a phase of "pragmatization" by integrating slowly into the Egyptian political system. In October 2000, the Ikhwan won seventeen seats in the People's Assembly although the Mubarak regime forced its candidates to run as independents.[51] In February 2000, the leader of the Ikhwan Asam al-Eryan had said that the Brotherhood's call for an Islamic state was "a slogan that has passed its time. . . . The constitution already says that Egypt is an Islamic state and that Sharia is the basis of legislation."[52] The organization continued to operate in a state of semiclandestinity but became increasingly vocal. In the parliamentary elections of 2005, the Ikhwan came in second in votes and seats; this time the organization did not refrain from using religious slogans like "it's not for position, nor for power, not for money, nor for party . . . it's for Islam and for God."[53] Its electoral successes in a constrained political environment increased the Brotherhood's visibility and confidence. During an interview in late June 2010, a member of the Ikhwan's Executive Bureau, Essam al-Arian, argued that "the rules of politics in Egypt must be changed by ending the state of emergency and allowing the freedom to form parties without limitations or conditions; allowing parliament to hold the government accountable; selecting the government from the parliamentary majority; and preventing electoral fraud."[54]

Despite this call for political openness, the Brotherhood has always represented the community of pious Muslims. In 2014, for example, a Pew Research opinion poll showed that those supporting the Muslim Brotherhood are more likely to say that laws should follow the Quran.[55] Its appeal is not confined to economically disadvantaged citizens who depend on the Brotherhood's welfare programs. Actually, the Ikhwan has enjoyed high levels of support from the professional classes and the student population.[56]

The overthrow of the Mubarak regime in February 2011 paved the way for the liberalization of the country's political system. On February 21, 2011, the Brotherhood formed the Freedom and Justice Party (hizb al-hurrya wa al-adala) to participate in the 2011–2012 parliamentary elections. The party managed to win 37.5 percent of the votes and 235 out of 508 seats in the People's Assembly.[57] Consequently, the secretary-general of the party, Saad el-Katami, became Speaker of the People's Assembly.

Although the Brotherhood had promised not to participate in the presidential elections of 2012, it finally decided to take advantage of the political climate and have its own candidate. Khairat al-Shater was disqualified as the Brotherhood's presidential candidate by the Electoral Commission because he had a criminal conviction. The organization had to nominate another candidate. Finally, Mohamed Morsi won the election by 51 percent of the vote.[58] The election of Morsi as president of Egypt in May 2012 confirmed the Ikhwan's growing popularity in Egyptian society. According to Hesham al-Awadi, his victory can be attributed not only to his personal abilities but also to the Ikhwan's mobilizational competence.[59] The new president sought to assure the opposition that the Brotherhood did not intend to take over the state. Therefore, the cabinet of Prime Minister Hesham Qandil, appointed by Morsi on August 2 2012, consisted of thirty-five ministers but only five were affiliated with the Brotherhood.[60]

This political coming out was the result of two factors. First, the Ikhwan had to deal with Egyptian society's newly discovered mode of democratic participation. The Brotherhood decided to engage more in participatory politics in order to remain relevant. Second, there have been important demographic changes within the Ikhwan that have inevitably affected its approach to democracy. Even though there is no youth division within the organization, students have increasingly played an important role in the postrevolution period. Indeed, the younger members of the Brotherhood participated in the protest movement against the Mubarak regime. Hence they "received hands-on training on how to organize civil disobedience campaigns and offered their experience to the group's leadership, which replied unenthusiastically."[61]

For many years, its clandestine or semilegal status did not permit the development of a robust political program offering solutions for everyday problems. The Muslim Brotherhood has favored gradualism (*tadarruj*), while implementing reforms in the social sphere (e.g., education). That being said, its ideology has evolved over the years and has never been coherent. Some hard-line elements have supported the idea of confronting the state and imposing Islam on the society. But this has not always been the case. According to Richard Mitchell, the Brotherhood has even praised Western countries for respecting individual freedoms and rights of workers, and affirming the responsibility of rulers to their people.[62]

Besides, the post-Mubarak Brotherhood declared its intention to transform the Egyptian economy. Hence it did not oppose privatization and understood the need to reform the public welfare and subsidies system.[63] Also, the Ikhwan followed a pragmatic economic policy cultivating ties with the West and international organizations. Accordingly, the Brotherhood agreed to a $3.2 billion loan from the International Monetary Fund in February 2012.[64] In fact, President Morsi followed a rather liberal economic policy that contributed to the increase of Egyptian exports and the growth of the national economy.[65]

Morsi's government lasted only a year. During the final months of 2012 and the first six months of 2013, hundreds of thousands of Egyptians protested against Mohamed Morsi demanding his resignation. The military coup d'état on July 3, 2013, did not come as a surprise. The army has been the most powerful institution in post-1952 Egypt; actually, all Egypt's preceding presidents (i.e., Nasser, Sadat, and Mubarak) were former officers.[66]

It is not known yet why the army decided to intervene in July 2013 and not earlier. The protests against the Morsi government were clearly the pretext for the military coup. The situation in Turkey probably weighed heavily in this decision. One lesson to be drawn from the rise of Islamists in Turkey is that time works in their favor so the army has to act early on before it is too late. To put it simply, Egypt's military leaders did not want to have the fate of their Turkish colleagues. The crushing of the July 2016 coup attempt by Erdoğan seems to confirm this perception.

As of this writing, it is not clear how the coup and the subsequent banning of the Muslim Brotherhood in the summer of 2013 will affect its long-term status. Many of its senior officials have been arrested and activities have been banned. Abdel Fattah el-Sisi, the former army chief of staff and current president of Egypt, has indicated that the Ikhwan will remain a banned group. He has argued that "their ideological structure makes confrontation with us inevitable. . . . [They believe] that we are not real Muslims and they are real Muslims. . . . An ideology like that cannot come back."[67] Despite the government crackdown, the Ikhwan is likely to survive as an organization; its long history of clandestine existence and grassroots support can only strengthen its will to remain active.

The Political Adaptability of Al-Nahda

Tunisia has been typically described as the most westernized Arab country. Under the leadership of Habib Bourguiba (1956–1987), Tunisian authorities imposed a militant secularism that severely restricted the public role of Islam. Bourguiba's Personal Status Code significantly enhanced women's rights in the country. His reforms amounted to a social revolution resembling Kemal Ataturk's westernization project. In the late 1970s, however, the Tunisian leader did not hesitate to use the Islamists to counter the growing influence of leftists on university campuses.[68]

Rachid al-Ghannouchi has been the leading figure in the Islamist movement since the early 1980s. He was born in a small town of southern Tunisia and studied in Cairo and Damascus. In April 1981, al-Ghannouchi established the Islamic Tendency Movement (Harakat al ittijah al-Islami), which campaigned for the end of the single-party system and the introduction of political pluralism in Tunisia. The party was inspired by the Muslim Brotherhood, but it had no formal links to the Egyptian organization. Three months later he was arrested together with some of his followers and sent to prison, from which he was released in 1987.

Following the overthrow of Habib Bourguiba in November 1987, the new leader, Zine El Abidine Ben Ali, tried to normalize relations with Tunisian Islamists. As a consequence, political prisoners were released from prison and Rachid al-Ghannouchi was pardoned. The Islamic Tendency

Movement was renamed the Renaissance Movement. Al-Nahda sought recognition as a legitimate political force because al-Ghannouchi argued that "participation by the Islamists in elections is a testimony to their willingness to abide by the rules of the democratic process."[69] Indeed, the party participated in the April 1989 parliamentary elections through independent candidates and won 14.5 percent of the vote; yet it failed to win any seats due to the electoral system.[70] Ben Ali continued to enforce the exclusion of Islamists from the political system. Indeed, he gradually resorted to his predecessor's policy of repression against political opponents. Consequently, al-Ghannouchi and other senior Islamist leaders were forced into exile.

He returned to Tunisia on January 30, 2011, following the collapse of the Ben Ali regime. Al-Nahda was legalized two months later and participated in the Tunisian Constituent Assembly elections in October 2011, when it received 37 percent of the votes and won 89 of the 217 seats.[71] The party formed a coalition government with two secular, left-of-center parties, the Congress for the Republic and Ettakatol.[72]

Al-Ghannouchi and other senior figures have portrayed al-Nahda as a moderate political force that combines Islamic and liberal values. He once asked, "why are we put in the same place as a model that is far from our thought, like the Taliban or the Saudi model, while there are other successful Islamic models that are close to us, like the Turkish, the Malaysian and the Indonesian models, models that combine Islam and modernity?"[73] Moreover, he has been keen to emphasize the universal applicability of democratic ideals. In an article titled "Tunisia Shows That There Is No Contradiction Between Islam and Democracy," the leader of al-Nahda argued that "despite what some believe, there is no 'Arab exception' to democracy, nor is there any inherent contradiction between democracy and Islam. The Middle East can indeed achieve stability and peace through a process of democratic reconciliation and consensus. . . . Unlike in Libya, Egypt or Iraq, Tunisia's new political system has turned away from exclusion; rather, we put our faith in the ballot box. . . . The results of free and fair elections must be respected."[74] Thus, he dismissed culture-specific arguments to explain the lack of democracy in the Arab Middle East. Instead, he highlighted different national experiences and pointed out achievements of the past.

Al-Nahda's relatively liberal approach has been clearly demonstrated by its view on women. In general, it can be argued that gender relations in Tunisia are more equal than in other Arab societies. Tunisian women have a visible presence in the public sphere and have enjoyed rights similar to their counterparts in the Western world.[75] At the same time, Tunisian society has experienced a revival of conservative Muslim values that advocate gender segregation and traditional roles for women. Given the political and social sensitivities attached to the issue, al-Nahda has opted for a middle ground. The party has committed itself to the protection of women's rights in the country. Yet, as I show later, that this has not prevented some of its senior members from calling for conservative changes.

The party has tried hard to strike a balance between Tunisia's realities and its ideological orientation. Therefore, its ideologues have differentiated between Islamic and Islamist parties. During an interview, the party spokesman Samir Dilou stated that "We are not an Islamist party, we are an Islamic party, which is also inspired by the principles of the Quran, which states expressly, in matters of faith, there must be no coercion. . . . There are no rules in how people should dress, whether they wear the veil or not. . . . We do not want a theocracy. We want a democratic state that is characterized by the idea of freedom. People should decide for themselves how they live, the religious state model in the sense of Algeria or the Taliban has failed. If there is any model for us, then it is possibly Turkey."[76]

In maintaining this balance, the party leadership has accepted the competitive nature of parliamentary politics. Al-Nahda failed to win the October 2014 parliamentary elections. The secularists of the Nida Tunis (Tunis Calls) Party won the most seats and formed a new coalition government without al-Nahda.[77] Al-Nahda conceded defeat to its secular rival in those general elections.[78] The smooth political change indicated the maturity of the country's political system and the sincerity of al-Nahda's intentions. On the other hand, Monica Marks has argued that the party has adopted an approach based on compromise and defensive minimalism in order to ensure its long-term survival.[79]

In any case, al-Nahda has followed a gradualist approach to political transition and cultural transformation. It has clearly targeted religious voters who believe that Islam must have a more public role in the country. While the Tunisian society is ethnically homogeneous, it is divided mostly along the secular-Islamic axis. The party has come to represent the community that was politically marginalized and passive for many decades, namely religious Tunisians.

To sum up, al-Nahda has portrayed itself as a faith-oriented political party advocating certain Islamic principles, while being a pro-democracy

force. It has offered a relatively liberal interpretation of the Islamic traditions and norms in regard to personal freedoms; such an interpretation fits
well Tunisia's own social and cultural patterns. Hence the party is very
likely to survive and prosper politically as a moderate force that combines
pragmatism with religious assertion.

The Islamo-Democrats Between the Global and the Local

The emergence of Islamo-democracy is a bottom-up process resulting from
unique local conditions, described earlier, as well as larger technological
and societal developments. The spread of communication technology (e.g.,
cell phones, portable computers) has facilitated political mobilization both
within and across borders. In 2001, only 3.3 million Turks (5.20 percent)
had access to the Internet from home. One year later, the number of regular
Internet users doubled to almost 7.5 million (11.4 percent) and reached 46
million (58 percent) in 2016.[80] In Egypt, there has been a similar growth of
Internet connectivity. In 2001, there were only half a million regular
Internet users, who represented less than 1 percent of the total population;
in 2016, their number reached 30 million (30 percent of the population).[81]
In Tunisia, only 4 percent of the population had access to the Internet from
home in 2001, whereas 48 percent of Tunisians were regular users in 2016.[82]

With the spread of the Internet, the social media revolution has reached
the Middle East. In June 2012, for example, there were 55 million Arabs on
Facebook and 3.7 million on Twitter.[83] The use of social media has allowed
the formation of networks that cannot be infiltrated easily by security agencies because they lack the hierarchical structures of traditional organizations.[84] More importantly, they have created a new space of dialogue that
has challenged official narratives and regimes' monopoly of information,
while exposing human rights violations and state corruption.

The Internet has opened up societies to universal norms in ways that
were not thought possible some years ago. It is a bright new world of
knowledge and opportunities that cannot leave Muslim societies intact. As
a matter of fact, many Muslims have responded positively to the forces of
globalization. For example, an opinion poll conducted by the University of
Maryland in 2007 showed that 92 percent of Egyptians felt positively about
"the world becoming more connected through greater economic trade and
faster communication."[85] The Middle East has begun to come out from its

isolation and expose itself to a global marketplace of ideas and practices. And in this environment, the Islamo-democrats have moved fast to take advantage of the emerging situation and address local concerns from a global angle. They have used social media and other new communication technologies to spread their messages. Not surprisingly, Erdoğan, Morsi, and al-Ghannouchi have Twitter accounts with millions of followers.

Simultaneously, many middle-class Muslims from the Middle East have been able to travel and receive education in Western countries. According to a 2014 report released by the Institute of International Education, the number of students from the Middle East in U.S. universities has more than tripled since 2000.[86] Such experiences have made many Muslims more aware of civil liberties and democracy. Naturally, they have pushed for their home countries to follow a similar path. It is certainly not a coincidence that many Islamist politicians have studied and worked abroad.

Political stagnation has also been challenged by the growth of university education that has produced masses of graduates with rising expectations in the Middle East. In 2010, for instance, 23 percent of university graduates were unemployed in Tunisia.[87] In Egypt, unemployment among college graduates is ten times higher than among those who did not go to college.[88] These graduates are better informed of international developments than the previous generation. They can compare governments' performance and ability to tackle income inequality. Therefore, they are more likely to join protests because they tend to see more social and political problems.[89] Indeed, the youth has played an important role in the growth of Islamo-democracy, especially during the Arab Spring revolutions.

In spite of these cross-national dynamics, Islamo-democrats seem to have little in common. Local circumstances have clearly dictated their political development. The Brotherhood was founded in the 1920s, whereas al-Nahda and the AKP were established relatively recently. The Ikhwan has had many traumatic experiences with the Egyptian authorities; thousands of its members have been arrested and tortured by the security forces. It gained power only for a year before the army staged a coup against President Morsi. In contrast, al-Nahda is still a legal party in Tunisia, while the AKP has been the governing party of Turkey since 2002.

Also, there are major differences between the three parties' conceptualization of Islamo-democracy based on political and cultural differences. To start with, the AKP has not identified itself as an Islamist party but rather as a conservative one. During a speech at the Oxford Center for Islamic

Studies in April 2009, Erdoğan denied that Turkey is a representative of moderate Islam. In his words, "Islam cannot be classified as moderate or not."[90] In January 2005, the party became an observer member of the European People's Party in the European Parliament, which was established by Christian Democratic parties in 1976. The AKP's understanding of Islamo-democracy is probably comparable to the postwar European Christian Democracy that has dominated Western Europe for decades. The 2002 and 2007 election platforms, *Herşey Türkiye İçin* (Everything Is for Turkey) and *Nice Ak Yıllara* (To Many Bright Years), stressed the party's commitment to democracy, human rights, the rule of law, limited government, and respect for diversity.[91] Erdoğan has also defended Turkey's secularism on numerous occasions. In April 2016, for instance, the Speaker of Turkey's parliament, Ismail Kahraman, called for a religious constitution; Erdoğan reacted by saying that "the reality is that the state should have an equal distance from all religious faiths. . . . This is laicism."[92]

The party has been very keen to emphasize its role in the democratization of Turkey. In 2005, Hakan Yavuz argued that AKP parliamentarians, who had local political experience, were versed in global discourses of human rights and democracy; therefore, they represented the connection between the local and the global.[93] The AKP has switched from "political" to "social Islam" because it has learned from the experience of the Welfare Party, banned in 1997.[94] Therefore, the party has not endorsed an openly Islamist agenda. It has been argued that the AKP could pursue Muslim politics without establishing an Islamic state.[95] More specifically, it has favored "passive secularism" whereby the state has a passive role regarding the public role of Islam; in other words, the state does not recognize any official religion but it does not suppress public manifestations of religiosity.[96]

For many decades, the Ikhwan avoided deliberately discussing in detail the ideal system of governance. Hasan al-Banna favored the establishment of an Islamic polity governed by Sharia and vaguely supported Muslim unity. His successors have tried to strike a balance between a commitment to pursue the global aim of Islamization and the necessity to adapt to the local peculiarities of Egypt. The Brotherhood has promoted the Quranic concept of the *al-Wasatiyah* (the Middle Community) and its modern application. According to the Quran, "and thus We have made you an *ummat wasat* [i.e., a just, equitable, or good nation] that you may be the bearers of witness to the people and [that] the Messenger may be a bearer of witness to you" (2:143). Egyptian Islamists have interpreted the verse as a God-given request for moderation. Yusuf al-Qaradawi has argued that "Wasatiyya is the balance between mind and Revelation, matter and spirit, rights and duties, individualism and collectivism, inspiration and commitment, the Text [i.e., Quran and the Sunnah] and personal interpretation [*ijtihad*]."[97] As a result, the Muslim Brotherhood has moved to the political center, while facing tough opposition from Salafis.[98]

Furthermore, the Muslim Brothers have argued that the foundation of representative democracy can be found in the Islamic principle of shura, which was first analyzed by al-Banna. The Brotherhood has attempted to theorize the Islamicness of democracy, claiming that people are the source of all power; it follows that popular sovereignty could be practiced through free and fair elections, a limit on the number of a ruler's terms, and a strong parliament.[99] As opposed to the AKP, the Ikhwan has used the Quran extensively as a source of guidance for the development of its political doctrine. It reflects the organization's deep Islamic roots and the prominent role of ulama within it.

Unlike the AKP and the Brotherhood, al-Nahda has favored a more inclusive approach that comes closer to the Western paradigm. The party has been greatly influenced by the political thinking of Rachid al-Ghannouchi, who spent twenty-two years exiled in London. According to al-Ghannouchi, "Elections give a democratic mandate but that mandate must be exercised in an inclusive manner. For this reason the party refused to monopolize power when we won elections and shared key ministries with other parties and independents. . . . We are conscious that the practices we adopt now, of consensus-building and power-sharing between parties and between Islamists and secularists, provide a model for the future of democratic governance in the whole Arab world."[100]

These words could have come from any liberal European politician. His rhetoric is engaging and progressive. Also, it reveals that al-Nahda has aimed at establishing an alternative model of Islamo-democracy that can even be exported to the rest of the Arab world. It is fair to say that al-Nahda's perception of democracy is heavily influenced by the Tunisian political and cultural realities.

Despite these significant differences, the AKP, the Ikhwan, and al-Nahda have all relied heavily on the democracy master frame to propagate their messages and gather support. The component of political equality is particularly useful for Islamo-democrats who want to challenge the established political order and increase their appeal. The AKP has been keen to embrace it for reasons of political expediency. The party has reached out to pious Turks who were historically marginalized by the westernized secular elites. During a pre-election rally in Ankara in June 2014, Erdoğan stated that "they said we weren't good enough to be a village leader, that we couldn't be prime minister, that we couldn't be elected president. They didn't even deign to see us as an equal person in the eyes of the state."[101] In a clear reference to the old Kemalist establishment, the Turkish leader implied that there was systemic discrimination against religious citizens. In fact, the AKP has stressed the concept of political equality to capitalize on widespread feelings of injustice and exclusion. The governing party has even attempted to improve the rights of the Christian minority in order to strengthen its claim to political equality.[102]

The Muslim Brotherhood has taken a less clear position on this component. From its point of view, political equality is the acceptance of diversity. The Ikhwan has claimed to be an organization that is open to all citizens irrespective of their background. In the words of the supreme guide of the Muslim Brotherhood Mohamed Badie: "We respect everybody, no matter how much we disagree or agree with them; and we cooperate in common issues. . . . Diversity enriches life. The Prophet of Islam . . . nurtured and promoted diversity. Naturally, we must take into account the needs of the Egyptian people of all faiths and all political leanings and cultural orientations."[103]

In this way, Badie sought to increase the appeal of the Brotherhood among Egypt's secular urban dwellers and appease Western governments that worried about the spread of Islamism in the country. The commitment to political equality was reaffirmed by certain unprecedented steps. In late June 2014, Morsi's spokesman announced that the president-elect intended to appoint a Christian and a woman as vice presidents.[104] But the concept of political equality is not boundless. The Brotherhood has admitted it would ask its members, if needed, not to vote for a Christian or female president.[105]

In Tunisia, al-Nahda has long committed itself to political equality for all Tunisian citizens. According to article 6 of its statute, the party seeks to "reinforce the principle of sovereignty of the people by building a democratic state . . . to achieve equality between citizens and the development of structures of civil society and the liberalization of its mechanisms to perform [a] full role in contributing to the overall development."[106] The party has perceived this component as a safeguard against authoritarianism and political exclusion. Equality also means more accountability and transparency in government, something which is important for a party that still views itself as having a fiduciary duty to Tunisian Muslims.

Despite all this, for many Islamo-democrats political equality does not necessarily mean gender equality. For example, Erdoğan has claimed that "you cannot put women and men on an equal footing [because] it is against nature."[107] In Tunisia, female members of al-Nahda have called for changes in the country's Code of Personal Status, which has outlined women's family rights. Farida Laabidi, a female al-Nahda member of parliament, said in August 2012 that "we cannot speak of equality between man and woman in absolute terms. Otherwise, we will risk upsetting the family balance and distorting the social model in which we live."[108] Such views reflect a growing tendency in many Muslim countries to empower men and give them more responsibilities. But also it can be interpreted as part of a new Islamic anti-feminism movement that advocates traditional roles for women.

The component of majority rule has been adopted, albeit to varying degrees, by the three parties. The AKP has frequently stressed the importance of majority rule because many Turks have favored a democratic system with Islamic values. According to a 2012 opinion poll, conducted by Pew Research, 71 percent of Turkish citizens support democracy, but at the same time 61 percent of them want Islam to have some or much influence on their country's laws.[109] Therefore, Erdoğan has striven to build a majoritarian democracy whereby political minorities would not be able to hijack the state again. Not surprisingly, the Turkish government has not always tolerated opposition protests and has restricted press freedoms. In this effort, Erdoğan has been supported by the influential thinker Hayreddin Karaman, who once claimed that "the values of the majority" should be the basis of legislation, whereas minorities should "refrain from using some of their freedoms."[110] Following the failed coup of July 2016, Erdoğan called for the return of the death penalty. During the so-called Democracy and Martyrs' Rally he declared that "sovereignty belongs to the people, so if the people make this decision I am sure the political parties will comply."[111] Thus, he would be able to ostracize the coup plotters and their supporters from his imagined community of pious Muslims. More than anything else, this conflict is a struggle for the soul of Turkish Islam. The AKP seeks to monopolize control over Islamic activities and perceives competitors as a threat. Therefore, the Islamism of the AKP is increasingly exclusive and hostile to political minorities.

In Egypt, the Muslim Brotherhood has endorsed the component of majority rule as well. For instance, it has justified the application of Sharia on the basis of the country's religious demographics; the huge majority of Egyptians are Sunni Muslims. It follows that democracy has been conceptualized by the Brotherhood as the will of the majority.[112] At the same time, Yusuf al-Qaradawi has argued that "Islam does not concern itself with [the will of] the majority where there is a clear ruling in the Quran and the Sunnah, as opposed to [the] western democratic system which gives the majority the absolute right that its opinion is the law and the law is reformed if it is in violation of its opinion."[113] Thus, this component has been utilized to advance certain goals (e.g., application of Sharia); it is not really part of the Brotherhood's understanding of democracy.

Likewise, al-Nahda has not adopted wholeheartedly the concept of majority rule. After the outbreak of the Tunisian Revolution, the party presented itself as part of the new majority seeking democracy and freedom. Al-Nahda in power showed restraint and pragmatism, although it was accused of imposing "easternization" to revoke the results of decades-long westernization.[114] Following the defeat of al-Nahda in the October 2014 Tunisian parliamentary elections, al-Ghannouchi warned against one-party rule; from his point of view, "Tunisia's democracy is transitional, and cannot stand a return to conflict—a small majority is not enough to lead in the coming period. The solution is in an agreement based on mutual trust between various actors."[115] Thus, he has argued that majority rule in itself is not always fair and desirable. Instead, he has supported a pluralist system with power sharing and consensus building.

The democracy master frame has also provided political legitimacy to the AKP, the Ikhwan, and al-Nahda. The Turkish governing party has constantly used this component to support its policies vis-à-vis its domestic opponents. Initially, the party's commitment to democratization was meant to function as "a protective shield against the repressive actions of the secularist establishment."[116] But the electoral victories have gradually served as a source of unlimited legitimacy. During the summer 2013 Gezi Park protests, for example, then prime minister Tayyip Erdoğan declared that "we are opposed to violence, terror, vandalism. . . . For those who come to me with democratic demands, I'll sacrifice my life."[117] The Turkish leader knows that the lack of political legitimacy could impede government actions and eventually lead to his fall. Therefore, he has exaggerated his party's democratic nature in order to avoid criticism.

Similarly, the Brotherhood sought political legitimacy to strengthen its position in the political system. In this effort, the organization has stressed its endorsement of democracy and pluralism. According to Abdel Moneim Abou el-Fotouh, a senior member of the Ikhwan, the organization "has embraced diversity and democratic values. In keeping with Egypt's pluralistic society, we have demonstrated moderation in our agenda and have responsibly carried out our duties to our electoral base and Egyptians at large."[118] Thus, the Brotherhood hoped to counter accusations that it has a hidden agenda to turn the country into an Islamic state. The political legitimacy that derived from the election of Mohamed Morsi is still useful for juxtaposing against the anti-Ikhwan narrative produced by the Egyptian military and its supporters.

In Tunisia, al-Nahda has been keen to demonstrate its allegiance to democratic ideals and contribute to the democratization process. Following his decision to cede power to a caretaker government in January 2014, al-Ghannouchi said that "we've made sacrifices. We even sacrificed power for the sake of Tunisia and for democracy. . . . We have achieved the first goal of the revolution which is freedom."[119] In a country that has suffered from authoritarian rule, political generosity of that sort is self-beneficial because it produces political legitimacy. In turn, the acquired legitimacy can strengthen al-Nahda's claim that it is a party advocating a cause that is compatible with the country's political path.

Overall, the use of the democracy master frame has contributed to the indigenization of Islamism in Turkey, Egypt, and Tunisia. In spite of its modifications and imperfect application, the master frame has contributed to the popularity of the AKP, the Ikhwan, and al-Nahda. These political parties have experimented ideologically with democratic and Islamic values; as a result, they have experienced contradictions and duality. Even though there are different versions of this hybrid Islamism, it is obvious that the convergence of Islam and democracy is happening at different paces in different places. Therefore, the emergence of Islamo-democracy has changed the nature of Islamist politics in parts of the Middle East.

Conclusion

The rise of Islamo-democracy is a bottom-up development that points to the glocalization of Islamism. The Islamo-democrats neither seek the demolition of the existing state apparatus and the construction of a new Islamic state nor viciously reject democracy as a Western system that works against the spirit of Islam. This version of political Islam is closely identified with the existing state and does not support the abolition of borders. As opposed to Islamist globalists who have envisioned the establishment of a universal Islamic state that is not embedded in any particular territory, the Islamo-democrats tend to embrace the notion of bordered community. More importantly, they are prepared to accommodate local norms and practices into their ideological orbit. Their democraticness does not necessarily mean acceptance of liberal values (e.g., gender equality). It is rather defined as participation in elections and recognition of the constitutional process.

In Turkey, the AKP has dominated the political system for more than a decade. It came to power in the first decade of the century as a democratizing force against the old Kemalist elite that abandoned the country's Islamic tradition. Egypt's Muslim Brotherhood has not hidden its Islamist orientation and vision; yet Morsi did not push for the "Ikhwanization" of the state despite his clear electoral victories. In Tunisia, al-Nahda has become a responsible political party capable of endorsing Islamic values while acknowledging the country's peculiarities.

In spite of its shortcomings, Islamo-democracy has grown roots in the Middle East. New Islamist parties have been established that seek the blurring of democracy and Islam. Hence Islamists in Morocco (Justice and Development Party), Libya (National Forces Alliance), and Jordan (Islamic Action Front) have adopted a new political agenda, putting emphasis on pluralism, tolerance, and the economy. While every country is unique, the spread of this new version of Islamism has been facilitated by the use of the democracy master frame; its three components have been useful in helping to reshape Islamism as a pragmatic and humane ideology.

The wave of democratization sweeping through the Middle East could have a significant impact on the relations between the West and the Muslim world. The rise of Islamo-democrats is a challenge that the West can choose either to confront or to co-opt. In the first scenario, Western governments could spend vital resources in a conflict of civilizations, putting Muslim-majority nations in the arms of other anti-Western forces. In the second scenario, the West, principally the United States, could initiate a process of socializing Islamist or Islamist-leaning governments into the international community. In this way, the Islamo-democracy could almost function as the equivalent of the Christian Democrats in postwar Europe: a business-oriented force with a conservative, faith-based social agenda.

Chapter 4

The Politics of Electoral Salafism
in Egypt and Tunisia

[The Tunisian society should] take advantage of the
achievements of Western civilization and . . . work on . . .
the indigenization of them.

Reform Front, May 2012

Due to its global reach, Islam is a heterogeneous religion with many local
traditions and practices. The fragmentation of the Muslim faith has triggered revivalist movements like Salafiyya. The Salafi movement is calling
modern Muslims to revert to authentic Islam of the Prophet Muhammad
and his Companions, the *salaf* or "ancient ones."[1] According to a hadith,
the Prophet stated that "the people of my own generation are the best, then
those who come after them, and then those of the next generation."[2] Salafis
have argued that the first three generations of Muslims learned Islam
directly from the Prophet or those who knew him; therefore, early Islam
was pure and perfect. However, Islam was later infected with innovation
(*bid'a*) because many Muslims introduced elements of culture into the religion. Therefore, Salafis have recognized only the Quran, the *Ahadith*, and
the consensus of the Companions (*ijma al-sahabah*) as valid sources of
Islamic law. Salafis accept the teachings of the four *madhahib* (Hanafi, Hanbali, Maliki, Shafi'i), as long as they are based on the Quran and the Sunnah. However, most of them have denounced Shia Muslims as heretics and
have called them *rawafid* (rejectionists) because they do not recognize the
legitimacy of the first three caliphs.

Moreover, Salafis view themselves as members of the saved sect. A
hadith warns that "the *umma* will divide into 73 sects"[3] and another one

states, "Beware! The people of the Book [i.e., the Jews and the Christians])
before [you] were split up into seventy-two sects, and this community will
be split into seventy-three: seventy-two of them will go to Hell and one of
them will go to Paradise."[4] Consequently, Salafis believe that they have a
God-given mission to defend Islam from its enemies. They possess the
absolute truth because they follow a highly literalist approach to the Islamic
sources.

That being said, Salafis have often been misunderstood as seeking to live
under the conditions and circumstances of the early Muslims. Actually, what
is important for them is to imitate and re-enact the methodology (*manhaj*)
of the Salaf. From their point of view, this manhaj is "the only reason why
Islamic leaders of the early centuries were able to conquer the world. . . .
[They] professed Islam in its true and righteous form."[5] That means that
Salafism recognizes the achievements of modernity if they are compatible
with Sharia; the aim is the revival of orthodoxy in the present era.

Although Salafism is a modern movement, its intellectual roots lie in
the teachings of Ibn Taymiyaa (1263–1328) and Muhammad ibn Abd al-
Wahhab (1703–1792), two scholars of the Hanbali school of Islamic jurisprudence. They both accepted the Quran and the Sunnah as the only
sources of Islamic law. Taymiyaa was one of the first Islamic scholars who
criticized the existence of pre-Islamic practices within Islam and called for
a return to authentic Islam. In his famous work *Iqtida' as-Sirat al-Mustaqim*
(Following the Straight Path), Taymiyaa defended the uniqueness of Islam
against other monotheistic religions.[6] Therefore, he condemned certain
practices, such as the worshiping of Sufi saints.

The eighteenth-century preacher and scholar Muhammad ibn Abd al-
Wahhab also advocated purification of the faith and return to the Islam
practiced by the first generations of Muslims in the Arabian Peninsula. He
rejected religious innovations and polytheism (*shirk*). Instead, he emphasized the concept of *tawhid* (oneness of God).[7] Wahhab's ideas gained wider
acceptance when he allied himself with Muhammad bin Saud, the founder
of the first Saudi state in 1744. Since then, Wahhabism has been the dominant form of Islam practiced in Saudi Arabia.[8] The alliance between the
Wahhabi clerical establishment and the Saudi state has survived into the
twenty-first century.

However, Wahhabism is not identical to Salafism. According to Trevor
Stanley, "Wahhabism was a pared-down Islam that rejected modern influences, while Salafism sought to reconcile Islam with modernism."[9] Indeed,

the Salafi movement started in the mid- to late nineteenth century. The father of modern Salafism is considered to be the grand mufti of Egypt Muhammad Abduh (1849–1905), who advocated a return to the "simple" Islam of the Salaf.[10] Another influence was the Albanian-born Islamic scholar Muhammad Nasiruddin al-Albani (1914–1999), who specialized in the fields of hadith and *Fiqh* (Islamic jurisprudence), denounced Wahhabis' attachment to the Hanbali school, and criticized Wahhab for his weak knowledge of hadith.[11]

The Salafi movement grew popular in the 1960s and 1970s. At that time, a large wave of Salafi scholars moved from Egypt to Saudi Arabia. Most of them were forced in exile due to government repression. Once in Saudi Arabia, Salafis interacted with the all-powerful Wahhabi clerical establishment. Flush with petrodollars, the Saudi state embarked on a campaign to promote Salafism-Wahhabism throughout the Middle East and beyond.[12] The Mecca-based Muslim World League and other similar Saudi organizations have funded the construction of mosques and madrassas worldwide with the sole aim of promoting this fundamental version of Islam. Salafism has been spread across the world, including in Western countries such as the United States, Canada, Great Britain, and Australia.[13]

But the Salafi movement is far from being homogeneous. According to Quintan Wiktorowicz, there are three subgroups of Salafis: the purists, the jihadis, and the politicos.[14] Each one has its own strategy and agenda, although the common goal is to live under Sharia. Many Salafis have engaged only in *da'wa* (call to Islam) and education activities, while attempting to purify Islam from its non-Islamic elements; other Salafis have engaged in jihadi activities against foreign powers, Muslim regimes, or fellow Muslims; and some others believe that the Salafi movement can participate in the political life of a country. This chapter focuses on those Salafis who have been willing to join the democratic process. It describes the emergence of electoral Salafism in Egypt and Tunisia, then explains how Salafi parties have functioned as glocalizers of Islamism by adopting the democracy master frame.

The Rise of Electoral Salafism

Following the Arab Spring revolutions, Salafi parties were established in Egypt and Tunisia. In the former, the al-Nour Party came in second in votes in the 2011–2012 parliamentary election and established itself as the main opposition party to the Muslim Brotherhood-led government. In the latter, Salafi-oriented parties have joined the political system.

But Salafis have typically rejected democracy as a man-made system that goes against the spirit and tenets of Islam. Modern representative systems, such as parliamentary democracy, are based on the principle of free and fair elections; voters express their preferences and elect members of the parliament who legislate according to their desires and views. The only restriction to this is the constitution, which is the supreme law of the land. However, constitutions can be amended by a parliamentary or popular vote. Under democracy, people basically decide for themselves what is right and wrong. For Salafis this is hubris against God's wishes; Sharia is a God-given code of laws that men must always follow. Democracy is immoral because man does not abide by God's rules and becomes ignorant of his duties.

Therefore, many Salafi scholars have openly condemned democracy and elections. Salafi scholar Khamis Mejri has denounced elections because Tunisia "is not democracy, but 'deceptocracy.' . . . The solution is the implementation of Islam."[15] Likewise, the Salafi leader Abu Muhammad al-Tahawi called for a boycott of the 2013 Jordanian parliamentary elections since "the parliament [passes] laws and regulations that contradict God's law" and "choosing legislators other than God is forbidden."[16] Besides, Muhammad Nasiruddin al-Albani argued that "elections according to democracy are unlawful, and parliaments that do not govern in accordance with the Quran and the Sunnah, but rather on the basis of the majority's arbitrariness, are tyrannical."[17]

Furthermore, many Salafis believe that the Quran prohibits Muslims from overthrowing—even by democratic means—the ruler as long as he allows them to perform their religious duties. Indeed, the Quran demands from Muslims to "obey Allah and obey the Messenger and those in authority from among you" (4:59). The believers can only disobey the ruler if he asks them to commit sinful acts.[18] Those engaged only in da'wa and education activities have used this verse to justify their noninvolvement in politics. Against this background, the participation of Salafi parties in post-Arab Spring elections is a puzzle.

The Political Transformation of Egyptian Salafis

Salafism appeared in Egypt in the early to mid-1970s. In the city of Alexandria, the first Salafis organized themselves into groups to purify Islam of non-Islamic elements and propagate a literal interpretation of the Quran and the Sunnah. During the 1980s and 1990s, some of them came under the influence of al-Albani and other Salafi scholars who returned from Saudi Arabia.[19] For three decades, Salafis refused to be involved in Egyptian politics because, as noted earlier, they viewed democracy as a man-made system that goes against the will of God, and they wanted to avoid any confrontation with the Mubarak regime.

The Salafi scene of Egypt has been dominated by Alexandria-based al-Da'wa al-Salafiyya (the Salafi Call), which was founded in 1984. Al-Da'wa has focused on charity activities for years. It has established a large network of clinics, orphanages, and welfare projects to aid the poor and needy; in fact, this effort has been in competition with the Ikhwan's social programs. Salafi leaders have denied that they have received money from Gulf countries to finance their social programs, but they have revealed little information about the source of their funding.[20] The Mubarak regime sought to use them as a counterbalance against the Muslim Brotherhood. However, the Egyptian authorities from time to time banned their publications and arrested Salafi leaders.

During the 1980s and 1990s, Salafis maintained an apolitical image that clashed with reality because they were largely intolerant of the Other. They confronted not only non-Muslims like the Christian Copts but also those Muslims deemed as deviant. In particular, Salafis criticized Sufis for their pilgrimage to shrines (*ziyara*), which is viewed as a grave sin. They condemned Sufis' alleged lack of interest in the science of hadith and other Islamic sciences. Therefore, Salafism's supposedly apolitical nature concealed strong views on state and religion, relations between Muslims and non-Muslims, and the diversity within Islam.

Al-Daw'a did not participate in the January 25, 2011, revolution against Mubarak. One of the founding leaders of the movement, Yasser al-Burhami, specified that Muslims were not prohibited from participating in the protests against the Egyptian regime, but he advised them to avoid it.[21] The cautious stance adopted by Salafis can be explained as an act of political survival; in the words of another Salafi leader, "they would have bombed us from the air if they saw our beards in Tahrir."[22] As a result, Egypt's Salafi movement did not join the uprising against the Egyptian regime apart from individual members.

Despite their self-restraint, Salafis decided to join the post-Mubarak political system. The Party of Light (Hizb al-Nour—hereafter al-Nour) was established by the al-Daʿwa movement after the Egyptian revolution in January 2011. In October 2011, however, one of the official spokesmen of al-Daʿwa argued that "not only democracy is forbidden by religion but also that democracy is infidelity."[23] On November 2, 2011, the Salafi-oriented Alliance for Egypt was formed by three parties: al-Nour, Hizb al-Asala (the Authenticity Party), and Hizb el-Benna Wa El-Tanmia (the Building and Development Party—hereafter BDP). Hizb al-Asala was formed by Muhammad Abd al-Maqsud, a Salafi preacher from Cairo. The BDP was established by the former jihadi group Jammat al Islamiyya (the Islamic Group), which launched a campaign of terror against the Egyptian state during the 1990s. Yet its leaders renounced violence and established the BDP with the slogan "construction, development, Sharia, political freedom, and social justice."[24]

Yasser al-Burhami justified the participation of al-Nour in the parliamentary elections of 2011–2012 by arguing that "Islam must become involved in all aspects of life, even the political, and the Islamic movement must unite."[25] Farhad Khosrokhavar has argued that the participation of the Egyptian Salafis in the post-Mubarak political system signified a fundamental change in their strategy. By abandoning their nonpolitical stance and forming a political party, Salafis recognized implicitly the democratic process.[26] But other scholars have viewed this shift as a tactical rather than strategic decision. According to Kamran Bokhari and Farid Senzai, "their transformation stems more from political expediency than a natural ideological evolution. As a result, their commitment to the democratic process is tenuous."[27] Whatever the case may be, the decision to participate in elections is of great significance because it creates a political precedent for the future of Salafism.

In the 2011–2012 parliamentary election, the Alliance for Egypt finished second in votes, receiving 27.8 percent of the total. As a result, al-Nour won 111 of the 498 parliamentary seats contested; the Authenticity Party won 3 seats, and the BDP 13 seats.[28] In the presidential election of 2012, the al-Nour-nominated candidate Hazem Salah Abu Ismail was disqualified by the electoral authorities. Consequently, the party supported the moderate Islamist Abdel Moneim Aboul Fotouh in the first round and Mohamed Morsi in the second one.

In spite of its electoral success, the Salafi movement has been hit by antagonism between rival factions. The Salafi Front, a breakaway group from al-Dawʿa, established the People's Party (al-Shaʾab) in October 2012.[29]

Interestingly, the new Salafi party advocated left-wing policies; for instance, it stated that "Our Prophet was the prophet of the poor and marginalized. It is our role to promote their struggles and concerns, especially farmers and workers, by adopting legislation that establishes real social justice—not only through charity like the rest of the Islamist movements."[30] In effect, it has attempted to differentiate itself from other Salafi groups that have focused on charitable activities. Therefore, it has reached out to underprivileged and marginalized communities by favoring populist economic policies, like giving land to poor farmers and subsidizing fertilizers.[31] In this way, al-Sha'ab found itself competing not only with fellow Salafi parties but also with socialist and left-wing parties.

There has been a general tendency among Egyptian Salafis to abandon the activist approach to politics for a more professional one. Following the January 2011 revolution, Salafis had to form more concrete proposals regarding the political and economic issues of concern for Egyptian society. Al-Nour's electoral program of 2011 reveals a state-centric approach whereby the government is asked to provide most services to Egyptian citizens. The party has favored a planned economy with full employment provided by the state. In addition, al-Nour is preoccupied with public health and piety; it advocates the banning of smoking and alcohol.[32] The party has also included environmental issues in its program, claiming that the "absence of religious faith has allowed officials and citizens alike to pollute the environment."[33] In effect, al-Nour represents the Islamist Right in the Egyptian political system with the Brotherhood being near the political center. Al-Nour seeks to represent the community of pious Muslims who want to live under Sharia.

Politically speaking, however, al-Nour has become increasingly pragmatic and flexible. In the early post-Mubarak period, the party stressed its commitment to the implementation of Sharia as the law of the land. The competitive nature of Egyptian politics has forced it to change views; for example, former chairman Abdel Ghafour asserted that al-Nour "rejects the idea of a religious state. It is unacceptable."[34] Moreover, the party chairman invited Copts to join al-Nour since they are fellow Egyptians. Ghafour even served as assistant president of integration in the Morsi government.

Also, the party has developed a culture of internal democracy. In September 2012, polls were held to choose the leaders of the party's local committees throughout the country. When the then party chairman Abdel Ghafour suggested postponing the process, the party's supreme committee ruled that the process should go ahead in nineteen of the country's twenty-eight provinces.[35] However, Ghafour had complained about the lack of transparency and the manipulation of voters by the supporters of Yasser al-Burhami. In December 2012, finally, Abdel Ghafour resigned from the party and established his own political formation Hizb al-Watan (the Homeland Party) together with 150 other party members. The new Salafi party has welcomed Copts and women as members.

While in parliament, al-Nour has been open to collaboration with other political forces. Following the December 2012 constitutional referendum that strengthened the Morsi government, al-Nour worked together with the secularist National Salvation Front against the Brotherhood.[36] Even more surprisingly, al-Nour joined socialist parties in opposing loans from the International Monetary Fund because Sharia forbids the payment of interest for loans.[37]

Notwithstanding their political pragmatism, Salafis' relationship with the Muslim Brotherhood is at best ambivalent. There are historical roots to the tensions between them. Actually, al-Da'wa was established in Alexandria in the 1970s by students who opposed the Ikhwan in the local university. The Egyptian authorities tolerated its existence for many years because the movement did not seek political change; indeed, al-Da'wa claimed that it could not overthrow Mubarak because he was a Muslim leader. In contrast, the Ikhwan was heavily repressed by the regime because it was accused of conspiring against the state. Yet many Salafis have criticized the Ikhwan for being too secretive and prioritizing party interests over Islamic principles. In fact, they do not consider the Brotherhood an Islamic organization. Al-Nour has taken a more conservative view than the Brotherhood on social issues; for example it supports strict gender segregation.

During the 2012–2013 protests against the Morsi government, al-Burhami and other senior Salafi leaders called for the resignation of the Egyptian president.[38] Like other opposition parties, al-Nour claimed that the Ikhwan had attempted the brotherhoodization of the state (akhwanat al-dawla).[39] More importantly, to the astonishment of many of its members, al-Nour supported the military coup against the Morsi government. It was a politically risky decision because many supporters of the party sided with the Ikhwan and denounced the military coup. Yet the Salafi leadership did not remain united in this act of political maneuvering. Sheikh Ahmed Aboul Enein, a senior official, resigned from the party.[40] The decision of al-Nour to support the military coup against a democratically elected president can be explained by two factors. First, the party had faced harsh competition from the Ikhwan and grasped the opportunity to remain the only Islamist force in the country's political system. Second, the coup was supported by the Saudi government, which is al-Nour's main external sponsor. At that time, the kingdom was competing with Qatar for the hearts and minds of Egyptian Muslims. Therefore, Riyadh backed Salafis and Doha supported the Ikhwan.[41] Nevertheless, some Saudi Salafi scholars condemned al-Nour for this decision because it "has caused damage to the interests of Islam and Muslims inside and outside Egypt."[42]

Al-Nour's support for the coup plotters aroused the animosity of the Muslim Brothers. In the words of Gehad el-Haddad, a Muslim Brotherhood spokesman, "military coups are the highest levels of treason, and those who support them are traitors."[43] However, not all Egyptian Salafis supported the coup against Morsi. The Salafi Call joined the pro-Morsi Anti-Coup Alliance to protest against military interference in Egypt's political system and support the ousted president Morsi. In December 2014, the organization withdrew from the alliance, seeking to restore "Islamic identity" and oppose "all forms of Western hegemony and Zionist-American Plots to support the counter-revolution and the coup."[44]

In the 2015 parliamentary elections, al-Nour won only 11 seats. Three reasons can explain its poor performance. To start with, the new Egyptian regime reduced the number of party-list seats (only 120 out of 596) and increased the number of independent candidates (448 of 596). Moreover, 28 MPs were selected directly by President Sisi. Additionally, the overall voter turnout was very low and those casting their vote largely supported pro-regime candidates. The Salafi supporters 'punished' al-Nour for its ambiguous stance vis-à-vis the Egyptian military. Finally, the party itself decided to keep a low profile during the elections to avoid antagonizing the Sisi regime. During 2014, al-Nour had faced lawsuits seeking its dissolution because the Egyptian constitution states that it is 'not permissible to establish any political party on a religious basis'.[45]

Al-Nour has tried hard to survive politically in the post-Morsi political order that is dominated by the Egyptian army. Therefore, it has declared itself not a religious party but a party based on religion. In this way, its leaders have hoped to avoid the constitutional prohibition of religious parties. They have argued that the party is "consistent with the rules of the constitution and political parties' law."[46] Also, the party seeks to guarantee fundamental rights within the framework of Sharia, including rule of law, freedom of speech, and freedom of association.[47] While not abandoning the goal of adopting Sharia as the law of the land, al-Nour has campaigned for democracy and civil liberties. Thus it can present itself as part of the pro-democracy movement in Egypt.

Whatever the differences between parties, the participation of Salafis in the Egyptian political system constitutes an important departure from their previous isolationist stance. They constitute a relatively inexperienced political movement that tries to strike a balance between the dominance of the military and the popularity of the Ikhwan. The particular conditions of Egypt have influenced their orientation, strategy, and organizational culture. But every Salafi party and group has its own understanding of the situation based on its previous experiences and set of aims.

The Duality of Tunisian Salafis

Salafism appeared in Tunisia sometime in the mid-1990s, but it did not attract a massive following. It remained a clandestine movement with little influence in Tunisian society. The first generation of Tunisian Salafis avoided any involvement in politics and concentrated on personal morality and piety. Nevertheless, Salafis were heavily repressed by the Ben Ali regime, which espoused a strict secularism. The revolution of 2011 and the subsequent rise of al-Nahda changed the political realities for Tunisian Salafis.

The Salafi-oriented Reform Front (Hizb Jabhat al-Islah al-Islamiyya al-Tunisiyya) was established after the overthrow of the Ben Ali regime in January 2011. It has been viewed as the successor of the secretive group Islamic Front, which operated during the 1980s. Although its candidates ran as independents in the October 2011 parliamentary elections, the party failed to win any seats. The party was legalized in late March 2012 under the al-Nahda-led government. During 2011, the interim government had twice refused to recognize the Reform Front as a legitimate party due to national security concerns.[48] Therefore, Jabhat al-Islah has tried hard to portray itself as a party that endorses pluralism. Indeed, its electoral platform stated that "the door is open to all Tunisians who believe in the [Islamic] principles, without exclusion or marginalization."[49]

Moreover, the Reform Front has attempted to promote a new political vision for post-Ben Ali Tunisia. While it represents Salafis, the party advocates a more democratic political system with checks and balances. Therefore, it has committed to "The establishment of a pluralistic political climate . . . [to ensure the] transfer of power by appealing to the polls without exclusion or marginalization of any class of the society . . . [while] establishing the principle of the separation of the three powers and strengthening the independence of the judiciary within the limits of the provisions of the Sharia."[50] It appears that the Reform Front has not only accepted the basic tenets of democracy but has also used them to maintain its position in the postrevolution political system. Yet the party has not distanced itself from its Salafi roots. Hence it aims at "restoring the Islamic way of life to establish an Islamic state that implements Islam and Sharia."[51] Thus, the target audience is the community of devout Muslims who want the implementation of Sharia.

But even clandestine Salafi groups have not completely rejected democracy. The more confrontational group Partisans of Sharia (Ansar al-Sharia) was established in April 2011 by Saif Allah Bin Hussein, a veteran of the war against the Red Army in Afghanistan. As opposed to militant Salafis in other parts of the Arab world, Ansar al-Sharia does not reject the electoral process. In the words of a senior member, the group is not "absolutely in opposition to pluralism and elections. . . . The main point is that we could conceive of such a development, but only in the context of an Islamic state. . . . Within this framework, the existence of parties and elections would not be forbidden."[52] In effect, the group has attempted to blend its version of Islamism with some democratic norms and practices.

This innovative approach largely derives from the reality of modern Tunisia, which is the most westernized society in the Arab world, apart from Lebanon. There is a large middle class that maintains strong links with France and other European countries.[53] It is politically risky for the Salafis to reject totally the electoral process in the postrevolutionary Tunisia, where citizens' empowerment has become a defining element of the new political system. For example, Ansar al-Sharia has come to recognize that "Tunisia is a specific country and this specificity should be respected. . . . We have the Quran and the Sunnah, sure, which are universal. But we also have our own specific context. We are neither Afghanistan, nor Iraq."[54] Hence Tunisian Salafis have advocated the hybridization of Islamism.

Yet Ansar al-Sharia represents the most extreme version of Tunisian Salafism with links to the international Jihadi-Salafi movement. Members of Ansar al-Sharia allegedly assassinated two left-wing politicians, Chokri Belaid and Mohamed Brahmi, in February and June 2013 respectively.[55] The group has accused al-Nahda and the Reform Front of having links to the U.S. security services.[56] On September 14, 2012, a mob of Salafis attacked the U.S. embassy in Tunis. Consequently, Tunisian authorities decided to designate the group as a terrorist organization in August 2013.[57]

Nevertheless, Salafi groups have often set the political agenda in Tunisia. When a dispute broke out at the University of Manouba over whether female students can wear a niqab in the classrooms, Said Ferjani, the spokesman of al-Nahda, asserted that the university must find a solution "without infringing in any shape or form on a woman's fundamental right to choose her own clothing."[58] Interestingly, he compared the niqab issue with the controversy caused by women wearing bikinis on Tunisia's beaches because they "are two sides of the same issue. We live within the dynamics of a fledgling democracy and we must respect democratic principles."[59] At first sight, al-Nahda has followed a middle path between the Salafi conservatism and secular liberties. In reality, however, al-Nahda has maintained an ambiguous approach toward Salafi parties. It tried to build a tactical alliance with Salafis even before their parties were recognized as legal. During the October 2011 parliamentary elections, the Reform Front asked its supporters to vote for al-Nahda in those constituencies that had no Salafi candidates.[60] Moreover, hardline figures within al-Nahda have maintained links with Salafi groups; for example, Sadok Chourou participated in Ansar al-Sharia's congress in May 2011.[61] Yet the leader of the Reform Front, Mohamed Khouja, has accused al-Nahda of being too eager to compromise with its secular coalition partners.[62]

Indeed, it seems that Salafis have increasingly competed against the moderate al-Nahda for the votes of pious Muslims. According to Anne Wolf, there are three reasons for the defection of supporters from al-Nahda to Salafi groups: first, al-Nahda did not support a reference to Sharia in the new Tunisian constitution; second, it has not taken action against members of the Ben Ali kleptocratic regime; and finally, it did not support socioeconomic reforms to improve the lives of people.[63]

Other Salafis have become even more aggressive in their criticism of al-Nahda. In November 2012, for instance, Salafi imam Nasr al-Din Alawi accused the party of "wanting new elections on the bodies of members of the Salafi movement" and he asserted that he "will fight the interior minister and the other leaders of the al-Nahda [because] they have turned America, the Pharaoh and idol of this age, into their God."[64] Like their Egyptian counterparts, Salafis in Tunisia have tried to find their place in the political spectrum. Therefore, Salafis have often seen themselves in a

twofold struggle. On the one hand, they have to confront militant secularists who view Salafism as nothing else than fanaticism. On the other hand,
they compete against the more moderate Islamists of al-Nahda for the same
audience, namely the community of devout Muslims.

Their limited electoral appeal means that Tunisian Salafis tend to focus
on high-profile issues and launch attention-seeking campaigns. Ansar al-
Sharia initiated an "Occupy Mosques" campaign in order to evict imams
who collaborated with the Ben Ali regime.[65] Also, Salafis have accused the
secular media of blasphemy against Islam. In January 2012, they protested
against the broadcasting of the French animated movie *Persepolis*, which
had a scene depicting Allah.[66] In addition, they have been blamed for
attacks against cultural events that they deemed "un-Islamic."[67] In all cases,
Salafis portrayed themselves as local defenders of Islam against foreign
influences and secularism.

Electoral Salafis Between the Global and the Local

The followers of Salafism believe in a universal creed that is supposed to be
applicable to every Muslim society. Therefore, they do not tolerate local
traditions that are viewed as deviations from the true religion.[68] Their holis-
tic approach to Islam has led them to the rejection of alternative interpretations of Islamic sources. They advocate uniformity and perfection.
Moreover, they have a sense of moral superiority, viewing non-Salafis as a
threat to their eternal salvation.[69] Olivier Roy rightly points to the similarities between Salafism and Protestant fundamentalism: both favor a literal
reading of the sacred texts while rejecting diversity.[70] Like Protestant fundamentalists, Salafis believe in strict morals and personal responsibility. Protestant fundamentalists and Salafis are mission conscious because God has
given them a task to accomplish.

The rise of electoral Salafism in North Africa is not a unique development. The first Salafi parties were actually established in the Persian Gulf
region. In Kuwait, the Islamic Salafi Alliance (al-Tajammu al-Islami al-
Salafi) entered national politics in the 1990s. Salafis managed to get elected
as members of Kuwait's National Assembly in December 2012 and July
2013. One of them, Ali Saleh al-Umair, was moved to the position of minister for oil in a cabinet reshuffle in January 2014.[71] In neighboring Bahrain,
the Islamic Purity Party (al-Asalah al-Islamiyah) was founded in 2002 and

won three seats in 2010 parliamentary elections. The participation of Salafi parties in elections in Kuwait and Bahrain can be explained by three factors. First, there is a small but not insignificant Salafi community, which means that such parties have an electoral base and enjoy some degree of legitimacy. Second, Salafis have allied with the Sunni monarchies to oppose local Shia political forces in the two countries. Third, Salafi parties have received significant support from Saudi Arabia.[72] In other words, the emergence of electoral Salafism in the Gulf is mainly connected to the politics of Sunni-Shia antagonism.

In contrast to developments in the Gulf region, the emergence of electoral Salafism in North Africa is the result of cataclysmic political changes. The outbreak of the Arab Spring revolutions has led to a wave of democratization across the region. As a result, tens of political parties have been established to participate in the postrevolution political systems. The new Salafi parties in Egypt and Tunisia have chosen to campaign through the parliaments and within the constitutions. They have come to represent a particular community of Muslims. These parties have ultraconservative views on social and family issues, but they have denounced the use of violence. It is a new generation of Salafi politicians who have contributed to the glocalization of Islamism.

There are some important differences in the political priorities of Tunisian and Egyptian Salafis. The former have focused more than the latter on cultural and language issues because French still enjoys an important status in Tunisia as a widely spoken language.[73] As a result, Tunisian Salafis have advocated the Arabization of the educational system and social life. In contrast, Egyptian Salafis have not discussed language issues because they live in a society where Arabic is the main instrument of communication. Instead, they have focused on the role of Christians in Egypt because there is a large minority of Copts.[74] With the exception of Lebanon, Egypt is the only country where Salafis have extensively discussed relations between Islam and Christianity. Again, local circumstances dictate priorities and set the parameters of Salafis' actions.

In addition, Salafis' perceptions of Israel can indicate the degree to which particularization of Islamism has taken place. In general, Salafis of all orientations have refused to acknowledge the right of the Jewish state to exist; from their point of view, Israel is an artificial entity because Palestine is an Islamic *waqf* (mortmain property). In December 2011, however, the then al-Nour president Abdel Ghafour announced that "treaties Egypt has signed [i.e., Camp David Accords] must be upheld, we intend to respect them."[75] Although the al-Nour leaders have made hostile statements about Israel, it seems that the party has accepted the realities on the ground. In contrast, their Tunisian counterparts have advocated "the criminalization of all forms of normalization with the Zionist entity" and have frequently called for the destruction of the Jewish state.[76]

There are three reasons why Egyptian and Tunisian Salafis have different approaches toward Israel. First, Egypt shares borders with the Jewish state and has some pressing issues (e.g., low-level insurgency in Sinai, Hamas's tunnel strategy) to resolve through negotiation with Israeli authorities. Tunisia is a safe distance from Israel and the surrounding security issues. In other words, the reality of geographical proximity can change some hard-line Salafi positions. Second, Egypt's Salafi movement has been dominated by preachers who have advocated a nonviolent approach. In fact, even those who violently confronted the Mubarak regime, during the 1990s, have now denounced terrorism as a method of political change (e.g., BDP). In Tunisia, an important part of the Salafi movement is controlled by individuals who joined foreign insurgencies and still consider the use of violence a legitimate method (e.g., Ansar al-Sharia). Third, the relationship between Egypt and the Palestinians has historically been somewhat strained, especially after the signing of the Israeli-Egyptian Peace Agreement in 1979. On the other hand, Tunisian authorities gave refuge to the Palestinian Liberation Movement after its expulsion from Beirut in 1982 and Israeli warplanes bombed the organization's headquarters in Tunis in October 1985. As a result anti-Israeli sentiments still run deep in Tunisia. It is hardly a coincidence that the moderate leader of al-Nahda, Rachid al-Ghannouchi, has used anti-Israeli rhetoric, accusing Ben Ali of "betraying the Palestinian cause" and being "a collaborator with the Zionists."[77]

Irrespective of their differences, both Egyptian and Tunisian Salafis have striven to "Salafize" the masses by demonstrating flexibility toward democracy. Their isolationist position was overcome by the speed of political events in Egypt and Tunisia. Consequently, Salafis decided to participate in the electoral process because they came to recognize the new political reality. More importantly, they have seen a political opportunity for themselves to promote their agenda and later even gain power. The larger sociopolitical environment is another crucial factor in the rise of electoral Salafism. Egypt and Tunisia are among the most diverse countries in the Arab world. As opposed to tribal societies like Libya and Yemen, both have a large middle class of educated professionals and businessmen who have been exposed to globalization for two decades. The two countries have large tourist industries; in fact, millions of tourists visit Egypt and Tunisia every year. Many young Tunisians and Egyptians speak a foreign language and follow foreign media. It is a new generation of computer-literate people that can engage in discussions in social media. These factors, separate and combined, can explain the unique political circumstances that confronted the Salafi movement in these two countries.

As a result, Salafis in both countries have developed a more consensual approach to society and politics. The Reform Front has urged the society to "take advantage of the achievements of the Western civilization and to work on . . . the indigenization of them."[78] From its point of view, Muslims could learn from the West and adopt some good things. Moreover, the Reform Front has presented a pro-democracy platform. Hence its leader, Muhammad al-Khawjah, a former professor at the University of Tunis, stated that "it is no longer the time for armed jihad. . . . We believe Islam is a religion of democracy and freedom."[79] Nevertheless, his understanding of democracy is unique. In his words, "in Europe, democracy gives sovereignty to the people, but in Muslim countries, we prefer to emphasize the sovereignty of Islamic legislation. . . . The job of the lawmaker is to distinguish the *haram* (illicit) from what is *halal* (licit) according to Islamic law."[80] His version of democracy is tailored for religious Tunisians who wish to support electoral Salafism.

Likewise, Egyptian Salafis have attempted to strike a balance between the tenets of global Salafism and the local political realities. In general, the application of Sharia is the primary goal of Salafis because it is God's law. Al-Nour and other Salafi parties have called for Sharia to be the sole source of legislation in post-Mubarak Egypt. Hence Salafis strongly supported the 2012 constitution, prepared by the Brotherhood-controlled Constituent Assembly, because its article 219 stated that legislation will be based on Sharia as prescribed by Sunni Islam. Following the coup against Morsi in June 2013, the 2012 constitution was suspended by the Egyptian army. Although al-Nour joined a committee that had the aim of preparing a new constitution, it failed to prevent the removal of article 219; yet it decided to support the 2013 draft constitution because al-Azhar University, the oldest Sunni academic institution in the Muslim world, ruled in favor of abolishing this article.[81] Instead, the Supreme Constitutional Court's interpretation of Sharia will serve as the principal source of legislation. The prevailing political circumstances forced Egyptian Salafis to change position in a way that reflects their growing capacity to compromise.

In this context of political transition, Salafis have utilized democracy as a master frame to mobilize support and increase their appeal among Muslim communities. The adoption of the democracy master frame is a necessary step for the political survival of those Salafis who decided to follow a nonviolent approach and take advantage of the postrevolutionary momentum. This master frame combines the struggle for representation with recognition of identity and culture.

At first sight, it appears that Salafi parties have been reluctant to accept the principle of political equality because it implies female participation in politics. Yet Tunisian and Egyptian Salafis have recognized implicitly the existence of this component. Al-Nour was obliged to include female candidates on the party lists for the 2011 parliamentary elections; yet party leaders stressed that they support gender segregation and women remained at the bottom of the lists to minimize their chances of getting elected.[82] Moreover, al-Nour selected female candidates based on their "good reputation" and commitment to wear the niqab.[83] Since then, al-Nour has shifted toward a more inclusive approach. In April 2015, the party announced that its electoral list would include 120 female candidates, including Christians and niqab-wearing women.[84] However, Salafis would accept neither a Christian nor a female as a head of state. The Salafi rationale was provided by Mohamed Mokhtar al-Mady, a senior official of al-Nour: a Christian president would not know how to apply Sharia, while a woman can "go weak when [she] gets her period."[85]

In Tunisia, Salafis have faced similar dilemmas because their antiwomen bias is not well received by the society. Due to the electoral laws, the Reform Front was forced to include female candidates in its lists during the October 2014 parliamentary elections. Some of these women have been vocal about their rights and role in Tunisian politics. For instance, Rabiaa Smaali declared, "I want to represent all Tunisian women. I took my own decision to participate in these elections. Nobody added my name to gain votes for veiled women."[86] While women do not play a leadership role in the movement, it seems that there is a Salafi variation of feminism in the making.

Although global Salafism has propagated a conservative and traditional view on women's rights, local followers have preferred to meet legal requirements and acknowledge societal realities. Consequently, the participation of female Salafi candidates in elections broke a long-standing taboo and set a precedent for Salafis to accept the political equality of the female population. One could argue that the adoption of the democracy master frame entails an obligation to accept the component of political equality, which undermines Salafi beliefs about gender relations.[87]

Despite being a political minority, Salafis have endorsed the component of majority rule. Since they are trapped in their own reality, many Salafis tend to overestimate their potential influence in their respective societies. During an interview on February 9, 2014, al-Burhami argued that the "al-Nour party's support base is expanding every day."[88] Similarly, Tunisian Salafis believe that their popularity is on the rise; for example, Rabiaa Smaali claimed that "I am sure that if a popular referendum is held on the application of Sharia, the majority of Tunisians would vote for it."[89] A young Tunisian Salafi scholar admitted that "I am myself confident about my religious discourse and my popular influence, which is my major source of power to achieve my goal of spreading the message of Islam."[90] This misinterpretation of political reality can be explained by two factors. First, long isolation and clandestine experiences have contributed greatly to the loss of political perspicacity. Second, Salafis strongly believe in the eventuality of their success, thus they support majority rule as a principle.

In any case, democracy is not understood by electoral Salafis only as an expression of people's will to choose their leaders. It is an opportunity for a soul-searching exercise that could lead to authentic Islam. In fact, it is centered on an Islamist equivalent of Jean-Jacques Rousseau's general will that suppresses individualism and encourages conformity.[91] The participation in the post-Arab Spring democratic transition is a means to an end. By patronizing *demos* (the citizenry), Salafis could one day control *kratos* (the state).

This component can also explain the political strategy of some Egyptian Salafis in the post-Mubarak political system. Al-Nour first allied itself to the Muslim Brothers and then to the all-powerful military. In both cases, the party used this component to justify its strategy of shifting alliance. In 2012, the decision to support Morsi in the second round of the presidential elections was presented as the only option for Egyptian Salafis; the second candidate, Ahmed Shafik, was a former senior officer of the air force and a former minister under Hosni Mubarak. Despite their long history of competition and mutual suspicion, Salafis and Muslim Brothers supported each other against members of the previous regime to safeguard majority rule. But when the new president became increasingly partisan and protests erupted against him, the Salafis utilized the same master frame to defend their alliance with their former foes. An al-Nour official justified the party's pro-army stance by claiming that Egypt under Morsi "was on the brink of a civil war and he was not accepting any proposals or compromises that would save the situation."[92] In this way, their political struggle has been framed as a democratizing effort against both the remnants of the previous regime and the Brotherhood's authoritarianism for the sake of the majority of the people.

Finally, the democracy master frame has the powerful component of political legitimacy that offers Salafis recognition for being part of the party system. Thus, they can gain more acceptance in the eyes of the general public, which has been skeptical or even hostile toward them and become more attractive to potential allies. Indeed, this component has allowed the formation of broader political alliances with parties and groups that do not share the core values of Salafism. As has already been mentioned, al-Nour has cooperated with socialist parties in the Egyptian parliament and the Reform Front has maintained a close relationship with al-Nahda.[93] The use of this component can also deter state repression because it raises the political cost of confronting Salafis. However, Salafis are free riding on democracy. They do not contribute much to democratic politics, but they still enjoy the legitimacy that comes with participating in it. It follows that having political legitimacy can become an instrument to undermine adversaries who oppose Salafi demands.

The Egyptian and Tunisian Salafis are not the only ones who use the democracy master frame. As the previous chapter showed, Islamist parties and organizations like the AKP, the Ikhwan, and al-Nahda have also been keen to make use of the democracy master frame. Yet electoral Salafis and Islamo-democrats do not necessarily share the same understanding of democracy. Islamo-democrats have a more genuine interest in consensual politics. In contrast, Salafis view democracy more as a tool that can reshape their image and portray them as a force of change.

Furthermore, Salafism is not the only conservative religious movement entering electoral politics in the Middle East. In Israel, political parties have been formed by the ultra-Orthodox movement. The Jewish Home (HaBayit HaYehudi) is a religious party established in November 2008; it supports the establishment of a state governed by Jewish law. Haredi Judaism has been represented by the Union of Israel (Agudat Yisrael) and its splinter group Flag of the Torah (Degel HaTorah). The two parties have participated in many elections and have even joined coalition governments. Both electoral Salafism and the ultra-Orthodox movement have condemned the secular lifestyle and have claimed to have God-given solutions to everyday problems and issues. Moreover, they are part of larger movements that have a nonpolitical stance and focus on personal morality.

Still, the endorsement of the democracy master frame by Salafis in Egypt and Tunisia represents a significant development that differentiates them from their counterparts in other Muslim-majority countries. The adopted frame has led to the socialization of Salafis into the new political culture that includes elements of pluralism. Although the master frame has been used selectively by Salafis to reach out to Muslim communities, it has also enforced on them new norms of conduct and behavior. In effect, the master frame of democracy has encouraged participation, accountability, and consensus building. This development puts electoral Salafis on a collision course with those who still condemn democracy as man-made system that goes against Sharia. Ironically, the organization of electoral campaigns, the drafting of the party's list of candidates in accordance with state laws, and frequent interactions with the media could shape the political behavior of Salafi actors who function as glocalizers: they adapt the idea of democracy to local conditions in order to achieve political goals and remain relevant. The outcome of this is the rise of electoral Salafism, a hybrid form of Salafism that combines global tenets with an acknowledgment of local conditions.

Conclusion

Salafis have been known for their denouncement of politics and the focus on da'wa. However, Salafi parties have been established in Tunisia and Egypt. It is a localized event that can be explained by the particularities of these two countries. The post-Arab Spring political culture of both countries has facilitated the rise of an electoral Salafism that includes both conservative Islamic values and democratic practices.

The master frame of democracy has been applied by Egyptian and Tunisian Salafis to their local environments in order to gain legitimacy at a time of increased participatory politics. But this decision comes with a price since it entails the participation of Salafi parties in the electoral process. As a result, Salafis must abide by the constitution and the laws that they seek to change. Moreover, they have to take into account not only other political forces but also public opinion. One may claim that their endorsement of democracy is not genuine, since Salafis support democratic politics only as long as this serves their political goals.

Yet the effort of electoral Salafis to gain recognition through elections could encourage their counterparts in other parts of world to express their views in the same fashion. Indeed, the participation of Salafis in the electoral arena can lead to the socialization of the larger Salafi movement.[94] In this case, electoral Salafism could become a force of moderation and stability in some Muslim-majority counties that usually suffer from chronic corruption, political instability, and nepotism. In 2012, a Saudi Salafi scholar, Sheikh Salman al-Awdah, asserted that "democracy might not be an ideal system, but it is the least harmful, and it can be developed and adapted to respond to local needs and circumstances."[95] In Indonesia, local Salafis have proposed a system to appoint the ruler that resembles the institution of shura; they suggested the establishment of a special body, the ahl al-halli wa al-'aqd or Majlis al-Shura, consisting of knowledgeable people in different fields: religion, defense, economics, and so on.[96] Based on these developments, it can be argued that electoral Salafism is on the rise in the Muslim world.

Nevertheless, the future of electoral Salafism will depend on state responses: political repression will inevitably bring resistance and confrontation, whereas political accommodation can encourage moderation. Salafi parties are often viewed as the long arm of clandestine groups that espouse jihadi-Salafism. But such a view ignores the diversity that exists within Salafism, which is a large and acephalous movement. Electoral Salafism can be viewed as a new political trend that ought to be recognized on its own terms.

PART III

Islamist Militancy and
the Master Frame of Justice

Justice is a fundamental virtue of any society. The *Republic* of Plato offered one of the first definitions of justice; according to the ancient Greek philosopher, justice is "giving to each what is owed."[1] In *Nicomachean Ethics*, Aristotle explained that justice has two different, but closely related, forms: general justice regarding whether a man deals fairly with other people and particular justice that can be either distributive or corrective. The former type of particular justice implicates the proportional distribution of things based on merit, while the latter restores equality among victims of wrongdoing irrespective of merit.[2] The topic of justice was discussed extensively during the Age of Enlightenment. David Hume claimed famously that "public utility is the sole origin of justice."[3] Immanuel Kant argued that "the universal law of justice is: act externally in such a way that the free use of your will is compatible with the freedom of everyone according to a universal law."[4] John Stuart Mill suggested that "justice implies something which it is not only right to do, and wrong not to do, but which some individual person can claim from us as his moral right."[5]

Yet the idea of justice has deep religious origins since all three Abrahamic religions have preached about it. Judaism has viewed justice (*mishpat*) as an attribute of God that men have to adopt for themselves.[6] The Book of Deuteronomy calls for "justice, justice you should pursue" (16:20). It is a religious obligation that has to be constantly fulfilled by the faithful. From a Hebrew perspective, justice is to treat all people equitably.[7] The concept was incorporated in the Ten Commandments given by God to the Jews as rules of conduct. In fact, one could argue that the last five of the

Ten Commandments emphasize the importance of social justice in human relations.[8]

Christian theology has also repeatedly affirmed the centrality of justice to God's desires for humankind. For instance, every believer is obliged to "hunger and thirst for justice" (Matthew 5:6). The Catholic theologian Thomas Aquinas (1225–1274) considered justice one of the four cardinal virtues (the others being prudence, fortitude, and temperance) that can be practiced by anyone regardless of their religious affiliation.[9] For theological and historical reasons, the Roman Catholic Church has focused on a specific form of justice: the one that regulates social relations. Therefore, it has a long tradition of getting involved in social justice issues, especially in Latin America. In contrast, the Eastern Orthodox Church asserts that justice issues are "an integral part of the Gospel, but they are not the soul of the Gospel" since it has concentrated more on spiritual needs.[10]

The concept of justice ('adl) has also been at the heart of Islamic tradition and thought. Two of the ninety-nine names of God relate to justice: the "Equitable" (Al-Muqsit) and the "Just" (Al-Adl). In addition, the main aim of Islamic revelation is to create an ethical and just social order on earth.[11] The concept itself can be found throughout the Quran; for example, a verse states that "certainly We sent Our messengers with clear arguments, and sent down with them the Book and the measure [mizan] that men may conduct themselves with equity" (57:25). According to Sa'id ibn Jubayr, an early Islamic scholar, 'adl could have four significations: "[First] al-'adl in the administration of justice in accordance with God's command "and when you judge between the people, judge with justice" (4:61). [Second] al-'adl in speech, as construed in this command "and when you speak, be just" (6:153). [Third] al-'adl [in the meaning of] ransom [because] God said 'and beware a day when no soul will in aught avail another; and no counterpoise shall be accepted from it [the soul], nor any intercession shall be profitable to it' (2:113). [Fourth] al-'adl in the sense of attributing to God [because] 'the unbelievers ascribe equals to their Lord'" (6:1).[12]

Although all Muslims believe that justice is a God-given virtue, there are different perceptions of its essence. Most Sunnis view justice as compliance with God's actions and commands, which can be understood only through revelation.[13] Therefore, it is not possible to provide a rationale for God's wishes and decisions. It follows that human reason cannot fully comprehend or explain the nature of divine justice.

The Shia perspective on justice is different. Most Shias argue that human reason can explain and understand God's actions and his divine commands. Thus, godly justice must align with human notions of justice.[14] Moreover, al-'adl has been connected to the return of the Mahdi (i.e., the hidden imam, discussed in Chapter 5).[15] According to one Shia hadith, the Mahdi "would fill up the earth with equity and justice as it would have been fraught with injustice and tyranny."[16] He will rule for some years before the Judgment Day (*Yawm al-Din*); although each individual has a responsibility for his actions, God will judge them according to his will.

To sum up, justice is the foundation of every society because it defines the nature of relations between people. Therefore, it has preoccupied religion and philosophy for millennia. While Abrahamic religions view justice as a God-given obligation that must be fulfilled by believers, ancient and modern philosophy has adopted a humancentric understanding of it. In both cases, justice is about fairness and equity. It is a necessary virtue for the conduct of a pious life.

*   *   *

The claim to justice has been a powerful normative-ideational framework accompanying political changes and upheavals through the ages. For this reason, justice has been used as a master frame by contemporary parties and movements to gain support for political causes. According to Hank Johnston and Sebastian Haunss, it includes certain elements such as working conditions, job security, and transnational labor solidarity.[17] At first sight, it seems like a Western-oriented cognitive schema aiming at the promotion of a socialist agenda for working-class people nationally and internationally. But the master frame addresses deeper issues as well. It is a master frame deriving from the critical theory of justice.[18] It contains a certain analysis of social relations based on power asymmetries and inequalities between groups.[19] It also offers a critique of the justifications provided for these relations, focusing on their reciprocity and generality; the former suggests that no party involved can claim rights or privileges it denies to others, while the latter means that all those affected have the right to ask for justifications.[20]

I argue that the master frame of justice consists of three main components. The first one includes moral and ethical principles that could outline the meaning of justice for movements, groups, and parties. These principles are not exclusively definable, which means that they are open to interpretations and additions. They have been overtly secularized, but in reality some of them have a religious basis. For example, the Brazilian Landless Workers' Movement (Movimento dos Trabalhadores Sem Terra) has called for access of poor people to arable land; yet it is the liberation theology of the Catholic Base Communities (Comunidades Eclesiais de Base) and the organization's option for the poor principle that have fueled the movement's demands for social justice.[21] In Israel, the organization Peace Bloc (Gush Shalom) has campaigned for Palestinian rights and a long-lasting peace between the two peoples. Although it has been viewed by many as a left-wing secular organization, the Peace Bloc's campaign has been based on the concept of *Tikkun olam*; it literally means repairing the world, but is to be understood as the pursuit of social justice. The phrase is mentioned in the oral Torah (Mishnah).

The issue of equality is the second component. The promotion of any type of justice (general or particular) is only possible if there is equality among human beings. Only then can justice be realized without any compromise. Without equality before the law, justice would favor the strong and punish the weak. During the period of apartheid, for example, the justice master frame was heavily used by political forces that fought for equality among different racial and ethnic groups in South Africa. In his autobiography, Nelson Mandela described the triumph of the African National Congress in the 1994 elections as a "victory of justice" because black South Africans gained political equality.[22] Likewise, the Black Panthers movement in the United States demanded equality for African Americans who faced discrimination and racism.[23] Through such equality, the Afro American community could have enjoyed justice and security.

The third component is the responsibility to protect those who suffer from injustice. Accordingly, it is the duty of all socially aware and concerned individuals to provide help and support to those who live under injustice. There are plenty of examples whereby movements employed the justice master frame by invoking the responsibility-to-protect component. For example, the pro-Palestinian International Solidarity Movement has recruited supporters from Western countries, including the Unites States, to travel to the Palestinian Territories and protest against the confiscation of Arab land by Jewish settlers.[24] For another example, antiabortion groups in the United States have mobilized supporters to fight the "injustice of abortion" by protecting "unborn human lives."[25] The structure of the justice master frame is described in Figure 5.

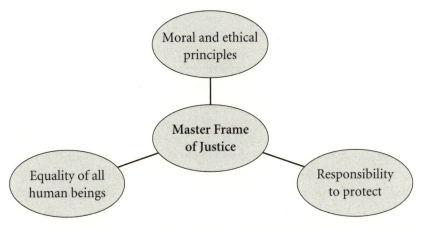

Figure 5. Components of the master frame of justice

The concept of justice has preoccupied contemporary Islamic political thought. In his book *Fi Zilal al Qu'ran* (In the Shadow of the Quran), the famous Egyptian scholar Sayyid Qutb analyzed the Islamic view on justice. From his point of view, the application of justice depends on three principles: freedom of conscience, defined as freedom from servitude and submission to God only; human equality, because all men and women, who descended from Adam and Eve, share the same rights and responsibilities; and social solidarity, which includes not only cooperation between individuals and society but also social responsibility toward the family and the community or even between the umma and other nations.[26] From his point of view, all of these principles are guaranteed by Sharia. More importantly, Qutb envisioned a new mission for Islam that can save humanity from the unjust rule of "earthly lords" (*al arbab al-ardiyyah*) like tyrants, regimes, and institutions.[27] Consequently, Islam cannot ignore injustice and oppression. Muslims have the duty to fight for the universal spread of justice.

Given the importance of justice in Islam, it is hardly a surprise that some jihadi groups have adopted the word *justice* in their title; Morocco's al-Adl wal-Ihsan (Justice and Benevolence) and the Iranian Sunni group Jaish ul-Adl (the Army of Justice) are only two of them. In this way they emphasize the rightness of their cause against unjust opponents. Even the archaic group of postponers (Murji'a) was initially called ahl al-'adl wa-l-sunnah (the people of justice and Sunnah).[28]

Furthermore, militant groups have attempted to theorize the centrality of justice in their campaigns of violence. From al-Qaeda's point of view there are two types of justice: general and reciprocal. This categorization of justice resembles, to a certain extent, Aristotle's two forms of justice, the general and the particular. In an open letter to Americans, for example, Osama bin Laden stated that "the first thing we are calling you to is Islam. . . . It is the religion of showing kindness to others, establishing justice between them, granting them their rights and defending the oppressed and the persecuted."[29] The leader of al-Qaeda believed that the call to Islam will bring general justice to all individuals who decide to convert. There is a theological dimension to this offer. According to an al-Qaeda commander, Muslims "are the people of justice, we embrace it, believe in it. . . . Injustice in our religion is *haram* (prohibited) . . . so, we will not be unjust with you."[30]

In addition, bin Laden claimed that there is reciprocal justice between enemies that includes some proportionality. He once asked rhetorically, "in what creed are your dead considered innocent but ours worthless? By what logic does your blood count as real and ours as no more than water? Reciprocal treatment is part of justice, and he who commences hostilities is the unjust one."[31] In this way, he attempted to justify the targeting of Western civilians by al-Qaeda and affiliated groups: terrorist attacks are just an application of reciprocal justice against the enemies of Islam. Therefore, al-Qaeda has portrayed the United States as an immoral country that has conspired against the umma. It is the source of all injustice and violence. In the words of Ayman al-Zawahiri, "the crimes America perpetrates against Muslim prisoners [i.e., referring to the Abu Ghraib torture scandal] will not be forgotten by the Muslim umma. . . . All these crimes give Muslims more rights to stand in the face of the American aggression."[32]

The desire to achieve justice of any form derives from an idealization of the early Islamic life. In his essay "Milestones," Sayyid Qutb argued that the Medinan society "was freed from all oppression, and the Islamic system was established in which justice was God's justice. . . . The banner of social justice was raised in the name of One God, and the name of the banner was Islam."[33] Likewise, Sayyid Abu A'la Mawdudi argued that the Prophet "succeeded in setting up a model Islamic society and became head of the state. The new social order was a perfect manifestation of the Islamic teachings—of morality and social justice."[34] Therefore, Islamists have called for the re-creation of a past utopia where justice prevails.

Ayatollah Khomeini contributed to this effort by portraying Prophet Muhammad as the model of a just military leader. In his words, "when he gave orders for the conquest of a certain area, the burning of a certain place, or the destruction of a certain group whose existence was harmful for Islam, the Muslims, and the mankind in general, his orders were just."[35] Thus the founder of the Islamic Republic of Iran expanded the meaning of justice to include the responsibility to defend Muslims against other groups, which could involve the conquest of territories and the annihilation of the opponents. This interpretation of the Prophet's actions after the establishment of the first Islamic state in Medina serves as a guide for Shia militias in Iraq and Syria. In the name of justice, they must engage in warfare against those who constitute a threat against the umma and eventually humanity.

The Iranian intellectual and father of the so-called Red Shiism, Ali Sariati, also discussed the concept of justice from a Shia perspective. He argued that "Shi'ites, who represent the oppressed, justice-seeking class in the caliphate system" have viewed Ali as "the manifestation of a justice which serves the oppressed."[36] Hence he understood justice as a dividing issue between the two main branches of the Muslim faith; his approach to justice was largely sectarian. Sariati supported the view that Ali is the eternal symbol of justice for Shia Muslims who are deprived of their liberty and dignity.

Islamist militants have incorporated elements of all such thinking into their adopted master frame of justice, which provides them with a cognitive umbrella under which they can gather support against their adversaries. Due to its strong religious basis, this master frame has the potential to rally large segments of society behind Islamist militants. Although it is loosely specified, the justice master frame can be used for mobilization and recruitment purposes. Indeed, both Sunni and Shia militant groups in Syria and Iraq have utilized it to organize sectarian campaigns.

Chapter 5

The Militancy of Shia Groups
in Lebanon, Iraq, and Syria

> The believers and the oppressed people . . . have declared
> their eternal hostility, especially the escalating statements of
> Trump against Islam and Muslims. He does not distinguish
> between radical and moderate Islamic movements. . . . If
> America does not distinguish between the radical and the
> moderate, we will not be silent and we will resist it as before.
>
> Muqtada al-Sadr, November 10, 2016

The Shia branch of Islam has its roots in the death of Prophet Muhammad in 632. The question of his succession divided the Muslim community.[1] Those who believed that the Prophet died without appointing a successor (caliph) to lead the umma called themselves *ahl al-sunnah* or Sunni Muslims. They claimed that Muslims could select the new leader by following the Sunnah (the tradition). The appointment of Abu Bakr (632–634) as first caliph by some of the Companions of the Prophet Muhammad was disputed by those who supported his cousin and son-in-law Ali as the legitimate leader.[2] The supporters of Ali argued that he was designated by the Prophet himself to become his successor and they came to be known as Shi'atu 'Ali (the Party of Ali). He eventually became the fourth caliph in 656.

After the death of Ali in 661, the question of succession came to the surface again in a dramatic way. First Hasan and then Hussein, the two sons of Ali and grandsons of the Prophet Muhammad, claimed the leadership of the caliphate against the Umayyad family. The martyrdom of Hussein in the Battle of Karbala in 680 was a defining incident in the history of Islam because it widened the divide between Sunnis and Shias.[3] From the Shia point of view, Hussein chose to get sacrificed for a just cause instead of submitting to an illegitimate ruler.[4] According to Lesley Hazelton, "if Ali was the foundation figure of Shia Islam, Hussein was to become its sacrificial icon."[5] The former has been viewed as more of a spiritual than a political leader, while the latter has been presented as a fearless warrior who sacrificed himself for the most noble of causes: justice against the evildoers. The question of succession led to the theological and political fragmentation of the umma.[6]

The figure of the Mahdi is another important tenet of the Shia doctrine. The adherents of Shia Islam believe that the Mahdi was the twelfth imam, or the so-called hidden imam, who disappeared and will return one day to bring justice.[7] Due to the Shias' deep sense of persecution and injustice, the Mahdi has become a perpetual symbol of hope.[8] Being a minority in the Muslim world, most Shias developed a siege mentality vis-a-vis the Sunni majority. Therefore, Shias living in some Sunni-dominated states practiced *taqiya* (Islamic deception). The concept refers to a dispensation allowing Shias to hide their faith when under threat or prosecution. Yet the Shia branch of Islam managed to survive and even became the state religion of Persia under the Safavid dynasty in 1501.

The schism between the two branches of Islam remained a theological, rather than a political, constant in the Muslim world. That being said, Sunnis and Shias do share many beliefs and practices. In certain countries, such as Iraq and Azerbaijan, there has even been a high rate of intermarriage between members of the two denominations.[9] In fact, the politicization of the Sunni-Shia divide is a relatively recent event that was reinforced after the outbreak of the Iranian Revolution.[10]

This chapter describes the origins of modern Shia militancy in the Middle East, focusing on the role of prominent Shia clerics in Iraq, Lebanon, and Iran. Then it examines two Shia groups currently considered the most powerful and influential of all: Hizb'allah and the Mahdi Army. It covers their origins and development, as well as their involvement outside national borders. Moreover, the chapter attempts to explain how Shia militants have acted as glocalizers of Islamism by adopting the master frame of justice.

The Origins of Modern Shia Militancy in the Middle East

Despite its great authority, the Shia clergy had traditionally maintained a mainly religious and spiritual role. This changed in the late 1950s when the

Hizb al-Da'wa al-Islamiyya (Islamic Call Party) was established by a group of Iraqi Shia clerics, including Muhammad Baqir al-Sadr.[11] The new party campaigned for an Islamic state in the face of growing communist influence within the Shia community.[12] Moreover, al-Da'wa objected to the passing of new secular and socialist-oriented legislation by the new Baathist regime, which had overthrown the Hashemite monarchy in July 1958.

Simultaneously, the Shia population in Lebanon was in turmoil following the constitutional crisis of 1958. Imam Musa al-Sadr, cousin of Muhammad Baqir al-Sadr, went to Lebanon to take a leadership position in the local Shia community. He managed to mobilize his co-religionists by offering a political interpretation of Shia tenets and history.[13] In 1974, he founded Harakat al-Mahrumin (the Movement of the Dispossessed) to support Shia Muslims.[14] One year later, this movement evolved into a militia known by its acronym Amal (Afwaj al-Muqawamah al-Lubnaniyyah—Battalions of the Lebanese Resistance). The disappearance of Sadr en route to Libya in August 1978 left a political vacuum that was later filled by Hizb'allah.

But Imam Musa al-Sadr did not envision the transformation of Shiism into a revolutionary ideology; he rather promoted the political instrumentalization of Shia tenets. He was not the only one attempting that. Ali Shariati attempted to blend Shiism with Marxist concepts in the early 1970s. Shariati framed early Islamic history in Marxist terms when he wrote that "as soon as the chain of the prophetic mission reached the Prophet Muhammad, he began his struggle with the aristocracy, slave-owners, land-owners of Taif and the Qoraish merchants."[15] Therefore, Shariati defined Shiism "as the struggle for justice against foreign rule, tyranny, feudalism, and exploitation."[16]

Yet most Western politicians and scholars did not understand before the late 1970s the dynamics of Shia militancy in the greater Middle East. It is not a coincidence that the French government gave refuge to Ayatollah Khomeini in 1978. He was considered, at the time, as only a religious man who went into exile because of the shah's growing authoritarianism. Very few people thought that he could establish a new regime. In the early 1970s, however, Khomeini had proposed the system of *vilayat-i faqih* (the guardianship of Islamic jurist), claiming that power in a true Islamic state must rest with ulama and only a *faqih* (jurist) possessing knowledge can assume rulership. He proposed a system of governance derived from the imamate, namely a fundamental belief of Shia Islam about universal leadership by a single individual in religious and secular matters.[17]

The 1979 Iranian Revolution led to the overthrow of the shah and the return of Ayatollah Khomeini from France. His version of Islamism became a revolutionary force for the defense of Shia rights. Ayatollah Khomeini followed up Shariati's interpretation of Islamic history when he argued that "the imperialists have imposed on us an unjust order, and thereby divided our people into two groups: *mustakbirin* [oppressors] and *mustad'afin* [oppressed]."[18] Both terms can be found in the Quran. The establishment of an Islamic republic was supposed to be only the first step toward a global conquest. In classic Trotskyite fashion, Khomeini believed that the export of the revolution would eventually lead to the establishment of a pan-Islamic state where justice would prevail. In effect, he viewed Shias as the representatives of oppressed peoples of all religions.[19]

Revolutionary Iran sought to export its ideology to Lebanon because the country had a sizable Shia community and its clerics maintained strong links with their Iranian counterparts. In the early 1980s, Lebanon was in the middle of a bloody civil war and the Shia population largely relied on the Amal militia to protect itself. Following the disappearance of Imam Sadr, Amal broke up into two different factions, one pro-Syrian and one pro-Iranian. With the help of Iran's Revolutionary Guards, Hizb'allah was established in the early to mid-1980s.[20]

The Khomeini regime also supported various Shia groups in Iraq following the outbreak of the Iran-Iraq War in 1980. The Supreme Council for the Islamic Revolution in Iraq (Al-Majlis al-A'ala al-Islami al-'Iraqi, hereafter SCIRI) was set up in Tehran in 1982 by members of the al-Da'wa Party. The latter had a long history of confrontation against President Saddam Hussein, but never seriously challenged the Baathist rule. Under the leadership of Muhammad Baqir al-Hakim, an Iraqi Shia cleric, the Supreme Council was established to assist Tehran in winning the war against the Baathist regime and to create an Iranian-style government in the country.[21]

After the end of the Iran-Iraq War, the new priority for the Iranian regime was to rebuild the economy and consolidate its power domestically. The death of Ayatollah Khomeini in 1989 signified the beginning of a new era for Iranian diplomacy. The new president, Akbar Hashemi Rafsanjani, advocated a more pragmatic and less ideological foreign policy in the region and beyond. As a result, Tehran prioritized the development of its economic relations with neighboring countries like Turkmenistan and Russia.[22] Yet the Islamic Republic remained isolated throughout the 1990s due to the U.S. dual containment policy.[23]

The 9/11 terrorist attacks reshaped dramatically the geopolitical balance of power in the Middle East. The 2003 U.S. invasion of Iraq paved the way for the political empowerment of local Shias and the return of Iran as a regional great power. In the summer of 2004, Vali Nasr warned that "the change in the sectarian balance of power [in Iraq] is likely to have a far more immediate and powerful impact on politics in the greater Middle East than any potential example of a moderate and progressive government in Baghdad."[24] Indeed, the regime change in Iraq has led to unprecedented conflict between Sunnis and Shias, drawing in neighboring countries like Saudi Arabia and Iran. But while Iraqi Shia politicians and religious leaders have been known for their pan-Shia tendency, they have also espoused a hybrid local identity. In fact, they have attempted to negotiate between global Shiism and local realities.

Concurrently, the Lebanese Shia community has become more integrated into the country's political system. Hizb'allah decided to assume a minor governing role in 2005; indeed, two of its senior members took ministerial posts in Fouad Siniora's cabinet. Since then, as I explain later, the group has joined national unity governments. Nevertheless, Hizb'allah has not been transformed into a peaceful political party. Actually, it has expanded its military activities in neighboring Syria and elsewhere.

Following the 2010–2012 Arab Spring revolutions, relations between Sunnis and Shias have been strained further. The overthrow of Arab regimes took the Iranian leadership by surprise, which had faced a similar situation during 2009 with the so-called Green Revolution after the rigged presidential elections.[25] Therefore, Tehran was initially reluctant to endorse the massive protests in Tunisia and Egypt. When the wave of democratization hit Syria, which is Tehran's closest ally in the Middle East, the Iranian leadership became even more alert. The outbreak of a full-scale civil war in Syria between the Alawite-controlled regime and the Sunni-dominated opposition has been viewed by Iran and its allies in Lebanon and Iraq as an organized effort to undermine Shia power in the Middle East.[26]

The "Lebanonization" and the Re-Shiafication of Hizb'allah

Hizb'allah was officially created in 1985, but began to take shape in the early to mid-1980s. The group draws its origins from a breakaway faction of the Amal movement, the Lebanese branch of al-Da'wa, and other radical Shia organizations. The very adoption of the name Hizb'allah derived from the Quranic verse 5:56: "And whosoever takes Allah and His messenger and those who believe for friend—surely *the party of Allah*, they shall triumph."[27]

According to Islamic theology, there are two parties: the Party of God (Hizb'allah) and the Party of Satan (Hizbu'shaytan). Thus, Hizb'allah is more than just a party; it represents God on earth. Central to Hizb'allah's ideology is Khomeini's concept of vilayat-i faqih.

The 1989 Taif Agreement signaled the end of the Lebanese civil war, but did not achieve the disarmament of Hizb'allah, which has maintained a militia in the southern part of the country. Regardless of military setbacks, such as the assassination of the party's second general-secretary, Sayyed Abbas Mussawi, in 1992, Hizb'allah continued throughout the 1990s its guerilla campaign against the Israeli army, which had declared a security zone in south Lebanon. However, under the new leadership of Sayyed Hassan Nasrallah, the group participated in the Lebanese political system and initiated a rapprochement with non-Islamist parties, prompting some analysts to claim that Hizb'allah was going through a process of "Lebanonization."[28]

The Israeli unilateral withdrawal from south Lebanon in May 2000 was hailed as a victory of Hizb'allah, which achieved its primary goal of unifying the country. The group subsequently attempted to play a greater role in the Lebanese political system. At the same time, Hizb'allah opened itself more to the world, reaching out to the antiglobalization movement.[29] Despite its growing normalization, the group did not abandon its militant character. On July 12, 2006, the group ambushed an Israeli patrol on Lebanon's border with Israel, provoking an invasion by the Israeli Defense Forces. Muhammad Ayoob supports the view that Hizb'allah's actions in 2006 indicated its "unwillingness to undergo a total transformation into a normal political party abjuring the use of arms."[30] Although many Arab governments criticized the group for initiating a war that led to the destruction of Lebanon's infrastructure, Arab public opinion largely supported the group.[31]

Following the 2006 war, Hizb'allah has progressed politically and has gained popularity among Lebanese Shias. Since 2009, it has held 14 seats in the 128-member Lebanese parliament. Moreover, Hizb'allah provides an assortment of social services for Lebanon's sizable Shia community, including hospitals, schools, orphanages, and youth centers. The group also owns several media, including the magazine *Qubth Ut Alla* (The Fist of God), the radio station al-Nour (the Light), the TV station al-Manar (the Light-house), and various Internet sites.[32] Additionally, the group has used social media to spread its messages. It is fair to say that Hizb'allah is the most well organized and sophisticated Shia group in the Middle East. Eitan Azani has described Hizb'allah as a hybrid terrorist organization that operates at three levels: the civilian level, which consists of da'wa, social welfare, and religious education; the political level; and the military one.[33]

Despite its efforts to integrate into the Lebanese political system, the group has not escaped from the reality of armed conflicts. Even though it has been keen to emphasize its national character and aspirations, Hizb'allah has participated in the Syrian civil war. The relationship between the group and Damascus is more complex than it may seem at first. Many analysts have viewed Hizb'allah as the long arm of Syria in Lebanon. During an interview with Egypt's daily *al-Ahram* in February 2000, Nasrallah acknowledged the ideological differences between his party and the Syria regime; he said that "we agree with the Syrians on a number of fundamental political and strategic issues with regard to the fate of Lebanon, Syria, and the region as a whole, in spite of the fact that the Arab Ba'ath Socialist Party and Hizb'allah each have their own different ideologies."[34] Yet Nasrallah revealed that he feels "a certain affinity with Syria, not only in the political domain, but also on many other levels, including psychologically and emo-tionally, thanks to our shared interests and fate."[35]

After the U.S. invasion of Iraq in March 2003, Nasrallah reaffirmed his alliance with the Syrian regime, which was targeted by American neocon-servative politicians.[36] During a speech in the Hizb'allah-controlled south-ern suburbs of Beirut on March 13, 2003, he declared his support for Bashar al-Assad: "This young leader has his finger on the pulse of the Arab street and reflects his conscience, spirit, and feelings of anger and dejection. Nobody can simply or easily disregard him or his words, especially since he is president of a country being threatened by the United States. . . . In the Arab world we need men like him—men who know how to lead. . . . From here in Beirut, we address ourselves to Damascus and tell Syria and its courageous Arab leader: You are not alone; the whole nation is with you . . . the whole Lebanon supports you, and this resistance has fought, and is still fighting with you."[37]

Despite these rhetorical overtures to the Assad regime, the party initially tried to hide its involvement in the Syrian civil war. In regard to media reports about Hizb'allah fighters taking part in battles against Sunni militants, the group's leadership continuously denied such involvement.[38] There are a number of reasons for this. First, Hizb'allah has often claimed to be a nonsectarian resistance group fighting for the independence and sovereignty of Lebanon;[39] support for a dictatorial regime that has massacred thousands of its citizens is not an easily defensible position. Second, Hizb'allah understood that its participation in the Syrian civil war would probably have serious security repercussions inside Lebanon. Indeed, Sunni militants have attacked Shia-populated districts of Beirut as retaliation for Hizb'allah's support for the Assad regime.[40] Third, Hizb'allah's involvement in Syria could damage its image as a movement confronting what it calls U.S. imperialism and Israeli colonialism because its adversary now is neither of them.[41]

After many months of speculation, finally, Hizb'allah acknowledged the presence of its fighters in the neighboring country in May 2013.[42] The group has attempted to justify its participation in the Syrian civil war by claiming to defend Shia-populated villages near the Lebanese-Syrian border and protect Shia pilgrimage sites like the Sayyida Zaynab Mosque in Damascus. According to Matthew Levitt and Aaron Zelin, the mosque was used by Hizb'allah during the 1980s for the purpose of recruiting Saudi Shias who later may have been involved in the Khobar Towers bombing against U.S. troops in 1996.[43] The party leadership has recognized the downside of Hizb'allah's intervention in Syria. In a message to Lebanese Sunni militants fighting alongside the Syrian opposition, Nasrallah stated that "we renew our call for sparing Lebanon any internal clash or conflict. We disagree over Syria. You fight in Syria; we fight in Syria; then let's fight there. Do you want me to be more frank? Keep Lebanon aside."[44]

Some analysts have emphasized the political and military rationale behind the organization's involvement in the Syrian civil war. Chris Zambelis has argued that Hizb'allah got involved into the conflict in order to retain the strategic depth that Syria has provided to the group over the years. Since the country serves as a "logistical land bridge" between Lebanon and Iran, it is vital for the Lebanese group to support President al-Assad.[45] If the Syrian regime falls, one less friendly to Hizb'allah leadership with sectarian biases may come to power.[46] In addition, the alliance with Syria is helping the group to sustain pressure against Israel and anti-Hizb'allah forces within Lebanon. Indeed, Hizb'allah's military campaign in Syria is its first major foreign adventure. By mid-2013, the French government estimated the number of Hizb'allah fighters at about four thousand.[47] In particular, the battle for the strategically located town of Qusayr revealed the extent of Hizb'allah's involvement in the conflict. The participation of Hizb'allah forces was a crucial factor in the victory of the Syrian army.[48]

But for a group that has defined itself as a resistance organization defending Lebanon, such involvement cannot be easily dismissed as the result of geopolitical upheaval. While this explanation is plausible, it tends to underestimate the commitment of Hizb'allah to Shia causes in the Middle East. After all, the group has been involved in distant sectarian conflicts like Yemen without any apparent geopolitical rationale.[49] Hizb'allah is trapped between a globalized agenda and a localized constituency.

The Rise, Fall, and Reemergence of the Mahdi Army

For decades, the political and social status of Iraq's Shia community was inferior to that of Sunnis. The majority of the latter rallied around Saddam Hussein, while the Baath Party enforced top-down secularism and imposed a secular Iraqi identity on its citizens.[50] The Saddam regime questioned the loyalty of Shias, viewing them as Iran's fifth column in the country. Consequently, Shias were systematically discriminated against and marginalized. After the end of the 1991 Gulf War, Shias revolted in southern Iraq against the regime. The rebel forces consisted of army conscripts, members of the SCIRI and other antiregime elements such as the Iraqi Communist Party. Nonetheless, the well-equipped Republican Guard, loyal to Saddam, managed to crush the uprising in April 1991.[51] Tens of thousands of Shias were killed and hundreds of thousands were forced to leave their homes.

The Iraqi regime survived UN sanctions against it and remained in power during the 1990s. Following the 9/11 attacks, the Bush administration adopted an interventionist policy in the Middle East, focusing on the promotion of democracy and regime change. Washington accused Iraq of being part of an axis of evil together with Iran and North Korea. In March 2003, finally, the United States launched an invasion against Iraq.

The fall of the Saddam regime and the subsequent de-Baathification eventually led to the establishment of a Shia-dominated political system in Iraq. Since the first free parliamentary election in January 2005, the Iraqi government has been controlled by Shia parties. Notwithstanding widespread media and public perceptions, the Iraqi Shias are not a coherent group. On the contrary, they have been divided by power struggles and personality clashes. This fragmentation is largely reflected in their post-Saddam political behavior. Iraqi Shias are split into three different political factions: the SICRI, the al-Da'wa, and the Sadrist Movement. Each of them has its own ideological platform representing different schools of thought within the community.

The Mahdi Army (Jaish al-Mahdi) was founded by the young Shia cleric Muqtada al-Sadr in June 2003. Its name refers to the hidden twelfth imam who Shias believe is still on earth in occultation. Muqtada established the group in Sadr City (formerly known as Saddam City), a Shia-populated slum on the outskirts of Baghdad. He is the son of Muhammad Sadiq al-Sadr and the son-in-law of Muhammad Baqir al-Sadr. Both were influential Shia clerics who were assassinated by Saddam Hussein because they were outspoken and critical of his regime. Sadiq al-Sadr was killed, alongside two of his sons, in southern Iraq in 1999. Baqir al-Sadr had been arrested and tortured by secret police officers in 1980. The tragic history of his family has certainly influenced Muqtada's thinking.

He initially welcomed the overthrow of the Saddam regime by the U.S. forces. However, Muqtada later became increasingly critical and eventually confronted the Bush administration and its local allies. It seems that the young Shia leader and his supporters felt excluded from the post-Saddam political system, since the U.S. government largely collaborated with Iraqi Shia who had been in exile during Saddam's rule. Yet Sadrists attempted to enter the new Iraqi political system. During the December 2005 parliamentary elections, they joined the United Iraqi Alliance and won thirty seats.[52] Consequently, Sadrists received ministerial positions in the new Shia-controlled Iraqi government. In late November 2006, Muqtada decided to withdraw his ministers from the Maliki government.[53]

The Mahdi Army attempted to follow the successful example of Hizb'allah in Lebanon. Therefore, it offered social services in neighborhoods and places where the Iraqi government proved unable or unwilling to do it. In the words of a Sadr City resident, "this is an army of volunteers. . . . They are clerics at night and heroes during the day. . . . This army is helping society. They clean the streets, protect our schools and distribute fuel."[54] Yet the group never fully transformed itself into an organization of Hizb'allah's size and structure. Instead, it remained an armed group serving the interests of Muqtada.

The 2006 bombing of the al-Askari Mosque in the city of Samarra paved the way for growth of the Mahdi Army. Although Shia shrines had been targeted before the attack, that was the first time that a sacred mosque of such symbolic resonance was destroyed by Sunni militants. Under these circumstances, the Mahdi Army took advantage of the widespread climate of fear produced by the bombing to fill a political vacuum. Muqtada heavily criticized the rival Shia parties of al-Da'wa, led by Nouri al-Maliki, and the SCIRI, led by Sayyid Abdul Aziz al-Hakim (brother of Muhammad Baqir al-Hakim), for being incapable of defending Shias. As a result, the Mahdi Army fought against the Badr Brigade, affiliated with the Supreme Council, in the holy city of Karbala in the summer of 2007.

At that moment, Sadrists were facing a three-front conflict in Iraq: the first was against Sunni militants, the second against fellow Shias who dominate the post-Saddam political system, and the third against the U.S. forces. Yet Muqtada did not entirely control the Mahdi Army; criminal and rogue elements managed to profit from the collapse of the Iraqi state and the subsequent "mafiaization" of the economy.[55] Muqtada himself viewed the growing division between Sunnis and Shias as a distraction from the larger goal of forcing the withdrawal of U.S. forces. He once complained that "death squads that say they kill on behalf of the Mahdi Army are trying to destroy us and divide us and prevent us from raising arms against the forces of occupation."[56]

Following a new round of fighting between the Mahdi Army and the Iraqi army in Karbala in August 2007, Muqtada declared a six-month ceasefire. On June 13, 2008, a letter from Sadr was read in a mosque in Kufa, whereby the Shia cleric explained his strategy:

- Transforming the Mahdi Army into a civilian movement dealing with religious, social, and cultural affairs.
- Establishing a special branch of experienced fighters for defensive purposes.
- Using the new civilian movement to fight Western ideology and globalization.
- Disowning anyone in the Mahdi Army who did not follow his orders.[57]

Therefore, an organization called Mumahidoon, which means "those who paved the path," was established to implement the new strategy. It delivered social services, such as Quranic lessons and trash collection after pilgrimages, and organized youth activities like soccer tournaments.[58] Muqtada himself left the country and went to Iran to continue his studies; he eventually returned to Iraq in early 2011. But he never stopped exercising influence on Iraqi politics. His bloc won 40 seats out of 325 in the March 2010 parliamentary elections; thus, Prime Minister Maliki came to depend on Muqtada.[59]

The Mahdi Army has been perceived by most Iraqi Sunnis as a sectarian group organizing reprisals against them.[60] Yet Sadrists have always been keen to emphasize "Iraqiness" and nationalism as opposed to sectarianism and Iranophilia. According to Patrick Cockburn, who extensively investigated Muqtada and the Mahdi Army, the Shia leader even enjoyed popularity among some Sunnis before 2006 due to his anti-American rhetoric.[61] In reality, the Mahdi Army and Muqtada's followers advocated the formation of a new identity that would include some aspects of Iraqi nationalism (e.g. territorial integrity), Arab cultural pride, and certain Shia elements (e.g. pilgrimage to Shia shrines).

But the al-Askari Mosque bombing and suicide attacks against Shia neighborhoods led to the rapid sectarianization of the Mahdi Army. The growing Iranian influence was an additional factor contributing to the ideological transformation of the Mahdi Army. Even though Tehran welcomed the overthrow of Saddam, it was alarmed by the presence of tens of thousands of U.S. troops in the neighboring country. Some analysts have described how Iranian intelligence penetrated the Mahdi Army and other Shia militias to launch a proxy war against the United States.[62] Following the withdrawal of U.S. troops from Iraq in December 2011, the Mahdi Army became inactive but it was not disbanded. It remained the personal army of Muqtada. At the same time, he increased his presence on the Internet with the launching of a personal website.

The military victories of ISIS led to the revival of the Mahdi Army in June 2014. In particular, the fall of Mosul made obvious that the Iraqi army had suffered from low morale and weak leadership. The (new) Mahdi Army, which was now called "Peace Companies" (Saraya al-Salaam), was better equipped and trained and had already been engaged in the fighting against ISIS.[63] Yet Muqtada decided to withdraw his forces from the battle against the Islamic State in February 2015 because Shia militias were accused of atrocities against Sunni civilians.[64] The fall of Ramadi, a town strategically located between Baghdad and Samarra, on May 14, 2015, brought ISIS close to Shia shrines. As a result, Muqtada warned Sunni militants that "his supporters will fill Iraq's land with their rotting bodies if they tried to desecrate any sacred place of this Holy Land."[65]

The rise of the Islamic State has forced Iraqi Shia groups to fight Sunni militants, with Syria being the new battleground.[66] That being said, the initial reason for the mobilization of Iraqi Shia volunteers does not seem to be the support for the Assad regime. Instead, they arrived in Syria to guard Shia mosques and shrines. These volunteers have formed different groups, including the Abu al-Fadl al-Abbas Brigade, named after the son of Imam Ali. The main mission of the brigade has been to protect the Sayyida Zeinab Mosque in south Damascus from Sunni militants. Zeinab is an important figure within Shia history because she was the daughter of Ali and Fatima and granddaughter of the Prophet Muhammad, and she survived the Battle of Karbala. The al-Abbas Brigade has produced propaganda videos relying heavily on historical narratives. One of its YouTube videos, for example, states that "the Umayyad descendents are back with their injustice, O Zeinab."[67] The slogan "Labayka Ya Zaynab!" (We are here for you, Zaynab) has been very popular among Shia fighters.

The brigade has recruited fighters from the Iraqi Shia community by capitalizing on the Shia narratives of persecution and suffering. Therefore, its fighting units have been named after the Twelve Imans and other important figures from Shia history. The instrumentalization of Shia history is aimed at stirring emotions of solidarity and empathy among pious Shias. Nevertheless, not all Shia volunteers are idealists; some have received a salary to join armed groups fighting in Syria.[68] The Mahdi Army has not been involved, officially speaking, in the Syrian civil war. However, its actions or inactions are bound to influence developments in neighboring Syria.

The Shia Militants Between the Global and the Local

Shia militant groups have often attempted to balance global sectarian solidarity with local political realities. In fact, they are involved in a constant effort to address their communities' own concerns and demands, while remaining part of the embattled Shia world. This double nature of Shia militancy has led to contradictions and inconsistencies because allegiance to the ethnic community does not always triumph over sectarian loyalties.

In Lebanon, a country created by the French colonial authorities, identity conflicts have been particularly evident.[69] Due to its religious composition, Lebanon is culturally divided and politically polarized. Lebanese Shias now compete for power and influence with other communities, such as the Sunnis and the Maronites. But this was not always the case. For decades, the institutionalized Maronite-Sunni dominance marginalized the large Shia community.[70] In spite of the systematic discrimination they suffered, Shias remained loyal to the Lebanese state and built their collective identity in relation to it.

The rise of Hizb'allah during the 1980s challenged the existing political conformity. In its "Open Letter," published on February 16, 1985, the group declared that "we are a community connected to Muslims from every corner of the world. . . . Whatever assails the Muslims in Afghanistan, in Iraq, in the Philippines, or anywhere else assaults the body of the Muslim nation, of which we are an indivisible part."[71] Therefore, Hizb'allah initially presented itself as a pan-Islamic organization with a global mission. Its yellow flag incorporates an image of the globe because it aspires to an international reach and influence. Moreover, the group questioned the legitimacy of the Lebanese state and offered a new broader identity to local Shias that transcended national borders. In April 1987, then secretary-general of Hizb'allah Shaykh Subhi al-Tufayli declared that "[the group does] not work or think within the borders of Lebanon, this little geometric box, which is one of the legacies of imperialism. Rather, we seek to defend Muslims throughout the world."[72]

Since the early 1990s, however, the group has largely refrained from such rhetoric and has advocated Lebanese independence. Hizb'allah's decision to participate in the 1992 parliamentary elections signaled its gradual transformation into a more localized organization. Hence its 1992 election program stated that "it is now imperative to cooperate with other devoted parties in order to complete the necessary steps towards . . . the forging of internal peace on the basis of political concord that is furthest as could be from abominable sectarian biases or narrow confessional discriminations."[73] The gradual "Lebanonization" of Hizb'allah became more obvious when the party decided, for the first time, to join the Lebanese government in July 2005. The "Political Chapter" of Hizb'allah, published in 2009, came to confirm the party's new Lebanese-centric orientation; it states that Iran is a "state of central importance in the world of Islam," whereas according to its 1985 "Open Letter" the country was "the nucleus of the Islamic state in the world."[74]

The ideological transformation of Hizb'allah has coincided with a vibrant debate about the future of the Shia community in the country. For example, the Lebanese Shia cleric Hani Fahs, a critic of Hizb'allah, favored the establishment of a strong nation-state to pacify sectarian tensions. In his words: "The first reason for the pathological awakening of sub-identities is the weakness, or absence, of the state. States are reduced to one party, race or sect. In this type of state, the citizen resorts to fanaticism to get protection from his group. However, [this protection] can only be achieved through a strong and fair inclusive and sponsoring state."[75]

More importantly, Fahs asked Lebanese Shias to give priority to their national identity, cooperate with other religious groups, and support the state despite its weaknesses.[76] In fact, he was not the first Shia cleric advocating a stronger Lebanese state. Muhammad Mehdi Shamseddine, head of the Higher Islamic Shia Council between 1994 and 2001, favored the establishment of a civic state (al-dawla al-madaniyya) where citizens would view themselves as Lebanese first and then as members of different religious groups. Therefore, he asked Shias in the Arab world to develop their national identities as Lebanese, Iraqis, or Bahrainis and integrate into their respective countries.[77]

In Iraq, Shias were historically excluded from positions of power. Although they have been under more Iranian cultural influence than Shias in Saudi Arabia and Yemen, their relationship with Tehran is very complex. On the one hand, many prominent Iraqi Shia clerics are of Iranian origin and the Iranian presence in the holy cities of Najaf and Karbala has been historically very strong. On the other hand, many Iraqi Shias have resented the Iranian influence and have been fierce proponents of Iraqi nationalism. In effect, the community is torn between its strong relationship with Iran and the preservation of a unique ethnoreligious identity. The status of community is of paramount importance for regional stability because Iraq has the largest population of Shias in the Arab world.

The Iraqi Shia clergy does not hold a single view on identity and state. Ayatollah Ali Sistani has supported the idea of a modern nation-state governed by politicians; in fact, the spiritual leader of Iraqi Shias has not accepted Khomeini's vilayat-i faqih model, which constitutes a political innovation that breaks a centuries-old Shia clerical tradition of disengagement from political affairs.[78] Sistani has recognized the unique character of Iraq as a multiethnic and multiconfessional state that could be bound together by a strong national identity. Muhammad Baqir al-Hakim, the founder of the Iranian-supported SCIRI, came to agree with this approach, although he had earlier advocated an Iranian-style Islamic republic.[79]

In spite of their tactical alliance with Iran, Iraqi Shia groups have become increasingly domestic in their thinking.[80] When Muqtada took over the Sadrist movement after the overthrow of Saddam Hussein, he initiated a campaign of confronting the Shia religious leaders of Iranian origin; in effect, he advocated the Arabization of the Iraqi Shia clergy. In this case, ethnic affiliation prevailed over sectarian loyalties. Laurence Louer has argued that "the Sadrists are a phenomenon deeply rooted in the specificity of Iraqi Shiism as it had developed following the Gulf War of 1990–1991. . . . It illustrated, furthermore, that the Arab and Iraqi nationalist ideology of the Ba'athist regime was not without impact on Shia society."[81] It is not a coincidence that the Mahdi Army and the greater Sadrist movement have used almost exclusively Iraqi flags in public demonstrations and public gatherings, while making propaganda movies depicting symbolically images of Mecca and Arab horseman.[82] Muqtada has called for the creation of an Islamic state in Iraq, while rejecting Iranian interference in Iraqi political affairs.[83] Moreover, his dedication to Iraqiness indicates that the young Shia cleric has not fully accepted the idea of a global Islamic state.

On balance, it is fair to argue that Shia militancy is not a monolithic trend. The interrelationship between sectarian identity and ethnicity has produced different political outcomes. What Shia militants have in common is the cognitive framework of justice. Both Hizb'allah and the Mahdi Army are justice-seeking groups. In effect, they have functioned as agents of glocalization by adopting the master frame of justice, which conveys a universal idea that can be applied locally.

Their perspective of justice is based on moral and ethical principles provided by Shia narratives and tenets. In particular, the concept of Mahdi has allowed Shia militants to define the essence of general and reciprocal justice. To start with, Nasrallah once claimed that the "divine state of justice realized on part of this earth will not remain confined within its geographic borders, and is the dawn that will lead to the appearance of the Mahdi, who will create the state of Islam on earth."[84] Similarly, during an interview with al-Jazeera TV, Muqtada claimed that his group "will be the army of the Reformer [Mahdi]. At the end of time Mahdi will appear . . . and if we are capable mentally, physically and militarily, and in terms of faith, we will all be his soldiers. Hence the Al-Mahdi Army is a matter of faith, and it cannot be disbanded."[85] In both cases, Mahdi is perceived as a politicospiritual guide and a symbol of moral perfection. His justice is applicable to everyone but it is defendable only by the chosen ones.

According to Shia eschatology, the Mahdi will return on earth to judge the living and dead; at that time justice will finally triumph. The implication is that the outcome of this struggle is rigidly determined, since there is a heavenly purpose and a predetermined time schedule. It is evident that Nasrallah and Muqtada have been influenced by Ayatollah Khomeini's vision of Shia Islam's eventual triumph; for instance, the Iranian leader once claimed that "God willing, with the spread of the Islamic Revolution the Satanic Powers will be isolated and the government of the downtrodden will pave the ground for the global government of the Mahdi at the end of time."[86]

The so-called Karbala narrative has also offered a pool of moral and ethical principles connected to justice, such as courage, responsibility, self-sacrifice, integrity, and altruism. Hussein and his seventy-two devout followers fought against a much larger army sent by Yazid of the Umayyad family that had taken over the caliphate in 661. Kamran Aghaie maintains that the Karbala narrative depicts these men "as courageous warriors who fought for the sake of God and divine justice and willingly gave up their lives as martyrs."[87] It was the moment of absolute pride and honor.

Not surprisingly, Hizb'allah has embraced the Karbala narrative to justify its actions. Nasrallah has compared the group's 2006 assault against Israel with Hussein's rebellion against Yezid. In his words, Hizb'allah "was told" that it had two choices: "Either for the war to continue and that you be crushed, or, to surrender, to turn over your weapons, to free the two [Israeli] captives, to abandon Palestine, to abandon the sovereignty of your country . . . to abandon the dignity of your people. . . . At that moment . . . what came directly to my conscience, my mind, my heart, was the 10th Day [of Muharram holy month], when Imam Hussein stood and said: 'You have made me choose between two—between battle and humiliation. And it is impossible for us to be humiliated.' "[88]

Thus, the death of Hussein still serves as the ultimate example of martyrdom against oppression and injustice. It is a powerful narrative that has delineated the content of justice through its underlying moral and ethical principles. More importantly, it can become the basis for the justification of reciprocal actions against opponents. The martyrdom of Hussein must be avenged by his true followers irrespective of the time that has passed. Indeed, the Karbala narrative has been internalized by Hizb'allah's fighters in Syria. As one of them stated, "what is happening in Syria today is a repetition of what happened over 1,000 years ago during the battle of Karbala, which ended with the killing of Hussein, the grandson of the Prophet

Muhammad. Imam Hussein was killed by the Umayyad Caliph, which heralded the schism between Sunnis and Shiites. We will not allow that to happen another time."[89]

But the justice master frame cannot be adopted without the second component of equality. For this purpose, Hizb'allah has tried to portray itself as a group open to all Lebanese citizens. Thus, its leadership has made a conscious strategic decision to deemphasize its Shia heritage. Despite being an almost exclusive Shia organization, the group has portrayed itself as nonsectarian. Indeed, the integration of Hizb'allah into the Lebanese political system forced the group to emphasize the component of equality. According to its 1996 electoral program, "Achieving justice and equality among the Lebanese is considered one of the main bases for establishing a stable dignified and prosperous country in which all the Lebanese engage in the process of construction with drive and solidarity under equality of opportunities, equality of all, individuals, classes and areas, in rights and duties, whether political, economical or social."[90]

Likewise, Muqtada has frequently mentioned equality as a fundamental issue for the post-Saddam Iraqi society. During an interview with the Iraqi newspaper *Al-Hayat* in December 2014, he said that "personally, I believe that there are several ways to resolve the crisis with our [Sunni] brothers. . . . I believe that everyone is responsible—first and foremost religious and governmental figures. . . . I will not accept for there to be first and second-class citizens in Iraq. . . . Everyone is equal, no one is better than the other, except in terms of piety and patriotism."[91]

Thus the Shia cleric has attempted to reach out to the Iraqi Sunnis by calling for equality among different communities. In this way, he could gain recognition for being a leader for all Iraqis. Muqtada has understood that Sunni political marginalization comes at a high price for security and stability. As long as the Iraqi political system is based on the principle of one-man, one-vote, Shias will continue to control the government. Nevertheless, it is vital to ensure equal treatment and opportunities for all Iraqi citizens.

Finally, Shia militant groups have evoked the component of the responsibility-to-protect to gain legitimacy and acceptance. Nasrallah has often used this component to justify Hizb'allah's strategy of confronting Jihadi-Salafi groups in Syria. In a speech on the eighth anniversary of the 2006 war, Nasrallah claimed that Hizb'allah's intervention in Syria is aimed at safeguarding Lebanon from ISIS; therefore, he stressed that "we are ready to sacrifice, as we are presenting martyrs and injured in this battle, so we will not refrain from protecting our people and sanctities. This is a battle of honor and existence, and we are ready for sacrifice."[92] Likewise, during the 2005–2008 civil war, Muqtada claimed that "it is the duty of the al-Sadr movement and the Iraqi people to strive to gradually liberate Iraq. The liberation of Iraq does not mean only bearing arms. There is also cultural liberation, social liberation, military liberation, and so on."[93] Both leaders have stressed the responsibility-to-protect component because it can justify actions being taken against local adversaries; it is intentionally vague and not specific in order to adjust to different goals or scenarios.

Furthermore, Shia groups have discovered for themselves a new mission to support those who live under injustice. As a result, Hizb'allah and the Mahdi Army have extended the responsibility-to-protect norm to other Muslim communities in the Middle East and beyond. Nasrallah has declared that "Hizb'allah . . . will not abandon Palestine, al-Quds [i.e., Jerusalem], and the holy sites of the nation. We were born and [have] arisen on bearing the responsibility of defending Palestine and al-Quds."[94] Additionally, he has increasingly paid attention to Bahrain's Shias. In January 2015, Nasrallah argued that "world governments, and many of those who stood with the Arab Spring, stop at Bahrain and the injustice against the Bahraini people. . . . The day will come when Bahrain will be dwelt by another people [referring to the Bahraini regime's policy of bringing Sunni settlers], just like the Zionists in Palestine inhabited it."[95] His statement indicated a deep concern about the future of Shiism in Bahrain and implied Hizb'allah commitment to support the Shia cause in the island country.

Similarly, Muqtada has claimed that "the al-Sadr movement is Islamic even more than it is Iraqi. . . . An attack against any Islamic or Arab country will mean that the al-Sadr movement will become an interested party. . . . It will defend Islam however necessary."[96] The first indication of that came after a Danish newspaper published cartoons depicting the Prophet Muhammad in January 2006; the Shia cleric stated that "this is a Western crusade and campaign against Islam."[97] Therefore, Sadrists held protests against Denmark in the city of Kut and demanded the withdrawal of Danish troops from the country.[98] It appears that, despite their localized political and cultural foundations, Muqtada and the Sadrists have sought to build an organization that will surpass the borders of Iraq.

In recent years, Muqtada has tried to present himself as a religious leader who is above Iraqi sectarian politics.[99] For this reason, he has showed interest in developments outside Iraq and the Middle East. In December 2014, he issued a statement condemning the arrest of the Shia cleric Shaikh Ali Salman, declaring, "I advise the [Bahraini] officials to release him. Otherwise, his arrest will be the start of an unjust regime and an end of any dialogue principles."[100] In November 2016, he condemned the election of Donald Trump as the forty-fifth president of the United States by stating that "the believers and the oppressed people . . . have declared their eternal hostility, especially the escalating statements of Trump against Islam and Muslims. He does not distinguish between radical and moderate Islamic movements."[101] This level of interest is not surprising given his glocal approach to politics; Muqtada's ambitions within Iraq could be realized if he manages to rebrand himself and his group from being sectarian to being ecumenical.

Shia leaders and groups have found themselves at the nexus of global and local. Hizb'allah and the Mahdi Army have adopted a Shia version of Islamism that advances a globalized agenda; yet the main target audience remains their own ethnic community. In fact, the indigenization of Islamism has made the concept of imamate as obsolete as that of socialist utopia. It is the master frame of justice that has bridged the gap between the tenets of globalized Shiism and the political realities of local communities. This convergence has been achieved with the help of moral and ethical principles that derive from Shia theology, the component of equality for all that can conceal sectarian goals, and the responsibility to protect those who face injustice and need help. In this way, Shia militants have been able to remain relevant and influential in their own communities.

Conclusion

Shia militant groups have played an increasingly important political role in the Middle East since the 1980s. They are armed organizations with complex internal structures and a religious sense of mission. Due to their Shia origin and orientation, the top leadership consists of Islamic scholars and jurists. But Shia militant groups have not been immune to the effects of global processes.

Hizb'allah has constantly tried to balance its position between the global and the local. It has come to represent a great portion of Lebanese Shias. At the beginning the group advocated the utopian goal of establishing a global Islamic state; yet it later took up the cause of Lebanese sovereignty. However, the outbreak of the Syrian civil war has created new dilemmas for Hizb'allah. The group decided to intervene in order to protect one of its major sponsors, the Assad regime.

The Iraqi Shia community has been traditionally marginalized by Sunni rulers in Baghdad. But there is also a long history of mobilization and resilience. The Mahdi Army was formed to defend the interests of Muqtada al-Sadr and the Sadrist movement against pro-Iranian parties, the U.S. occupation authorities, and Sunni militants. Despite its sectarian origin, the group has been keen to emphasize its Iraqiness. Simultaneously, it has attempted to remain part of the greater Shia world without abandoning the local Iraqi community. Indeed, Muqtada has striven to become a leader with both national and regional recognition.

To sum up, Shia armed groups are the epitome of glocalization. They have adhered to a version of Islamism that has a global claim, while promoting a localized Shia identity. The issue of justice has featured heavily in the Shia discourses. Sayyed Hassan Nasrallah of Hizb'allah and Muqtada al-Sadr of the Mahdi Army have constantly utilized the master frame of justice to mobilize support and promote their political goals.

The fate of Shia militants will depend on the outcome of the civil wars in Syria and Iraq. Not only have they invested strategic resources (e.g. fighters, weapons) in a life-or-death struggle but they have also been more exposed to ideational influences from the global system. Hizb'allah and the Mahdi Army have been entrapped in a cycle of sectarian violence and revenge that they cannot escape easily without undermining their raison d'être. Nonetheless, they have demonstrated adaptability and flexibility in facing new challenges and realities.

Chapter 6

The Militancy of Sunni Groups
in Iraq and Syria

[We will impose] the Sharia rules [so that] justice prevails,
injustice is removed, and a judicious Islamic government is
established following the course of the Prophet. It shall be
a government that seeks to liberate the Muslim land, apply
the Sharia of God, treat people equally, and remove
injustice.

Abu Mohammad al-Julani, December 22, 2013

The first two decades after 2000 have witnessed the outbreak of more
Sunni-supported insurgencies than ever before. The rebellion against the
Assad regime in Syria, the civil war in Libya, the insurgency in the Sinai
Peninsula, and the low-intensity conflict in Mali have been instigated by
Sunni militant groups. Therefore, it is not an exaggeration to claim that
Sunni militancy is becoming a major security issue in the greater Middle
East and beyond.

While they largely act independently from each other, these groups are
part of the larger Jihadi-Salafi movement (al-haraka al-jihadiyya al-
Salafiyya).[1] This is a highly diverse and heterogeneous movement with a
global reach that has embarked on an armed struggle allegedly to defend
Sunni communities under threat. Violence is its defining characteristic; participation in elections and nonviolent activism are alien concepts.[2] Sunni
violence is not a new challenge, far from it. Indeed, the 9/11 terrorist attacks
and the subsequent wars in Afghanistan and Iraq gave a new momentum
to the Jihadi-Salafi movement.

Defining the movement is a prerequisite for understanding its essence. The term *Jihadi-Salafism* has been used by many scholars, but only a few have attempted to define it. According to Quintan Wiktorowicz, the movement "believes that violence can be used to establish Islamic states and confront the United States and its allies."[3] This definition was probably valid during the immediate post-9/11 period when jihadi groups focused largely on the United States. Gilles Kepel defines Jihadi-Salafis as those who have "a supercilious respect for the sacred texts in their most literal form, but they combine it with an absolute commitment to jihad whose number one target has to be America, perceived as the greatest enemy of the faith."[4] These two definitions imply that the Jihadi-Salafi movement is synonymous with al-Qaeda and its globalist approach. Mohammed Hafez provides a shorter, but perhaps more accurate, definition of the Jihadi-Salafi movement as one that "represents an extreme form of Sunni Islamism that rejects democracy and Shia rule."[5]

The scale of its engagement is another issue of discussion in the literature. Frazer Egerton argues that Jihadi-Salafis have adhered to the deterritorialization of the umma because of the prevalence of movement among them. More specifically, many of them have traveled to conflict zones, receiving training from local groups and fighting alongside other Mujahidin.[6] In their eyes, this experience alone confirms the existence of an embattled umma that needs their support and dedication. In effect, it can be argued that Jihadi-Salafism is an unintended side effect of globalization, which has created a new class of international warriors with loyalty only to their imagined umma. Hence al-Qaeda has fought for the purpose of establishing a global caliphate for all Muslims.

In recent years, however, the Jihadi-Salafi movement has become increasingly sectarian in nature. Sunni militants do not focus anymore on the far enemy of the West, but rather on a nearer enemy. The Paris and Brussels attacks during the winter of 2015–2016 were isolated incidents of jihadi terrorism on European soil. Despite external support for the perpetrators, both attacks can be described as homegrown terrorism since they were mainly committed by French and Belgian nationals. The involvement of the Islamic State of Iraq and Syria was largely defensive in nature; it has sought to raise the cost of Western military action in the Middle East, rather than occupying European territory.

Indeed, Sunni militants aim at overthrowing Shia-dominated or secular regimes in the Middle East. Their approach is openly divisive since they seek to establish a localized Sunni theocracy clear of its religious minorities. The localization of Jihadi-Salafism is a recent development that has been understudied because many analysts still interpret Jihadi-Salafism as a glob-alized force without any territorial attachment. However, Sunni militancy has evolved into a phenomenon of political and cultural complexity that has drawn on historical narratives, selective theological interpretations, and global influences.

This chapter describes the development of Sunni militancy in Iraq and Syria since 2003, focusing on al-Qaeda's Middle Eastern strategy and Abu Musab al-Zarqawi's jihad in Iraq. It then covers the rise of two Jihadi-Salafi groups that currently dominate the Sunni militant scene in Syria and Iraq: ISIS and the al-Qaeda-affiliated al-Nusra Front. Finally, it examines how Sunni militants have become agents of glocalization by adopting the justice master frame.

The Origins of Modern Sunni Militancy in the Middle East

The outbreak of Sunni militancy was largely triggered by two events that took place in 1979: the Iranian Revolution and the Soviet invasion of Afghanistan. The departure of the shah in February 1979 paved the way for the return of Ayatollah Khomeini and the establishment of the Islamic Republic. While attempting to consolidate his power domestically, Kho-meini pronounced his intention to export the revolution.[7] Although the Iranian leader espoused pan-Islamism, he used terms and concepts deriving from the Shia tradition and theology.[8] Naturally, the Shia populations of Arab countries were susceptible to Khomeini's revolutionary messages. Saudi Arabia felt threatened by the rise of Khomeini because it has a sizable Shia minority that has been discriminated against for many years.[9] There-fore, the Saudi regime intensified its effort to promote Wahhabism and to counter Shiism throughout the region.

Since the kingdom was considered to be a close U.S. ally, its aggressive pursuit of Sunni dominance was viewed as a blow to Iranian aspirations in the Middle East. Indeed, Washington and its European allies failed to understand the potential that Sunni militancy had to become a major anti-Western force. The Iranian hostage crisis during 1979–1980 and the sub-sequent kidnapping of Western citizens in Lebanon by pro-Iranian groups had already created an image about the Islamic Republic that was completely negative. Riyadh had a free hand to assist Sunni militants in the Middle East and South Asia, both financially and morally.

Simultaneously, the Soviet invasion of Afghanistan and the Mujahidin resistance against the Red Army were the catalyst for the formation of militant Sunni groups like al-Qaeda. Arab volunteers joined the ranks of the Afghan resistance in order to fight against the Soviet superpower. After the withdrawal of the Soviet troops in 1988, some of them decided to continue the jihad against the far enemy of the United States, which was blamed for the Muslim world's misfortunes.[10]

Osama bin Laden's al-Qaeda gradually increased its international jihadi activities by attacking Western targets and interests.[11] Al-Qaeda reached its zenith with the September 11, 2001, attacks in New York and Washington. Following the U.S. invasion of Afghanistan in October 2001, the group withdrew to the border areas of Pakistan to regroup. With the fall of the Taliban regime, al-Qaeda lost not only a vital ally but also its territorial base. Not being able to launch another major 9/11-type attack, it became a franchise-operated group providing nothing more than ideological coverage to jihadi groups operating in the West, the Middle East, and elsewhere.[12]

The U.S. invasion of Iraq in March 2003 offered al-Qaeda a new opportunity to revive itself in that part of the Muslim world that had more strategic and symbolic importance than any other, namely the Middle East. After all, the organization's top echelons have always been occupied by ethnic Arabs. While being isolated in the tribal areas of Pakistan, the organization's leadership decided to outsource the launching of a jihad in Iraq.

The branch of al-Qaeda in Iraq was established by Abu Musab al-Zarqawi, a Jordanian national. Al-Zarqawi, who was known as a street criminal in Jordan, traveled to Afghanistan in the late 1980s to join the insurgency against the Red Army. In Afghanistan, he met Osama bin Laden and decided to bring jihad to his native Jordan. He was arrested upon his return to Jordan in 1993 and was sent to prison for six years. There he met Abu Muhammad al-Maqdisi, a Jordanian-Palestinian radical cleric and theorist of jihad.[13] After his release, he traveled back to Afghanistan, where he established his own organization called Jama'at al-Tawhid wal-Jihad (Organization of Monotheism and Jihad). The organization recruited radicals from Jordan, Syria, Palestine, and Lebanon and took responsibility for several attacks against Jordanian and U.S. targets. Following the U.S. invasion of Iraq in March 2003, Zarqawi decided to expand the group's activities into the neighboring country.

In August 2003, Jama'at al-Tawhid attacked the Jordanian Embassy in Baghdad, the United Nations Mission to Iraq, and Imam Ali Mosque in the holy Shia city of Najaf. The timing of Zarqawi's campaign of terror was not coincidental; it started when it became obvious that Sunnis had lost their privileged position in post-Saddam Iraq. The political and economic marginalization of Iraqi Sunnis came as a shock to them; the Baathist regime had established a strong patron-client relationship with the Sunni community. Consequently, Sunnis had largely dominated the public sector and the security services. The lion's share of public spending had gone to members of the community. Under Saddam's rule, Sunnis were the winners and the Shias were the losers.[14] The U.S. occupation and the dismantlement of the Baathist regime dramatically changed the balance of power inside the country.

In October 2004, Zarqawi pledged allegiance to Osama bin Laden and became the emir of the al-Qaeda in Iraq (hereafter—AQI). From the beginning of his engagement in Iraq, Zarqawi demonstrated a vicious hate for the Shias. In a letter to Osama bin Laden in January 2004, he wrote: "[Shias] are an insurmountable obstacle, a lurking snake, a crafty and malicious scorpion, a spying enemy, and a mortal venom. . . . History's message, confirmed by the current situation, demonstrates most clearly that Shiism is a religion that has nothing in common with Islam except in the way that Jews have something in common with Christians as people of the Book. From patent polytheism, tomb worship . . . to calling the companions of the Prophet infidels and insulting the mother of the believers [i.e., Aisha] and the best of Muslim nation, they arrive at distorting the Quran . . . in addition to claiming that the imams are infallible."[15]

Here Zarqawi attempted to enforce upon Osama bin Laden an anti-Shia agenda that al-Qaeda at that moment clearly did not have. His letter cited anti-Shia fatwas by Ibn Taymiyya and Ibn Hazm, who have been considered as prominent Sunni ulama. In addition, Zarqawi attempted to capitalize on the growing Sunni anger over Shia empowerment in post-Saddam Iraq. His aim was to provoke a civil war between Sunnis and Shias. Indeed, his letter admitted that "if a sectarian war were to break out, a large part of the Muslim community worldwide would support the Iraqi Sunnis."[16] The bombing at the al-Askari Mosque in Samarra in February 2006 and the indiscriminate targeting of Shia civilians brought Iraq to the brink of civil war during 2006–2009.

The leader of AQI was eventually denounced by al-Qaeda for his anti-Shia strategy; instead, Osama favored an insurgency exclusively against the

U.S. and coalition troops. Nevertheless, AQI's strategy poisoned the relations between Sunni and Shia in Iraq and paved the way later for ISIS's campaign against the Shia-dominated regime. A few months before his death, Zarqawi outlined his rationale behind the anti-Shia strategy, claiming that "the Muslims will have no victory or superiority over the aggressive infidels such as the Jews and the Christians until there is a total annihilation of those under them such as the apostate agents headed by the [Shia] *Rafidi* [i.e., rejector]."[17]

In other words, he prioritized the jihad against the near enemy of Shias over al-Qaeda's global jihad against the United States. His strategy was essentially localist, although al-Qaeda viewed jihad in Iraq as only part of a larger project. The then deputy leader of al-Qaeda, Ayman al-Zawahiri, sent a letter to Zarqawi in July 2005, outlining the organization's strategy: first, expulsion of U.S. occupation troops from Iraq; second, establishment of an Islamic state in Iraq; third, invasion of neighboring countries; and fourth, an attack against Israel.[18] Apparently, al-Zawahiri did not find Iraqi Shias an enemy worthy to fight with al-Qaeda.

Notwithstanding al-Qaeda's pan-Islamic approach, the larger Jihadi-Salafi movement has harbored strong anti-Shia sentiments. According to Vali Nasr, the "anti-Shia violence is not just a strategic ploy used by al-Qaeda operatives . . . to create instability in Iraq and undermine Washington's plans for that country's future; it is a constituent part of the ideology of Sunni militancy."[19] For instance, the same day that several bombs killed Shia pilgrims in Baghdad and Karbala, during the celebration of Ashura in March 2004, the Kuwaiti Wahhabi leader Hamed al-Ali condemned the Shia rite as the "biggest display of idolatry" and accused the Shia of joining an evil axis linking Washington, Tel-Aviv, and the Shia holy city of Najaf to grab Persian Gulf oil and disenfranchise Sunnis.[20]

Due to his disrespect for the local tribal culture and use of indiscriminate violence against civilians, Zarqawi found himself increasingly isolated from the Sunni community. Therefore, Fawaz Gerges has observed that the Iraqi branch of al-Qaeda, under Zarqawi, "lost a historic opportunity to integrate itself with an aggrieved Sunni community that initially had tolerated its presence."[21] During 2006–2009, the U.S. military took the opportunity to organize the Sunni Awakening Movement (Ḥarakat al-Inqadh al-Sunni), which battled AQI in western Iraq.

In January 2006, Zarqawi allied AQI with other jihadi groups and established an umbrella organization, the Iraqi Mujahidin Council (Majlis Shura al-Mujahidin fi al-Iraq). However, Zarqawi was killed in a U.S. air strike on June 7, 2006. His successor, Abu Hamza al-Muhajir, an Egyptian, brought AQI back to its intended purpose, namely to act as the local affiliate of al-Qaeda. The Iraqi Mujahidin Council was disbanded for unknown reasons in October 2006 and was renamed as Islamic State of Iraq (Dawlat al-Iraq al-Islamiyyah). The group attacked coalition troops and Iraqi government forces.

In April 2010, al-Muhajir was killed in a joint U.S.-Iraqi operation near the Sunni city of Tigrit. The following month, the Shura Council of the Islamic State of Iraq appointed Abu Bakr al-Baghdadi as the new leader. There is little information about al-Baghdadi. He was born in the Iraqi city of Samarra in 1971. He has a PhD in Islamic sciences and served four years in a U.S. prison camp in southern Iraq.[22] Al-Baghdadi has benefited from his tribal affiliation because he is from the al-Bu'badri tribe, which is descended from the Prophet's Quraysh tribe.[23] As I discuss below, al-Baghdadi later established ISIS and declared himself caliph.

The Sunni-Supported Insurgency and the Arrival of Al-Qaeda in Syria

Syria has been a country of political complexities and divisions due to the heterogeneity of the population. The coup of 1970 brought to power the air force general Hafez al-Assad, who came from an Alawite family in Latakia.[24] During Hafez al-Assad's rule, the armed forces and the internal security agencies went through a process of "Alawitization" whereby the Shia sect of Alawites came to dominate the top echelons of the security apparatus. The Assad regime also formed alliances with prominent Sunni families in Damascus and Aleppo, and allowed members of other religious minorities like Christians and Druze to prosper economically.

The divide-and-rule strategy worked relatively well, but there were occasional Sunni revolts. Members of the Syrian branch of the Muslim Brotherhood, which had been established during the 1940s, participated in civil disobedience actions against the Baathist regime during the 1960s. The group gradually shifted to violence in the mid- to late 1970s. In June 1979, for example, a Muslim Brotherhood-affiliated group attacked the Aleppo Artillery School, killing many cadets. There were more attacks between 1979 and 1981 targeting members of the security forces, Baathist officials, and pro-regime Muslim leaders. The organization was also blamed for an assassination attempt against Hafez al-Assad on June 26, 1980. During this period, the Muslim Brotherhood clearly adopted an anti-Alawite stance.

The confrontation came to a climax in early February 1982, when the Brotherhood staged an uprising in Hama.[25] The response of the Assad regime was extremely violent: the army besieged the city for three weeks killing thousands of insurgents and civilians. The Hama massacre ended the Muslim Brotherhood-led rebellion and solidified the regime. The Syrian branch became a marginal force in Syria politics, although Hafez al-Assad released some of its members from prisons in the mid-1990s. The organization had denounced the use of violence and advocated democratization.

After Hafez al-Assad's death in 2000, his son Bashar al-Assad had come to power promising reforms. The outbreak of the Arab Spring revolutions during 2010 took Bashar al-Assad by surprise and he decided to react to protests with repression.[26] The Syrian uprising was started by apolitical sections of the society. Initially, protestors demanded more opportunities and improved living conditions, rather than democracy and regime change. The Brotherhood was not visibly involved in the eruption of the Syrian uprising. Yet the Assad regime responded with disproportionate violence against unarmed civilians. The security crackdown backfired as opposition groups started arming themselves to defend neighborhoods and villages by the summer of 2011. Opposition activists were largely mobilized by informal networks and social media.[27] The Baathist regime has closely monitored religious services and attendance at officially registered mosques. Many Sunni clerics in Syria's big cities refused to allow opposition demonstrations in their mosques because they feared regime retaliation; yet in small cities and rural areas, mosques did become the strongholds for opposition activities.[28]

The Assad regime did not control quickly enough a game changer factor: the widespread availability of satellite television, Internet, and mobile phones. According to David Lesch, opposition-in-exile groups sent to Syrian activists large quantities of satellite modems, mobile phones, computers, and other electronic devices.[29] In particular, the use of social media (e.g., Twitter, Facebook, YouTube) enabled the opposition activists to avoid detection by the security agencies and organize themselves against the regime. This movement had an amorphous structure with no hierarchical leadership. The social media created a new political space for the opposition activists to criticize the regime and propagate their antiregime messages in a domain beyond the state's control; in effect, the security agencies could not control the flow of information coming from largely anonymous cyber activists and citizen journalists. As a result, state-controlled media narratives were rejected by the majority of Syrians.

Initially the Syrian opposition consisted of secular groups (e.g., the Free Syrian Army), but it was later hijacked by Sunni militants. Most of them can be classified as followers of Jihadi-Salafism. There are several reasons why Jihadi-Salafi groups emerged in the country, such as the presence of Syrian migrants in Saudi Arabia, tribal links between Syria and Gulf countries, and the indoctrination of Syrian clerics in Salafi-oriented institutions.[30] Moreover, the severity of the Assad regime's reprisals against the civilian population inevitably increased the popularity of those who were willing to fight a religious war.

In January 2012, the al-Qaeda-affiliated group Jabhat al-Nusra li Ahl al Sham (the Support Front for the People of Syria) was formed by Abu Mohammad al-Julani and other Syrian members of Zarqawi's jihadi network in Iraq. Charles Lister argued that "al-Nusra's comparatively pragmatic, localized, and socially-integrated approach has secured it both al-Qaeda affiliate status and strong levels of support—or at least acceptance—inside Syria."[31] Despite being part of the global al-Qaeda network, al-Nusra has concentrated its efforts on confronting the Assad regime. It has tried to control territory and develop state structures in northwestern Syria.

Since Assad has increasingly relied on the Alawite-dominated security services for survival, the conflict has gradually turned into a sectarian one with the opposition drawing on the Sunni majority for support.[32] Consequently, Sunni militants have been able to call for outside support; for instance, Yusuf al-Qaradawi issued a fatwa calling on Muslims to help rebels in Syria.[33] Indeed, thousands of foreign fighters have traveled to Syria to join the insurgency. According to a study published by the King's College International Centre for the Study of Radicalization, approximately four thousand Muslims from Western Europe have gone to Syria since early 2011 to join jihadi groups, representing 20 percent of the foreign fighter total.[34] It appears that most of them come from Great Britain, Germany, Belgium, and the Netherlands. Moreover, thousands of Sunni militants from neighboring countries like Saudi Arabia and Jordan, but also more distant Muslim countries such as Libya and Tunisia, have answered the call to arms.

The new media and the Internet have played a crucial role in mobilizing support for the Sunni insurgency in Syria. Videos depicting murdered civilians, including children, have been widely circulated on jihadi websites and forums. Visual images of civilian suffering have provoked strong feelings of anger, guilt, and desire for revenge. In fact, many Western fighters joined the insurgency in Syria after watching these videos. During a TV interview in March 2013, for example, a Dutch convert to Islam explained that he decided to join the Sunni resistance because he "could not sit and watch [videos of] his sisters in Syria being raped and his brothers being beheaded."[35] The flow of foreign fighters to Syria indicates that the country has come to be the new battleground for Sunni militancy.

The Rise and Expansion of ISIS

The Islamic State of Iraq took advantage of the anti-Assad insurgency to reach neighboring Syria.[36] Al-Baghdadi tried to take over al-Nusra in April 2013, but al-Julani referred the issue to Ayman al-Zawahiri. In November 2013, the leader of al-Qaeda attempted to mediate between the two al-Qaeda-affiliated groups. More specifically, he suggested that al-Nusra focus on the war against the Assad regime and that the Islamic State fight only in Iraq.[37] Although the leader of al-Qaeda ruled against this merger, al-Baghdadi decided to rename his organization as the Islamic State in Iraq and Syria (al-Dawlah al-Islamiyah fi al-Iraq wa-al-Sham) in order to stress his claim to Syria. In February 2014, Zawahiri decided to disavow the group and keep the al-Nusra Front as the sole affiliate in Syria.[38]

The rapid growth of ISIS is an unprecedented event in the history of the modern Middle East. As a result of its spectacular military victories, the group has held sway over vast territory in Syria and Iraq and millions of people have come under its rule. ISIS has a solid source of funding, ranging from extortion and kidnappings to tax collection. The June 2014 capture of Mosul led to the looting of many banks; consequently, hundreds of millions of dollars were confiscated by ISIS. The group has also seized oil fields in northern Syria. Thus its financial assets were estimated at 1.1 billion British pounds in June 2014.[39] ISIS has even published an annual report since 2012, called *An-Naba*, in which it has listed all its activities. In 2013, the group claimed almost ten thousand operations, including one thousand assassinations and four thousand bomb attacks.[40]

ISIS has followed a strict interpretation of Sharia in the territories that have come under its control. It has imposed harsh punishment on alleged criminals and homosexuals. Also, the group has banned music and has forced women to cover themselves completely in order to restrict their participation in public life. Yet it does not reject modern technology. Actually, ISIS has been one of the most active clandestine groups on the Internet given that its Twitter accounts have thousands of followers.[41]

But ISIS is not just another jihadi group. It has tried to build a quasi state in the occupied territories. Its state-building process includes the establishment of a new court system of Sharia and the construction of post offices and police stations.[42] In the northern Syrian city of ar-Raqqa, the so-called capital of ISIS, the group has provided social services to win the hearts and minds of the local population. For example, it has opened mills to produce more bread and managed to improve the electricity and water supply.[43] In addition, it has run its own schools and kindergartens imposing a new curriculum on teachers and pupils.

As opposed to al-Qaeda, which has been a deterrorialized organization, ISIS measures its success by the ability to control territory. Its statecentric strategy resembles that of the Taliban during the 1990s: military victories have led to the control of vast territories.[44] ISIS has been keen to establish a Sunni-majority state in the Levant and Mesopotamia. Such a new state could become the nucleus of a caliphate that would unite all Sunni Muslims. The new entity would be the defender of all Sunnis in the world who have been "persecuted by infidels." In the words of a Belgian Muslim ISIS fighter in Syria, "the enemies of Allah and of Islam have gathered worldwide, starting with the so-called 'peaceful' Buddhists who exterminate . . . Muslims in Asia, or the Africans in Central Africa who kill the Muslims, or the Westerners, or the Shia may Allah curse them. They are all gathered against the Sunni Muslims."[45] Moreover, ISIS has claimed authority over all other jihadi groups. In June 2014, ISIS spokesman Abu Muhammad Al-Adnani declared that "the legality of all emirates, groups, states, and organizations, becomes null by the expansion of the khilafah's authority and arrival of its troops to their areas."[46]

In spite of its ambitious goals, the group has produced limited literature on ideology and political strategy. The third issue of *Dabiq Magazine*, produced by ISIS's Al-Hayat Media Center, gave some insights about the group's political aims and objectives in Syria and Iraq. The Islamic State aims at "waging its jihad alongside a *da'wa* campaign. . . . It fights to defend the Muslims, liberate their lands, and bring an end to the *tawaghit* [idolatry], while simultaneously seeking to guide and nurture those under its authority and ensure that both their religious and social needs are met."[47]

It appears that ISIS adheres to an extreme version of Salafism which could serve as the state ideology of the new caliphate.

Yet the eventual aim is to create a proper Islamic society, although it is not clear what that means in practice. For this purpose, the group "actively works to educate its citizens, preach to and admonish them, enforce their strict adherence to Islamic obligations, judge their disputes . . . eradicate all traces of *shirk* [polytheism] and heresy, incite the people to jihad and call them to unite behind [Abu Bakr al-Baghdadi]."[48] In effect, ISIS has envisioned the establishment of a totalitarian state and the radical transformation of the society. ISIS's revolutionary vision resembles that of early Bolsheviks in Russia or the Nazi Party in Germany. The declaration of a caliphate serves a higher cause: to bring back Islam to its original state and fulfill the wishes of God. While the group has adopted a theological approach to statehood, it has also warned its adherents about future failures; for example, an ISIS ideologue asserted that "the Khilafah is a state whose inhabitants and soldiers are human beings. They are not infallible angels. You may see things that need improvement and that are being improved . . . but remember that the Khilafah is at war with numerous kafir state and their allies . . . so be patient."[49]

In his informative report *The Islamic State* Richard Barrett compared the Jihadi-Salafism of ISIS with the ideology of Baathism. Interestingly, the two ideologies share "the idea of a state run by a small group of the enlightened."[50] Moreover, both seek to privilege an extended group of people who ought to dominate the planet; for the Baathists this is the Arab race and for ISIS it is the Sunni umma. Following the U.S. invasion in 2003, Baathists and Sunni militants viewed the presence of coalition forces as a proof of Western imperialism against not only Iraq but also the Arab nation as a whole. Furthermore, they understood Shia political empowerment as an existential threat against the Sunni community.

ISIS has not recognized the borders established by the Sykes-Picot Agreement of 1916. In a largely symbolic move, it destroyed border posts between Iraq and Syria in the summer of 2014. In doing so, the group appealed to three different constituencies: the local tribes who live across the borders and resent the artificial borders, former Baathists who advocate Arab unity, and fellow Islamists seeking unification of all Muslim-populated territories.[51] Additionally, ISIS has fostered a personality cult around its self-declared Caliph al-Baghdadi in the occupied areas. ISIS's declaration of a caliphate stated that "the Islamic State . . . resolved to

Figure 6. Stages in reestablishing the caliphate in Abu Musab al-Zarqawi's strategy

announce the establishment of the Islamic khilafah, the appointment of a khalifah for the Muslims, and the pledge of allegiance to the sheikh, the mujahid, the scholar who practices what he preaches, the worshipper, the leader, the warrior, the reviver, descendent from the family of the Prophet, the slave of Allah, Ibrahim Ibn Awwad ibn Ibrahim ibn Ali al-Badri al-Samarrai."[52] The statement obviously attempted to reshape the image of al-Baghdadi by drawing parallels with the life of the Prophet Muhammad. The post of the caliph has been associated with collective memories of Islamic glory. Thus, it is vital for the new leader to appear qualified.

The group has largely avoided acknowledging the role of Osama bin Laden in the Jihadi-Salafi movement. Instead, there are many references to the role of Abu Musab al-Zarqawi, who has been portrayed by ISIS ideologues as a *mujaddid* (reviver).[53] This is an honorable and prestigious title given to those who are sent by Allah at the turn of every century of the Islamic calendar to revive true Islam.[54] Zarqawi is also credited with the strategy of re-establishing the caliphate that now has been adopted by ISIS. More specifically, his strategy consisted of five pillars: *hijrah* (emigration for the cause of Allah); the formation of a *jama'ah* (community); *tawahhush* (destabilization of nonbelievers); *tamkin* (consolidation); and finally the establishment of the khilafah (caliphate).[55] Zarqawi's strategy is represented in figure 6.

Al-Baghdadi's first public appearance in Mosul in June 2014 revealed more about his thinking and aims. He used Quranic phrases to demonstrate his religious knowledge and establish his legitimacy. Chase Robinson is of the opinion that his address was similar to the letters, sermons, and speeches of caliphs in the seventh, eighth, and ninth centuries.[56] Yet he spoke about a range of issues, including the mistreatment of Muslims in Burma, the veil issue in France, and the relationship between democracy and secularism. In so speaking, he could have been viewed as well informed and suitable for the post. But this presentation involves more than the personality of al-Baghdadi. ISIS has been engaged in a war of words and symbols. The choice of the new name, Abu Bakr, is not coincidental; the father-in-law of the Prophet Muhammad and first caliph, was chosen over Ali, the preferred one by those who believe that the successor must be a relative of the Prophet. Al-Baghdadi also promised to march on Rome like the Muslim warriors of the seventh century. Such symbolism is connected to the golden era of Islam.

The group has drawn cultural and ideational resources from Islamic eschatology. Hadiths have elaborated on how the end of time would happen. According to one of them, a great battle between Muslims and the nonbelievers will take place near the Syrian town of Dabiq during the time of Malahim (the Islamic equivalent of Armageddon).[57] ISIS ideologues have named their electronic magazine after Dabiq in order to emphasize the group's divine mission and the inevitability of victory against the enemies. Moreover, they have cited the battle between Isa (Jesus) and the Masih ad-Dajjal (Antichrist) because "kufr and its tyranny will be destroyed [and] Islam and its justice will prevail on the entire earth."[58] It is an event leading to the end of the world when all humans stand before God to be judged. The Quran discusses the Day of Judgment, or Resurrection (al-Qiyama), when those who did good deeds would go to paradise (al-Janna) and those who did unrighteous deeds who go to hell (Jahannam). ISIS has adhered to the concept of the Judgment Day because it represents the ultimate endpoint. Jean-Loup Samaan makes an interesting point about the group's state-building effort; its leadership does not want a state that would join the international community, but one that would mark the end of history as we know it.[59]

In early June 2014, the collapse of the Iraqi army in Mosul presented a new opportunity for ISIS to arm itself with U.S.-manufactured weapons like Humvees and artillery pieces.[60] In late June 2014, a parade of the confiscated tanks and SCUD missiles took place in ar-Raqqa to boost morale and demonstrate the might of the Islamic State.[61] However, it is not clear whether ISIS seeks to transform itself into a regular army; so far, it has used a combination of conventional and asymmetric tactics against its opponents, including ambushes, suicide bombings, detonations of improvised explosive devices, and mortar and rocket attacks.

The speed of the ISIS advance in northern Iraq in the summer of 2014 can be explained by several factors. First, the group was probably aided by former Baathists who have resented the loss of privileged status and have blamed the Shia-dominated government for their misfortunes. The Maliki government was largely viewed as sectarian and pro-Iranian. As a result, a growing number of Sunni Arabs have come to see violence as the only available tool for political change. The marginalization of the Iraqi Sunni community has created a political opportunity for ISIS to portray itself as a champion of the Sunni cause. Second, ISIS could have received some support from Gulf countries that worry about the strategic implications of the resurgent Iranian foreign policy in the region.[62] For its foot soldiers, however, the military victories are the proof of a predetermined outcome that is bound to happen; as a British member put it "look where we started and where we are today. . . . These kuffars fear from us the Khilafah, they see this coming but they cannot prevent it, they cannot delay it."[63]

The spectacular military victories of ISIS during 2014 and 2015 increased its appeal among other jihadi groups in the Middle East and beyond. In late June 2014, for example, the Kurdish jihadi group Ansar al-Islam (Helpers of Islam) pledged allegiance to the Islamic State and dissolved itself. Its last official announcement stated that "this is a state that established the laws of Allah, carried out the *hudud* [Sharia-sanctioned punishments for serious crimes], set up the various administrative offices, and brought justice to the oppressed."[64] In August 2014, members of the militant Filipino group Abu Sayyaf swore an oath of loyalty to ISIS too.[65] In early October 2014, the Libyan jihadi group Majlis Shura Shabab al Islam (the Islamic Youth Shura Council) announced that the city of Darnah was part of ISIS's caliphate.[66] A few weeks later, six leading figures of the Tehreek-e-Taliban in Pakistan pledged allegiance to al-Baghdadi, but their decision was not approved by the top leadership and most members.[67] In March 2015, the Nigerian jihadi group Boko Haram joined ranks with ISIS to integrate West Africa into the self-declared caliphate.[68]

ISIS has bolstered its influence in the Middle East on the basis of sectarianism and religious bigotry. In July 2014, the group issued an ultimatum to the Christians of occupied Mosul to convert to Islam, pay a special tax (*jizya*), or face death.[69] As a result, the remaining Christian population left the city and found refuge in the Kurdish-controlled areas of northern Iraq.[70] In effect, ISIS has attempted to reinstitutionalize the old system of *dhimma* (writ of protection), whereby non-Muslims were obliged to pay a religious levy to the caliphate for their own security. In addition, ISIS has attacked members of the Yezidi community, who have been viewed as apostates.[71]

Furthermore, ISIS's ideologues have presented their struggle against Shia-dominated regimes as part of a perpetual conflict for the soul of Islam.

Consequently, it has showed no mercy for prisoners of war. For instance, the group was accused of killing 670 Shia prisoners in Mosul while releasing the Sunni ones.[72] The genocidal tactics employed by ISIS have resulted in ethnic cleansing and mass killings. It has not tolerated the presence of other jihadi groups in the area. For example, the relationship between al-Nusra and ISIS can be described as confrontational. The two groups have fought fierce battles in northern and central Syria during 2014.[73] Indeed, they represent different jihadi schools of thought: the former is part of the al-Qaeda network, which has fought for the utopian aim of establishing a global Islamic state, while the latter has the less ambitious goal of establishing a hegemonic Islamic state in the Sunni-populated areas of the Middle East.[74] Yet the battle for the hearts and minds of Sunni Muslims is now fought locally, not globally.

Since late 2016, ISIS had lost more than a quarter of the territory it once controlled in the two countries.[75] The group has been weakened by its territorial overextension and the increased military coordination among its adversaries. On October 16, 2016, Iraqi and Kurdish forces began a Mosul offensive with the backing of U.S.-led air strikes. ISIS will almost certainly be defeated in northern Iraq. However, the group is likely to maintain a presence in Syria and certain Sunni-populated areas of Iraq in the foreseeable future. Although substantial military capability will be lost as a result of the offensive operations against ISIS, the group will have enough resources to resume a low-level insurgency.

The Sunni Militants Between the Global and the Local

The new jihad of Sunni militants is a more narrowly defined political project. It is a territorial, not postterritorial, quest that can only be achieved by a localized force of determined and highly motivated fighters. Most Sunni militants have now focused on the establishment of a Sunni state in the Middle East. For this purpose, there are two important steps that must be taken: control of territory and homogenization of the population. This vision is in line with the concept of nation-state. But instead of ethnicity being coterminous with territory, it is the religious denomination that sets the limits of territorial expansion. In this political entity, there is no place for non-Muslims or Muslims who deviate from the beliefs and canons of

Jihadi-Salafism. Such a nation-building process almost resembles the force-ful nation-building in Europe from the eighteenth century to the twentieth: conducting ethnic cleansing against minorities, pursuing homogenization of culture, and creating a heroic past.

Despite the fact that most senior leaders of ISIS are of Arab origin, the group is keen to emphasize its pan-Sunni membership and postethnic ethos. For instance, al-Baghdadi released a statement on July 1, 2014, that "it is a khilafah that gathered the Caucasian, Indian, Chinese, Shami [i.e., Syrians], Iraqi, Yemeni, Egyptian, Maghribi [i.e., North African], American, French, German, and Australian. . . . Their blood mixed and became one, under a single flag and goal, in one pavilion, enjoying this blessing, the blessing of faithful brotherhood. . . . The State is a state for all Muslims. The land is for the Muslims, all the Muslims. O Muslims everywhere, whoever is capable of performing hijrah [emigration] to the Islamic State, then let him do so, because hijrah to the land of Islam is obligatory."[76]

By acknowledging the diversity within ISIS, al-Baghdadi attempted to encourage more foreigners to join the group. The flow of foreign-born Muslims could not only strengthen ISIS forces but also alter the demo-graphic makeup of the new state. Indeed, a number of Moroccan and Tuni-sian jihadis have brought their families to settle in ar-Raqqa and other ISIS-controlled Syrian cities, and foreign preachers have been appointed in mosques.[77] The ISIS propaganda machine has encouraged Muslims to immigrate to ISIS-controlled territories in Syria and Iraq by publishing photos of a well-organized communal life.[78] It has framed the new state as a heaven on earth for Sunni Muslims who want to practice their religion free of foreign interference. This is an attractive possibility for those who wish to become pioneers of a new political entity.

This identification of nationality (or subnationality) with religion is not unusual in the region. The Lebanese political system, for instance, is based on confessionalism, whereby political power is allocated proportionally among the country's religious groups.[79] Based on the political history of Lebanon, it is fair to argue that subnationality in the form of registered religious affiliation either brings benefits or incurs costs. The nonseparation of nationality and religion is probably clearer in the case of Israel. Despite being a democratic and pluralistic country, Israel is a self-identified Jewish state. Indeed, the Law of Return gives every Jew the right to immigrate to Israel and acquire citizenship of the state.[80] Accordingly, the new caliphate aspires to become a pan-Sunni state in the Middle East, hence the call for Sunni Muslims to immigrate there.

Moreover, the group has attempted to foster a sense of Sunni patriotism among the local population and the foreign fighters. In March 2015, for instance, ISIS spokesman Abu Muhammad Al-Adnani said that "if the Islamic State is broken, God forbid, then no Mecca or Madina will be for you O Sunnis after that" and "Sunnis will be the slaves of Shias."[81] ISIS has sought the development of a common identity for those who live under its control. If the identity-formation process is successful, it could secure the loyalty of an ethnically diverse population. For this purpose, the group could draw valuable ideational and cultural resources from Sunni Islam, which has a history of imperial expansionism.[82]

Likewise, the al-Nusra Front could establish its own Sunni ministate in northwestern Syria. For this purpose, it has started a top-down Islamization process; for example, the group has implemented strict rules regarding women's dress.[83] In addition, militants from al-Nusra and other groups have attacked Alawite villages near the Syrian coast in order to create a homogenous territory.[84] Indeed, the capture of the northwestern city of Idlib by al-Nusra forces in March 2015 could pave the way for the creation of a second quasi state.[85] Thus, the group has provided water and electricity services, built roads, and helped in the running of hospitals.[86]

But these localized state-building efforts have coincided with the hybridization of Islamism. Sunni militants have functioned as glocalizers by adopting the master frame of justice. More specifically, they have transferred global ideas of justice into local Muslim communities. They have done this in the hope of gaining legitimacy and acceptance because demands for justice are shared by almost everyone. The use of the justice master frame can facilitate mobilization and recruitment, since it has strong religious roots and can appeal to the majority of the local Muslim population.

The justice of Sunni militancy is not a vague concept; it is based on moral and ethical principles provided by Sunnis' understanding of Sharia, such as piety, accountability to God, fairness, solidarity, and the welfare of society. For instance, al-Julani has stated that his group aims at imposing "the Sharia rules [so that] justice prevails, injustice is removed, and a judicious Islamic government is established following the course of the Prophet. It shall be a government that seeks to liberate the Muslim land, apply the Sharia of God, treat people equally, and remove injustice."[87] From his point of view, the application of Sharia is the only way to achieve justice because it is the manifestation of divine righteousness. The underlying belief is that the pursuit of justice forms part of a teleology of Islamic progress. Jihadi-Salafis not only claim to possess the absolute truth but also assert they have a mission to bring about God's justice in the world.

Therefore, fighting for justice is more than just a responsibility. It is an epic journey for personal and collective salvation. When members of al-Nusra were asked by an *al-Jazeera* journalist whether they are part of the al-Qaeda network, their response focused on the delivery of justice as an end in itself. They argued that "we are against injustice and anyone who commits injustice. So if justice is al-Qaeda, then we are with al-Qaeda. And if al-Qaeda is injustice, we are against al-Qaeda. If the U.S. is acting for justice, then we are with America. And if America is for injustice, we are against them."[88]

In effect, the local branch of al-Qaeda has portrayed itself as a justice-seeking group, fighting without prejudice for the sake of the people. However, al-Nusra's commitment to Sharia-sanctioned justice has been disputed by ISIS. For instance, a former member of the al-Nusra Front who joined ISIS claimed that "[while being member of al-Nusra] I did not see implementation of Allah's Sharia nor did I see justice between an emir and an ordinary member."[89]

Instead, ISIS has claimed to be the only "entity in [Syria] actively implementing Sharia."[90] It follows that an authentic Islamic state can only exist if ISIS's version of Sharia is fully applied. The establishment of the caliphate would create a society where justice would prevail. ISIS has declared that the "flag of Khilafah will rise over [the al-Aqsa Mosque in Jerusalem] and Rome. . . . The shade of this blessed flag will expand until it covers all eastern and western extents of the Earth, filling the world with the truth and justice of Islam and putting an end to the falsehood and tyranny of jahiliyyah."[91] Thus, the group has promoted a dichotomy between the khilafah (the caliphate) that enforces justice and the jahiliyyah (the time of ignorance) which is identified with injustice.

Sunni militants have stressed the issue of equality among Muslims, which is the second component of the justice master frame. For example, an ISIS spokesman has described the self-declared caliphate as a place where there is "no difference between Arab and foreigner, white or black. Here, the American and the Arab became brothers, and the African and European, and the Eastern and Western."[92] The new entity is framed as a land of equality and fairness for Sunni Muslims from all over the world.

Nevertheless, it is clear that ISIS has developed a distorted understanding of equality that, while it is postracial and postethnic in character, has also a strong sectarian content. Not surprisingly, it has even criticized al-Qaeda's leadership for "treating Shias as Muslims."[93] The group has framed the targeting of the Shia population as a just act of retribution. The Shia opponents have been called "idolaters" (*taghut*) and "rejectionists" (*rafidi*). Both words have a very negative meaning. The former describes those who worship anything except God. The latter refers to a core belief of the Shia theology, that is, Shias' refusal to recognize the first three caliphs. For both accusations, Shias must be punished. The de-Muslimization of the Shia population has paved the way for its extermination. During June 2014, ISIS posted dozens of photos on its Twitter accounts, depicting the execution of captured Iraqi army soldiers. Some photos had captions like "this is the destiny of Maliki's Shias" or "the filthy Shias are killed in the hundreds."[94]

From the Sunni militants' perspective, the content and application of equality is determined by God's law. Equality is not based on the will of the people and democracy, but is what Sharia dictates. In the words of al-Nusra's military commander, Zahran Alloush, "The democracy we see in the world today is the dictatorship of the strong. We do not believe that democracy equals justice. This is an illusion. . . . We refuse to have the supra-constitutional principle of democracy imposed upon us. We know from the people of our country that the Muslims dream of the blessing of a life of justice under Islam. The state that we strive to establish will emerge from the will of our people who want the Quran and the Sunnah. . . . Our nation has a great thirst for an Islamic state, in which justice prevails as in the glorious days of the early Muslims."[95]

While he does not define its content, Alloush connects equality with the early Islam of the Prophet and his Companions. His dismissal of democracy does not derive from a typical Salafi line of thinking that views it as a man-made system; in his opinion, democracy is hateful because it favors the strong while the concept of justice is applicable to all people under God.

The third component of the justice master frame is particularly important because it has been used to rationalize the involvement of Sunni militants in Syria and Iraq. The responsibility to protect has been constantly evoked by Jihadi-Salafi groups to justify their actions in the battle zones. Although this responsibility is rooted in international law, the United Nations has evidently failed to stop the mass killing of civilians in Syria. ISIS has provided its own account of events. Following the outbreak of the anti-Assad uprising, "the Islamic State quickly got involved, answering the cries of the weak and oppressed Muslims by sending a mission from Iraq to activate its units in Sham [i.e., Syria] and later make the announcement of its official expansion."[96] The group has attempted to portray its involvement in Syria not as a strategic calculation to control new territories but as an effort to save Muslims.

More importantly, ISIS has attempted to describe itself as a champion of justice for all Muslims. In June 2014, it proclaimed a caliphate for all Muslims in Sunni-populated parts of Syria and Iraq. Its declaration stated that "the time has come for those generations that were drowning in oceans of disgrace, being nursed on the milk of humiliation, and being ruled by the vilest of all people, after their long slumber in the darkness of neglect— the time for them to rise. The time has come for the umma of Muhammad to wake up from its sleep, remove the garments of dishonor, and shake off the dust of humiliation and disgrace . . . and the dawn of honor has emerged anew. The sun of jihad has risen."[97]

The use of such emotional language aimed at evoking memories of a traumatized past, when the glorious years of Muslim expansion were replaced by Western colonialism. It is not a coincidence that ISIS leadership used words like *humiliation* and *dishonor* to recruit fighters. In this way, it has presented its campaign as a just cause for the sake of defending the umma against its enemies. It portrays Westerners as unbelievers and Arab leaders and Shia Muslims as apostates in order to delegitimize them. Moreover, the group has claimed that the execution of Western hostages is a tit-for-tat response to Western aggression that brings justice to Muslims. In effect, ISIS has sought to exact reciprocal justice on those who are deemed a threat.

The responsibility-to-protect component is confirmed by testimonies of individual jihadi fighters who said that they have a duty to save Muslims from evildoers. According to a former Royal Netherlands soldier of Turkish origin who has trained foreign fighters, "these people [i.e., foreign fighters] came here with the noble purpose of helping Syrian people."[98] A British female convert who moved to Syria with her husband, a jihadi fighter, called other Muslims to join the war because "these are your brothers and sisters as well and they need our help, so instead of sitting down and focusing on your families or focusing on your studies, you need to stop being selfish because the time is ticking."[99] In the words of a French fighter, "I resented the world's indifference toward my Muslim brothers. . . . In French mosques, you cannot talk about it. . . . They never talk about the context of confrontation. Islam calls for an eye for an eye, a tooth for a tooth."[100] From their statements, it is clear that the responsibility to protect has both a religious and ideological reasoning.

Furthermore, ISIS has claimed a responsibility to protect those Muslims who live under foreign occupation. The Palestinian problem is typically viewed by all militants as a matter of great concern due to the suffering of the local population and the religious importance that is attached to the area. Therefore, ISIS has condemned "the massacres taking place in Gaza against the Muslim men, women, and children" and has committed itself "to do everything within its means to continue striking down every apostate who stands as an obstacle on its path towards Palestine."[101] ISIS has even attempted to portray itself as the protector of new Muslims. In January 2015, for instance, the Libyan branch of ISIS brutally murdered twenty-one Egyptian Coptic Christians. In a video titled "A Message Signed with Blood to the Nation of the Cross," a member of the group explained that the beheading of the hostages was retaliation for the abduction of Camilia Shehata, a Coptic woman who was allegedly kidnapped by her family because she converted to Islam.[102]

In contrast to ISIS, the al-Nusra Front has avoided discussing the protection of Muslims outside Syria as such. Instead, it has stressed that its mission is "to fight the regime and its agents on the ground, including Hizb'allah and others."[103] In reality, al-Nusra has accepted the division of labor within the al-Qaeda network. Al-Zawahiri may not be as charismatic as Osama bin Laden, but he enjoys enough respect from his co-ideologues to lead al-Qaeda. Therefore, he is solely responsible for decisions regarding the umma as a whole and its constituencies. In the view of Abdel Bari Atwan, a British journalist who interviewed bin Laden in the late 1990s, "the writings and statements of both Osama bin Laden and Ayman al-Zawahiri testify that they always expected their struggle to be multigenerational."[104] In the meantime, al-Nusra has taken on the task of overthrowing the Assad regime in the name of justice.

From all the above, it is clear that the justice master frame has been utilized by militants in Iraq and Syria to mobilize members of the Sunni community. Their understanding of justice is compatible with the local situation and cultural context. In a state of war, people are looking for security that only justice could bring. Sunni militants have capitalized on the desperation of Syrians and Iraqis and depicted their actions as a justice-seeking campaign. They know that justice can be used as a powerful cognitive tool because of its three main components: moral and ethical principles defined by Sharia, equality for all Sunni Muslims, and responsibility to protect them. Hence Sunni militants have transmitted the global idea of justice to local constituencies, albeit with serious modifications that reflect political and cultural realities.

Conclusion

In the post-9/11 period, Sunni militancy is on the rise in the Middle East. Al-Nusra and ISIS have sought to overthrow Shia-dominated regimes in Syria and Iraq. Even though they share the same anti-Shia sentiments, the two groups have also competed against each other for power and influence.

ISIS has grown dramatically over the past few years to the point that it now controls significant portions of territory in Syria and Iraq. The transformation of ISIS from an insurgent group to a self-declared state has changed the nature of Islamist militancy. The main goal is now the establishment of a Sunni-only state at the heart of the Middle East that could attract fellow Sunnis from elsewhere. It is a grandiose project of state and nation building that has a strong theological and apocalyptic basis.

Al-Nusra has been part of the al-Qaeda network, but it has engaged in a localized effort to build an Islamic state in Syria. It has managed to survive al-Baghdadi's attempt to monopolize the Jihadi-Salafi movement and has retained its autonomy. Al-Nusra has adopted an anti-Alawite and anti-Iranian rhetoric that utilizes a logic of an existential conflict where violence takes precedence over peace. While it is militarily weaker than ISIS, it represents a distinct version of Sunni militancy.

Both groups have functioned as Islamist glocalizers because they have utilized the justice master frame. More specifically, Sunni militants have managed to adopt the global idea of justice and adapt it to local conditions. They have sought to establish a polity where justice will prevail. This can only be achieved with the implementation of Sharia, which provides the necessary moral and ethical principles. They have also embraced the principle of equality among Sunni Muslims who constitute the true umma. Shias and other religious communities are viewed as enemies. The justice master frame also incorporates the responsibility-to-protect norm that militants have embraced to justify their campaigns in Syria and Iraq.

It is difficult to predict the future of ISIS and al-Nusra. While Western countries will certainly try to defeat them, the rise of Sunni militancy is foremost a political problem. It is highly likely that Jihadi-Salafism will remain active and resolute. It is an evolving movement rather than static and disciplined. Moreover, its dynamism and sustainability have been affirmed by its ability to endorse universal ideas and disseminate them locally.

Conclusion

The rise of Islamism is a modern phenomenon characterized by heterogeneity and complexity. Political Islam can best be described as a social movement embodied by three generations: the Islamist nationalists, the Islamist globalists, and the Islamist communitarians. Each one of them had or currently has its own scale of engagement with the Muslim world. Islamist nationalists fought for liberation from foreign or despotic rule in localized struggles. In spite of their pan-Islamic rhetoric, they were confined within the national borders. The Islamist globalists attempted to confront their adversaries throughout the world in the name of the umma.

This book focuses on the third generation of Islamists who represent Muslim communities within and beyond national borders. What differentiates them from the other two is that they have functioned as glocalizers of universal ideas and norms. Apart from the technological aspects, the new Islamists have endorsed cognitive and ideational aspects of globalization. In this way, they have contributed to the particularization of Islamism. This is an ideology with global reach and local relevance, since it has incorporated different political and cultural realities.

The glocalization of political Islam has been happening for several years. It is the outcome of broader developments, such as the post-9/11 notion of pan-Islamism, the social media revolution, and the fragmentation of Muslim identity, especially after the Arab Spring revolutions. The new political Islam is situated between global processes and local environments. In this context, I make three main claims concerning the new generation of Islamists.

First, I argue that human rights are not only a fundamental set of rights and freedoms for individuals but also a powerful master frame. This frame consists of three main components: a generic framework of rights and freedoms, ethical legitimacy, and moral obligation to help human beings. This master frame has been utilized by Islamist activists of different sorts to achieve a variety of political goals.

The 9/11 attacks and other acts of jihadi terrorism have affected public perceptions of Islam in Europe. Consequently, there has been a dramatic increase of physical and verbal attacks against Muslims in many European countries. Under these circumstances, Islamist activists of convert origin have adopted the human rights master frame to propagate their messages to Muslim communities. They have avoided a direct confrontation with authorities, concentrating their efforts on activism. Hence convert-activists have promoted a hybrid Islamism among the continent's Muslim communities that fiercely denounces integration and assimilation policies.

The nonviolent activist group Hizb ut-Tahrir has also embraced the master frame of human rights to appeal to Muslims worldwide. Being a transnational group, it has faced the challenge of operating in diverse political and cultural environments. As a consequence, it has to address multiple audiences that have different perspectives. The master frame of human rights serves a double mission: it presents the establishment of the caliphate as itself a right worth fighting for, while promoting the new state as the future guarantor of rights. In other words, the caliphate of Hizb ut-Tahrir would be a global solution to local problems. The group is the epitome of glocalization because its different branches have endorsed a powerful master frame emphasizing actual or alleged human rights violations against Muslim communities.

Second, I maintain that the global idea and practice of democracy has been used by several Islamist parties and groups as a master frame to mobilize support and wage a political struggle. It consists of three main components: political equality, majority rule, and political legitimacy. The democracy master frame can address local concerns from a global angle. It provides Islamists with crucial legitimacy at a time of increased tensions between the West and the Muslim world.

The Islamo-democrats have sought change from within the system and have largely advocated consensual politics. Turkey's AKP, Egypt's Muslim Brotherhood, and Tunisia's al-Nahda have attempted the blending of Islamic and some democratic values. The AKP has employed the master frame of democracy to defend itself from domestic foes and strengthen its position in the Turkish political system. In Egypt, the Muslim Brotherhood joined the electoral process in order to gain power by democratic means. For this reason, it relied heavily on the democracy master frame to propagate its messages inside and outside the country. In neighboring Tunisia, al-Nahda has tried to fuse elements of the Tunisian political and social exceptionalism with its version of Islamism. In every case, the target audience is the community of pious Muslims who advocate the empowerment of Islam in public life.

The democracy master frame has also been embraced by electoral Salafis. Although most Salafis have typically condemned democracy as an alien system imported from the West, Egypt's al-Nour and Tunisia's Reform Front have espoused a hybrid Islamism that includes a commitment to Sharia and participation in the democratic process. The decision to enter politics was not easily taken because it goes against their core beliefs; yet it represents an opportunity to defend the religious values of the Salafi community. Interestingly, the exposure of electoral Salafism to democratic ideas and norms could possibly influence the future of the larger Salafi movement.

Third, I argue that justice is a universal idea with religious and philosophical foundations that Islamist militants have utilized as a master frame. It consists of three main components: moral and ethical principles, equality, and the responsibility to protect. Both Shia and Sunni groups have employed justice as a master frame because it can mobilize Muslims and legitimize their sectarian cause.

Hizb'allah and the Mahdi Army have systematically used the justice master frame for the purpose of gathering support and gaining legitimacy against adversaries. They have engaged in sectarian campaigns in Syria and Iraq, although they are supposed to represent all Muslims. This apparent paradox has been reconciled by the employment of the justice master frame. The concept of justice has been deep-rooted in the Shia tradition since the early Islamic period. Despite the targeting of heterodox populations, Shia militants stress equality among Muslims and claim a responsibility to protect their communities and allies.

Likewise, the Sunni militants of ISIS and al-Nusra have embraced justice as a master frame and have attempted to apply it locally. In this way, they could defend their actions in Syria and Iraq as a justice-seeking quest sanctioned by Sharia and defined by its moral and ethical principles. Sunni militants have endorsed the component of equality selectively, since they do not consider non-Sunni Muslims as part of the umma. They have affirmed their intent to protect Sunni communities because they carry a godly mission. From their point of view, justice is both a means and an end.

The use of human rights, democracy, and justice master frames shows that political Islam is not that different from other social movements. However, the application of these cognitive schemata is not always a well-defined exercise. Islamist activists have often instrumentalized human rights in the name of pursuing a Sharia-based justice. Some Islamo-democrats have viewed respect for human rights, however they define them, as a necessary prerequisite for the democratization of authoritarian regimes and the creation of a just society. And Islamist militants have sought justice to safeguard collective rights.

Furthermore, the list of Islamist parties and groups that have functioned as agents of glocalization is far from exhaustive. In fact, it can be argued that most Islamists negotiate between the global and the local. Yet the particularization of Islamism precludes any meaningful convergence among activists, politicians, and militants. The growing divisions within the Muslim world make the much-desired return to the authentic Islam of the seventh century an almost impossible endeavor. Globalization, Mahmood Monshipouri writes, poses a central challenge to the issue of authenticity: Muslim communities have to balance tenets and traditions with modern standards and practices in order to exercise their power and maintain their values in global contexts.[1] Consequently, the new political Islam stands between global ideas and local realities. It is a dynamic manifestation of our glocalized world.

The question that naturally arises is what approach Western democracies should take toward the new political Islam. In the immediate post-9/11 period, there was a heated debate in the United States and Europe emphasizing the role of Islamist militants over those who do not use violence. However, the new political Islam is a diverse and acephalous movement that has proved to be highly adaptive to global processes and local circumstances.

For instance, Islamist politicians have joined the democratic process and in some cases even won power and gained the dismissal of secularists. The political victories of Islamists in Turkey, Egypt, and Tunisia have proved that Islam can coexist with democracy. The drive toward democracy reflects the new realities in some parts of the Muslim world. An opinion poll conducted by the University of Maryland found that an overwhelming 82 percent of Egyptians believed that democracy was a good way of governing the country.[2] Yet it may take years for democracy to take root in the

Middle East. It is hard to disagree with Eytan Gilboa's suggestion that "elections should be the last step in the democratization transition, not the first, and that they should be held only after most of the conditions for a viable democracy are put in place."[3] While Islam is certainly compatible with democracy, some Islamists will never accept an ideology and system supported by the West.

Liberal democracies can relatively easily formulate a strategy vis-à-vis militants, but it is more difficult when it comes to those who eschew violence. Islamist politicians now use concepts and norms that the Western world cherishes. Fawaz Gerges has argued that there are two schools of thoughts in the United States in regard to political Islam: the confrontationalists and accommodationists. The former a priori view Islamists as an expansionist and monolithic enemy, while the latter consider political Islam as a highly diverse movement with many different expressions.[4]

During George W. Bush's presidency, the United States was drawn into a conflict with Islamist militants in Afghanistan, Iraq, and elsewhere. As result, U.S. relations with the Muslim world reached a low point. The Obama administration tried to contain the damage. On June 4, 2009, Barack Obama gave a historic speech in Cairo. The U.S. president asked for "a new beginning between the United States and Muslims around the world, one based on mutual interest and mutual respect, and one based upon the truth that America and Islam are not exclusive and need not be in competition. Instead, they overlap, and share common principles—principles of justice and progress; tolerance and the dignity of all human beings."[5] It was not a coincidence that he mentioned human rights, justice, and the democratic principle of tolerance. President Obama emphasized those concepts and norms that are gaining acceptance in Muslim societies.

Nonetheless, the United States has maintained an ambiguous stance toward some Islamo-democrats. Although the Obama administration initially condemned the military coup against the democratically elected president Morsi in Egypt, it finally came to recognize the new authorities.[6] Geopolitical considerations seem to have played some role in this decision. At the same time, the United States has refused to designate the Muslim Brotherhood as a terrorist group.[7] The logic is obvious: the power of Islamo-democrats is a challenge for Islamist militants. Indeed, al-Qaeda was taken by surprise by the events of the Arab Spring; Osama bin Laden himself admitted that "the umma always directed its face in expectation of victory which began to show in the east, and all of a sudden the sun of revolutions came from the west."[8] Although al-Qaeda welcomed the overthrow of Mubarak and Ben Ali, it did not endorse democracy and human rights. The empowerment of people through the electoral process could undermine the raison d'être of Islamist militants and marginalize them politically.

Therefore, it is essential to acknowledge the diversity that exists within the world of political Islam. Militants represent in absolute numbers only a tiny minority of Islamists. In fact, the demonization of Islamism is counterproductive and morally wrong. Several religions have given birth to social movements and ideologies; Islam has been hardly unique in this regard. In the United States, the Christian Right has fought many cultural wars over education and family. Many organizations and prominent Christian leaders have campaigned for the banning of abortion and have supported a Christian curriculum in American public schools. In France, the legalization of same-sex marriages created a huge wave of protests in 2013. Despite decades of secularization, an important part of French society remains deeply religious and attached to traditional Catholic values. In Israel, ultra-Orthodox Jews have become an important force in the society and the political system. In Sri Lanka, Burma, and Thailand, Buddhist monks have taken a leading political role in confronting religious minorities, particularly Muslims. The Bharatiya Janata Party, which openly campaigned for the rights of the Hindu population over Muslims and Christians, won the Indian parliamentary elections of 2014.

Since political Islam is a diverse movement, a monolithic treatment of Islamists is not the most suitable approach. Hizb ut-Tahrir and other similar groups stand as an example of nonviolent Islamist activism that Western governments should tolerate. Moreover, Islamo-democrats can almost be viewed as the equivalent of Christian Democrats in the postwar period. Like them, they support religion-based ethics and favor a probusiness agenda without seeking to abolish the secular character of the state. The recognition of Islamo-democrats as potential partners can become a game-changing factor for U.S. policy in the Middle East. Some analysts have already accepted the prominence of the Islamist factor in Middle Eastern politics. Jonathan Broder has rightly pointed out that "the West will have to get used to political Islam as a major force in the Middle East."[9]

Unfortunately, the recent election of Donald Trump as the president is likely to stir new tensions between the United States and Islamists. Although he has advocated a more isolationist foreign policy, his political investment in Islamophobia leaves little hope for a modus vivendi with Islamist activists and politicians. But confrontation does not have to be the only outcome. Indeed, accommodation is possible if the United States and other Western countries acknowledge the glocalization of political Islam. This movement of movements has been susceptible to changes and influences like the rest of the world, but is here to stay.

Notes

Preface

1. Farhad Khosrokhavar, *The New Arab Revolutions That Shook the World* (London: Paradigm, 2012), 103.

2. Charles Hirschkind, "What Is Political Islam," *Middle East Report* 27 (1997), http://www.merip.org/mer/mer205/what-political-islam.

3. On Sufi Islam, see Annemarie Schimmel, *Mystical Dimensions of Islam* (Chapel Hill: University of North Carolina Press, 1975).

4. Ammar Ali Hassan, "Anatomy of Sufism," *Al-Ahran*, August 27, 2009, http://weekly.ahram.org.eg/2009/962/feature.htm.

5. Nazih Ayobi, *Political Islam: Religion and Politics in the Arab World* (London: Routledge, 1991), ix.

6. Guilain Denoeux, "The Forgotten Swamp: Navigating Political Islam," *Middle East Policy* 9, no. 2 (June 2002): 61.

7. Frederic Volpi, "Critically Studying Political Islam," in *Political Islam: A Critical Reader*, ed. Frederic Volpi (London: Routledge, 2011), 1.

8. Daniel M. Varisco, "Mitigating Misrepresentation," in *Islamism: Contested Perspectives on Political Islam*, ed. Richard C. Martin and Abbas Barzegar (Stanford, Calif.: Stanford University Press, 2010), 130.

9. Charles Tripp, "All (Muslim) Politics Is Local," *Foreign Affairs*, September-October 2009, http://www.foreignaffairs.com/articles/65229/charles-tripp/all-muslim-politics-is-local.

10. Paul M. Lubeck, "The Islamic Revival: Antinomies of Islamic Movements Under Globalization," in *Global Social Movements*, ed. Robin Cohen and Shirin M. Rai (London: Athlone Press, 2000), 154.

11. "The Future of World Religions: Population Growth Projections, 2010–2050," Pew Research Center, April 2, 2015, http://www.pewforum.org/2015/04/02/religious-projections-2010-2050/.

12. Sunni Islam has four schools of jurisprudence, namely Hanafi, Maliki, Shafi'i, and Hanbali. Shia Islam has two main schools of jurisprudence: the Ja'fari and the Ismaili.

13. Olivier Leaman, "Is Globalization a Threat to Islam? Said Nursi's Response," in *Globalization, Ethics and Islam: The Case of Bediuzzaman Said Nursi*, ed. Ian Markham and Ibrahim Ozdemir (London: Ashgate, 2005), 123.

14. See, for example, J. Spencer Trimingham, *Islam in Ethiopia* (London: Routledge, 1965); Bruce Privratsky, *Muslim Turkistan: Kazak Religion and Collective Memory* (London: Routledge, 2001); Rajeswary Ampalavanar Brown, *Islam in Modern Thailand: Faith, Philanthropy and Politics* (London: Routledge, 2013).

15. The Central Media Office of Hizb ut-Tahrir, "Open Communiqué to the Mayors of Antwerp, Mechelen, Vilvoorde, and Mazaak and to the Intellectuals and Politicians in Belgium," September 29, 2013, http://www.hizb-australia.org/global-da-wah/item/921-open-communique-to-the-mayors-of-antwerp-mechelen-vilvoorde-and-mazaak-and-to-the-intellectuals-and-politicians-in-belgium.

16. Gudrun Kramer, "Islamist notions of Democracy," *Middle East Report* 23, no. 4 (1993), http://www.merip.org/mer/mer183/islamist-notions-democracy.

17. "FJP: We Defend Democracy, Elected President a Red Line," *IkhwanWeb: The Muslim Brotherhood's Official English web site*, June 30, 2013, http://www.ikhwanweb.com/article.php?id=31063&ref=search.php.

18. "Muslim Brotherhood Praises Pro-Democracy Brussels Declaration," *Ikhwan-Web*, May 13, 2014, http://www.ikhwanweb.com/article.php?id=31653&ref=search.php.

19. "President Morsi—Symbol of Freedom, Icon for Democracy," *IkhwanWeb*, November 8, 2013, http://www.ikhwanweb.com/article.php?id=31406.

20. Lina Khatib, Dina Matar, and Atef Alshaer, *The Hizbullah Phenomenon: Politics and Communication* (Oxford: Oxford University Press, 2014), 49.

21. "Sayyed Nasrallah: Resistance Might Take Control of Galilee in Future War," February 18, 2011, http://www.almanar.com.lb/english/adetails.php?eid=2651&cid=23&fromval=1&frid=23&seccatid=14&s1=1.

22. "Sayyed Nasrallah: As I Always Promised You Victory, I Now Promise You Another One," May 29, 2013, http://www.almanar.com.lb/english/adetails.php?fromval=3&cid=101&frid=23&seccatid=14&eid=95549.

23. Maulana Muhammad Ali, *The Holy Quran*, 4th revised ed. (Lahore: Ahmadiyya Anjuman Isha'at Islam Lahore, 1951).

24. Richard Netton, *A Popular Dictionary of Islam* (London: RoutledgeCurzon, 1997).

Introduction

Note to epigraph: Zareena Grewal, *Islam Is a Foreign Country: American Muslims and the Global Crisis of Authority* (New York: New York University Press, 2013), 152.

1. See, for example, Joel Beinin and Joe Stork, eds., *Political Islam* (Berkeley: University of California Press, 1997); John L. Esposito, ed., *Political Islam: Revolution, Radicalism or Reform?* (Boulder, Colo.: Lynne Rienner, 1997); Valentine M. Moghadam, *Globalization and Social Movements: Islamism, Feminism and the Global Justice Movement*, 2nd ed. (Lanham, Md.: Rowman and Littlefield, 2013).

2. See, for example, Robert Gilpin, *The Challenge of Global Capitalism* (Princeton, N.J.: Princeton University Press, 2002); John Baylis, Steve Smith, and Patricia Owens, *The Globalization of World Politics*, 4th ed. (Oxford: Oxford University Press, 2008).

3. Gilles Trudeau, "Industrial Relations and Globalization: Some Reflections Based on the Canadian Experience," in *Which "Global Village"? Societies, Cultures and Socio-Political Systems in a Euro-Atlantic Perspective*, ed. Valeria Gennaro Lerda (Westport, Conn.: Praeger, 2002), 63.

4. Victor Roudometof, "Transnationalism, Cosmopolitanism and Glocalization," *Current Sociology* 53, no.1 (2005): 115.

5. Riccardo Fiorentini and Guido Montani, *The New Global Political Economy: From Crisis to Supranational Integration* (Cheltenham, U.K.: Edward Elgar, 2012), 79.

6. See, for example, Paul Hirst and Grahame Thompson, *Globalization in Question: The International Economy and the Possibilities of Governance* (Cambridge: Polity Press, 1996), 2.

7. See, for example, Jan A. Scholte, *Globalization: A Critical Introduction* (London: Macmillan, 2000); John Tomlinson, *Globalization and Culture* (Cambridge: Polity Press, 2000).

8. Anthony Giddens, *The Consequences of Modernity* (Stanford, Calif.: Stanford University Press, 1990), 64.

9. Alex Inkele, *One World Emerging* (Boulder, Colo.: Westview Press, 1998), xiv.

10. On ontological security, see Catarina Kinnvall, "Globalization and Religious Nationalism: Self, Identity, and the Search for Ontological Security," *Political Psychology* 25, no. 5 (2004): 741–763.

11. Susan Olzak, "Does Globalization Breed Ethnic Discontent?" *Journal of Conflict Resolution* 55, no. 1 (2011): 3–32.

12. Julia Elliott and Elizabeth Knowles, *The Oxford Dictionary of New Words* (Oxford: Oxford University Press, 1997).

13. See, for example, Ronald Robertson, "Situating Glocalization: A Relatively Autobiographical Intervention," in *Global Themes and Local Variations in Organization and Management: Perspectives on Glocalization*, ed. Gili S. Drori, Markus A. Hollerer, and Peter Walgenbach (New York: Routledge, 2014), 25–36.

14. See, for example, Marwan Kraidy, "The Local, the Global, and the Hybrid: A Native Ethnography of Glocalization," *Critical Studies in Media Communication* 16, no. 4 (1999): 456–477; Alice Y. L. Lee, "Between the Global and the Local: The Glocalization of Online News Coverage on the Transregional Crisis of SARS," *Asian Journal of Communication* 15, no. 3 (2005): 255–273; Richard Giulianotti and Roland Robertson, "Forms of Glocalization: Globalization and Migration Strategies of Scottish Football Fans in North America," *Sociology* 41, no. 1 (2007): 133–152; Isabel Jijon, "The Glocalization of Time and Space: Soccer and Meaning in Chota Valley, Ecuador," *International Sociology* 28 (2013): 373–390.

15. Barry Wellman, "Little Boxes, Glocalization and Networked Individualism," in *Digital Cities II: Computational and Sociological Approaches*, ed. Makoto Tanabe, Peter van den Besselaar, and Toru Ishida (New York: Springer, 2002), 13.

16. Fruma Zachs, "Cross-Glocalization: Syrian Women Immigrants and the Founding of Women's Magazines in Egypt," *Middle Eastern Studies* 50, no. 3 (2014): 353.

17. Wayne Gabardi, *Negotiating Postmodernism* (Minneapolis: University of Minnesota Press, 2001), 33.

18. William H. Thornton, "Mapping the 'Glocal' Village: The Political Limits of Glocalization," *Continuum: Journal of Media and Cultural Studies* 14, no. 1 (2000): 82.

19. Ronald Robertson, "Glocalization: Time-Space and Homogeneity-Heterogeneity," in *Readings in Globalization: Key Concepts and Major Debates*, ed. George Ritzer and Zeynep Atalay (Oxford: Wiley-Blackwell, 2010), 334.

20. Charles Tilly, *Social Movements 1768–2004* (London: Paradigm, 2004), 102.

21. Robertson, "Glocalization," 342.

22. Sayyid Jamal al-Din al-Afghani, "An Islamic Response to Imperialism," in *Islam in Transition: Muslim Perspectives*, ed. John J. Donahue and John L. Esposito (New York: Oxford University Press, 1982), 16–20.

23. Hunt Janin, *The Pursuit of Learning in the Islamic World, 610–2003* (Jefferson, N.C.: McFarland, 2005), 144.

24. Antony Black, *The History of Islamic Political Thought: From the Prophet to the Present* (Edinburgh: Edinburgh University Press, 2011), 314–317.

25. Souad T. Ali, *A Religion, Not a State: Ali Abd al-Raziq's Islamic Justification of Political Secularism* (Salt Lake City: University of Utah Press, 2009).

26. On Hasan al-Banna's internationalism, see A. Z. al-Abdin, "The Political Thought of Hasan al-Banna," *Islamic Studies* 28, no. 3 (Autumn 1989): 219–234.

27. Carrie Rosefsky Wickham, *The Muslim Brotherhood: Evolution of an Islamist Movement* (Princeton, N.J.: Princeton University Press, 2013), 27–33.

28. See Raphaël Lefèvre, *Ashes of Hama: The Muslim Brotherhood in Syria* (London: Hurst, 2013); Marion Boulby, *The Muslim Brotherhood and the Kings of Jordan, 1945–1993* (Atlanta: Scholars Press, 1999).

29. On the Iranian Revolution, see John L. Esposito, *The Islamic Revolution: Its Global Impact* (Miami: Florida International University Press, 1990).

30. See Imam Khomeini, *Islam and Revolution: Writings and Declarations of Imam Khomeini* (Berkeley, Calif.: Mizan Press, 1981).

31. See Jonathan Randal, *Osama: The Making of a Terrorist* (New York: Vintage, 2005).

32. On the limited role of the Arabs in the anti-Soviet insurgency, see Thomas Hegghammer, "The Rise of Muslim Foreign Fighters: Islam and the Globalization of Jihad," *International Security* 35, no. 3 (Winter 2010–2011): 63.

33. See chapter 5.

34. On Hamas, see Matthew Levitt and Dennis Ross, *Hamas: Politics, Charity, and Terrorism in the Service of Jihad* (New Heaven, Conn.: Yale University Press, 2007).

35. Olivier Roy was probably the first to use the term *Islamo-nationalists* to describe the blurring of nationalism and Islamism in the Middle East. See Olivier Roy, *Globalized Islam: The Search for New Ummah* (New York: Columbia University Press, 2004), 62–66.

36. See, for example, Fawaz Gerges, *The Far Enemy: Why Jihad Went Global* (Cambridge: Cambridge University Press, 2005); Gilles Kepel, *Jihad: The Trail of Political Islam* (London: I. B. Tauris, 2006).

37. Ahmed Rashid, *Militant Islam, Oil and Fundamentalism in Central Asia*, 2nd ed. (New Haven, Conn.: Yale University Press, 2010), 128–142.

38. Roy, *Globalized Islam*, 63 and 238.

39. Madawi al-Rasheed, "The Local and the Global in Saudi Salafi-Jihadi Discourse," in *Global Salafism: Islam's New Islamic Movement*, ed. Roel Meijer (London: Hurst, 2009), 307.

40. Roy, *Globalized Islam*, book synopsis.

41. Frederic Volpi, "Introduction: Critically Studying Political Islam," in *Political Islam: A Critical Reader*, ed. Frederic Volpi (London: Routledge, 2011), 5.

42. Peter Mandaville, *Transnational Muslim Politics: Reimagining the Umma* (London: Routledge, 2001), 188.

43. On the importance of the Bosnian war for Muslim awareness, see Akbar S. Ahmed and Hastings Donnan, "Islam in the Age of Postmodernity," in *Islam, Globalization and Postmodernity*, ed. Akbar S. Ahmed and Hastings Donnan (London: Routledge, 1994), 7.

44. See, for example, Marc Sageman, *Leaderless Jihad: Terror Networks in the Twenty-First Century* (Philadelphia: University of Pennsylvania Press, 2008); Mariam Abou Zahab and Olivier Roy, *Islamist Networks: The Afghan-Pakistan Connection* (New York: Columbia University Press, 2006).

45. Davot Malet, *Foreign Fighters: Transnational Identity in Civil Conflicts* (Oxford: Oxford University Press, 2013), 203.

46. See Michael Willis, *The Islamist Challenge in Algeria: A Political History* (New York: New York University Press, 1999).

47. See Cerwyn Moore and Paul Tumelty, "Foreign Fighters and the Case of Chechnya: A Critical Assessment," *Studies in Conflict and Terrorism* 31, no. 5 (May 2008): 412–433.

48. David D. Kirkpatrick, "In Egypt, No Alliance with Ultraconservatives, Islamist Party Says," *New York Times*, December 1, 2011, http://www.nytimes.com/2011/12/02/world/middleeast/egypts-muslim-brotherhood-keeps-distance-from-salafis.html.

49. Hasnain Kazim and Maximilian Popp, "Dangerous Friends: Power Struggle Splits Turkish Ruling Party," *Spiegel Online International*, August 21, 2013, http://www.spiegel.de/international/europe/power-struggle-splits-erdogan-ruling-akp-party-in-turkey-a-917823.html.

50. Aaron Y. Zelin, "The War Between ISIS and Al-Qaeda for Supremacy of the Global Jihadist Movement," Washington Institute, *Research Notes* 20, June 2014, http://www.washingtoninstitute.org/policy-analysis/view/the-war-between-isis-and-al-qaeda-for-supremacy-of-the-global-jihadist.

51. Victor Roudometof, "Glocalization, Space, and Modernity," *European Legacy* 8, no. 1 (2003): 45.

52. J. K. Gibson-Graham, "Beyond Global vs. Local: Economic Politics Outside the Binary Frame," in *Geographies of Power: Placing Scale*, ed. Andrew Herod and Melissa W. Wright (Malden, Mass.: Wiley-Blackwell, 2002), 32–33.

53. See Bernard Lewis, *What Went Wrong? The Clash Between Islam and Modernity in the Middle East* (New York: HarperCollins, 2003).

54. Kant argued that the modern world is one in which "the peoples of the earth have entered in varying degrees into a universal community, and it has developed to the point where a violation of the rights in one part of the world is felt everywhere." See Immanuel Kant, *Political Writings* (Cambridge: Cambridge University Press, 1991), 107–108.

55. Johan Meulemanv, "South-East Islam and the Globalization Process," in *Islam in the Era of Globalization*, ed. Johan Meulemanv (London: Routledge, 2002), 16.

56. Anthony Giddens, *The Consequences of Modernity* (Stanford, Calif.: Stanford University Press, 1990), 150.

57. See Amitai Etzioni, "Communitarianism," in *From the Village to the Virtual World*, ed. Karen Christensen (London: Sage, 2003), 226.

58. On Islamism and communitarianism, see Filippo Dionigi, *Hezbollah, Islamist Politics, and International Society* (London: Palgrave Macmillan, 2014), 65–81.

59. "9/11 George Bush—This Crusade is Gonna Take A While," NBC, September 16, 2001, https://www.youtube.com/watch?v = 7TRVcnX8Vsw.

60. See, for example, "Muslim-Western Tensions Persist," Pew Research Global Attitudes Project, July 21, 2011, http://www.pewglobal.org/2011/07/21/muslim-western-tensions-persist/.

61. Steven Kull, "Muslim Public Opinion on U.S. Policy, Attacks on Civilians and Al-Qaeda," WorldPublicOpinion.Org, April 24, 2007, 16, http://www.worldpublicopinion.org/pipa/pdf/apr07/START_Apr07_rpt.pdf.

62. See Emmanuel Karagiannis, "When the Green Gets Greener: Political Islam's Newly Found Environmentalism," *Small Wars and Insurgencies* 25, no. 5 (November 2014): 181–201.

63. Lauren Russell, "Church Plans Quran-Burning Event," CNN, July 31, 2010, http://edition.cnn.com/2010/US/07/29/florida.burn.quran.day/.

64. Samuel P. Huntington, *The Clash of Civilizations and the Remaking of the World Order* (New York: Simon and Schuster, 1996), 211.

65. Dale F. Eickelman and Jon W. Anderson, "Redefining Muslim Publics," in *New Media in the Muslim World: The Emerging Public Sphere*, ed. Dale F. Eickelman and Jon W. Anderson, 2nd ed. (Bloomington: Indiana University Press, 2003), 9.

66. Scott Shane and Ben Hubbard, "ISIS Displaying a Deft Command of Varied Media," *New York Times*, August 30, 2014, http://www.nytimes.com/2014/08/31/world/middleeast/isis-displaying-a-deft-command-of-varied-media.html?_r = 0.

67. Jason Gainous and Kevin M. Wagner, *Tweeting the Power: The Social Media Revolution in American Politics* (Oxford: Oxford University Press, 2013), 1–2.

68. Benjamin Barber, *Jihad vs. Mcworld: Terrorism's Challenge to Democracy* (London: Corgi Books, 1995).

69. Robert D. Kaplan, "The Coming Anarchy: How Scarcity, Crime, Overpopulation, Tribalism, and Disease Are Rapidly Destroying the Social Fabric of Our Planet," *Atlantic Monthly*, February 1, 1994, 44–76.

70. Tariq Ramadan, *Western Muslims and the Future of Islam* (Oxford: Oxford University Press, 2004), 4.

71. Asef Bayat, "Islamism and Social Movement Theory," *Third World Quarterly* 26 (2005): 891–908; Mohammed Hafez, *Why Muslims Rebel* (London: Lynne Rienner, 2004); Philip W. Sutton and Stephen Vertigans, "Islamic 'New Social Movements'? Radical Islam, Al-Qaeda and Social Movement Theory," *Mobilization: An International Journal* 11 (2006): 101–115; Quintan Wiktorowicz, ed., *Islamic Activism: A Social Movement Theory Approach* (Bloomington: Indiana University Press, 2004).

72. Mario Diani, "Networks and Social Movements: A Research Programme," in *Social Movements and Networks: Relational Approaches to Collective Action*, ed. Mario Diani and Doug McAdam (Oxford: Oxford University Press, 2003), 301.

73. There is an extensive literature on social movement theory. See Doug McAdam, John D. McCarthy, and Mayer Zald, ed., *Comparative Perspectives on Social Movements* (Cambridge: Cambridge University Press, 1996); Sidney Tarrow, *Power in Movement: Social Movements and Contentious Politics* (Cambridge: Cambridge University Press, 1998); David A. Snow, Sarah A. Soule, and Hanspeter Kriesi, eds., *The Blackwell Companion to Social Movements* (Oxford: Blackwell, 2004).

74. Huntington, *Clash of Civilizations*, 217–218.

75. Peter Mandaville, *Islam and Politics*, 2nd ed. (London: Routledge, 2014), 414.

76. Abdulaziz Sachedina, "Political Islam and the Hegemony of Globalization: A Response to Peter Berger," *Hedgehog Review* 4, no. 2 (Summer 2002): 28.

77. Ahmed and Donnan, "Islam in the Age of Postmodernity," 2.

78. Robertson, "Glocalization," 342.

79. George Ritzer, *Globalization: A Basic Text* (London: Wiley-Blackwell, 2009), 254.

80. International Crisis Group, *Understanding Islamism* (Brussels: IGC, 2005), 3–4.

81. See Hakan Yavuz, *Islamic Political Identity in Turkey* (New York: Oxford University Press, 2003), 15–36.

82. Gili S. Drori, Markus A. Hollerer, and Peter Walgenbach, "Unpacking the Glocalization of Organization: From Term, to Theory, to Analysis," *European Journal of Cultural and Political Sociology* 1, no. 1 (2014): 92.

83. Wiktorowicz, *Islamic Activism*, 2.

84. International Crisis Group, *Understanding Islamism*, 1.

85. Joshua D. Hendrick, "The Regulated Potential of Kinetic Islam: Antitheses in Global Islamic Activism," in *Muslim Citizens of the Globalized World: Contributions of*

the Gülen Movement, ed. Robert A. Hunt and Yüksel A. Aslandogan (Somerset, N.J.: The Light, 2007), 12.

86. Samuel Moyn, *The Last Utopia: Human Rights in History* (Cambridge, Mass.: Harvard University Press, 2010), 118.

87. Francis Fukuyama, "The West Has Won: Radical Islam Cannot Beat Democracy and Capitalism: We're Still at the End of History," *Guardian*, October 11, 2001, http://www.theguardian.com/world/2001/oct/11/afghanistan.terrorism30.

88. On the liberal idea, see Francis Fukuyama, *The End of History and the Last Man* (London: Hamish Hamilton, 1992), 45.

89. See Khalid al-Anani, "Islamist Parties Post-Arab Spring," *Mediterranean Politics* 17, no. 3 (2012): 466–472 and Tarek Chamkhi, "Neo-Islamism in the post-Arab Spring," *Contemporary Politics* 20, no. 4 (2014): 453–468.

90. See Olivier Roy, *The Failure of Political Islam* (Cambridge, Mass.: Harvard University Press, 1994).

91. I borrowed this idea from Thomas Olesen, "The Uses and Misuses of Globalization in the Study of Social Movements," *Social Movement Studies* 4, no. 1 (2005): 50.

92. Doug McAdam, "Introduction: Opportunities, Mobilizing Structures, and Framing Processes –Toward a Synthetic, Comparative Perspective on Social Movements," in McAdam, McCarthy, and Zald, *Comparative Perspectives on Social Movements*, 6.

93. Doug McAdam, "Culture and Social Movements," in *New Social Movements: From Ideology to Identity*, ed. Enrique Larana, Hank Johnston, and Joseph R. Gusfield (Philadelphia: Temple University Press, 1994), 37.

94. See Erving Goffman, *Frame Analysis* (Cambridge, Mass.: Harvard University Press, 1974).

95. See Scott A. Hunt, Robert D. Benford, and David A. Snow, "Identity Fields: Framing Processes and the Social Construction of Movement Identities," in *New Social Movements: From Ideology to Identity: From Ideology to Identity*, ed. Enrique Larana, Hank Johnston, and Joseph R. Gusfield (Philadelphia: Temple University Press, 1994), 185–208.

96. David A. Snow and Robert D. Benford, "Ideology, Frame Resonance, and Participant Mobilization," *International Social Movement Research* 1 (1988): 197–218.

97. Members of Hizb ut-Tahrir in Britain, *The Method to Re-establish the Khilafah and Resume the Islamic Way of Life* (London: Al-Khilafah Publications, 2000), 120.

98. David A. Snow and Robert D. Benford, "Master Frames and Cycles of Protest," in *Frontiers in Social Movement Theory*, ed. Aldon D. Morris and Carol McClurg Mueller (New Haven, Conn.: Yale University Press, 1992).

99. Pamela E. Oliver and Hank Johnston, "What a Good Idea! Ideologies and Frames in Social Movement Research," in *Frames of Protest: Social Movements and the Framing Perspective*, ed. Hank Johnston and John A. Noakes (Lanham, MD.: Rowman and Littlefield, 2005), 189.

100. William K. Carroll and R. S Ratner, "Master Framing and Cross-Movement Networking in Contemporary Social Movements," *Sociological Quarterly* 37, no. 4 (1996): 602–603.

101. Hank Johnston, *Tales of Nationalism: Catalonia, 1939–1979* (New Brunswick, N.J.: Rutgers University Press, 1991).

102. Stella M. Capek, "Environmental Justice Frame: A Conceptual Discussion and Application," *Social Problems* 40, no. 1 (1993): 5–24.

103. Shoshana Blum-Kulka and Tamar Liebes, "Frame Ambiguities: Intifada Narrativization of the Experience by Israeli Soldiers," in *Framing the Intifada: People and Media*, ed. Akiba A. Cohen and Gadi Wolsfeld (Norwood, N.J.: Ablex, 1993), 27–52.

104. Oliver and Johnston, "What a Good Idea!" 198.

105. Lawrence P. Markowitz, "How Master Frames Mislead: The Division and Eclipse of Nationalist Movements in Uzbekistan and Tajikistan," *Ethnic and Racial Studies* 32, no. 4 (May 2009): 716–738.

106. Emmanuel Karagiannis, "Making New Friends: Explaining Greek Radical Left's Political Support for Middle Eastern Islamists," *Dynamics of Asymmetric Conflict* 5, no 3 (2012): 183–195.

107. Robert D. Benford and David A Snow, "Framing Processes and Social Movements: An Overview and Assessment, *Annual Review of Sociology* 26, (2000): 618.

108. Hank Johnston, "Verification and Proof in Frame and Discourse Analysis," in *Methods of Social Movement Research*, ed. Bert Klandermans and Suzanne Staggenborg (Minneapolis: University of Minnesota Press, 2002), 66.

109. Ralph H. Turner, "Ideology and Utopia After Socialism," in *New Social Movements: From Ideology to Identity*, ed. Enrique Larana, Hank Johnston, and Joseph R. Gusfield (Philadelphia: Temple University Press, 1994), 79.

110. Carol Anderson, *Eyes Off the Prize: African Americans, the United Nations, and the Struggle for Human Rights, 1944–1955* (Cambridge: Cambridge University Press, 2003).

111. Olesen, "Uses and Misuses of Globalization," 56.

112. Anthony Oberschall, "Opportunities and Framing in the Eastern European Revolts of 1989," in *Comparative Perspectives on Social Movements*, ed. Doug McAdam, John D. McCarthy, and Mayer Zald (Cambridge: Cambridge University Press, 1996), 104.

113. On the eightieth anniversary of the Easter Rising of 1916, the Irish Republican Army declared that "the British denial of democracy in Ireland is at the core of the conflict. The resolution of that conflict demands justice." See Irish Republican Army, "Easter Statement," April 7, 1996, http://cain.ulst.ac.uk/events/peace/docs/ira070496.htm.

Part I

1. See Louis Henkin, *The Age of Rights* (New York: Columbia University Press, 1990).

2. Thorsten Bonacker et al., "Human Rights and the (De)securitization of Conflict," in *Civil Society, Conflicts and the Politicization of Human Rights*, ed. Raffaelle Marchetti and Nathalie Tocci (New York: United Nations University Press), 31.

3. Nisrine Abiad, *Shariah, Muslim States and International Human Rights Treaty Obligations: A Comparative Study* (London: British Institute of International and Comparative Law, 2008), 60.

4. Ibid.

5. David G. Littman, "Human Rights and Human Wrongs," *National Review Online*, January 19, 2003, http://www.nationalreview.com/articles/205577/human-rights-and-human-wrongs/david-g-littman.

6. See Zayn al-Abidin, *The Treatise on Rights: Risalat-al-huquq* (Hyderabad: Al-Shaheed Publications, 1992).

7. Muhammad Khalid Masud, "Muslim Perspectives on Global Ethics," in *The Globalization of Ethics: Religious and Secular Perspectives*, ed. William M. Sullivan and Will Kymlicka (Cambridge: Cambridge University Press, 2007), 98.

8. Ibid., 100.

9. Valerie Hoffman, "Islam, Human Rights and Interfaith Relations: Some Contemporary Egyptian Perspectives," in *Islamic Political and Social Movements*, ed. Barry Rubin (London: Routledge, 2013), 87.

10. Ibid.

11. Abdolkarim Soroush, *Reason, Freedom, and Democracy in Islam* (Oxford: Oxford University Press, 2000), 129–130.

12. Syed Abul A'la Maududi, "Human Rights in Islam," *vazhionline.com*, 3, http://vazhi.vazhionline.com/files/elibrary/english/003_Human%20Rights%20in%20Islam.pdf.

13. Ibid.

14. Masud, "Muslim Perspectives on Global Ethics," 107.

15. Ibid., 108.

16. Ali Unal and Alphonse Williams, eds., *Fethullah Gülen: Advocate of Dialogue* (Fairfax, Va.: The Fountain, 2000), 135–138.

17. Justin Gest, *Apart: Alienated and Engaged Muslims in the West* (London: Hurst, 2010), 23.

18. Yasemin Soysal, *Limits of Citizenship: Migrants and Postnational Membership in Europe* (Chicago: University of Chicago Press, 1996), 4.

19. Roderick Leslie Brett, *Social Movements, Indigenous Politics and Democratisation in Guatemala, 1985–1996* (Leiden: Brill, 2008), 189.

20. Min Sook Heo and Cathy A. Rakowski, "Challenges and Opportunities for a Human Rights Frame in South Korea: Context and Strategizing in the Anti-Domestic Violence Movement," *Violence Against Women* 20, no. 5 (May 2014): 581–606.

21. Ronald Holzhacker, "Gay Rights Are Human Rights: The Framing of New Interpretations of International Human Rights Norms," in *The Uses and Misuses of*

Human Rights: A Critical Approach to Advocacy, ed. George Andreopoulos and Zehra F. Kabasakal Arat (New York: Palgrave Macmillan, 2014), 56.

22. See "Russian FM Urges Ukraine to Stop Human Rights Violations of Russian-Speaking Population," Tass—Russian News Agency, April 11, 2014, http://tass.ru/en/world/727499.

23. Frans Viljoen, "International Human Rights Law: A Short History," *UN Chronicle: The Magazine of the United Nations* 46, no. 1–2 (January 2009), http://unchronicle.un.org/article/international-human-rights-law-short-history/.

24. Benjamin O. Arah, "Dr. King: Politics of Civil Disobedience and the Ethics of Nonviolent Action," in *The Liberatory Thought of Martin Luther King Jr.*, ed. Robert E. Birt (Lanham, MD: Lexington Books, 2012), 281.

25. David McKittrick and David McVea, *Making Sense of the Troubles: The Story of the Conflict in Northern Ireland* (Chicago: New Amsterdam Books, 2002), 147–148.

26. Turan Kayaoglu, "Trying Islam: Muslims Before the European Court of Human Rights," *Journal of Muslim Minority Affairs* 34, no. 3 (2014): 355.

27. Mohammad Mazher Idriss, "R (Begum) v Headteacher and Governors of Denbigh High School: A Case Note," *Judicial Review* 10, no. 4 (2005): 296–302.

28. "Burqini Ruling: Court Says Schools Can Require Co-Ed Swims," *Spiegel Online International*, September 11, 2013, http://www.spiegel.de/international/germany/burqini-ruling-german-court-says-schools-can-require-co-ed-swims-a-921743.html.

29. Ivan Rioufol, "Pourquoi je suis convoqué par la Police Judiciaire," *Le Figaro*, June 10, 2013, http://blog.lefigaro.fr/rioufol/2013/06/tandis-que-la-gauche-alerte.html.

30. Kate Zebiri, "Orientalist Themes in Contemporary British Islamophobia," in *Islamophobia: The Challenge of Pluralism in the 21st Century*, ed. John L. Esposito and Ibrahim Kalin (Oxford: Oxford University Press, 2011), 175.

31. Max Fisher, "Saudi Arabia's Oppression of Women Goes Way Beyond Its Ban on Driving," *Washington Post*, October 28, 2013, http://www.washingtonpost.com/blogs/worldviews/wp/2013/10/28/saudi-arabias-oppression-of-women-goes-way-beyond-its-ban-on-driving.

32. For example, see Saeed Paivandi, *Discrimination and Intolerance in Iran's Textbooks* (Washington, D.C.: Freedom House, 2008); Farah Mihlar, "Ethnic and Religious Discrimination Big Challenge for Malaysia's Minorities," Minority Rights Group, May 25, 2011, http://www.minorityrights.org/10815/comment-amp-analysis/ethnic-and-religious-discrimination-big-challenge-for-malaysias-minorities.html; Amnesty International, "Pakistan," *Annual Report 2013*, http://www.amnesty.org/en/region/pakistan/report-2013; "Islam and Homosexuality: Straight but Narrow," *Economist*, February 4, 2012, http://www.economist.com/node/21546002.

Chapter 1

1. Emmanuel Karagiannis, "European Converts to Islam: Mechanisms of Radicalization," *Politics, Religion and Ideology* 13, no. 1 (2012): 99–100.

2. Kevin Brice, *A Minority Within a Minority: A Report on Converts to Islam in the United Kingdom* (London: Faith Matters), 2010, 24–29.

3. The word *Sufi* probably originates from the Arabic word *saaf,* meaning pure or clean. On Sufi Islam, see J. Spencer Trimingham, *The Sufi Orders in Islam* (Oxford: Oxford University Press, 1998).

4. On hybrid identities, see Keri E. Iyall Smith and Patricia Leavy, *Hybrid Identities: Theoretical and Empirical Examinations* (Leiden: Brill, 2008).

5. See John Lofland, *Doomsday Cult: a Study of Conversion, Proselytization and Maintenance of Faith* (Englewood Cliffs, N.J.: Prentice-Hall, 1966); Merrill Singer, "The Use of Folklore in Religious Conversion: The Classidic Case," *Review of Religious Research* 22, no. 2 (1980): 170–185; Lewis R. Rambo, *Understanding Religious Conversion* (New Haven, Conn.: Yale University Press, 1993).

6. John Lofland and Rodney Stark, "Becoming a World Saver: A Theory of Conversion to a Deviant Perspective," *American Sociological Review* 30 (1965): 862.

7. See Larry Poston, *Islamic Da'wah in the West: Muslim Missionary Activity and the Dynamics of Conversion of Islam* (Oxford: Oxford University Press, 1992); Anne Sophie Roald, *New Muslims in the European Context: The Experience of Scandinavian Converts* (Boston: Brill, 2004). For jihadi converts, see Farhad Khosrokhavar, *Suicide Bombers: Allah's New Martyrs* (London: Pluto Press, 2002), 206–217; Olivier Roy, "Al-Qaeda in the West as a Youth Movement: The Power of a Narrative," in *Ethno-Religious Conflict in Europe: Typologies of Radicalisation in Europe's Muslim Communities,* ed. Michael Emerson (Brussels: CEPS, 2009), 16–17; Milena Uhlmann, "European Converts to Terrorism," *Middle East Quarterly* 15 (2008): 31–37.

8. Ron Geaves, *Islam in Victorian Britain: The Life and Times of Abdullah Quilliam* (Markfield: Kube, 2010), 59–95.

9. Ali Kose, *Conversion to Islam: A Study of Native British Converts* (London: Kegan Paul International, 1996), 14.

10. Jonathan Laurence and Justin Vaisse, *Integrating Islam: Political and Religious Challenges in Contemporary France* (Washington, D.C.: Brookings Institution Press, 2006), 43.

11. See "How Many People Convert to Islam," *Economist,* September 29, 2013, http://www.economist.com/blogs/economist-explains/2013/09/economist-explains -17; Veronique Mistiaen, "Converting to Islam: British Women on Prayer, Peace and prejudice," *Guardian,* October 11, 2013, http://www.theguardian.com/world/2013/oct/ 11/islam-converts-british-women-prejudice.

12. On the concept of a religious market, see Henri Gooren, "The Religious Market Model and Conversion: Towards a New Approach," *Exchange* 35, no. 1 (2006): 39–60.

13. Olivier Roy, *Globalized Islam: The Search for New Ummah* (New York: Columbia University Press, 2004), 317.

14. Maia de la Baume, "More in France Are Turning to Islam, Challenging Nation's Idea of Itself," *New York Times,* February 3, 2013, http://www.nytimes.com/

2013/02/04/world/europe/rise-of-islamic-converts-challenges-france.html?pagewanted
=1&_r=0.

15. Bob Smietana, "Muslim Music for a New Generation? Who Says Hip-Hop Can't be Islamic?" *Huffington Post*, July 8, 2013, http://www.huffingtonpost.com/2013/07/08/muslim-music-hip-hop-country_n_3561487.html.

16. Anna Pukas, "Hunt for the White Widow," *Express*, March 7, 2012, http://www.express.co.uk/expressyourself/306587/Hunt-for-the-white-widow.

17. Veronique Mistiaen, "Converting to Islam: British Women on Prayer, Peace and Prejudice," *Guardian*, October 11, 2013, http://www.theguardian.com/world/2013/oct/11/islam-converts-british-women-prejudice.

18. Olivier Roy, "Islam in the West or Western Islam? The Disconnect of Religion and Culture," in *Political Islam: A Critical Reader*, ed. Frederic Volpi (London: Routledge, 2011), 244.

19. Gilles Kepel, *Allah in the West: Islamic Movements in America and Europe* (Stanford, Calif.: Stanford University Press, 1997), 130.

20. See "About IHRC," Islamic Human Rights Commission, http://www.ihrc.org.uk/about-ihrc.

21. Douglas Murray, "The Truth About the Islamic Human Rights Commission, Recommended by Britain's Muslim Police," *Telegraph*, January 21, 2010, http://blogs.telegraph.co.uk/news/douglasmurray/100023272/the-truth-about-the-islamic-human-rights-commission-recommended-by-britains-muslim-police/.

22. See Bradford North, *wikipedia.org*, http://en.wikipedia.org/wiki/Bradford_North_%28UK_Parliament_constituency%29#Elections_in_the_1990s.

23. Islamic Party of Britain, "Our Policies," no date, http://www.islamicparty.com/policies/policies.pdf.

24. See the Association of British Muslims, "Our Aims," http://www.aobm.org/our-aims/.

25. Jonathan Northcroft, "Service Marks Brave Devotion of Aid Worker," *Herald Scotland*, August 25, 1995, http://www.heraldscotland.com/sport/spl/aberdeen/service-marks-brave-devotion-of-aid-worker-1.665017.

26. Bureau of Democracy, Human Rights and Labor, "Finland—International Religious Freedom Report for 2013," U.S. Department of State, http://www.state.gov/j/drl/rls/irf/religiousfreedom/index.htm#wrapper.

27. Hietaneva Panu, "Leader of Finnish Islamic Party Says He was a Soviet Spy," *Helsingin Sanomat* (International Edition), November 4, 2008, http://www.hs.fi/english/article/Leader+of+Finnish+Islamic+Party+says+he+was+a+Soviet+spy/1135240796149.

28. Finnish Islamic Party, "Suomen Islamilaisen Puolueen Kannanotto Viron Rasismia Ja Fasismia Vastaan," March 3, 2009, http://www.suomenislamilainenpuolue.fi/tiedotteet.html.

29. From 711 to 1492, a great part of the Iberian Peninsula was controlled by Muslim kingdoms. For many centuries, the Andalusian city of Cordoba in southern Spain was one of the most important centers of Islamic culture.

30. Marta Dominguez Diaz, "The Islam of 'Our' Ancestors: An 'Imagined' Morisco Past Evoked in Today's Andalusian Conversion Narratives," *Journal of Muslims in Europe* 2, no. 2 (2013): 159–160.

31. "Het recht om gewoon moslim te kunnen zijn," Islam Democraten—Partijprogramma, http://stem.islamdemocraten.nl/het-recht-om-gewoon-moslim-te-kunnen-zijn/.

32. Maurits S. Berger, "The Netherlands," in *The Oxford Handbook of European Islam*, ed. Jocelyne Cesari (Oxford: Oxford University Press, 2014), 181.

33. Naim el-Ghandour, "Mosque and Cemetery: Too Much to Ask?" islamonline.net, February 13, 2009, http://archive.islamonline.net/?p=5722.

34. Bureau of Democracy, Human Rights and Labor, "Greece—International Religious Freedom Report for 2013," U.S. Department of State, http://www.state.gov/j/drl/rls/irf/religiousfreedom/index.htm#wrapper.

35. Paul Goble, "Why Are Russian Converting to Islam?" islamicity.org, 2009, http://www.islamicity.org/3551/why-are-russians-converting-to-islam/.

36. "Islamskaya Grazhdanskaya Hartiya,"ansar.ru, 2012, http://www.ansar.ru/person/islamskaya-grazhdanskaya-hartiya.

37. Ibid.

38. Khalida Khamidullina, "Musulmane trebuyut peremen," *Tatarskaya Gazeta*, 2012, http://www.tatargazeta.ru/index.php?option=com_content&view=article&id=233:2012-01-10-10-37-45&catid=4:2010-11-04-15-26-09&Itemid=11 (original link is broken).

39. Respect Party, "Civil Liberties," 2010, http://www.therespectparty.net/manifesto.php?category=CivilLiberties.

40. Yvonne Ridley, "The Passing of a Chechen," yvonneridley.org, July 10, 2006 (original link is broken: http://yvonneridley.org/yvonne-ridley/articles/the-passing-of-a-chechen-4.html), http://yvonne-ridley.blogspot.com/.

41. Yvonne Ridley, "Something Rather Repugnant," freepublic.com, November 23, 2005 (original link is broken: http://www.freerepublic.com/focus/f-news/1529185/posts).

42. Christoph Ehrhardt, "Ich bin ein Muslim jeworden," *Frankfurter Allgemeine*, September 6, 2007, http://www.faz.net/aktuell/politik/konvertiten-ick-bin-ein-muslim-jeworden-1459407.html.

43. Pierre Vogel, "16,000 Deutsche Konvertierenzum Islam," 2008, http://www.youtube.com/watch?v=Ega020cGJMc.

44. Andrea Brandt and Maximilian Popp, "Will Efforts to Train Homegrown Muslim Leaders Fail?" *Der Spiegel*, September 16, 2010, http://www.spiegel.de/international/germany/0,1518,717512,00.html.

45. Jaap van Essen, "Interview met Abdul-Jabbar in De Gelderlander," *Nova TV*, November 24, 2004, http://www.novatv.nl/page/detail/nieuws/7759/Interview+met+Abdul-Jabbar+in+De+Gelderlander+%2820+november%29.

46. See Mitchell D. Silber, *The Al Qaeda Factor: Plots Against the West* (Philadelphia: University of Pennsylvania Press, 2012).

47. Robert Mendick and Ben Lazarus, "Anti-Semitic' Charity Under Investigation," *Telegraph*, May 24, 2014, http://www.telegraph.co.uk/news/10854579/Anti -Semitic-charity-under-investigation.html.

48. Abdurraheem Green, "Mustafa Kemal Ataturk," https://videopress.com/v/ B3T4Gsli; Abdurraheem Green, "Homosexuality," https://videopress.com/v/SnW6 XKaT.

49. Souad Mekhennet, "German Officials Alarmed by Ex-Rapper's New Message: Jihad," *New York Times*, August 31, 2011, http://www.nytimes.com/2011/09/01/world/ europe/01jihadi.html?_r = 1&pagewanted = all.

50. See Benjamin Weinthal, "The Rise of a 'German Salafist Colony' in Egypt," *Long War Journal*, August 15, 2012, http://www.longwarjournal.org/archives/2012/08/ the_opening_of_a_ger.php; "Berlin Rapper in 'Islamic State' Beheading Video," *Deutsche Welle*, November 5, 2014, http://www.dw.de/about-dw/profile/s-30688.

51. Christine Hauser, "Deso Dogg, Ex-Rapper Who Joined ISIS, Is Killed by U.S. Airstrike," *New York Times*, October 15, 2015, http://www.nytimes.com/2015/10/31/ world/europe/deso-dogg-denis-cuspert-ex-rapper-who-joined-isis-is-killed-by-us -airstrike.html?_r = 1.

52. Reto Wissmann, "Islamischer Zentralrat campiert am Bielersee," *Der Bund*, June 9, 2010, http://www.derbund.ch/bern/stadt/Islamischer-Zentralrat-campiert-am -Bielersee/story/31948320.

53. Beat Rechsteiner, "Wiegefahrlichist der IslamischeZentralrat?" *Aargauer Zeitung*, May 15, 2010, http://www.aargauerzeitung.ch/schweiz/wie-gefaehrlich-ist-der -islamische-zentralrat-8621169.

54. Katia Murmann, "Hinter dem Schleier," *Der Sonntag*, June 25, 2011, http:// www.sonntagonline.ch/ressort/aktuell/1708/.

55. Ann Guenter, "Wie Extrem Sind Schwizer Islamisten?" Blick.ch, January 14, 2012, http://www.blick.ch/news/schweiz/wie-extrem-sind-schweizer-islamisten-id416 14.html.

56. "Hamza Andreas Tzortzis, Former Catholic, Greece," Islamreligion.com, October 14, 2013, http://www.islamreligion.com/videos/10368/.

57. Andrew Gilligan, "Speaker with Extremist Links to Address Detroit Bomber's Former Student Group," *Daily Telegraph*, January 18, 2010, http://www.telegraph .co.uk/education/educationnews/7012827/Speaker-with-extremist-links-to-address -Detroit-bombers-former-student-group.html.

58. Hamza Andreas Tzortzis, "A Note on the England Riots," hamzatzortzis.com, no date, http://www.hamzatzortzis.com/essays-articles/politics-current-affairs/a-note -on-the-england-riots/.

59. See Bassam Tibi, "Muslim Migrants in Europe: Between Euro-Islam and Ghettoization," in *Muslim Europe or Euro-Islam: Political Culture and Citizenship in*

the Age of Globalization, ed. Nezar Alsayyad and Manuel Castells (Boulder, Colo.: Lexington Books, 2002), 31–52.

60. Joan Smith, "The Veil Is a Feminist Issue," *Independent*, October 8, 2006, http://www.independent.co.uk/voices/commentators/joan-smith/joan-smith-the-veil -is-a-feminist-issue-419119.html.

61. Dan Bloom, "France Embroiled in Free Speech Row After Islamophobic TV Presenter Is Sacked for Saying Muslims Should Be Deported to Prevent Civil War," *MailOnLine*, December 22, 2014, http://www.dailymail.co.uk/news/article-2883275/ France-embroiled-free-speech-row-Islamophobic-TV-presenter-sacked-saying-Muslims -deported-prevent-civil-war.html.

62. Gas Mudde, *Populist Radical Right Parties* (Cambridge: Cambridge University Press, 2007), 84–86.

63. Jocelyne Cesari, "The Securitisation of Islam in Europe," CEPS Challenge Pro-gramme, Research Paper no. 15, April 2009, Centre for European Policy Studies, Brussels.

64. Ingrid Ramberg, *Islamophobia and Its Consequences on Young People* (Buda-pest: Council of Europe, 2004), 6.

65. Ann-Sofie Nyman, *Intolerance and Discrimination Against Muslims in the EU: Developments Since September 11* (Vienna: International Helsinki Federation for Human Rights, 2005), 30.

66. Pew Research Center, "Muslims in Europe: Economic Worries Top Concerns About Religious and Cultural Identity," 2006, http://www.pewglobal.org/2006/07/06/ muslims-in-europe-economic-worries-top-concerns-about-religious-and-cultural -identity/.

67. Brice, *Minority Within a Minority*, 14.

68. Ibid., 25.

69. Ibid., 30.

70. Yvonne Ridley, "How I Came to Love the Veil," yvonneridley.org, October 22, 2006 http://yvonneridley.org/2006/how-i-came-to-love-the-veil.

71. Van Essen, "Interview met Abdul-Jabbar."

72. European Monitoring Centre on Racism and Xenophobia, *Muslims in the European Union: Discrimination and Islamophobia* (Brussels: EUMC, 2006), 78.

73. The tradition of *hijrah* dates from the early Islamic period when Prophet Muhammad and his followers migrated to Medina to establish the first Islamic state.

74. "Interview mit Pierre Vogel," *20 Minuten Online*, December 10, 2009, http:// www.20min.ch/news/dossier/minarett/story/-Das-wird-ein-Erdbeben-ausloesen--11 801151.

75. Andrea Sommer, "Ich komme aus einem links-grunen Elternhaus," *Berner Zeitung*, February 16, 2012, http://www.bernerzeitung.ch/schweiz/standard/Ich-komme -aus-einem-linksgruenen-Elternhaus/story/19946069.

76. Yvonne Ridley, "Re-drawing the Battle Lines," *Analysis and Opinion*, no date, http://yvonneridley.org/analysis-and-opinion/re-drawing-the-battle-lines/.

77. Von Abdel Azziz Qaasim Illi, "Fall Christine Dietrich: Islamophobie ist Keiner Politischen Gesinnung Eigen," Islamischer Zentralrat Schweiz, September 28, 2011, http://www.izrs.ch/fall-christine-dietrich-islamophobie-ist-keiner-politischen-gesin nung-eigen.html.

78. Katia Murmann, "Hinter dem Schleier," *Der Sonntag*, June 25, 2011, http:// www.sonntagonline.ch/ressort/aktuell/1708/.

79. Pierre Vogel, "Holocaust gegen Muslime und die Propagandamethoden von Adolf Hitler," December 26, 2012, https://www.youtube.com/watch?v = QDUiq45 waKA.

80. Abdurraheem Green, "Freedom to Choose or Not to Choose Religion," June 1, 2014, http://tifrib.com/2014/06/01/abdurraheem-green-rejects-universal-declara tion-of-human-rights/.

81. Gilligan, "Speaker with Extremist Links."

82. Hamza Andreas Tzortzis, "Is Jihad Terrorism?" June 20, 2010, https://www .facebook.com/notes/worshippers-of-allah-the-one-and-only/is-jihad-terrorism/397 315383308.

83. Hamza Andreas Tzortzis, "Edifying Statement on Islamic State Group and Islamic Values," *iera.org*, September 4, 2014, http://www.iera.org/media/press-releases/ edifying-statement-islamic-state-group.

84. Pierre Vogel, "Menschenrechte im Islam: Rechte für die ganze Menschheit," September 2, 2013, https://www.facebook.com/PierreVogelOffiziell/posts/531898736 889864.

85. Ibid.

86. Green, "Freedom to Choose."

87. Islamic Central Council of Switzerland, "Islamophobie in der Schweiz," June 20, 2011, http://www.izrs.ch/islamophobie-in-der-schweiz.html.

88. Yvonne Ridley, "Stay Human—Support Gaza," *Analysis and Opinion*, no date, http://yvonneridley.org/analysis-and-opinion/stay-human-support-gaza/.

89. Finnish Islamic Party, suomenislamilainenpuolue.fi, October 27, 2014, http:// www.suomenislamilainenpuolue.fi/etuen.html.

Chapter 2

1. See Reza Pankhurst, *Hizb Ut Tahrir: The Untold History of the Liberation Party* (London: Hurst, 2016), 17–35.

2. Taqiuddin an-Nabhani, *Concepts of Hizb ut-Tahrir* (London: Al-Khilafah, no date), 76.

3. Suha Taji-Farouki, *A Fundamental Quest: Hizb ut-Tahrir and the Search for the Islamic Caliphate* (London: Grey Seal, 1996), 6.

4. Amnon Cohen, *Political Parties in the West Bank Under the Jordanian Regime, 1949–1967* (Ithaca, N.Y.: Cornell University Press, 1982), 210.

5. Members of Hizb ut-Tahrir in Britain, *The Method to Re-establish the Khilafah and Resume the Islamic Way of Life* (London: Al-Khilafah Publications, 2000), 120.

6. Hizb ut-Tahrir, *The Methodology of Hizb ut-Tahrir for Change* (London: Al Khilafah Publications, 1999), 32.

7. "British Born Tel-Aviv Bombers," *Khilafah Magazine*, June 2003, 18.

8. Manuela Paraipan, "Hizb ut-Tahrir: An Interview with Imran Waheed," Worldpress.org, September 12, 2005, http://www.worldpress.org/Europe/2146.cfm.

9. Mamdooh Abu Sawa Qataishaat, "Media Statement Regarding ISIS's Declaration in Iraq," Media Office of Hizb ut-Tahrir, Wilayah of Jordan, July 1, 2014, http://www.hizb.org.uk/current-affairs/media-statement-regarding-isiss-declaration-in-iraq.

10. Taqiuddin an-Nabhani, *The Ruling System in Islam* (London: Al-Khilafah Publications, 5th edition, 1996), 43–49.

11. Hizb ut-Tahrir, *The Draft Constitution or the Necessary Evidences for It* (London: Dar al-Ummah Publishing House, 2010), 58.

12. See Imran Waheed, "Who Killed Farhad Usmanov?" *Khilafah Magazine*, July 2002, 10.

13. On Hizb ut-Tahrir in Great Britain, see Ihsan Yilmaz, "The Varied Performance of Hizb ut-Tahrir: Success in Britain and Uzbekistan and Stalemate in Egypt and Turkey," *Journal of Muslim Minority Affairs* 30, no. 4 (December 2010): 501–517.

14. Ed Husain, *The Islamist: Why I Joined Radical Islam in Britain, What I Saw Inside and Why I Left* (London: Penguin Books, 2007), 80.

15. Imran Waheed, Representative of Hizb ut-Tahrir, Britain, "Egypt/Uzbekistan 'Crooked' Partners in War Against Terrorism," ummah.com, July 4, 2002, http://www.ummah.com/forum/showthread.php?5149-Egypt-Uzbekistan-crooked-partners-in-War-against-Terrorism&s=69ed788c49bbd06355c69d68b9db9087.

16. "Muslim Leader Condemns Protesters," *BBC News*, February 4, 2006, http://news.bbc.co.uk/2/hi/uk/4676524.stm.

17. "Women Protest the Subjugation of Veiled Muslim Women Under French Secularism," Hizb ut-Tahrir Britain, September 26, 2010, http://www.hizb.org.uk/dawah/women-protest-the-subjugation-of-veiled-muslim-women-under-french-secularism.

18. Peter Walker, "Anti-U.S. Protesters in London Condemn Controversial Film," *Guardian*, September 16, 2012, http://www.theguardian.com/uk/2012/sep/16/anti-us-protesters-london.

19. Bruno De Cordier, "Why Was Hizb ut-Tahrir Protest in Brussels the Biggest?" Neweurasia.net, January 28, 2011, http://www.neweurasia.net/photoblog/why-was-hizb-ut-tahrir-protest-in-brussels-the-biggest/.

20. Hizb ut Tahrir Nederland, Khilafah Conference, "It Is Time for Khilafah," March 17, 2013, http://www.youtube.com/watch?v=6Nndz3r1yGw.

21. Kirstine Sinclair, "Same Old Message, New Wrapping: Hizb ut-Tahrir's Activities in Denmark," Report, Center for Mellemøststudier, University of Southern Denmark, March 2011, 4.

22. See Hizb ut-Tahrir Denmark, *The Environmental Problem: Its Causes and Islam's Solution* (Copenhagen: Hizb ut-Tahrir, 2009).

23. Madeleine Gruen, "Hizb ut-Tahrir's Activities in the United States," *Terrorism Monitor* 5, no. 16 (2007), http://www.jamestown.org/single/?no_cache = 1&tx_ttnews %5Btt_news%5D = 4377#.VyT4bPl97IU.

24. "World 'Deserves' an Islamic Caliphate, Says Bankstown Sheik Ismail Al-Wahwah," *Guardian*, October 11, 2014, http://www.theguardian.com/world/2014/oct/11/muslims-ready-to-sacrifice-everything-for-caliphate-says-ismail-al-wahwah.

25. Michael Kugelman, "Another Threat in Pakistan, in Sheep's Clothing," *New York Times*, August 3, 2012, http://www.nytimes.com/2012/08/04/opinion/hizb-ut-tahrir-threatens-pakistan-from-within.html.

26. "19 Hizb ut-Tahrir Men Booked Under Sedition Law, Jailed," *Nation*, April 14, 2012, http://www.nation.com.pk/pakistan-news-newspaper-daily-english-online/national/14-Apr-2012/19-hizb-ut-tahrir-men-booked-under-sedition-law-jailed.

27. Ishaan Tharoor, "Behind Bangladesh's Failed Coup Plot: A History of Violence," *Time Magazine*, January 19, 2012, http://world.time.com/2012/01/19/behind-bangladeshs-failed-coup-plot-a-history-of-violence/?xid = rss-topstories.

28. "Bangladesh Hasina Government Fires Bullets at Hizb ut-Tahrir Protest Outside National Press Club," December 29, 2012, http://www.youtube.com/watch?v = HUltMhjEmdU.

29. Hizb ut-Tahrir Afghanistan, "Hizb ut-Tahrir Wilayah Afghanistan Organizes Conference in the Capital on Corruption, Causes and Solution," news release, April 5, 2012, http://www.hizb-ut-tahrir.info/info/english.php/contents_en/entry_17159.

30. See "Annual Women's Conference Organized by the Women of Hizb ut-Tahrir Malaysia: Save Women and Children with Shariah and Khilafah," *khilafah.com*, May 4, 2014, http://www.khilafah.com/index.php/activism/asia/18646-annual-womens-conference-organised-by-the-women-of-hizb-ut-tahrir-malaysia-qsave-women-and-children-with-Shariahh-and-khilafahq.

31. On Hizb ut-Tahrir in Indonesia, see Mohammad Iqbal Ahnaf, "Between Revolution and Reform: The Future of Hizb ut-Tahrir Indonesia," *Dynamics of Asymmetric Conflict* 2, no. 2 (July 2009): 69–85; Mohamed Nawab Mohamed Osman, "Reviving the Caliphate in the Nusantara: Hizb ut-Tahrir Indonesia's Mobilization Strategy and Its Impact in Indonesia," *Terrorism and Political Violence* 22, no. 4 (September 2010): 601–622.

32. "Muslims Meet in Jakarta for Pan-Islamic State Talks," *Reuters*, August 12, 2007, http://www.reuters.com/article/2007/08/12/us-indonesia-muslim-idUSJAK280 49220070812.

33. Mairbek Vatchagaev, "Moscow Recognizes Hizb ut-Tahrir Operates Inside Russia," *Eurasia Daily Monitor* 9, no. 213, November 20, 2012, https://jamestown.org/program/moscow-recognizes-hizb-ut-tahrir-operates-inside-russia-2/.

34. "Hizb ut-Tahrir Palestine: Protest at the Russian Representative Office in Ramallah," khilafah.com, December 6, 2012, http://www.khilafah.com/index.php/activism/middle-east/15116-hizb-ut-tahrir-palestine-protest-at-the-russian-represent ative-office-in-ramallah; "Hizb ut-Tahrir Demands Russia Release Members," *RFE/*

RL, November 29, 2012, http://www.rferl.org/content/hizb-ut-tahrir-russia-indonesia/24784504.html.

35. "Hizb ut-Tahrir al-Islami vi Dagestane," *Caucasian Knot*, July 30, 2014, http://www.kavkaz-uzel.ru/articles/235276/.

36. See Central Intelligence Agency, *The World Factbook—Ukraine* (Washington, D.C.: CIA, 2006).

37. "Islamic Radical Party Hosts Conference in Ukraine's Crimea," *BBC Monitoring Service*, August 17, 2007.

38. Ben Blanchard, "Radical Islam Stirs in China's Remote West," Reuters, July 6, 2008, http://www.reuters.com/article/us-china-politics-islam-idUSPEK13637820080707.

39. Hizb ut-Tahrir Australia, "Protest Against Chinese Repression of Uyghur Muslims," March 14, 2015, https://www.youtube.com/watch?v=pEmcfFbN45s.

40. On Hizb ut-Tahrir in Central Asia, see Emmanuel Karagiannis, *Political Islam in Central Asia: The Challenge of Hizb ut-Tahrir* (London: Routledge, 2010), 58–72.

41. Bureau of Democracy, Human Rights, and Labor, "Uzbekistan—2013," *International Religious Freedom Report*, http://www.state.gov/j/drl/rls/irf/religiousfreedom/index.htm#wrapper.

42. On the evening of May 12, 2005, while some pro-Islamist businessmen were facing trial, a crowd attacked a local police station, seized weapons, took hostages, and broke into a nearby jail and released prisoners. Next day, armored cars entered Bobur Square, where thousands of unarmed civilians demonstrated against President Karimov, and fired indiscriminately into them. It is not clear how many people were killed that day, with estimates ranging from 170 to more than 700. See C. J. Chivers, "Tales of Uzbek Violence Suggest Larger Tragedy," *New York Times*, May 19, 2005, http://www.nytimes.com/2005/05/19/international/asia/19uzbekistan.html?.

43. "Kyrgyz Imam Arrested for Belonging to Banned Islamic Group," *RFE/RL'S Kyrgyz Service*, October 2, 2012, http://www.rferl.org/content/kyrgyzstan-hizb-ut-tahrir/24726253.html.

44. Jacob Zenn, "Hizb ut-Tahrir Takes Advantage of Ethnic Fault Lines in Tatarstan, Kyrgyzstan," *Eurasia Daily Monitor* 9, no. 218, November 29, 2012, http://www.jamestown.org/single/?no_cache=1&tx_ttnews%5Btt_news%5D=40174.

45. Head of the Media Office of Hizb ut-Tahrir in Kyrgyzstan, "Uzbek Intelligence Roams Kyrgyzstan Looking to Kill Muslims," May 5, 2014, http://www.khilafah.com/uzbek-intelligence-roams-kyrgyzstan-looking-to-kill-muslims/.

46. Central Media Office of Hizb ut-Tahrir, "Parliamentary Elections in Tajikistan," March 7, 2015, http://www.khilafah.com/index.php/analysis/asia/20854-parliamentary-elections-in-tajikistan.

47. See Hizb ut-Tahrir Tajikistan, "O Muslims in Tajikistan Your Constitution Is the Book and Sunnah and Not the Manmade Constitution, Which Enslaves Mankind," November 13, 2014, http://www.khilafah.com/index.php/analysis/asia/20130-o-mus

lims-in-tajikistan-your-constitution-is-the-book-and-sunnah-and-not-the-manmade
-constitution-which-enslaves-mankind.

48. "Protest in Aleppo, Syria by Hizb ut-Tahrir," *khilafah.com*, November 9, 2012, http://www.khilafah.com/index.php/activism/middle-east/14986-video-protest-in -aleppo-syria-by-hizb-ut-tahrir.

49. Hizb ut-Tahrir, "Hundreds of Women to Gather at a Critical Press Conference in Jordan Organised by Hizb ut-Tahrir," news release, April 24, 2013, http:// www.hizb-ut-tahrir.info/info/english.php/contents_en/entry_24835.

50. The Media Office of Hizb ut-Tahrir Jordan, "Protest Invites Outside Mosques Condemning the Tyrant Bashar's Massacres and Plea to the Sleeping Armies," news release, August 22, 2013, http://www.hizb-uttahrir.info/info/english.php/contents_en/ entry_28434.

51. Hizb ut-Tahrir Britain, "Syria's Islamic Alliance," October 13, 2013, http:// www.hizb.org.uk/current-affairs/syrias-islamic-alliance.

52. Hizb ut-Tahrir Australia, "Speech by the Ameer of Hizb ut-Tahrir to the People of Al-Shaam and the Sincere Revolutionaries," January 24, 2013, http://www.hizb -australia.org/global-da-wah/item/621-speech-by-the-ameer-of-hizb-ut-tahrir-to-the -people-of-al-shaam-and-the-sincere-revolutionaries.

53. On Hizb ut-Tahrir in the Palestinian Territories, see Jacob Høigilt, "Prophets in Their Own country? Hizb al-Tahrir in the Palestinian Context," *Politics, Religion and Ideology* 15, no. 4 (October 2014): 504–520.

54. Hizb ut-Tahrir Britain, "How Dare They Even Suggest That Political Islam Has Failed," May 19, 2014, http://www.hizb.org.uk/islamic-culture/how-dare-they -even-suggest-that-political-islam-has-failed.

55. Hizb ut-Tahrir Britain, "The Myths of the 'Turkish Model'," May 19, 2014, http://www.hizb.org.uk/current-affairs/the-myths-of-the-turkish-model.

56. Hizb ut-Tahrir Yemen, "Hizb ut Tahrir Wilayah Yemen Rallies the People of Yemen to Rise and Work for the Establishment of the Khilafah on the 93rd Anniversary of Its Destruction," June 15, 2014, http://www.khilafah.com/index.php/activism/ middle-east/19002-hizb-ut-tahrir-wilayah-yemen-rallies-the-people-of-yemen-to -rise-and-work-for-the-establishment-of-the-khilafah-on-the-93rd-anniversary-of -its-destruction.

57. See International Crisis Group, "Yemen at War," *Crisis Group Middle East Briefing* no. 45, March 27, 2015, http://www.crisisgroup.org/~/media/Files/Middle %20East%20North%20Africa/Iran%20Gulf/Yemen/b045-yemen-at-war.pdf.

58. "Interview with Member of Hizb ut-Tahrir in Iraq," *Khilafah,* August 17, 2008, http://www.khilafah.com/interview-with-member-of-hizb-ut-tahrir-in-iraq/.

59. Hizb ut-Tahrir, *The American Campaign to Suppress Islam* (London: Al-Khilafah Publications, 1996), 20.

60. Ahmad Abu Hayyan, "The Claim of the Rise of Anti-Semitism in the UK: Stirring One Community Against the Other," Hizb ut-Tahrir Britain, January 19, 2015,

http://www.hizb.org.uk/current-affairs/the-claim-of-the-rise-of-antisemitism-in-the
-uk-stirring-one-community-against-another.

61. Hizb ut-Tahrir America, "Irvine 11—Muslim and Guilty," no date, presumably September 2011, http://hizb-america.org/index.php/culture/comment/123-irvine
-11-muslim-and-guilty.

62. Hizb ut-Tahrir America, "Anwar al-Awlaki Death: America—Judge, Jury and Executioner," no date, http://hizb-america.org/index.php/culture/comment/110-an
war-al-awlaki-death-america-judge-jury-and-executioner.

63. Hizb ut-Tahrir Scandinavian (Denmark), "Stigende Islamofobi og Politisk Hykleri," January 15, 2015, http://www.hizb-ut-tahrir.dk/content.php?contentid = 637
&caller = http://hizb-ut-tahrir.dk/.

64. For a socialist perspective on Islamophobia in Denmark, see Ellen Brun and Jacques Hersh, "The Danish Disease: A Political Culture of Islamophobia," *Monthly Review* 60, no. 2 (June 2008), https://monthlyreview.org/2008/06/01/the-danish-dis
ease-a-political-culture-of-islamophobia/.

65. Daniel Stacey, "Australia Struggles Over Role of Hizb ut-Tahrir Islamic Group," *Wall Street Journal*, November 17, 2014, http://www.wsj.com/articles/austra
lia-struggles-over-role-of-hizb-ut-tahrir-islamic-group-1416280803.

66. Chris Uhlmann and James Glenday, "Number of Australian Jihadists Serving with Terrorists in Iraq and Syria Prompts Security Rethink," *ABC News*, June 23, 2014, http://www.abc.net.au/news/2014–06–23/australian-jihadists-prompt-government
-to-consider-new-security/5542738.

67. See, for example, Hizb ut-Tahrir Australia, "Insight, ISIS and Intervention," August 13, 2014, http://www.hizb-australia.org/media-centre/press-releases/item/1375
-insight-isis-and-intervention.

68. Hizb ut-Tahrir Australia, "Government Crackdown on Muslims Heading to Syria Hypocritical," December 3, 2013, http://www.hizb-australia.org/media-centre/
press-releases/item/967-government-crackdown-on-muslims-heading-to-syria-hypo
critical.

69. Women Hizb ut-Tahrir Australia, "Burqa Bans and Bogus Plans: How Should the Muslim Women Respond?" October 16, 2014, http://www.hizb-australia.org
/sisters/articles/item/1454-burqa-bans-and-bogus-plans-how-should-the-muslim
-woman-respond.

70. Hizb ut-Tahrir Indonesia, "The Representatives of the French Embassy in Jakarta 'Speechless' Debating with HTI over the Issue of Freedom of Speech," January 20, 2015, http://hizbut-tahrir.or.id/2015/01/22/the-representatives-of-the-french-em
bassy-in-jakarta-speechless-debating-with-hti-over-the-issue-of-freedom-of-speech/.

71. See Priyambudi Sulistiyanto, "Politics of Justice and Reconciliation in Post-Suharto Indonesia," *Journal of Contemporary Asia* 37, no. 1 (2007): 73–94.

72. See Philip Eldridge, "Human Rights in Post-Suharto Indonesia," *Brown Journal of World Affairs* 9, no. 1 (Spring 2002): 127–139.

73. Hizb ut-Tahrir Malaysia, "Detainees' Torture: The Brutality of CIA and Malaysia's Involvement," news release, December 17, 2014, http://www.mykhilafah .com/index.php/dari-meja-jurucakap/5029-press-release-detainees-tortures-the-bru tality-of-cia-and-malaysia-s-involvement.

74. Ibid.

75. Abdul Wahid, "On the Recent Events in Paris," *Current Affairs*, Hizb ut-Tahrir Britain, January 8, 2015, http://www.hizb.org.uk/current-affairs/dr-abdul-wahid-on -the-recent-events-in-paris.

76. See Anti-Defamation League, "Attitudes Towards Jews in Ten European Countries," March 2012, http://archive.adl.org/anti_semitism/adl_anti-semitism_ presentation_february_2012.pdf.

77. See, for example, Linda Grant, "What British Jews Think of Israel," *Independent*, July 18, 2006, http://www.independent.co.uk/news/uk/this-britain/what-british -jews-think-of-israel-408400.html.

78. Osman Bakhach, "FSB v Krimu dopitue 150 musulman," *hizb.org.ua*, May 13, 2014, https://hizb.org.ua/uk/hizb-ut-tahrir-in-ukraine/hizb-ut-tahrir-ukraine/crisis/ 2170-crimea.html.

79. Women's Section of the Central Media Office of Hizb ut-Tahrir, "Women of Hizb ut-Tahrir Announce Campaign Highlighting the Genocide of Muslim Women and Children in the Central African Republic," February 24, 2014, http://www.khila fah.com/index.php/analysis/africa/18152-women-of-hizb-ut-tahrir-announce-cam paign-highlighting-the-genocide-of-muslim-women-and-children-in-the-central-afri can-republic-car.

80. Hizb ut-Tahrir Britain, "The Oppression of Rohinya Muslims in Burma," August 7, 2012, http://www.hizb.org.uk/current-affairs/the-oppression-of-rohingya -muslims-in-burma.

Part II

1. Samuel P. Huntington, *The Third Wave: Democratization in the Late Twentieth Century* (Norman: University of Oklahoma Press, 1993).

2. See Philip N. Howard and Muzammil M. Hussain, *Democracy's Fourth Wave? Digital Media and the Arab Spring* (New York: Oxford University Press, 2013).

3. Robert A. Dahl, *On Democracy* (New Haven, Conn.: Yale University Press, 2000), 37–38.

4. On sovereign democracy, see Andrey Okara, "Sovereign Democracy: A New Russian Idea or a PR Project?" *Russia in Global Affairs*, no. 2 (July-September 2007), http://eng.globalaffairs.ru/number/n_9123.

5. Geir Helgesen and Li Xing, "Democracy or Minzhu: The Challenge of Western Versus East Asian Notions of Good Governance," *Asian Perspective* 20, no. 1 (Spring-Summer 1996): 95–124.

6. Thomas Olesen, "The Uses and Misuses of Globalization in the Study of Social Movements," *Social Movements Studies* 4, no. 1 (2005): 56.

7. Kavitha A. Davidson, "Democracy index 2013: Global Democracy Still at a Standstill the Economist Intelligence Unit's Annual Report Shows," *Huffington Post*, March 21, 2013, http://www.huffingtonpost.com/2013/03/21/democracy-index-2013 -economist-intelligence-unit_n_2909619.html.

8. Paul Hirst, "Representative Democracy and Its Limits," *Political Quarterly* 59, no. 2 (April-June 1988), 190.

9. Eugene Rogan, *The Fall of the Ottomans: The Great War in the Middle East* (New York: Basic Books, 2015), 2.

10. Tadeusz Swietochowski, *Russian Azerbaijan, 1905–1920: The Shaping of a National Identity in a Muslim Community* (Cambridge: Cambridge University Press, 2004), 144–146.

11. Graham E. Fuller, *The Future of Political Islam* (New York: Palgrave Macmillan, 2003), 29.

12. Rita K. Noonan, "Women Against the State: Political Opportunities and Collective Action Frames in Chile's Transition to Democracy," *Sociological Forum* 10, no. 1 (1995): 98–103.

13. Alana Mann, *Global Activism in Food Politics: Power Shift* (New York: Palgrave Macmillan, 2014), 115.

14. Sharon N. Barnartt, "The Arab Spring Protests and Concurrent Disability Protests: Social Movement Spillover or Spurious Relationship?" *Studies in Social Justice* 8, no. 1 (2014): 67–78.

15. "Assad Wins Syria Election with 88.7 Percent of Votes," Reuters, June 4, 2014, http://www.reuters.com/article/2014/06/04/uk-syria-crisis-election-assad-iduskbn0ef 21C20140604.

16. Sadek J. Sulaiman, "Democracy and Shura," in *Liberal Islam*, ed. Charles Kurzman (Oxford: Oxford University Press, 1998), 98.

17. Abu A'la Maududi, *The Islamic Law and Constitution*, 2nd ed. (Lahore: Islamic Publications, 1960), 219.

18. Yusuf al-Qaradawi, *Priorities of the Islamic Movement in the Coming Phase* (Cairo: al-Dar, 1992), also available at http://www.islambasics.com/view.php?bkID = 48&chapter = 6.

19. See Yusuf al-Qaradawi, "Does Islam Allow Democracy?" fatwa no. 85826, May 11, 2003, http://www.islamweb.net/emainpage/index.php?page = showfatwa&Option = FatwaId&Id = 85826.

20. Yusuf al-Qaradawi, "Shura in Islam," fatwa no. 84768, September 4, 2002, http://www.islamweb.net/emainpage/index.php?page = showfatwa&Option = FatwaId &Id = 84768.

21. Yusuf Qaradawi, "What Is the Rule in Entering into Parliaments?" fatwa no. 81429, March 27, 2000, http://www.islamweb.net/emainpage/index.php?page = show fatwa&Option = FatwaId&Id = 81429.

22. Ibid.

23. Ibid.

24. Qatar E-Government, *The Constitution of Qatar 2003*, http://portal.www .gov.qa/wps/wcm/connect/5a5512804665e3afa54fb5fd2b4ab27a/Constitution + of + Qatar + EN.pdf?MOD = AJPERES.

25. State Information Service of Egypt, *Constitution of the Arab Republic of Egypt 2014*, http://www.sis.gov.eg/Newvr/Dustor-en001.pdf.

26. Fethullah Gülen, "A Comparative Approach to Islam and Democracy," *SAIS Review* 21, no. 2 (Summer-Fall 2001), http://www.fountainmagazine.com/Issue/detail/ A-Comparative-Approach-to-Islam-and-Democracy.

27. Ibid.

28. Leonid Sykiainen, "Democracy and the Dialogue Between Western and Islamic Legal Cultures: The Gülen Case," in *Muslim Citizens of the Globalized World*, ed. Robert A. Hunt and Yüksel A. Aslandogan (Somerset, N.J.: The Light, 2007), 126.

Chapter 3

Note to epigraph: Mohammad Mursi, "This Is Egypt's Revolution, Not Ours," *Guardian*, February 8, 2011, https://www.theguardian.com/commentisfree/2011/feb/ 08/egypt-revolution-muslim-brotherhood-democracy.

1. Roy Jackson, *Mawlana Mawdudi and Political Islam* (New York: Routledge, 2011), 73.

2. Constitution of Jamaat-e-Islami, Pakistan, jamaat.org, 2016, http://jamaat.org/ beta/site/page/5.

3. Bassam Tibi, *Political Islam, World Politics and Europe: From Jihadist to Institutional Islamism* (London: Routledge, 2014), 73.

4. Joshua Teitelbaum, "The Muslim Brotherhood and the 'Struggle for Syria', 1947–1958: Between Accommodation and Ideology," *Middle Eastern Studies* 40, no. 3 (2004), 137–138.

5. See Raphaël Lefèvre, *Ashes of Hama: The Muslim Brotherhood in Syria* (London: Hurst, 2013), 30.

6. On the history of the Muslim Brotherhood in Syria, see chapter 6.

7. See, for example, Abdul Qadeem Zalloom, *Democracy Is a System of Kufr* (London: Al-Khilafah, 1995).

8. One of them, Ahmad al-Daur, managed to win a seat in both elections, but he was expelled from the parliament in 1958, charged with carrying out antigovernment activities, and he was jailed for two years. See Amnon Cohen, *Political Parties in the West Bank Under the Jordanian Regime, 1949–1967* (Ithaca, N.Y.: Cornell University Press, 1982), 216.

9. Hizb ut-Tahrir, *Political Thoughts* (London: Al-Khilafah Publications, 1999), 117.

10. On Islamist parties, see Julie Chernov Hwang, ed., *Islamist Parties and Political Normalization in the Muslim World* (Philadelphia: University of Pennsylvania Press, 2014).

11. Olivier Roy, "Islam: The Democracy Dilemma," in *The Islamists Are Coming: Who They Really Are*, ed. Robin Wright (Washington, D.C.: Woodrow Wilson Center Press, 2012), 13.

12. Gudrun Kramer, "Islamist Notions of Democracy," *Middle East Report* 23, no. 4, 1993, http://www.merip.org/mer/mer183/islamist-notions-democracy.

13. Michael Zantovsky, "1989 and 2011: Compare and Contrast," *World Affairs*, July-August 2011, http://www.worldaffairsjournal.org/article/1989-and-2011-compare-and-contrast.

14. On the causes of the Arab Spring revolutions, see Robert Springborg, "The Political Economy of the Arab Spring," *Mediterranean Politics* 16, no. 3 (2011): 427–433; Katerina Dalacoura, "The 2011 Uprisings in the Arab Middle East: Political Change and Geopolitical Implications," *International Affairs* 88, no. 1 (2012): 63–79.

15. Quinn Mecham, "Islamist Movements," in *The Arab Uprisings Explained: New Contentious Politics in the Middle East*, ed. Marc Lynch (New York: Columbia University Press, 2014), 202.

16. For a debate about the future of the Arab Spring revolutions, see Hillel Fradkin, "Arab Democracy or Islamist Revolution?" *Journal of Democracy* 24, no. 1 (January 2013): 5–13; Olivier Roy, "There Will Be No Islamist Revolution," *Journal of Democracy* 24, no. 1 (January 2013): 14–19.

17. See Turkish Statistical Organization, "Results of the General Election of Representatives (1983–2011)," http://www.turkstat.gov.tr/VeriBilgi.do?alt_id = 1061.

18. Ibid.

19. Ibid.

20. Ömer Taşpinar, "Turkey: The New Model?" in *The Islamists Are Coming: Who They Really Are*, ed. Robin Wright (Washington, D.C.: Woodrow Wilson Center Press, 2012), 128.

21. On the Anatolian Tigers, see Evren Hosgor, "Islamic Capital/Anatolian Tigers: Past and Present," *Middle Eastern Studies* 47, no. 2 (March 2011): 343–360.

22. European Stability Initiative, *Islamic Calvinists: Change and Conservatism in Central Anatolia* (Istanbul: ESI, 2005), 23–25.

23. See Turkish Statistical Organization, "Results of the General Election."

24. Ibid.

25. Ayhan Kaya, "Moderning, Secularism, Democracy and the AKP in Turkey," *South European Society and Politics* 16, no. 4 (December 2011): 583.

26. See Daniel Dombey, "Turkey's Ergenekon Trial: Q & A," *Financial Times*, August 5, 2013, http://www.ft.com/intl/cms/s/0/4a9e370a-fdbc-11e2-a5b1–00144feabdc0.html#axzz3djVJ1FED.

27. "Recep Tayyip Erdogan Wins Turkish Presidential Election," *BBC News*, August 14, 2014, http://www.bbc.com/news/world-europe-28729234.

28. Oguzhan Tekin, "Turkey's 2015 Election Results," *Today's Zaman*, June 11, 2015, http://www.todayszaman.com/blog/oguzhan-tekin/turkeys-2015-election-results_384983.html.

29. "Turkey Election: Ruling AKP Regains Majority," *BBC News*, November 2, 2015, http://www.bbc.com/news/world-europe-34694420.

30. Kemal Kaya, "Welfare Policies Are the Key to the AKP's Electoral Successes," *Turkey Analyst*, April 30, 2014, http://www.turkeyanalyst.org/publications/turkey-analyst-articles/item/106-welfare-policies-are-the-key-to-the-akp%E2%80%99s-electoral-successes.html.

31. See, for example, William Hale, "Christian Democracy and the AKP: Parallels and Contrasts," *Turkish Studies* 6, no. 2 (2005): 293–310.

32. "Erdogan Stands for Presidency, Invokes Allah," *EurActiv.com*, July 1, 2014, http://www.euractiv.com/sections/enlargement/erdogan-stands-presidency-invokes-allah-303212.

33. "Irked by 'Tipsy Youth,' Turkish PM Defends Booze Restrictions," *Hurriyet Daily News*, May 24, 2013, http://www.hurriyetdailynews.com/irked-by-tipsy-youth-turkish-pm-defends-booze-restrictions.aspx?pageID = 238&nID = 47577&NewsCatID = 338.

34. "Interview with Turkish Prime Minister Erdogan: Leader Says Headscarf Ban at Universities 'Unfortunate,'" *Spiegel Online*, September 20, 2007, http://www.spiegel.de/international/world/turkish-prime-minister-erdogan-leader-says-headscarf-ban-at-universities-unfortunate-a-506896.html.

35. M. Hakan Yavuz, *Toward an Islamic Enlightenment: The Gülen Movement* (Oxford: Oxford University Press, 2013), 218–219.

36. "Turkish Politics: A Challenge to Erdogan's Rule," *Economist*, December 17, 2013, http://www.economist.com/blogs/charlemagne/2013/12/turkish-politics.

37. Caroline Mortimer, "Turkey: Fethullah Gulen's Brother Arrested in Erdogan's Ongoing Crackdown After Coup," *Independent*, October 2, 2016, http://www.independent.co.uk/news/world/europe/turkey-coup-fethullah-gulen-police-arrest-brother-qutbadin-gulen-crackdown-erdogan-a7341471.html.

38. Tracy Wilkinson, "Turkey Pushes for Extradition of U.S.-based Cleric Who They Say Directed Failed Coup," *Los Angeles Times*, October 14, 2016, http://www.latimes.com/world/middleeast/la-fg-us-turkey-coup-extradition-snap-story.html.

39. Senem Aslan, "Different Faces of Turkish Islamic Nationalism," *Washington Post*, February 20, 2015, http://www.washingtonpost.com/blogs/monkey-cage/wp/2015/02/20/different-faces-of-turkish-islamic-nationalism/.

40. Emre Toros, "Social Indicators and Voting: The Turkish Case," *Social Indicators Research* 115, no. 3 (2014): 1021.

41. Ali Çarkoğlu, "Political Preferences of the Turkish Electorate: Reflections of an Alevi–Sunni Cleavage," *Turkish Studies* 6, no. 2 (2005): 287.

42. Tagip Erdogan, "Masum yavrucakların hesabı sorulacak," *akparti.org*, November 17, 2012, http://www.akparti.org.tr/site/haberler/masum-yavrucaklarin-hesabi-sorulacak/33711#1.

43. John Hooper, "Turkish Hopes Offer Hope of Peace with Kurdish Militants," *Guardian*, December 31, 2012, http://www.theguardian.com/world/2012/dec/31/turkish-peace-talks-kurdish-militants-pkk.

44. Ömer Taşpinar, "Turkey: An Interested Party" in *The Arab Awakening: America and the Transformation of the Middle East*, ed. Kenneth Pollack et al. (Washington, D.C.: Brookings Institution Press, 2011), 270–272.

45. See subsection on "Turkey and Erdogan Popular" in Pew Research Center's Survey titled "Most Muslims Want Democracy, Personal Freedoms and Islam in Political Life," July 10, 2012, http://www.pewglobal.org/2012/07/10/most-muslims-want -democracy-personal-freedoms-and-islam-in-political-life/.

46. There is an extensive bibliography on the Muslim Brotherhood. See Barry Rubin, *The Muslim Brotherhood: The Organization and Policies of a Global Islamist Movement* (London: Palgrave Macmillan, 2010); Tarek Osman, *Egypt on the Brink: From Nasser to the Muslim Brotherhood* (New Haven, Conn.: Yale University Press, 2011).

47. Husain Haqqani and Hillel Fradkin, "Islamist Parties: Going Back to the Origins," *Journal of Democracy* 19, no. 3 (July 2008): 15.

48. On the Secret Apparatus, see Richard P. Mitchell, *The Society of the Muslim Brothers* (Oxford: Oxford University Press, 1969), 30–31.

49. On the history of the Muslim Brotherhood, see Carrie Rosefsky Wickman, *The Muslim Brotherhood: Evolution of an Islamist Movement* (Princeton, N.J.: Princeton University Press, 2013).

50. Eric Trager, "The Unbreakable Muslim Brotherhood: Grim Prospects for a Liberal Egypt," *Foreign Affairs*, September-October 2011, https://www.foreignaffairs .com/articles/north-africa/2011–09–01/unbreakable-muslim-brotherhood.

51. As'ad Ghanem and Mohanad Mustafa, "Strategies of Electoral Participation by Islamist Movements: The Muslim Brotherhood and Parliamentary Elections in Egypt and Jordan, November 2010," *Contemporary Politics* 17, no. 4 (December 2011): 400.

52. Valerie Hoffman, "Islam, Human Rights and Interfaith Relations: Some Contemporary Egyptian Perspectives," in *Islamic Political and Social Movements*, ed. Barry Rubin (London: Routledge, 2013), 84.

53. International Republican Institute, "2005 Parliamentary Election Assessment in Egypt," November 15–21, 2005, http://www.iri.org/sites/default/files/fields/field_ files_attached/resource/egypts_2005_parliamentary_elections_assessment_report.pdf.

54. "Interview with Essam al-Arian, member of the Muslim Brotherhood's Executive Bureau," *ikhwanweb.com*, June 24, 2010, http://www.ikhwanweb.com/article .php?id = 25402&ref = search.php.

55. "One Year After Morsi's Ouster, Divides Persist on El-Sisi, Muslim Brotherhood," Pew Research Center, May 22, 2014, http://www.pewglobal.org/2014/05/22/ chapter-3-democratic-values-in-egypt/.

56. Wickham, *Muslim Brotherhood*, 34–42 and 58–70.

57. Gamal Essam El-Din, "Egypt's Post-Mubarak Legislative Life Begins Amid Tension and Division," *AhramOnLine*, January 23, 2012, http://english.ahram.org.eg/

NewsContent/33/100/32384/Elections-/News/Egypts-postMubarak-legislative-life
-begins-amid-te.aspx.

58. "Muslim Brotherhood's Mursi Declared Egypt President," *BBC News*, June 24, 2012, http://www.bbc.com/news/world-18571580.

59. Hesham al-Awadi, "Islamists in Power: The Case of the Muslim Brotherhood in Egypt," *Contemporary Arab Affairs* 6, no. 4 (2013): 545.

60. Noha el-Hennawy et al., "The Brothers of the Cabinet," *Egypt Independent*, August 10, 2012, http://www.egyptindependent.com/news/brothers-cabinet.

61. Al-Awadi, "Islamists in Power," 541.

62. Mitchell, *Society of the Muslim Brothers*, 246–247.

63. Stephen Glain, "Ikhwanomics: The Muslim Brotherhood Has a Plan for Egypt's Economic Recovery," *Majallah*, February 20, 2012, http://www.majalla.com/eng/2012/02/article55229570.

64. Charles Levinson, "Muslim Brotherhood Looks West in Bid to Revive Egyptian Economy," *Wall Street Journal*, February 12, 2012, http://www.wsj.com/articles/SB10001424052970204062704577220454030969184.

65. "Egypt's Interim Government Recognises Morsi's Economic Achievement," *Middle East Monitor*, September 16, 2013, https://www.middleeastmonitor.com/news/africa/7379-egypts-interim-government-recognises-morsis-economic-achievements.

66. It has been argued that the army's influence declined after the late 1970s to the benefit of internal security forces under the Ministry of Interior and the ruling National Democratic Party. See Philippe Droz-Vincent, "The Security Sector in Egypt: Management, Coercion and External Alliances Under the Dynamics of Change," in *The Arab State and Neo-Liberal Globalization: The Restructuring of State Power in the Middle East*, ed. Laura Guazzone and Daniela Poppi (Reading, UK: Ithaca Press, 2009).

67. David D. Kirkpatrick, "Egypt's New Strongman, Sisi Knows Best," *International New York Times*, May 24, 2014, 8.

68. Youcef Bouandel, "Political Islam in North Africa," in *Political Islam: Context Versus Ideology*, ed. Khaled Hroub (London: London Middle East Institute at SOAS, 2010), 100.

69. Rachid al-Ghannouchi, "Towards Inclusive Strategies for Human Rights Enforcement in the Arab World—A Response," *Encounters* 2 (1996): 191.

70. Dale F. Eickelman and James Piscatori, *Islamist Politics* (Princeton, N.J.: Princeton University Press, 1996), 133.

71. Eymen Gamha, "Final Results of Tunisian Elections Announced," *Tunisialive*, November 14, 2011, http://www.tunisia-live.net/2011/11/14/tunisian-election-final-results-tables/.

72. On the Left-Islamist coalition government, see Bruce Maddy-Weitzman, "Historic Departure or Temporary Marriage? The Left-Islamist Alliance in Tunisia," *Dynamics of Asymmetric Conflict* 5, no. 3 (November 2012): 196–207.

73. Anthony Shadid and David D. Kirkpatrick, "Activists in the Arab World Vie to Define Islamic State," *New York Times*, September 29, 2011, http://www.nytimes

.com/2011/09/30/world/middleeast/arab-debate-pits-islamists-against-themselves
.html?pagewanted = all&_r = 0.

74. Rachid Ghannouchi, "Tunisia Shows That There Is No Contradiction Between Democracy and Islam," *Washington Post*, October 24, 2014, http://www.washington post.com/opinions/tunisia-shows-there-is-no-contradiction-between-democracy-and -islam/2014/10/24/2655e552–5a16–11e4-bd61–346aee66ba29_story.html.

75. See Amel Grami, "Gender Equality in Tunisia," *British Journal of Middle Eastern Studies* 35, no. 3 (2008): 349–361.

76. Joachim Scholl, "Interview with Samir Dilou—'Wir wollen keinen Gottes-staat,'" *Deutchland Radio Kultur*, May 18, 2011, http://www.deutschlandradiokul tur.de/wir-wollen-keinen-gottesstaat.954.de.html?dram:article_id = 146287.

77. "Tunisia Elections Results: Nida Tunis Wins Most Seats, Sidelining Islamists," *Guardian*, October 30, 2014, http://www.theguardian.com/world/2014/oct/30/tunisia -election-results-nida-tunis-wins-most-seats-sidelining-islamists.

78. Tarek Amara and Patrick Markey, "Tunisian Islamists Concede Election Defeat to Secular Party," Reuters, October 27, 2014, http://www.reuters.com/article/ 2014/10/27/us-tunisia-election-idUSKBN0IG0C120141027.

79. Monica Marks, "Tunisia's Ennahda: Rethinking Islamism in the Context of ISIS and the Egyptian Coup," *Project on U.S. Relations with the Islamic World at Brook-ings*, August 2015, http://www.brookings.edu/~/media/Research/Files/Reports/2015/ 07/rethinking-political-islam/Tunisia_Marks-FINALE.pdf?la = en.

80. Turkey Internet Users, internetlivestats.com, 2016, http://www.internetlive stats.com/internet-users/turkey/.

81. Egypt Internet Users, internetlivestats.com, 2016, http://www.internetlivestats .com/internet-users/egypt/.

82. Tunisian Internet Users, internetlivestats.com, 2016, http://www.internetlive stats.com/internet-users/tunisia/.

83. Hind Mustafa, "Social Media Trending as 10 Million Arabs Join Facebook," *Al-Arabiya*, June 23, 2013, http://english.alarabiya.net/en/business/technology/2013/ 06/23/Social-media-trending-as-10-million-Arabs-join-Facebook-.html.

84. Lin Noueihed and Alex Warren, *The Battle for the Arab Spring: Revolution, Counter-Revolution and the Making of a New Era* (New Haven, Conn.: Yale University Press, 2012), 59.

85. Steven Kull, "Muslim Public Opinion on U.S. Policy, Attacks on Civilians and al-Qaeda," Program on International Policy Attitudes at the University of Maryland, April 24, 2007, 22, http://www.worldpublicopinion.org/pipa/pdf/apr07/START_Apr07 _rpt.pdf.

86. Devon Haynie, "More Middle Eastern Students Come to the U.S., Find Sur-prises," *U.S. News*, February 18, 2015, http://www.usnews.com/education/best -colleges/articles/2015/02/18/more-middle-eastern-students-come-to-the-us-find -surprises.

87. "Tunisia: High Rate of Unemployment Among Youth and Women," *Tunis Times*, May 25, 2014, http://www.thetunistimes.com/2014/05/tunisia-high-rate-unem ployment-youth-women-5551/.

88. Akira Murata, "Designing Youth Employment Policies in Egypt," *Global Economy and Development at Brookings*, Working Paper 68, January 2014, 7, http://www.brookings.edu/~/media/research/files/papers/2014/01/31-youth-employment-egypt-murata/arab-econpaper3murata-v5.pdf.

89. Sonia L. Alianak, *The Transition Towards Revolution and Reform: The Arab Spring Realised?* (Edinburgh: Edinburgh University Press, 2014), 9.

90. "Prime Minister Objects to 'Moderate Islam' Label," *Hurriyet Daily News*, April 3, 2009, http://www.hurriyet.com.tr/english/domestic/11360374.asp.

91. William Hale and Ergun Özbudun, *Islamism, Democracy and Liberalism in Turkey: The Case of the AKP* (London: Routledge, 2011), 20.

92. Samuel Osborne, "Turkish Parliament Speaker Prompts Outrage with Call to Replace Secularism with Religious Constitution," *Independent*, April 27, 2016, http://www.independent.co.uk/news/world/europe/turkish-parliament-speaker-prompts-outrage-with-call-to-replace-secularism-with-religious-a7002901.html.

93. M. Hakan Yavuz, *Islamic Political Identity in Turkey* (New York: Oxford University Press, 2005), 260.

94. Ihsan Dagi, "The Justice and Development Party: Identity, Politics, and Discourse of Human Rights in the Search of Security and Legitimacy," in *The Emergence of a New Turkey: Democracy and the AK Parti*, ed. M. Hakan Yavuz (Salt Lake City: University of Utah Press, 2006), 90.

95. Ahmet Kuru, "Muslim Politics Without an Islamic State: Can Turkey's Justice and Development Party Be a Model for Arab Islamists?" Brookings Doha Center, Policy Briefing, February 2013, 3.

96. Ibid., 2.

97. Qtd. in Ana Belen Soage, "Yusuf al-Qaradaqi: The Muslim Brothers' Favorite Ideological Guide," in Rubin, *Muslim Brotherhood*, 30.

98. See Robert Leiken and Steven Brooke, "The Moderate Muslim Brotherhood," *Foreign Affairs*, March-April 2007, https://www.foreignaffairs.com/articles/2007–03–01/moderate-muslim-brotherhoodsocial.

99. Annette Ranko, *The Muslim Brotherhood and Its Quest for Hegemony in Egypt* (Wiesbaden: Springer, 2015), 132.

100. Rachid Ghannouchi, "Tunisians Must Choose Ballots Over Bullets if We Are to Secure the Revolution," *Guardian*, October 28, 2013, http://www.theguardian.com/commentisfree/2013/oct/28/tunisians-ballots-not-bullets-secure-revolution#start-of-comments.

101. Jonny Hogg and Orhan Coskun, "Turkey's Erdogan Position Himself for More Powerful Presidential Role," Reuters, July 1, 2014, http://www.reuters.com/article/2014/07/01/us-turkey-election-erdogan-idUSKBN0F63NN20140701.

102. See, for example, "Turkish PM Erdoğan's Steps 'Not Enough', Greek Ortho-dox Patriarch Says," *Hurriyet Daily News*, May 9, 2014, http://www.hurriyetdailynews.com/turkish-pm-erdogans-steps-not-enough-greek-orthodox-patriarch-says.aspx?pageID = 238&nID = 66215&NewsCatID = 393.

103. "Dr. Badie Interview with Freedom and Justice Newspaper," ikhwanweb.com, February 22, 2012, http://www.ikhwanweb.com/article.php?id = 29722.

104. Abdel-Rahman Hussein, "Mohamed Morsi to Pick Woman and Christian as Egypt's Vice Presidents," *Guardian*, June 26, 2012, http://www.theguardian.com/world/2012/jun/26/mohamed-morsi-christian-woman-egypt.

105. Mariz Tadros, *The Muslim Brotherhood in Contemporary Egypt: Democracy Redefined or Confined?* (London: Routledge, 2012), 107.

106. "Alnzam alasasy" (The Statute After the Revision of the Ninth Conference)," 2016, http://www.ennahdha.tn/.

107. Jessica Sarhan, "Women Blast Erdogan Over 'Hate Crime,'" *Al Jazeera*, November 27, 2014, http://www.aljazeera.com/news/middleeast/2014/11/women-blast-erdogan-over-hate-crime-20141126104444682533.html.

108. Dorra Megdiche Meziou, "Tunisia's Ennahda Reconsiders Gender Equality," *Al-Monitor*, August 13, 2013, http://www.al-monitor.com/pulse/politics/2013/08/tunisia-ennahda-women-rights-threat.html#.

109. "Most Muslims Want Democracy, Personal Freedoms, and Islam in Political Life," *Pew Research Center*, July 10, 2012, http://www.pewglobal.org/2012/07/10/most-muslims-want-democracy-personal-freedoms-and-islam-in-political-life/.

110. Mustafa Akyol, "Erdogan Counts on Karaman's Islamic Counsel," *Al-Monitor*, January 29, 2014, http://www.al-monitor.com/pulse/tr/originals/2014/01/erdogan-karaman-counsel.html#.

111. "Turkey Coup: Erdogan Backs Return of Death Penalty at Vast Istanbul Rally," *BBC News*, August 8, 2016, http://www.bbc.co.uk/news/world-europe-37003819.

112. Tadros, *Muslim Brotherhood*, 97.

113. Ibid., p. 59.

114. Kareem Fahim, "Ruling Islamists, Under Attack, Reject Blame for Tunisia's Woes," *New York Times*, February 11, 2013, http://www.nytimes.com/2013/02/12/world/africa/memo-from-tunis-ennahda-party-rejects-blame-for-tunisias-troubles.html?_r = 0.

115. "Ennahda Leader Raises Concerns of One-Party Rule After Tunisia Polls," *Middle East Eye*, October 31, 2014, http://www.middleeasteye.net/news/ennahda-leader-hits-out-nidaa-tounes-after-tunisia-polls-587053990.

116. Hale and Özbudun, *Islamism*, 27.

117. In 2013, protests and riots erupted after the government declared its inten-tion to develop the Gezi Park project in central Istanbul. What started as a protest against the government's decision to build a shopping mall in the area eventually became an uprising defending secularism and liberal values. See Selcan Hacaoglu and

Taylan Bilgic, "Erdogan Denounces Protest Violence, Says Demands Welcome," *Bloomberg Business*, June 8, 2013, http://www.bloomberg.com/news/articles/2013–06–07/erdogan-slams-protest-violence-says-democratic-demands-welcome.

118. Abdel Moneim Abou el-Fotouh, "Democracy Supporters Should Not Fear the Muslim Brotherhood," *Washington Post*, February 9, 2011, http://www.washing tonpost.com/wp-dyn/content/article/2011/02/09/AR2011020905222.html.

119. Ines Bel Aiba, "Ennahda Leader Says 'Tunisia Model' Way to Defeat Islamic State," *Yahoo News*, October 23, 2014, http://news.yahoo.com/ennahda-leader-says -tunisia-model-way-defeat-islamic-000837755.html.

Chapter 4

1. On the doctrinal content of Salafism, see Roel Meijer, introduction to *Global Salafism: Islam's New Religious Movement*, ed. Roel Meijer (London: Hurst, 2009), 3–13.

2. Sahih al-Bukhari, vol. 7, book 76, no. 437, *sunnah.com*, http://sunnah.com/ bukhari/81/18.

3. Abu Dawud, book 41, no. 4579, *sunnah.com*, http://sunnah.com/abudawud/42.

4. Ibid., no. 4580.

5. Nico Prucha, "An Interview with Islamist Scholar Abd al-Mu'nim Moneep," *Perspectives on Terrorism* 6, no. 3, 2012, http://www.terrorismanalysts.com/pt/index .php/pot/article/view/prucha-abd-al-munim-moneep/html.

6. Muhammad Umar Menon, ed., *Ibn Taimiya's Struggle Against Popular Religion—with an Annotated Translation of His Kitab iqtida as-sirat al-mustaqim* (Berlin: De Gruyter, 2012), 89–332.

7. There are three types of tawhid: *tawhid ar-Ruboobiyyah*, whereby power rests in one God alone; *tawhid al-Uloohiyyah*, which dictates that all worship is directly solely to God; and *tawhid al-asmaa wa'al-sifat*, obliges the believer to accept literally the names and attributes of God found in the Quran and the hadith without inquiring about their exact nature. See Natana J. DeLong-Bas, *Wahhabi Islam: From Revival and Reform to Global Jihad* (Oxford: Oxford University Press, 2004), 56–58.

8. On the modern history of Wahhabism, see David Commins, *The Wahhabi Mission and Saudi Arabia* (London: Tauris, 2006).

9. See Trevor Stanley, "Understanding the Origins of Wahhabism and Salafism," *Terrorism Monitor: In-Depth Analysis of the War on Terror* 3, no. 14, July 15, 2005, http://www.jamestown.org/programs/tm/single/?tx_ttnews%5Btt_news%5D = 528& #.VfcuFBGqqko.

10. Abdullah Saeed, "Salafiya, Modernism, and Revival," in *The Oxford Handbook of Islam and Politics*, ed. John L. Esposito and Emad El-Din Shahin (Oxford: Oxford University Press, 2013), 33.

11. Stephane Lacroix, "Between Revolution and Apoliticism: Nasir al-Din al-Albani and His Impact on the Shaping of Contemporary Salafism," in *Global Salafism: Islam's New Religious Movement*, ed. Roel Meijer (London: Hurst, 2009), 68.

12. Karen Armstrong, "Wahhabism to ISIS: How Saudi Arabia Exported the Main Source of Global Terrorism," *New Statesman*, November 27, 2014, http://www.new statesman.com/world-affairs/2014/11/wahhabism-isis-how-saudi-arabia-exported -main-source-global-terrorism.

13. Adis Duderija, "Constructing the Religious Self and the Other: Neo-Traditional Salafi Manhaj," *Islam and Christian-Muslim Relations* 21, no. 1 (January 2010): 76.

14. Quintan Wiktorowicz, "Anatomy of the Salafi Movement," *Studies in Conflict and Terrorism* 29, no. 3 (2007): 207.

15. "Tunisian Salafi Cleric Khamis Mejri Rejects Democracy and Praises Bin Laden," Hannibal TV, December 2, 2012, http://www.memritv.org/clip/en/3860.htm.

16. Alaa Elayyan, "Democracy, Elections Are Forbidden in Islam: Salafist Leader," *AmmonNews*, January 6, 2013, http://en.ammonnews.net/article.aspx?articleNO = 19880#.VILrccn xUdU.

17. Robert G. Rabil, *Salafism in Lebanon: From Apoliticism to Transnational Jihadism* (Washington D.C.: Georgetown University Press, 2014), 37.

18. Din Wahid, "The Challenge of Democracy in Indonesia: The Case of Salafi Movement," *Islamika Indonesiana* 1, no. 1 (2014): 60.

19. Richard Gauvain, *Salafi Ritual Purity: In the Presence of God* (London: Routledge, 2013), 34.

20. Kristen McTighe, "The Salafi Nour Party in Egypt," Al Jazeera Center for Studies, April 10, 2014, http://studies.aljazeera.net/en/reports/2014/03/201432612833 62726.htm#e20.

21. "Yasser Borhami," *Ahramonline*, November 19, 2011, http://english.ahram .org.eg/NewsContent/33/102/26714/Elections-/Whos-who/Yasser-Borhami.aspx.

22. Omar Ashour, "Egypt's Salafi Challenge," Project Syndicate, January 3, 2012, http://www.project-syndicate.org/commentary/egypt-s-salafi-challenge.

23. "Democracy Is Not Only Haram but Also Kafr," http://www.youtube.com/ watch?v = 4kFirseQTQE&noredirect = 1.

24. Ramazan Yildirin, "Politicization of Salafism in Egypt," *SETA Analysis*, no. 6 (June 2014): 17.

25. "Yasser Borhami."

26. Farhad Khosrokhavar, *The New Arab Revolutions That Shook the World* (London: Paradigm, 2012), 114.

27. Kamran Bokhari and Farid Senzai, *Political Islam in the Age of Democratization* (New York: Palgrave Macmillan, 2013), 93.

28. "Interactive: Full Egypt Election Results," *Al Jazeera*, February 1, 2012, http:// www.aljazeera.com/indepth/interactive/2012/01/20121248225832718.html.

29. Nouran El-Behairy, "Salafi Front Launches 'Al-Shaab' Party," *Daily News Egypt*, October 20, 2012, http://www.dailynewsegypt.com/2012/10/20/salafi-front -launches-al-shaab-party/.

30. Mai Shams el-Din, "New Salafi Party Has Curious Policy Mix," *Egypt Independent*, October 23, 2012, http://www.egyptindependent.com//news/new-salafi-party -has-curious-policy-mix.

31. Ibid.

32. Al-Nour Party, "Albrnamj" (program), May 30, 2011, 16, https://archive.org/ details/hezb_alnoor.

33. Ibid., 17.

34. Jocelyne Cesari, *The Awakening of Muslim Democracy: Religion, Modernity and the State* (Cambridge: Cambridge University Press, 2014), 142.

35. Alaa Bayoumi, "Polls Expose Rift in Egypt's Al-Nour Party," *Al-Jazeera*, September 18, 2012, http://www.aljazeera.com/news/middleeast/2012/09/2012918155 941524869.html.

36. Nagwan El Ashwal, "Egyptian Salafism Between Religious Movement and Realpolitik," *SWP Comments 27*, German Institute for International and Security Affairs, Berlin, August 2013, 6.

37. Ibid.

38. Al Masry al Youm, "Salafi Leader: Morsy Should Step Down if Millions Protest," *Egypt Independent*, June 5, 2013, http://www.egyptindependent.com/news/salafi -leader-morsy-should-step-down-if-millions-protest.

39. Stephane Lacroix, *Egypt's Pragmatic Salafis: The Politics of Hizb al-Nour*, Carnegie Endowment for International Peace, Report, Washington D.C., November 2016, 11.

40. Patrick Kingsley, "Egypt's Salafist al-Nour Party Wields New Influence on Post-Morsi Coalition," *Guardian*, July 7, 2013, http://www.theguardian.com/world/ 2013/jul/07/egypt-salafist-al-nour-party.

41. On the Saudi-Qatari competition, see Elizabeth Dickinson, "How Qatar Lost the Middle East," *Foreign Policy*, March 5, 2014, http://foreignpolicy.com/2014/03/05/ how-qatar-lost-the-middle-east/.

42. "Saudi Religious Scholars Accuse Egyptian Salafist Al-Nour Party of Obstructing Shariah," *Middle East Monitor*, January 13, 2014, https://www.middleeastmonitor .com/news/africa/9200-saudi-religious-scholars-accuse-egyptian-salafist-al-nour-party -of-obstructing-Shariah.

43. Dahlia Kholaif, "Egypt's Islamic Divide," *Al Jazeera*, July 7, 2013, http:// www.aljazeera.com/indepth/features/2013/07/201377162839192812.html.

44. Adham Youssef, "More Islamist Groups Withdraw from Anti-Coup Alliance," *Daily News Egypt*, December 6, 2014, http://www.dailynewsegypt.com/2014/12/06/ islamist-groups-withdraw-anti-coup-alliance/.

45. Auf Yussef, "Political Islam's Fate in Egypt Lies in the Hands of the Courts," Atlantic Council, Report, November 25, 2014, http://www.atlanticcouncil.org/blogs/ menasource/political-islam-s-fate-in-egypt-lies-in-the-hands-of-the-courts.

46. Alaa Bayoumi, "Egypt's Salafi Party Faces Growing Isolation: The Future of the Salafi al-Nour Is Fraught with Uncertainty," *Al Jazeera*, May 18, 2004, http://

www.aljazeera.com/news/middleeast/2014/05/egypt-salafi-party-faces-growing-isola
tion-2014514111139164795.html.

47. Dietrich Jung, *Islamist Parties After the Spring: What Do Salafist Parties Want?*
Center for Mellemoststudier, University of Southern Denmark, January 2012, 3.

48. Aaron Zelin, "Who Is Jabhat al-Islah?" Carnegie Endowment for International
Peace, July 18, 2012, http://carnegieendowment.org/sada/2012/07/18/who-is-jabhat
-al-islah/cuxo.

49. Reform Front Party, "Political Program," May 2012, https://www.facebook
.com/photo.php?fbid = 386989028010382&set = a.360978077278144.79259.36097339
7278612&type = 1.

50. Ibid.

51. Ibid.

52. Fabio Merone, "Salafism in Tunisia: An Interview with a Member of Ansar al-
Shariah," April 11, 2013, *jadaliyya.com*, http://www.jadaliyya.com/pages/index/11166/
salafism-in-tunisia_an-interview-with-a-member-of-.

53. Alcinda Honwana, *Youth and Revolution in Tunisia* (London: Zed Books,
2013), 8.

54. Merone, "Salafism in Tunisia."

55. Yasmine Ryan, "The Benghazi Link to Tunisia's Assassinations," *Al Jazeera*,
September 12, 2013, http://www.aljazeera.com/indepth/features/2013/09/201391212
3114596685.html.

56. "The Salafist Struggle," *Economist*, January 1, 2014, http://www.economist
.com/blogs/pomegranate/2014/01/dispatch-tunisia.

57. "Tunisia Declares Ansar al-Shariah a Terrorist Group," *BBC News*, August 27,
2013, http://www.bbc.com/news/world-africa-23853241.

58. Monica Marks, "Tunisia's Student Salafis," in *The New Salafi Politics*, ed. Marc
Lynch, POMEPS Briefings 14, October 16, 2012, 23, https://pomeps.org/wp-content/
uploads/2014/06/POMEPS_Studies2_Salafi.pdf.

59. Ibid.

60. Zelin, "Who Is Jabhat al-Islah?"

61. Raphaël Lefèvre, "Current Events in North Africa," *Journal of North African
Studies* 17, no. 5 (December 2012): 926.

62. Shadi Hamid, *Temptations of Power: Islamists and Illiberal Democracy in a New
Middle East* (Oxford: Oxford University Press, 2014), 201.

63. Anne Wolf, "The Salafist Temptation: The Radicalization of Tunisia's Post
Revolution Youth," *CTC Sentinel*, April 29, 2013, https://www.ctc.usma.edu/posts/the
-salafist-temptation-the-radicalization-of-tunisias-post-revolution-youth.

64. "Tunisian Salafi Imam Nasr al-Din Alawi Displays His Shrouds and Threatens
to Fight Islamic Al-Nahda Party," Attounissia TV, November 2, 2012, http://www
.memritv.org/clip/en/3639.htm.

65. Fabio Merone and Francesco Cavatorta, "The Emergence of Salafism in Tunisia," Jadaliyya.com, August 17, 2012, http://www.jadaliyya.com/pages/index/6934/the
-emergence-of-salafism-in-tunisia.

66. Anthony Shadid, "Tunisia Faces a Balancing Act of Democracy and Religion," *New York Times*, January 30, 2012, http://www.nytimes.com/2012/01/31/world/africa/tunisia-navigates-a-democratic-path-tinged-with-religion.html?pagewanted = all.

67. Monia Ben Hamadi, "Tunisian Parties Rush to Benefit from Art Exhibit Riots," *Al-Monitor*, June 18, 2012, http://www.al-monitor.com/pulse/politics/2012/06/tunisians-puppets-in-the-hands-o.html#.

68. See Harun Karcic, "Globalisation and Islam in Bosnia: Foreign Influences and Their Effects," *Totalitarian Movements and Political Religions* 11, no. 2 (June 2010): 164.

69. Shadee Elmasry, "The Salafis in America: The Rise, Decline and Prospects for a Sunni Muslim Movement Among African-Americans," *Journal of Muslim Minority Affairs* 30, no. 2 (June 2010): 225.

70. Olivier Roy, "Islam in Europe: Clash of Religions or Convergence of Religiosities?" in *Conditions of European Solidarity*, vol. 2: *Religion in New Europe*, ed. Krzysztof Michalski (Budapest: Central European University Press, 2006).

71. Kenneth Katzman, "Kuwait: Security, Reform and U.S. Policy," Congressional Research Service, 7–5700, April 29, 2014, 8, Washington, D.C.

72. See Sylvia Westall, "The Quiet Influence of Kuwait's Salafis," Reuters, June 27, 2012, http://www.reuters.com/article/2012/06/27/us-kuwait-salafi-idUSBRE85Q0Y22 0120627; Husain Marhoon, "Bahraini Salafists in Spotlight," *Al-Monitor*, June 18, 2013, http://www.al-monitor.com/pulse/originals/2013/06/bahrain-jihadists-syria -salafism.html#.

73. For the status of the French language in Tunisia, see Mohamed Daoud, "The Survival of French in Tunisian Identity," in *Handbook of Language and Ethnic Identities: The Success-Failure Continuum in Language and Ethnic Identity Efforts*, vol. 2, ed. Joshua A. Fishman and Ofelia Garcia (Oxford: Oxford University Press, 2011), 57–60. For the Salafi attacks against the French culture and language, see Andrew Hammond, " 'No God' Film Angers Tunisian Islamists," Reuters, July 6, 2011, http://www.reuters .com/article/2011/07/06/us-tunisia-islamists-tension-idUSTRE7652VZ20110706.

74. Mokhtar Awad, "The Salafi Dawa of Alexandria: The Politics of a Religious Movement," *Current Trends in Islamist Ideology*, August 14, 2014, http://www.hudson .org/research/10463-the-salafi-dawa-of-alexandria-the-politics-of-a-religious-move ment-.

75. Oren Kessler, "Egypt Salafist Party Will Honor Israel Peace," *Jerusalem Post*, December 21, 2011, http://www.jpost.com/Middle-East/Egypt-Salafist-says-party-will -honor-Israel-peace.

76. Reform Front Party, "Political Program," May 2012, https://www.facebook .com/photo.php?fbid = 386989028010382&set = a.360978077278144.79259.36097339 7278612&type = 1.

77. Elad Benari, "Tunisia Rules Out Normalization of Ties with Israel," Israel-nationalnews.com, April 2, 2012, http://www.israelnationalnews.com/News/News .aspx/154382#.VHcSccneaCw.

78. Reform Front Party, "Political Program," May 2012, Facebook post.

79. Zelin, "Who Is Jabhat al-Islah?"

80. Anne Wolf, "New Tunisian Salafist Party: A Threat to Democratic Transition?" Open Democracy, August 14, 2012, https://www.opendemocracy.net/anne-wolf/new-tunisian-salafist-party-threat-to-democratic-transition.

81. Aaron T. Rose and Fady Ashraf, "Al-Nour Party Changes Position on Article 219," Daily News Egypt, September 16, 2013, http://www.dailynewsegypt.com/2013/09/16/al-nour-party-changes-position-on-article-219/.

82. "Al-Nour Party," Jadaliyya, November 18, 2011, http://www.jadaliyya.com/pages/index/3171/al-nour-party.

83. "Egypt's Salafists Looking for 'Good' Women Candidates," Al Arabiya News, October 16, 2014, http://english.alarabiya.net/en/News/middle-east/2014/10/16/Egypt-salafist-party-looking-for-good-women-as-candidates.html.

84. "Nour Party to Include Christian Women on Its Electoral Lists: Nader Bakkar," Ahram Online, April 19, 2015, http://english.ahram.org.eg/NewsContent/1/64/128094/Egypt/Politics-/Nour-Party-to-include-Christian-women-on-its-elect.aspx.

85. Hamdi Dabash, "Opponents of Islamism Are Satan's Followers Says Islamist Leader," Egypt Independent, June 14, 2011, http://www.egyptindependent.com//news/opponents-islamism-are-satans-followers-says-islamist-leader.

86. Majdi Ouerfelli, "The Veiled Candidate," Correspondents.org, October 11, 2014, http://www.correspondents.org/node/5826.

87. Like Salafi parties, Haredi parties in Israel have objected to the participation of female candidates in the electoral process. The issue came to the forefront of Israeli politics in December 2014 when female activists initiated the campaign "No Female Candidate, No Female Vote" in an effort to put pressure on these parties to end their practice of female exclusion. See Allison Kaplan Sommer, "Threats and Backlash for Ultra-Orthodox Women Seeking Political Voice," Haaretz, December 8, 2014, http://www.haaretz.com/blogs/routine-emergencies/1.630630.

88. Emad El-Mahdy, "In Conversation with Salafist Sheikh Yasser al-Burhami," Asharq al-Awsat, February 9, 2014, http://www.aawsat.net/2014/02/article55328729/in-conversation-with-salafist-sheikh-yasser-al-burhami.

89. Ouerfelli, "The Veiled Candidate."

90. Aitemad Muhanna-Matar, Ahmad: Narrative of a Tunisian Salafist, Report, Middle East Centre, London, October 2014, 8.

91. On the meaning of the general will, see Jean Jacques Rousseau, The Social Contract (London: Penguin Books, 1968), 61–65.

92. Kholaif, "Egypt's Islamic Divide.

93. There is a growing literature on Islamist moderation; see Jillian Schwedler, Faith in Moderation: Islamist Parties in Jordan and Yemen (New York: Cambridge University Press, 2007); Suveyda Karakayaa and A. Kadir Yildirim, "Islamist Moderation

in Perspective: Comparative Analysis of the Moderation of Islamist and Western Communist Parties," *Democratization* 20, no. 7 (2013): 1322–1349.

94. On socialization of Islamist groups see Filippo Dionigi, *Hezbollah, Islamist Politics and International Society* (New York: Palgrave Macmillan, 2014), 6–9.

95. Aaron Y. Zelin, "Democracy, Salafi Style: One of Saudi Arabia's Most Popular Hardline Clerics Just Embraced Democracy; Should We Worry, or Applaud?" *Foreign Policy*, July 20, 2012, http://www.foreignpolicy.com/articles/2012/07/19/democracy_salafi_style.

96. Wahid, "Challenge of Democracy in Indonesia," 58.

Part III

1. Stefan Gosepath, "The Global Scope of Justice," in *Global Justice*, ed. Thomas W. Pogge (Oxford: Blackwell, 2001), 145–146. The original reads: το τα οφειλόμενα εκάστω αποδιδόναι δίκαιον εστί.

2. Samuel Fleischacker, *A Short History of Distributive Justice* (Cambridge, Mass.: Harvard University Press, 2005), 19.

3. Wayne P. Pomerleau, *Twelve Great Philosophers: A Historical Introduction to Human Nature* (New York: Ardsley House, 1997), 206.

4. Immanuel Kant, *Metaphysical Elements of Justice: The Complete Text of Metaphysics of Morals*, part 1, 2nd ed. (Indianapolis: Hackett, 1999), 30.

5. John Stuart Mill, "Utilitarianism," in *Justice: A Reader*, ed. Michael J. Sandel (Oxford: Oxford University Press, 2007), 39.

6. Edward Kessler, "The Jewish Concept of Justice," *The Way*, supplement 97 (2000): 69.

7. Tim Keller, *Generous Justice: How God's Grace Makes Us Just* (New York: Penguin Books, 2010), 3.

8. Joseph P. Hester, *The Ten Commandments: A Handbook of Religious, Legal and Social Issues* (Jefferson, N.C.: McFarland, 2003), 237.

9. Jean-Pierre Torrell, *Saint Thomas Aquinas: The Person and His Work*, vol. 1, 2nd ed. (Washington, D.C.: Catholic University of America Press, 2005), 149.

10. Father John Matusiak, "A Dialogue on Orthodoxy and Society," Orthodox Church in America, no date, http://oca.org/questions/society/a-dialogue-on-orthodoxy-and-society.

11. Abdulaziz Abdulhussein Sachedina, *The Just Ruler in Shi'ite Islam: The Comprehensive Authority of the Jurist in Imamite Jurisprudence* (Oxford: Oxford University Press, 1988), 120.

12. Ibid., 122.

13. Najam Haider, *Shi'i Islam: An Introduction* (Cambridge: Cambridge University Press, 2014), 18.

14. Ibid.

15. On the hidden imam see Chapter 5.

16. Bihar al-Anwar, *The Promised Mahdi*, vol. 13 (Mumbai: Ja'fari Propagation Centre, no date), 274.

17. Hank Johnston and Sebastian Haunss, "Economic Globalization and Repertoires of Protest," paper presented at International Sociological Association Conference, Brisbane, Australia, July 19, 2002.

18. On critical theory of justice, see Iris M. Young, "Towards a Critical Theory of Justice," *Social Theory and Practice* 7, no. 3 (Fall 1981): 279–302.

19. Rainer Forst, "Towards a Critical Theory of Transnational Justice," *Metaphilosophy* 32, no. 1–2 (2001): 177.

20. Ibid.

21. Edward L. Cleary, *How Latin America Saved the Soul of the Catholic Church* (Mahwah, N.J.: Paulist Press, 2009), 32.

22. Nelson Mandela, *Long Walk to Freedom: the Autobiography of Nelson Mandela* (Boston: Back Bay Books, 1995), 620.

23. Charles E. Jones and Judson L. Jeffries, "Do Not Believe the Hype: Debunking the Panther Mythology," in *Black Panthers Party Reconsidered*, ed. Charles E. Jones (Baltimore: Black Classic Press, 1998), 25–56.

24. On the International Solidarity Movement, see Ghassan Andoni et al., *Peace Under Fire: Israel, Palestine and the International Solidarity Movement* (London: Verso, 2004).

25. See Jennifer Jefferis, *Armed for Life: The Army of God and Anti-Abortion Terror in the United States* (Oxford: Praeger, 2011).

26. Asyraf Hj Ab Rahman, *The Concept of Social Justice as Found in Sayyid Qutb's Fi Zilal Al-Qur'an*, Ph.D. thesis, University of Edinburgh, October 2000, 117–130.

27. Richard Bonney, *Jihad: From Qu'ran to Bin Laden* (London: Palgrave Macmillan, 2004), 217.

28. The movement argued that only God can judge who is a true Muslim and that all Muslims should be accepted as members of the umma. See Joas Wagemakers, "Seceders and Postponers? An Analysis of the 'Khawarij' and 'Murji'a' Labels in Polemical Debates Between Quietist and Jihadi-Salafis," in *Contextualising Jihadi Thought*, ed. Jeevan Deol and Zaheer Kazmi (London: Hurst, 2011), 151.

29. Bruce Lawrence, *Messages to the World: The Statements of Osama bin Laden* (London: Verso, 2005), 166.

30. Qassim ar-Reimy, "Message to the American Nation," *Inspire Magazine* 11 (2013): 9.

31. Lawrence, *Messages to the World*, 234.

32. Ayman Al-Zawahiri, "Iman Defeats Arrogance," *Inspire Magazine* 12 (Spring 2014): 11.

33. Sayyid Qutb, "Milestones," in *Dissent—A Global Reader*, ed. Derek Malone-France (Lanham, Md.: Lexington Books, 2012), 228.

34. Sayyid Abul A'la Mawdudi, *Islam Today* (London: UKIM Dawah Centre, no date), 5.

35. Imam Khomeini, *Governance of the Jurist* (*Velayat-e Faqeeh*) (Tehran: Institute for Compilation and Publication of Imam Khomeini's Works, 2005), 53.

36. Ali Shariati, "Red Shi'ism: The Religion of Martyrdom—Black Shi'ism: The Religion of Mourning," shariahti.com, no date, http://www.shariahti.com/english/redblack.html.

Chapter 5

1. On the early history of Islam, see Fred M. Donner, "Political History of the Islamic Empire up to the Mongol Conquest," in *The Oxford History of Islam*, ed. John L. Esposito (Oxford: Oxford University Press, 1999), 1–60.

2. On the personality of Ali and his claim to succession, see Moojan Momen, *An Introduction to Shi'i Islam* (New Haven, Conn.: Yale University Press, 1985), 11–17.

3. On the Battle of Karbala, see Yasin T. al-Jibouri, *Kerbala and Beyond* (Qum: Ansariyan Publications, 2002).

4. Laurence Louer, *Transnational Shia Politics: Religious and Political Networks in the Gulf* (London: Hurst, 2008), 6.

5. Lesley Hazleton, *After the Prophet: The Epic History of the Shia-Sunni Split in Islam* (New York: Doubleday, 2009), 158.

6. The two branches eventually developed their own rituals, cultural practices, and theology. See Yann Richard, *Shi'ite Islam* (Oxford: Blackwell, 1995), 11–48.

7. The Occultation of the Mahdi can be divided into two periods: the minor occultation (874–941) when he used his deputies to maintain contact with followers and the major occultation (941 to the present) when the hidden imam is not in contact with the faithful.

8. Richard Martin, *Encyclopaedia of Islam and the Muslim World* (New York: Macmillan, 2004), 421.

9. See Musa al-Gharbi, "The Myth and Reality of Sectarianism in Iraq," *Al Jazeera Opinion*, August 18, 2014, http://america.aljazeera.com/opinions/2014/8/iraq-sectarianismshiassunniskurdsnourialmalaki.html; Hema Kotecha, "Islamic and Ethnic Identities in Azerbaijan: Emerging Trends and Tensions," discussion paper, OSCE Office in Baku, July 2006, 30, http://www.osce.org/baku/23809?download=true.

10. Olivier Roy, "The Impact of the Iranian Revolution on the Middle East," in *The Shi'a Worlds and Iran*, ed. Sabrina Mervin (London: Saqi, 2010), 29–30.

11. See Talib Aziz, "The Role of Muhammad Baqir al-Sadr in Shi'i Political Activism in Iraq from 1958 to 1980," *International Journal of Middle East Studies* 25 (1993): 207–222.

12. Louer, *Transnational Shi Politics*, 83.

13. Joseph Alagha, "Hezbollah's Conception of the Islamic State," in *The Shi'a Worlds and Iran*, ed. Sabrina Mervin (London: Saqi, 2010), 89–90.

14. See Fouad Ajami, *The Vanished Imam: Musa al Sadr and the Shia of Lebanon* (Ithaca, N.Y.: Cornell University Press, 1986).

15. See Ali Shariati, *An Approach to the Understanding of Islam* (Houston: Free Islamic Literatures, 1980).

16. Heinz Halm, *Shi'a Islam: From Religion to Revolution* (Princeton, N.J.: Markus Wiener, 1997), 134.

17. See Allama al-Hilli, "Imamate and Ijtihad," in *Authority and Political Culture in Shi'ism*, ed. Said Amir Arjomand (Albany: State University of New York Press, 1988), 240.

18. Imam Khomeini, *Islamic Government: Governance of the Jurist* (Tehran: Institute for Compilation and Publication of Imam Khomeini's works, 2002), 30.

19. Marvin Zonis and Daniel Brumberg, "Shi'ism as Interpreted by Khomeini: An Ideology of Revolutionary Violence," in *Shi'ism, Resistance and Revolution*, ed. Martin Kramer (Boulder, Col.: Westview Press, 1987), 57.

20. See Steven O'Hern, *Iran's Revolutionary Guards* (Dulles, Va.: Potomac Books, 2012).

21. Louer, *Transnational Shi Politics*, 174.

22. Mehrdad M. Mohsenin, "The Evolving Security Role of Iran in the Caspian Region," in *The Security of the Caspian Sea Region*, ed. Gennady Chufrin (Oxford: Oxford University Press, 2001), 166–167.

23. See Alex Edwards, *"Dual Containment" Policy in the Persian Gulf: The USA, Iran, and Iraq, 1991–2000* (New York: Palgrave Macmillan, 2014).

24. Vali Nasr, "Regional Implications of Shi'a Revival in Iraq," *Washington Quarterly* 27, no. 3 (Summer 2004): 7.

25. See Robert Tait and Julian Borger, "Iran Elections: Mass Arrests and Campus Raids as Regime Hits Back," *Guardian*, June 17, 2009, http://www.theguardian.com/world/2009/jun/17/iran-election-protests-arrests1.

26. The Alawites are an offshoot of Shia Islam and are mostly found in the coastal area and major cities of Syria. Although Alawites consider themselves Muslims, their doctrine has integrated many non-Islamic elements. However, their "Muslimness" has been recognized by prominent Muslim leaders, including the Lebanese Shia cleric Musa al-Sadr and the Sunni grand mufti of Jerusalem, Haj Amin al-Husseini.

27. Naim Qassem, *Hizb'allah: The Story from Within* (London: Saqi, 2005), 76.

28. Magnus Ranstorp, "The Strategy and Tactics of Hizballah's Current 'Lebanonization' Process," *Mediterranean Politics* 3, no. 1 (1998): 103–134.

29. Emmanuel Karagiannis and Clark McCauley, "The Emerging Red-Green Alliance: Where Political Islam Meets the Radical Left," *Terrorism and Political Violence* 25, no. 2 (2013): 175.

30. Mohammed Ayoob, *The Many Faces of Political Islam: Religion and Politics in the Muslim World* (Ann Arbor: University of Michigan Press, 2007), 123.

31. See, for example, Steven Stalinsky, "Arab World Divided Over Hezbollah," *New York Sun*, July 19, 2006, http://www.nysun.com/foreign/arab-world-divided-over-hezbollah/36281; Dan Murphy and Sameh NaGuib, "Hizbullah Winning Over

Arab Street," *Christian Science Monitor*, July 18, 2006, http://www.csmonitor.com/2006/0718/p01s03-wome.html.

32. See Gabriel Weimann, "Hezbollah Dot Com: Hezbollah's Online Campaign," in *New Media and Innovative Technologies*, ed. Dan Caspi and Tal Samuel-Azran (Beer-Sheva: Ben-Gurion University Press, 2008).

33. Eitan Azani, "The Hybrid Terrorist Organization: Hezbollah as a Case Study," *Studies in Conflict and Terrorism* 36, no. 11 (2013): 899–916.

34. Nicholas Noe, *Voice of Hezbollah: The Statements of Sayyed Hassan Nasrallah* (New York: Verso, 2007), 227.

35. Ibid.

36. On May 6, 2002, the U.S. undersecretary of state John Bolton gave a speech entitled "Beyond the Axis of Evil" in which he named Cuba, Libya, and Syria as state sponsors of terrorism that have ambitions for weapons of mass destruction.

37. Noe, *Voice of Hezbollah*, 284–285.

38. "Hezbollah Denies Role in Syria Unrest," PressTV, January 24, 2012, http://edition.presstv.ir/detail/222902.html.

39. Vali Nasr, *The Shia Revival: How Conflicts Within Islam Will Shape the Future* (New York: W. W. Norton, 2007), 233.

40. "Lebanon 'Suicide Bomber' Strikes Southern Beirut," *BBC News*, February 3, 2014, http://www.bbc.com/news/world-middle-east-26022425.

41. Hizb'allah has been keen to support foes of the United States, claiming to be part of an anticolonial bloc. See, for example, "Hezbollah: U.S.-Cuba Thaw Proof of Colonial Demise," *Daily Star*, December 24, 2014, http://www.dailystar.com.lb/News/Lebanon-News/2014/Dec-24/282187-hezbollah-us-cuba-thaw-proof-of-colonial-demise.ashx.

42. Amir Ahmed and Tom Watkins, "Hezbollah Leader Acknowledges Fighters' Presence in Syrian Town," CNN.com, May 27, 2013, http://edition.cnn.com/2013/05/25/world/meast/syria-violence/.

43. Matthew Levitt and Aaron Y. Zelin, "Hizballah's Gambit in Syria," *CTC Sentinel*, August 27, 2013.

44. Ibid.

45. See Chris Zambelis, "Hizballah's Role in the Syria Uprising," *CTC Sentinel*, November 28, 2012.

46. Matthew Levitt, *Hezbollah: The Global Footprint of Lebanon's Party of God* (London: Hurst, 2013), 371.

47. "France Says 3,000–4,000 Hezbollah Are Fighting in Syria," Reuters, May 29, 2013, http://www.reuters.com/article/us-syria-crisis-france-hezbollah-idUSBRE94S19U20130529.

48. See Nicholas Blanford, "The Battle for Qusayr: How the Syrian Regime and Hizballah Tipped the Balance," *CTC Sentinel*, August 27, 2013, https://www.ctc.usma.edu/posts/the-battle-for-qusayr-how-the-syrian-regime-and-hizb-allah-tipped-the-balance.

49. David Schenker, "Why a Houthi Leader Is Buried in Hezbollah Cemetery," *Weekly Standard*, April 24, 2015, http://www.weeklystandard.com/blogs/why-houthi -leader-buried-hezbollah-cemetery_929094.html.

50. Joseph Sassoon, *Saddam Hussein's Ba'th Party: Inside an Authoritarian Regime* (Cambridge: Cambridge University Press, 2012), 259–260.

51. On the 1991 uprising, see Lawrence E. Cline, "The Prospects of the Shia Insurgency Movement in Iraq," *Journal of Conflict Studies* 20, no. 1 (Fall 2000): 44–67.

52. Kenneth Katzman, "Iraq: Elections, Government and Constitution," *Congressional Research Service Report for Congress*, June 15, 2006, http://fpc.state.gov/docu ments/organization/68287.pdf.

53. Mark Kukis, "Iraq's Dance: Maliki, Sadr and Sunnis," *Time*, April 25, 2008, http://content.time.com/time/world/article/0,8599,1735034,00.html.

54. "Profile: The Mahdi Army," *Al Jazeera*, April 20, 2008, http://www.aljazeera .com/news/middleeast/2008/03/200861505611516526.html.

55. International Crisis Group. "Iraq's Civil War, the Sadrists and the Surge," *Middle East Report* February 7, 2008, 17.

56. Patrick Cockburn, *Muqtada al-Sadr and the Battle for the Future of Iraq* (New York: Scribner, 2008), 184.

57. Antony H. Cordesman and Jose Ramos, "Sadr and the Mahdi Army: Evolution, Capabilities, and a New Direction," Center for Strategic and International Studies, August 4, 2008, 13, http://csis.org/files/media/csis/pubs/080804_jam.pdf.

58. Martha Crenshaw, "Mapping Militant Organizations: Mahdi Army," Center for International Security and Cooperation, http://web.stanford.edu/group/mapping militants/cgi-bin/groups/view/57#note15.

59. Babak Rahimi, "The Return of Moqtada al-Sadr and the Revival of Mahdi Army," *CTC Sentinel*, June 3, 2010, https://www.ctc.usma.edu/posts/the-return-of -moqtada-al-sadr-and-the-revival-of-the-mahdi-army.

60. Fanar Haddad, *Sectarianism in Iraq: Antagonistic Visions of Unity* (London: Hurst, 2011), 160–161.

61. Cockburn, *Muqtada al-Sadr*, 166.

62. See, for example, Sudar san Raghavan, "Iran Said to Support Shiite Militias in Iraq," *Washington Post*, August 15, 2006, http://www.washingtonpost.com/wp-dyn/ content/article/2006/08/14/AR2006081400477.html.

63. Colin Freeman, "Inside Baghdad's Shia Slum of Sadr City: 'We Can Deal with ISIS Ourselves,'" *Telegraph*, June 21, 2014, http://www.telegraph.co.uk/news/world news/middleeast/iraq/10916632/Inside-Baghdads-Shia-slum-of-Sadr-City-We-can -deal-with-Isis-ourselves.html.

64. Loveday Morris and Mustafa Salim, "Iraqi Shiite Cleric Recalls Militiamen from Fight Against Islamic State," *Washington Post*, February 17, 2015, https://www .washingtonpost.com/world/middle_east/iraqi-shiite-cleric-recalls-militiamen-from -fight-against-islamic-state/2015/02/17/9e85321a-b6bb-11e4-bc30-a4e75503948a_ story.html.

65. Hamza Mustafa, "Iraq: Sadr Vows to Protect Shi'ite Holy Sites from ISIS," *Asharq al-Awsat*, May 20, 2015, http://www.aawsat.net/2015/05/article55343559/iraq -sadr-vows-to-protect-shiite-holy-sites-from-isis.

66. Christopher Anzalone, "Zaynab's Guardians: The Emergence of Shi'a Militias in Syria," *CTC Sentinel*, July 23, 2013; Michael Knights, "Iran's Foreign Legion: The Role of Iraqi Shiite Militias in Syria," Washington Institute, *PolicyWatch* no. 2096, June 27, 2013, http://www.washingtoninstitute.org/policy-analysis/view/irans-foreign -legion-the-role-of-iraqi-shiite-militias-in-syria.

67. Mariam Karouny, "Shi'ite Fighters Rally to Defend Damascus Shrine," Reuters, March 3, 2013, http://www.reuters.com/article/2013/03/03/us-syria-crisis-shiites -idUSBRE92202X20130303.

68. Patrick Cockburn, "The Road from Iraq to Damascus: Iraqis Fight to the Death to Defend Shia Shrines—They Show Less Zeal for Assad's Regime," *Independent*, December 4, 2013, http://www.independent.co.uk/news/world/middle-east/the -road-from-iraq-to-damascus-iraqis-fight-to-the-death-to-defend-shia-shrines--they -show-less-zeal-for-assads-regime-8983559.html.

69. On Lebanon's political history, see Kamal Salibi, *A House of Many Mansions: The History of Lebanon Reconsidered* (Berkeley: University of California Press, 1988).

70. Joshua L. Gleis and Benedetta Berti, *Hezbollah and Hamas: A Comparative Study* (Baltimore: Johns Hopkins University Press, 2012), 9.

71. Dominique Avon and Anais-Trissa Khatchadourian, *Hezbollah: A History of the "Party of God"* (Cambridge, Mass.: Harvard University Press, 2012), 106.

72. Speech by Shaykh Subhi al-Tufayli, Al-Ahd (Beirut), April 10, 1987, cited by Michael S. Krammer, *Hezbollah's Vision of the West* (Washington, D.C.: Washington Institute for Near East Policy, 1989), 26.

73. Qassem, *Hizb'allah*, 271–277.

74. Filippo Dionigi, *Hezbollah, Islamist Politics, and International Society* (London: Palgrave Macmillan, 2014), 169.

75. Ali Mamouri, "Lebanese Shiite Cleric Calls for Building Inclusive State," *Al-Monitor*, January 2, 2014, http://www.al-monitor.com/pulse/originals/2014/01/leba non-shiite-cleric-inclusive-state-interview.html##ixzz3AwsZ8J26.

76. Yitzhak Nakash, *Reaching for Power: The Shi'a in the Modern Arab World* (Princeton, N.J.: Princeton University Press, 2006), 141.

77. Ibid., 143.

78. Ibid., 7.

79. Lawrence Joffe, "Ayatollah Mohammed Baqir al-Hakim," *Guardian*, August 30, 2003, http://www.theguardian.com/news/2003/aug/30/guardianobituaries.iraq.

80. Laurence Louer, *Shiism and Politics in the Middle East* (London: Hurst, 2012), 90.

81. Ibid., 93.

82. Reidar Visser, "Iraq," in *Militancy and Political Violence in Shiism: Trends and Patterns*, ed. Assaf Moghadam (London: Routledge, 2012), 105.

83. Nicholas Krohley, "Moqtada's al-Sadr's Difficult Relationship with Iran," hurstpublishers.com, August 7, 2014, http://www.hurstpublishers.com/moqtada-al -sadrs-difficult-relationship-with-iran/.

84. Martin Kramer, "Hizbullah: The Calculus of Jihad," in *Fundamentalisms and the State: Remaking Polities, Economies, and Militance*, ed. Martin E. Marty and R. Scott Appleby (Chicago: University of Chicago Press, 1993), 545.

85. "Interview with Muqtada al-Sadr, Leader of the al-Mahdi Army in Iraq," Al-Jazeera TV, March 29, 2008, http://www.memritv.org/clip_transcript/en/1726.htm.

86. N. M. Tehrani, *Imam Khomeini and the International System: A Collection of Articles* (Tehran: Institute for Compilation and Publication of Imam Khomeini's Works, 2006), 121.

87. Kamran Aghaie, *The Martyrs of Karbala: Shi'i Symbols and Rituals in Modern Iran* (Seattle: University of Washington Press, 2004), 9.

88. "Sayyed Nasrallah: I Most Understood Imam Husayn and Ashura During the July War in 2006," Muslimtv.net, February 16, 2012, http://themuslimtv.net/view_ video.php?viewkey = 3375606f9b29bac0f9c9.

89. Mona Alami, "Meet One of Hezbollah's Teen Fighters," *Al-Monitor*, January 28, 2016, http://www.al-monitor.com/pulse/originals/2016/01/lebanon-hezbollah -teenagers-jihad-syria.html.

90. Joseph Elie Alagha, *The Shifts in Hizbullah's Ideology: Religious Ideology, Political Ideology and Political Program* (Amsterdam: Amsterdam University Press, 2006), 256.

91. Mushreq Abbas and Sarmad al-Taei, "Sadr Calls on Maliki to Visit Protest Sites in Anbar," *Al-Monitor*, January 5, 2014, http://www.al-monitor.com/pulse/poli tics/2014/01/muqtada-sadr-interview-iraq-syria-sectarian-conflict.html#.

92. "S. Nasrallah: Lebanon Facing Existential Threat, We Will Change Path of Region," *Al-Manar*, August 16, 2014, http://www.almanar.com.lb/english/wapadetails .php?eid = 165857.

93. "Interview with Muqtada al-Sadr."

94. Batoul Wehbe, "Sayyed Nasrallah: We, the Twelve Shia, Won't Abandon Palestine," *Almanar News*, August 2, 2013, http://www.almanar.com.lb/english/adetails.php ?eid = 104466&cid = 23&fromval = 1.

95. "Sayyed Nasrallah: Project Similar to the Zionist Scheme in Bahrain: There Is Colonization," International Shia News Association, January 10, 2015, http://en .shafaqna.com/other-services/middle-east/item/39600-sayyed-nasrallah-project-simi lar-to-the-zionist-scheme-in-bahrain-there-is-colonization.html.

96. "Interview with Muqtada al-Sadr."

97. Pierre-Jean Luizard, "The Sadrists in Iraq: Challenging the United States, the Marja'iyya and Iran," in *The Shi'a Worlds and Iran*, ed. Sabrina Mervin (London: Saqi, 2010), 278.

98. Ibid.

99. Eli Sugarman and Omar al-Nidawi, "The Return of Muqtada al-Sadr," *Foreign Affairs*, February 11, 2013, https://www.foreignaffairs.com/articles/iraq/2013–02–11/back-black.

100. "His Eminence Sayyid Muqtada al-Sadr Issues a Statement on Arrest of the Bahraini Shaikh Ali Salman," jawabna.com, December 29, 2014, http://jawabna.com/en/index.php/statements/3134-his-eminence-issues-a-statement-on-arrest-of-the-bahraini-shaikh-ali-salman.html.

101. "Sayyid Muqtada al-Sadr in a Written Statement: The Forty-fifth President, Trump, Will Be Surely Within the U.S. Policy Done Before," jawabna.com, November 10, 2016, http://jawabna.com/en/index.php/news/3295-sayyid-muqtada-al-sadr-in-a-written-statement-the-45th-president-trump-will-be-surely-within-the-us-policy-done-before.html.

Chapter 6

1. The term *Jihadi-Salafi movement* first appeared in an interview with Ayman al-Zawahiri in 1994. See Thomas Hegghammer, "Jihadi-Salafis or Revolutionaries? On Religion and Politics in the Study of Militant Islamism," in *Global Salafism: Islam's New Religious Movement*, ed. Roel Meijer (London: Hurst, 2009), 244–266.

2. Farhad Khosrokhavar has pointed to some former Jihadi-Salafis, such as the founder of Egyptian Islamic Jihad Abbud al-Zumar, who have denounced political violence and have joined peaceful movements struggling for democracy. See Farhad Khosrokhavar, *The New Arab Revolutions That Shook the World* (London: Paradigm, 2012), 221–222.

3. Quintan Wiktorowicz, "A Genealogy of Radical Islam," *Studies in Conflict and Terrorism* 28, no. 2 (2005): 75.

4. Gilles Kepel, *Jihad: The Trail of Political Islam* (London: I. B. Tauris, 2006), 220.

5. Mohammed Hafez, *Suicide Bombers in Iraq: The Strategy and Ideology of Martyrdom* (Washington, D.C.: U.S. Institute of Peace, 2007), 64.

6. See Frazer Egerton, *Jihad in the West: The Rise of Militant Salafism* (Cambridge: Cambridge University Press, 2011).

7. Mehran Kamrava, "Khomeini and the West," in *A Critical Introduction to Khomeini*, ed. Arshin Adib-Moghaddam (New York: Cambridge University Press, 2014), 161–162.

8. For instance, Khomeini used the term *Nasibi* (pl. *Nawasib*), which refers to those who hate Ahl al-Bayt (i.e., the family of Prophet Muhammad), to describe the enemies of the Iranian Revolution.

9. See Toby Matthiesen, *The Other Saudis: Shiism, Dissent and Sectarianism* (Cambridge: Cambridge University Press, 2014).

10. Fawaz Gerges, *The Far Enemy: Why Jihad Went Global* (Cambridge: Cambridge University Press, 2009), 56–67.

11. See Michael W. S. Ryan, *Decoding Al-Qaeda's Strategy: The Deep Battle Against America* (New York: Columbia University Press, 2013).

12. See, for example, Mitchell D. Silber, *The Al Qaeda Factor: Plots Against the West* (Philadelphia: University of Pennsylvania Press, 2012).

13. Like Zarqawi, Maqdisi had spent time in Afghanistan and Pakistan. He later returned to Jordan and denounced the King Hussein regime. As a result, he was arrested and imprisoned. Maqdisi broke off ties with his former apprentice when Zarqawi started targeting the Iraqi Shias.

14. Musa al-Gharbi, "The Myth and Reality of Sectarianism in Iraq," *Al Jazeera America*, August 18, 2014, http://america.aljazeera.com/opinions/2014/8/iraq-sectar ianismshiassunniskurdsnourialmalaki.html.

15. Gilles Kepel and Jean-Pierre Milelli, *Al Qaeda in Its Own Words* (Cambridge, Mass.: Harvard University Press, 2008), 253.

16. Ibid., 254.

17. Nibras Kazimi, "Zarqawi's Anti-Shia Legacy: Original or Borrowed?" *Current Trends in Islamist Ideology*, November 1, 2006, http://www.hudson.org/research/9908 -zarqawi-s-anti-shi-a-legacy-original-or-borrowed.

18. Brian Whitaker, "Revealed: Al-Qaeda Plan to Seize Control of Iraq," *Guardian*, October 13, 2005, http://www.theguardian.com/world/2005/oct/13/alqaida.iraq.

19. Vali Nasr, "Regional Implications of Shi'a Revival in Iraq," *Washington Quarterly* 27, no. 3 (Summer 2004): 8.

20. "The History of Shia Muslims: Why the Aggravation?" *Economist*, March 4, 2004, 41.

21. Fawaz A. Gerges, *The Rise and Fall of Al-Qaeda* (Oxford: Oxford University Press, 2011), 116.

22. Tim Lister, "ISIS: The First Terror Group to Build an Islamic State?" CNN, June 13, 2014, http://edition.cnn.com/2014/06/12/world/meast/who-is-the-isis/index .html?hpt = imi_t4.

23. Abdel Bari Atwan, *Islamic State: The Digital Caliphate* (London: Saqi Books, 2015), 111.

24. His father, Sulayman al-Assad, was a prominent Alawi leader who opposed Sunni rule. See Patrick Seale, *Asad of Syria: The Struggle for the Middle East* (Berkeley: University of California Press, 1988), 5.

25. See Raphaël Lefèvre, *Ashes of Hama: The Muslim Brotherhood in Syria* (London: Hurst, 2013).

26. Stephen Starr, *Revolt in Syria: Eye-Witness to the Uprising* (London: Hurst, 2012), 5.

27. Reese Erlich, *Inside Syria: The Backstory of Their Civil War and What the World Can Expect* (New York: Prometheus, 2014), 85.

28. Emile Hokayem, *Syria's Uprising and the Fracturing of the Levant* (London: Routledge, 2013), 95.

29. David W. Lesch, *Syria: The Fall of the House of Assad* (New Haven, Conn.: Yale University Press, 2012), 92.

30. Hokayem, *Syria's Uprising*, 94–95.

31. Charles Lister, "Dynamic Stalemate: Surveying Syria's Military Landscape," policy briefing, Brookings Doha Center, May 2014, 7.

32. For a different perspective, see Christopher Phillips, "Sectarianism and Conflict in Syria," *Third World Quarterly* 36, no. 2 (2015): 357–376.

33. Anne Barnard and Hwaida Saad, "Sunni Cleric Issues Appeal for World's Muslims to Help Syrian Rebels," *New York Times*, June 2, 2013, 8.

34. Peter R. Neumann, "Foreign Fighter Total in Syria/Iraq Now Exceeds 20,000; Surpasses Afghanistan Conflict in the 1980s," *ICSR Insight*, January 26, 2015, http://icsr.info/2015/01/foreign-fighter-total-syriairaq-now-exceeds-20000-surpasses-afghanistan-conflict-1980s/.

35. J. Van De Bildt, "West Concerned as European Muslims Join Syria Fight," *Jerusalem Post*, May 26, 2013, http://www.jpost.com/International/West-concerned-as-European-Muslims-join-Syria-fight-314382.

36. On the rise of ISIS, see Michael Weiss and Hassan Hassan, *ISIS: Inside the Army of Terror* (New York: Regan Arts, 2015), 131–152.

37. "Zawahiri Disbands Main Qaeda Faction in Syria," *Daily Star*, November 8, 2013, http://dailystar.com.lb/News/Middle-East/2013/Nov-08/237219-zawahiri-disbands-main-qaeda-faction-in-syria-jazeera.ashx#axzz2jVRVxOhD.

38. Liz Sly, "Al-Qaeda Disavows Any Ties with Radical Islamist ISIS Group in Syria, Iraq," *Washington Post*, February 3, 2014, http://www.washingtonpost.com/world/middle_east/al-qaeda-disavows-any-ties-with-radical-islamist-isis-group-in-syria-iraq/2014/02/03/2c9afc3a-8cef-11e3–98ab-fe5228217bd1_story.html.

39. Adrian Lee, "The New Dark Ages: The Chilling Medieval Society ISIS Extremists Seek to Impose in Iraq," *Sunday Express*, June 21, 2014, http://www.express.co.uk/news/world/483920/Iraq-Isis-Extremists-Dark-Ages-Muslim-Baghdad-Jihadist.

40. Roula Khalaf and Sam Jones, "Selling Terror: How ISIS Charts Its Brutality in Annual Report," *Financial Times*, June 18, 2014, http://www.ft.com/intl/cms/s/2/69e70954-f639–11e3-a038–00144feabd c0.html.

41. Jessica Stern and J. M. Berger, *ISIS: The State of Terror* (London: William Collins, 2015), 145–175.

42. Simeon Kerr and Erika Solomon, "'State of Aleppo' Brochure Reveals ISIS Visions for Islamic State," *Financial Times*, June 30, 2014, http://www.ft.com/cms/s/0/0e882b36–005e-11e4-a3f2–00144feab7de.html#axzz36LFk4LqF.

43. "A-Raqqa Student: 'Daily Life Is Good' Under ISIS," *Syria: Direct*, April 27, 2014, http://syriadirect.org/news/a-raqqa-student-%E2%80%98daily-life-is-good%E2%80%99-under-isis/.

44. On the similarities between the Taliban and ISIS, see Ahmed Rashid, "ISIS: The New Taliban," *New York Review of Books*, July 2, 2014, http://www.nybooks.com/blogs/nyrblog/2014/jul/02/iraqs-new-taliban/.

45. "Belgian Jihadist Fighting with ISIS in Syria: It's Nice to See Infidel Blood from Time to Time," *memritv.org*, March 2014, http://www.memritv.org/clip/en/4210.htm.

46. Jean-Loup Samaan, "An End-of-Time Utopia: Understanding the Narrative of the Islamic State," *National Defense College Research Report*, Rome, April 2015, 3.

47. "Da'wah and Hisbah in the Islamic State," *Dabiq Magazine*, no. 3, 2014, 16–17.

48. Ibid.

49. "Advice for Those Embarking upon Hijran," *Dabiq Magazine*, no. 3, 2014, 33.

50. Richard Barrett, "The Islamic State," Soufan Group, November 2014, 19, http://soufangroup.com/wp-content/uploads/2014/10/TSG-The-Islamic-State-Nov14.pdf.

51. Ibid., 23.

52. Scott Lucas, "Iraq and Syria Document: ISIS's Declaration of a Caliphate for All Muslims," *EA WorldView*, June 30, 2014, http://eaworldview.com/2014/06/iraq-text-isis-declaration-caliphate-muslims/.

53. "From Hijrah to Khilafah," *Dabiq Magazine*, no. 1, 2014, 35.

54. The concept of mujaddid is based on a hadith that states that "Allah will raise for this community at the end of every hundred years the one who will revive its religion for it". See Abu Dawud, book 38: Kitab al-Malahim (The Book of Battles), hadith number 4278, http://sunnah.com/abudawud/39.

55. "From Hijrah to Khilafah," 39.

56. Chase Robinson, "The Caliph Has No Clothes," *International New York Times*, July 17, 2014, http://www.nytimes.com/2014/07/17/opinion/the-caliph-has-no-clothes.html?_r=0.

57. The hadith states, "The Last Hour would not come until the Romans [i.e., Europeans] would land at al-A'maq or in Dabiq." See Muslim ibn al-Hajjaj, Sahih Muslim, book 41: Kitab Al-Fitan wa Ashrat As-Sa'ah (The Book Pertaining to the Turmoil and Portents of the Last Hour), hadith number 6924, http://www.unitedamericanmuslim.org/sahihmuslim/041_smt.html#011_b41.

58. "Islam Is the Religion of the Sword Not Pacifism," *Dabiq Magazine*, February 2015, 24.

59. Samaan, "An End-of-Time Utopia," 6.

60. Sam Jones, "Iraq Crisis: Sophisticated Tactics Key to ISIS Strength," *Financial Times*, June 26, 2014, http://www.ft.com/intl/cms/s/0/6436f754-fd18–11e3-bc93–00144feab7de.html#axzz36LFk4LqF.

61. "ISIS Parades SCUD Missile, Tanks in Al-Raqqa, Syria," MEHRI TV, June 30, 2014, https://www.youtube.com/watch?v=fjvxHCY26rk.

62. Andreas Becker, "Who Finances ISIS?" *Deutsche Welle*, June 19, 2014, http://www.dw.de/who-finances-isis/a-17720149.

63. "British and Australian Fighters with ISIS Explain Motivation, Call Others to Join War in Syria, Iraq," *memritv.org*, June 20, 2013, http://www.memritv.org/clip/en/4317.htm.

64. "Ansar al-Islam Pledges Allegiance to the Islamic State," *Dabiq Magazine*, no. 4, 2014, 22.

65. Jhoanna Ballaran, "Philippines Probes Alleged ISIS Links in South," *Institute for War and Peace Reporting*, September 26, 2014, http://iwpr.net/report-news/philip pines-probes-alleged-isis-links-south.

66. Aaron Y. Zelin, "The Islamic State's First Colony in Libya," *Policy Watch* 2325, Washington Institute for Near East Policy, October 10, 2014, http://www.washington institute.org/policy-analysis/view/the-islamic-states-first-colony-in-libya.

67. Dean Nelson and Ashfaq Yusufzai, "Pakistan Taliban Pledge Allegiance to ISIL," *Daily Telegraph*, October 14, 2014, http://www.telegraph.co.uk/news/world news/asia/pakistan/11162277/Pakistan-Taliban-pledges-allegiance-to-Isil.html.

68. "Islamic State 'Accepts' Boko Haram's Allegiance Pledge," *BBC News*, March 13, 2015, http://www.bbc.com/news/world-africa-31862992.

69. "Iraqi Christians Flee After ISIS Issue Mosul Ultimatum," *BBC News*, July 18, 2014, http://www.bbc.com/news/world-middle-east-28381455.

70. Dominic Evans, "Convert, Pay Tax, or Die, Islamic State Warns Christians," Reuters, July 18, 2014, http://uk.reuters.com/article/2014/07/18/uk-iraq-security-chris tians-idUKKBN0FN29N20140718.

71. Raya Jalabi, "Who Are the Yazidis and Why Is Isis Hunting Them?" *Guardian*, August 11, 2014, http://www.theguardian.com/world/2014/aug/07/who-yazidi-isis -iraq-religion-ethnicity-mountains.

72. Luke Harding and Fazel Hawramy, "ISIS Accused of Ethnic Cleansing as Story of Shia Prison Massacre Emerges," *Guardian*, August 25, 2014, http://www.theguard ian.com/world/2014/aug/25/isis-ethnic-cleansing-shia-prisoners-iraq-mosul.

73. See, for example, "Al-Nusra and ISIS Fight Over Border City," *Middle East Monitor*, June 29, 2014, https://www.middleeastmonitor.com/news/middle-east/12437 -al-nusra-and-isis-fight-over-border-city.

74. On differences between the two groups, see Daniel Byman and Jennifer Wil-liams, "Al-Qaeda vs. ISIS: The Battle for the Soul of Jihad," *Newsweek*, March 27, 2015, http://www.newsweek.com/al-qaeda-vs-isis-battle-soul-jihad-317414.

75. Caroline Mortimer, "ISIS Loses a Third of Its Territory in Syria and Iraq, Analysts Say," *Independent*, October 9, 2016, http://www.independent.co.uk/news/ world/middle-east/isis-territory-losing-syria-iraq-terror-jihadists-iraqi-forces-air-strikes -mosul-a7352401.html.

76. Abu Bakr al-Baghdadi, "A Message to the Mujahidin and the Muslim Ummah in the Month of Ramadan," July 2014, https://ia902501.us.archive.org/2/items/ hym3_22aw/english.pdf.

77. "The Islamic State of Iraq and Greater Syria: Two Arab Countries Fall Apart," *Economist*, June 14, 2014, 35.

78. "A Window into the Islamic State," *Dabiq Magazine*, no. 4, 2014, 27–29.

79. See Michael Kerr and Amal Hamdan, "Lebanon: The Hybridity of a Confes-sional State," in *Routledge Handbook of Regionalism and Federalism*, ed. John Loughlin, John Kincaid, and Wilfried Swenden (London: Routledge, 2013).

80. On Israel's Law of Return, see Dvora Hacohen, "The Law of Return as an Embodiment of the Link Between Israel and the Jews of the Diaspora," *Journal of Israeli History* 19, no. 1 (March 1998): 61–89.

81. "ISIS Spokesman Reaffirms the Group's Victory, Says 'We Want . . . Paris Before Rome . . . After [We] Blow Up Your White House, Big Ben, and Eiffel Tower,'" *MEMRI Jihad and Terrorism Threat Monitor*, March 12, 2015, http://www.memrijttm .org/isis-spokesman-reaffirms-the-groups-victory-says-we-want-paris-before-rome -after-we-blow-up-your-white-house-big-ben-and-eiffel-tower.html.

82. See Efraim Karsh, *Islamic Imperialism: A History* (New Haven, Conn.: Yale University Press, 2006).

83. Raja Abdulrahim, "Islamic State, Rival Al Nusra Front Each Strengthen Grip on Syria," *Los Angeles Times*, November 28, 2014, http://www.latimes.com/world/ middleeast/la-fg-syria-nusra-front-20141128-story.html#page = 1.

84. Mohammad Ballout, "Syrian Jihadists Move War to Alawite Stronghold," *Al-Monitor*, August 8, 2013, http://www.al-monitor.com/pulse/security/2013/08/syrian -war-jihadists-alawite-stronghold-coast.html#.

85. Lizzie Dearden, "Syria Conflict: Idlib City Falls to Jabhat al-Nusra as President Assad's Forces Flee, Jihadists Claim," *Independent*, March 28, 2015, http://www .independent.co.uk/news/world/middle-east/syria-conflict-idlib-city-falls-to-jabhat -alnusra-as-president-assads-forces-flee-jihadists-claim-10141020.html.

86. Jennifer Cafarella, "Jabhat al-Nusra in Syria," *Middle East Security Report*, December 2014, 15.

87. See "Syria's Al-Nusrah Front Leader Interviewed on Conflict, Political Vision," *BBC Monitoring Middle East*, December 22, 2013.

88. Sue Turton, "Jabhat al-Nusra Says It Stands for 'Justice,'" *Al Jazeera*, January 13, 2013, http://blogs.aljazeera.com/blog/middle-east/jabhat-al-nusra-says-it-stands -justice.

89. "Dozens of 'Nusrah' and 'Ahrar' Fighters Repent and Join the Islamic State," *Dabiq Magazine*, no. 7, 2015, 39.

90. Ibid., 38.

91. "Foreword," *Dabiq Magazine*, no. 5, 2015, 3.

92. "ISIS Spokesman Reaffirms the Group's Victory."

93. "The Situation After the Mubahalah," *Dabiq Magazine*, no. 2, 2014, 25.

94. Rod Nordland and Alissa J Rubin, "Massacre Claim Shakes Iraq," *New York Times*, June 15, 2014, http://www.nytimes.com/2014/06/16/world/middleeast/iraq. html.

95. "Islamic Front's Military Commander: No to Democracy as Syrians Are Thirsty for Islamic State," *youtube.com*, January 30, 2014, https://www.youtube.com/ watch?v = aSsNb8motGI.

96. "From Hijrah to Khilafah," 40.

97. Lucas, "Iraq and Syria Document."

98. "Dutch Former Royal Netherlands Army Soldier Trains Jihadists in Syria," *youtube.com*, January 27, 2014, http://www.youtube.com/watch?v = nWua3exa6rw.

99. "British Women Joining Jihad in Syria," *Channel 4*, July 23, 2013, http://www.youtube.com/watch?v = 5hAlKlQ2g1Q.

100. Charlotte Boitiaux, "Confessions of a French Jihadist in Syria," *France 24*, February 13, 2014, http://www.france24.com/en/20140212-france-24-exclusive-syria -french-jihadist-foreign-fighter-confessions.

101. "Foreword," *Dabiq Magazine*, no. 2, 2014, 4.

102. David K. Kirkpatrick and Rukmini Callimachi, "Islamic State Video Shows Beheadings of Egyptian Christians in Libya," *New York Times*, February 15, 2015, http://www.nytimes.com/2015/02/16/world/middleeast/islamic-state-video-beheadings -of-21-egyptian-christians.html?_r = 0.

103. "Nusra Leader: Our Mission Is to Defeat Syria Regime," *Al Jazeera*, May 28, 2015, http://www.aljazeera.com/news/2015/05/nusra-front-golani-assad-syria-hezbol lah-isil-150528044857528.html.

104. Abdel Bari Atwan, *After Bin Laden: Al-Qa'ida, the Next Generation* (New York: New Press, 2013), 263.

Conclusion

1. Mahmood Monshipouri, *Muslims in Global Politics: Identities, Interests and Human Rights* (Philadelphia: University of Pennsylvania Press, 2009), 261.

2. Steven Kull, "Muslim Public Opinion on U.S. Policy, Attacks on Civilians and al-Qaeda," Program on International Policy Attitudes at the University of Maryland, April 24, 2007, 23, http://www.worldpublicopinion.org/pipa/pdf/apr07/START_Apr07 _rpt.pdf.

3. Eytan Gilboa, "The United States and the Arab Spring," in *The Arab Spring, Democracy and Security: Domestic and International Ramification*, ed. Efraim Inbar (London: Routledge, 2013), 68.

4. Fawaz A. Gerges, *American and Political Islam: Clash of Cultures or Clash of Interests?* (Cambridge: Cambridge University Press, 1999), 21–31.

5. "Remarks of the President on a New Beginning at the Cairo University," Office of the Press Secretary, White House, June 4, 2009, http://www.whitehouse.gov/the -press-office/remarks-president-cairo-university-6-04-09.

6. See Lally Weymouth, "Rare Interview with Egyptian Gen. Abdel Fatah al-Sissi," *Washington Post*, August 3, 2013, http://www.washingtonpost.com/world/middle_east/ rare-interview-with-egyptian-gen-abdel-fatah-al-sissi/2013/08/03/a77eb37c-fbc4-11e2 -a369-d195 4abcb7e3_story.html; Michael R. Gordon and Kareem Fahim, "Kerry Says Egypt's Military Was 'Restoring Democracy' in Ousting Morsi," *New York Times*, August 1, 2013, http://www.nytimes.com/2013/08/02/world/middleeast/egypt-warns -morsi-supporters-to-end-protests.html?_r = 0.

7. "Washington Refuses to Blacklist Muslim Brotherhood," *Middle East Monitor*, December 3, 2014, https://www.middleeastmonitor.com/news/americas/15623-wash ington-refuses-to-blacklist-muslim-brotherhood.

8. "Bin Laden Praises Arab Spring from Beyond the Grave," Channel 4, May 19, 2011, http://www.channel4.com/news/bin-laden-praises-arab-spring-from-beyond -the-grave.

9. Jonathan Broder, "Unfinished Mideast Revolts," *National Interest*, May-June 2012, 54.

Selected Bibliography

Abdin, A. Z al-. "The Political Thought of Hasan al-Banna." *Islamic Studies* 28, no. 3 (Autumn 1989): 219–234.

Abuza, Zachary. *Militant Islam in Southeast Asia.* Boulder, Colo.: Lynne Rienner, 2003.

Afghani, Sayyid Jamal al-Din al-. "An Islamic Response to Imperialism." In *Islam in Transition: Muslim Perspectives*, ed. John J. Donohue and John L. Esposito, 16–20. New York: Oxford University Press, 1982.

Afshar, Haleh. *Iran: A Revolution in Turmoil.* Albany: State University of New York Press, 1985.

Aghaie, Kamran. *The Martyrs of Karbala: Shi'i Symbols and Rituals in Modern Iran.* Seattle: University of Washington Press, 2004.

Ahmed, Akbar S. *Journey into Islam: The Crisis of Globalization.* Washington, D.C.: Brookings Institution Press, 2007.

Ahmed, Akbar S. and Hastings Donnan. "Islam in the Age of Postmodernity." In *Islam, Globalization and Postmodernity*, ed. Akbar S. Ahmed and Hastings Donnan, 1–20. London: Routledge, 1994.

Ajami, Fouad. *The Vanished Imam: Musa al-Sadr and the Shia of Lebanon.* Ithaca, N.Y.: Cornell University Press, 1986.

Ali, Maulana Muhammad. *The Holy Quran*, 4th revised ed. Lahore: Ahmadiyya Anjuman Isha'at Islam Lahore, 1951.

Ali, Souad T. *A Religion, Not a State: Ali Abd al-Raziq's Islamic Justification of Political Secularism.* Salt Lake City: University of Utah Press, 2009.

Alianak, Sonia L. *The Transition Towards Revolution and Reform: The Arab Spring Realised?* Edinburgh: Edinburgh University Press, 2014.

Anani, Khalid al-. "Islamist Parties Post-Arab Spring." *Mediterranean Politics* 17, no. 3 (2012): 466–472.

Anderson, Carol. *Eyes Off the Prize: African Americans, the United Nations, and the Struggle for Human Rights, 1944–1955.* Cambridge: Cambridge University Press, 2003.

Atwan, Abdel Bari. *After Bin Laden: Al-Qa'ida, the Next Generation.* New York: New Press, 2013.

———. *Islamic State: The Digital Caliphate.* London: Saqi Books, 2015.

Auyero, Javier. "Glocal Riots." *International Sociology* 16 (2001): 33–54.

Avon, Dominique and Anais-Trissa Khatchadourian. *Hezbollah: A History of the "Party of God."* Cambridge, Mass.: Harvard University Press, 2012.

Ayobi, Nazih. *Political Islam: Religion and Politics in the Arab World.* London: Routledge, 1991.

Ayoob, Mohammed. *The Many Faces of Political Islam: Religion and Politics in the Muslim World.* Ann Arbor: University of Michigan Press, 2007.

Barber, Benjamin. *Jihad vs. Mcworld: Terrorism's Challenge to Democracy.* London: Corgi Books, 1995.

Bayat, Asef. "Islamism and Social Movement Theory." *Third World Quarterly* 26 (2005): 891–908.

Baylis, John, Steve Smith, and Patricia Owens. *The Globalization of World Politics.* 4th ed. Oxford: Oxford University Press, 2008.

Beinin, Joel and Joe Stork, eds. *Political Islam.* Berkeley: University of California Press, 1997.

Black, Antony. *The History of Islamic Political Thought: From the Prophet to the Present.* Edinburgh: Edinburgh University Press, 2011.

Blum-Kulka, Shoshana and Tamar Liebes. "Frame Ambiguities: Intifada Narrativization of the Experience by Israeli Soldiers." In *Framing the Intifada: People and Media*, ed. Akiba A. Cohen and Gadi Wolfsfeld, 27–52. Norwood, N.J.: Ablex, 1993.

Boulby, Marion. *The Muslim Brotherhood and the Kings of Jordan, 1945–1993.* Atlanta: Scholars Press, 1999.

Brown, Rajeswary Ampalavanar. *Islam in Modern Thailand: Faith, Philanthropy and Politics.* London: Routledge, 2013.

Capek, Stella M. "Environmental Justice Frame: A Conceptual Discussion and Application." *Social Problems* 40, no. 1 (1993): 5–24.

Carroll, William K. and R. S. Ratner, "Master Framing and Cross-Movement Networking in Contemporary Social Movements." *Sociological Quarterly* 37, no. 4 (1996): 602–603.

Chamkhi, Tarek. "Neo-Islamism in the Post-Arab Spring." *Contemporary Politics* 20, no. 4 (2014): 453–468.

Clark, Ian. *Globalization and International Relations.* Oxford: Oxford University Press, 1999.

Cockburn, Patrick. *Muqtada al-Sadr and the Battle for the Future of Iraq.* New York: Scribner, 2008.

Cohen, Amnon. *Political Parties in the West Bank Under the Jordanian Regime, 1949–1967.* Ithaca, N.Y.: Cornell University Press, 1982.

Commins, David. *The Wahhabi Mission and Saudi Arabia.* London: Tauris, 2006.

Denoeux, Guilain. "The Forgotten Swamp: Navigating Political Islam." *Middle East Policy* 9, no. 2 (June 2002): 56–81.

Diani, Mario. "Networks and Social Movements: A Research Programme." In *Social Movements and Networks: Relational Approaches to Collective Action*, ed. Mario Diani and Doug McAdam, 299–319. Oxford: Oxford University Press, 2003.

Dionigi, Filippo. *Hezbollah, Islamist Politics, and International Society*. London: Palgrave Macmillan, 2014.

Drori, Gili S., Markus A. Hollerer, and Peter Walgenbach. "Unpacking the Glocalization of Organization: From Term, to Theory, to Analysis." *European Journal of Cultural and Political Sociology* 1, no. 1 (2014): 85–99.

Egerton, Frazer. *Jihad in the West: The Rise of Militant Salafism*. Cambridge: Cambridge University Press, 2011.

Eickelman, Dale F. and Jon W. Anderson. "Redefining Muslim Publics." In *New Media in the Muslim World: The Emerging Public Sphere*, 2nd ed., ed. Dale F. Eickelman and Jon W. Anderson, 1–18. Bloomington: Indiana University Press, 2003.

Eickelman, Dale F. and James Piscatori. *Islamist Politics*. Princeton, N.J.: Princeton University Press, 1996.

Elliott, Julia and Elizabeth Knowles. *The Oxford Dictionary of New Words*. Oxford: Oxford University Press, 1997.

Ellis, Donald G. *Transforming Conflict: Communication and Ethnopolitical Conflict*. New York: Rowman and Littlefield, 2006.

Erlich, Reese. *Inside Syria: The Backstory of Their Civil War and What the World Can Expect*. New York: Prometheus, 2014.

Esposito, John L. *The Islamic Revolution: Its Global Impact*. Miami: Florida International University, 1990.

———, ed. *Political Islam: Revolution, Radicalism or Reform?* Boulder, Colo.: Lynne Rienner, 1997.

Euben Roxanne, *Enemy in the Mirror: Islamic Fundamentalism and the Limits of Modern Rationalism*. Princeton, NJ.: Princeton University Press, 1999.

Fiorentini, Riccardo and Guido Montani. *The New Global Political Economy: From Crisis to Supranational Integration*. Cheltenham, U.K.: Edward Elgar, 2012.

Fukuyama, Francis. *The End of History and the Last Man*. London: Hamish Hamilton, 1992.

———. *Political Order and Political Decay: From the Industrial Revolution to the Globalization of Democracy*. New York: Farrar, Straus and Giroux, 2015.

Fuller, Graham E. *The Future of Political Islam*. New York: Palgrave Macmillan, 2003.

Gabardi, Wayne. *Negotiating Postmodernism*. Minneapolis: University of Minnesota Press, 2001.

Gainous, Jason and Kevin M. Wagner. *Tweeting the Power: The Social Media Revolution in American Politics*. Oxford: Oxford University Press, 2013.

Geaves, Ron. *Islam in Victorian Britain: The Life and Times of Abdullah Quilliam*. Markfield: Kube, 2010.

Gerges, Fawaz. *The Far Enemy: Why Jihad Went Global*. Cambridge: Cambridge University Press, 2005.

Giddens, Anthony. *The Consequences of Modernity*. Stanford, Calif.: Stanford University Press, 1990.

Gilpin, Robert. *The Challenge of Global Capitalism.* Princeton, N.J.: Princeton University Press, 2002.

Giulianotti, Richard and Roland Robertson. "Forms of Glocalization: Globalization and Migration Strategies of Scottish Football Fans in North America." *Sociology* 41, no. 1 (2007): 133–152.

Gleis, Joshua L. and Benedetta Berti. *Hezbollah and Hamas: A Comparative Study.* Baltimore: Johns Hopkins University Press, 2012.

Goffman, Erving. *Frame Analysis.* Cambridge, Mass.: Harvard University Press, 1974.

Gul, Imtiaz. "Transnational Islamic Networks." *International Review of the Red Cross* 92, no. 880 (December 2010): 899–925.

Gunning, Jeroen. *Hamas in Politics: Democracy, Religion, Violence.* London: Hurst, 2008.

Haddad, Fanar. *Sectarianism in Iraq: Antagonistic Visions of Unity.* London: Hurst, 2011.

Hafez, Mohammed. "Jihad After Iraq: Lessons from the Arab Afghans." *Studies in Conflict and Terrorism* 32, no. 2 (2009): 73–94.

———. *Suicide Bombers in Iraq: The Strategy and Ideology of Martyrdom.* Washington, D.C.: U.S. Institute of Peace, 2007.

———. *Why Muslims Rebel.* London: Lynne Rienner, 2004.

Haider, Najam. *Shi'i Islam: An Introduction.* Cambridge: Cambridge University Press, 2014.

Hale, William and Ergun Özbudun. *Islamism, Democracy and Liberalism in Turkey: The Case of the AKP.* London: Routledge, 2011.

Halm, Heinz. *Shi'a Islam: From Religion to Revolution.* Princeton, N.J.: Markus Wiener, 1997.

Hamid, Shadi. *Temptations of Power: Islamists and Illiberal Democracy in a New Middle East.* Oxford: Oxford University Press, 2014.

Hegghammer, Thomas. "The Rise of Muslim Foreign Fighters: Islam and the Globalization of Jihad." *International Security* 35, no. 3 (Winter 2010–2011): 53–94.

Hendrick, Joshua D. "The Regulated Potential of Kinetic Islam: Antitheses in Global Islamic Activism." In *Muslim Citizens of the Globalized World: Contributions of the Gülen Movement,* ed. Robert A. Hunt and Yüksel A. Aslandogan, 12–33. Somerset, N.J.: The Light, 2007.

Henkin, Louis. *The Age of Rights.* New York: Columbia University Press, 1990.

Hirst, Paul and Grahame Thompson. *Globalization in Question: The International Economy and the Possibilities of Governance.* Cambridge: Polity Press, 1996.

Hizb ut-Tahrir. *The American Campaign to Suppress Islam.* London: Al-Khilafah Publications, 1996.

———. *The Methodology of Hizb ut-Tahrir for Change.* London: Al-Khilafah Publications, 1999.

Hokayem, Emile. *Syria's Uprising and the Fracturing of the Levant.* London: Routledge, 2013.

Hosgor, Evren. "Islamic Capital/Anatolian Tigers: Past and Present." *Middle Eastern Studies* 47, no. 2 (March 2011): 343–360.

Howard, Philip N. and Muzammil M. Hussain. *Democracy's Fourth Wave? Digital Media and the Arab Spring*. New York: Oxford University Press, 2013.

Hunt, Robert A. and Yüksel A. Aslandogan, eds. *Muslim Citizens of the Globalized World*. Somerset, N.J.: The Light, 2007.

Hunt, Scott A., Robert D. Benford, and David A. Snow. "Identity Fields: Framing Processes and the Social Construction of Movement Identities." In *New Social Movements: From Ideology to Identity*, ed. Enrique Larana, Hank Johnston, and Joseph R Gusfield, 185–208. Philadelphia: Temple University Press, 1994.

Huntington, Samuel P. *The Third Wave: Democratization in the Late Twentieth Century*. Norman: University of Oklahoma Press, 1993.

———. *The Clash of Civilizations and the Remaking of the World Order*. New York: Simon and Schuster, 1996.

Husain, Ed. *The Islamist: Why I Joined Radical Islam in Britain, What I Saw Inside and Why I Left*. London: Penguin Books, 2007.

Inkele, Alex. *One World Emerging*. Boulder, Colo.: Westview Press, 1998.

Janin, Hunt. *The Pursuit of Learning in the Islamic World, 610–2003*. Jefferson, N.C.: McFarland, 2005.

Jijon, Isabel. "The Glocalization of Time and Space: Soccer and Meaning in Chota Valley, Ecuador." *International Sociology* 28 (2013): 373–390.

Johnston, Hank. *Tales of Nationalism: Catalonia, 1939–1979*. New Brunswick, N.J.: Rutgers University Press, 1991.

———. "Verification and Proof in Frame and Discourse Analysis." In *Methods of Social Movement Research*, ed. Bert Klandermans and Suzanne Staggenborg, 62–91. Minneapolis: University of Minnesota Press, 2002.

Kant, Immanuel. *Political Writings*. Cambridge: Cambridge University Press, 1991.

Kaplan, Robert D. "The Coming Anarchy: How Scarcity, Crime, Overpopulation, Tribalism, and Disease Are Rapidly Destroying the Social Fabric of Our Planet." *Atlantic Monthly*, February 1, 1994, 44–76.

Karagiannis, Emmanuel. "Making New Friends: Explaining Greek Radical Left's Political Support for Middle Eastern Islamists." *Dynamics of Asymmetric Conflict* 5, no. 3 (2012): 183–195.

———. "When the Green Gets Greener: Political Islam's Newly Found Environmentalism." *Small Wars and Insurgencies* 25, no. 5 (November 2014): 181–201.

Karsh, Efraim. *Islamic Imperialism: A History*. New Haven, Conn.: Yale University Press, 2006.

Kepel, Gilles. *Allah in the West: Islamic Movements in America and Europe*. Stanford, Calif.: Stanford University Press, 1997.

———. *Jihad: The Trail of Political Islam*. London: I. B. Tauris, 2006.

Kepel, Gilles and Jean-Pierre Milelli. *Al Qaeda in Its Own Words*. Cambridge, Mass.: Harvard University Press, 2008.

Khatib, Lina, Dina Matar, and Atef Alshaer. *The Hizbullah Phenomenon: Politics and Communication.* Oxford: Oxford University Press, 2014.

Khomeini, Imam. *Islam and Revolution: Writings and Declarations of Imam Khomeini.* Berkeley: Mizan Press, 1981.

Khosrokhavar, Farhad. *The New Arab Revolutions That Shook the World.* London: Paradigm, 2012.

———. *Suicide Bombers: Allah's New Martyrs.* London: Pluto Press, 2002.

Kinnvall, Catarina. "Globalization and Religious Nationalism: Self, Identity, and the Search for Ontological Security." *Political Psychology* 25, no. 5 (2004): 741–763.

Knysh, Alexander. *Islamic Mysticism: A Short History.* Boston: Brill, 2000.

Kohlmann, Evan F. *Al Qaida's Jihad in Europe: The Afghan-Bosnian Network.* London: Berg, 2004.

Kose, Ali. *Conversion to Islam: A Study of Native British Converts.* London: Kegan Paul International, 1996.

Kraidy, Marwan. "The Local, the Global, and the Hybrid: A Native Ethnography of Glocalization." *Critical Studies in Media Communication* 16, no. 4 (1999): 456–477.

Krammer, Michael S. *Hezbollah's Vision of the West.* Washington, D.C.: Washington Institute for Near East Policy, 1989.

Kurzman, Charles. *Liberal Islam.* Oxford: Oxford University Press, 1998.

Laurence, Jonathan and Justin Vaisse. *Integrating Islam: Political and Religious Challenges in Contemporary France.* Washington, D.C.: Brookings Institution Press, 2006.

Leaman, Olivier. "Is Globalization a Threat to Islam? Said Nursi's Response." In *Globalization, Ethics and Islam: The Case of Bediuzzaman Said Nursi*, ed. Ian Markham and Ibrahim Ozdemir, 121–126. London: Ashgate, 2005.

Lee, Alice Y. L. "Between the Global and the Local: The Glocalization of Online News Coverage on the Transregional Crisis of SARS." *Asian Journal of Communication* 15, no. 3 (2005): 255–273.

Lefèvre, Raphaël. *Ashes of Hama: The Muslim Brotherhood in Syria.* London: Hurst, 2013.

Lesch, David W. *Syria: The Fall of the House of Assad.* New Haven, Conn.: Yale University Press, 2012.

Levitt, Matthew and Dennis Ross. *Hamas: Politics, Charity, and Terrorism in the Service of Jihad.* New Haven, Conn.: Yale University Press, 2007.

Lewis, Bernard. *What Went Wrong? The Clash Between Islam and Modernity in the Middle East.* New York: HarperCollins, 2003.

Louer, Laurence. *Shiism and Politics in the Middle East.* London: Hurst, 2012.

———. *Transnational Shia Politics: Religious and Political Networks in the Gulf.* London: Hurst, 2008.

Lubeck, Paul M. "The Islamic Revival: Antinomies of Islamic Movements Under Globalization." In *Global Social Movements*, ed. Robin Cohen and Shirin M. Rai, 146–164. London: Athlone Press, 2000.

Malet, Davot. *Foreign Fighters: Transnational Identity in Civil Conflicts.* Oxford: Oxford University Press, 2013.

Mandaville, Peter. *Islam and Politics.* 2nd ed. London: Routledge, 2014.

———. *Transnational Muslim Politics: Reimagining the Umma.* London: Routledge, 2001.

Markowitz, Lawrence P. "How Master Frames Mislead: The Division and Eclipse of Nationalist Movements in Uzbekistan and Tajikistan." *Ethnic and Racial Studies* 32, no. 4 (May 2009): 716–738.

Matthiesen, Toby. *The Other Saudis: Shiism, Dissent and Sectarianism.* Cambridge: Cambridge University Press, 2014.

Mawdudi, Sayyid Abul A'la. *Islam Today.* London: UKIM Dawah Centre, no date.

McAdam, Doug. "Culture and Social Movements." In *New Social Movements: From Ideology to Identity,* ed. Enrique Larana, Hank Johnson, and Joseph R. Gusfield, 36–57. Philadelphia: Temple University Press, 1994.

McAdam, Doug, John D. McCarthy, and Mayer Zald, eds. *Comparative Perspectives on Social Movements.* Cambridge: Cambridge University Press, 1996.

Meijer, Roel, ed. *Global Salafism: Islam's New Religious Movement.* London: Hurst, 2009.

Members of Hizb ut-Tahrir in Britain. *The Method to Re-establish the Khilafah and Resume the Islamic Way of Life.* London: Al-Khilafah Publications, 2000.

Meulemanv, Johan. "South-East Islam and the Globalization Process." In *Islam in the Era of Globalization,* ed. Johan Meulemanv, 9–21. London: Routledge, 2002.

Milton-Edwards, Beverley and Stephen Farrell. *Hamas: The Islamic Residence Movement.* London: Polity Press, 2010.

Mitchell, Richard P. *The Society of the Muslim Brothers.* Oxford: Oxford University Press, 1969.

Moghadam, Valentine M. *Globalization and Social Movements: Islamism, Feminism and the Global Justice Movement,* New York: Rowman and Littlefield, 2013.

Moore, Cerwyn and Paul Tumelty. "Foreign Fighters and the Case of Chechnya: A Critical Assessment." *Studies in Conflict and Terrorism* 31, no. 5 (May 2008): 412–433.

Moyn, Samuel. *The Last Utopia: Human Rights in History.* Cambridge, Mass.: Harvard University Press, 2010.

Nabhani, Taqiuddin An. *Concepts of Hizb ut-Tahrir.* London: Al-Khilafah, no date.

———. *The Ruling System in Islam.* 5th ed. London: Al-Khilafah Publications, 1996.

Nakash, Yitzhak. *Reaching for Power: The Shi'a in the Modern Arab World.* Princeton, N.J.: Princeton University Press, 2006.

Netton, Richard. *A Popular Dictionary of Islam.* London: RoutledgeCurzon, 1997.

Noe, Nicholas. *Voice of Hezbollah: The Statements of Sayyed Hassan Nasrallah.* New York: Verso, 2007.

Noueihed, Lin and Alex Warren. *The Battle for the Arab Spring: Revolution, Counter-Revolution and the Making of a New Era.* New Haven, Conn.: Yale University Press, 2012.

Olesen, Thomas. "The Uses and Misuses of Globalization in the Study of Social Movements." *Social Movement Studies* 4, no. 1 (2005): 49–63.

Oliver, Pamela E., and Hank Johnson. "What a Good Idea! Ideologies and Frames in
Social Movement Research." In *Frames of Protest: Social Movements and the Fram-
ing Perspective*, ed. John A. Noakes and Hank Johnson, 185–204. Lanham, Md.:
Rowman and Littlefield, 2005.

Olzak, Susan. "Does Globalization Breed Ethnic Discontent?" *Journal of Conflict Resolution* 55, no. 1 (2011): 3–32.

Osman, Tarek. *Egypt on the Brink: From Nasser to the Muslim Brotherhood*. New
Haven, Conn.: Yale University Press, 2011.

Pankhurst, Reza. *Hizb Ut Tahrir: The Untold History of the Liberation Party*. London:
Hurst, 2016.

Poston, Larry. *Islamic Da'wah in the West: Muslim Missionary Activity and the Dynamics of Conversion of Islam*. Oxford: Oxford University Press, 1992.

Privratsky, Bruce. *Muslim Turkistan: Kazak Religion and Collective Memory*. London:
Routledge, 2001.

Qassem, Naim. *Hizb'allah: The Story from Within*. London: Saqi, 2005.

Rabil, Robert G. *Salafism in Lebanon: From Apoliticism to Transnational Jihadism*.
Washington D.C.: Georgetown University Press, 2014.

Ramadan, Tariq. *Western Muslims and the Future of Islam*. Oxford: Oxford University
Press, 2004.

Randal, Jonathan. *Osama: The Making of a Terrorist*. New York: Vintage Books, 2005.

Ranko, Annette. *The Muslim Brotherhood and Its Quest for Hegemony in Egypt*. Wiesbaden: Springer, 2015.

Rao, Shakuntala. "I Need an Indian Touch: Glocalization and Bollywood Films." *Journal of International and Intercultural Communications* 3, no. 1 (February 2010):
1–19.

Rasheed, Madawi al-. "The Local and the Global in Saudi Salafi-Jihadi Discourse." In
Global Salafism: Islam's New Islamic Movement, ed. Roel Meijer, 301–320. London:
Hurst, 2009.

Rashid, Ahmed. *Militant Islam, Oil and Fundamentalism in Central Asia*. 2nd ed. New
Haven, Conn.: Yale University Press, 2010.

Ritzer, George. *Globalization: A Basic Text*. London: Wiley-Blackwell, 2009.

Roald, Anne Sophie. *New Muslims in the European Context: The Experience of Scandinavian Converts*. Boston: Brill, 2004.

Robertson, Ronald. "Glocalization: Time-Space and Homogeneity-Heterogeneity." In
Readings in Globalization: Key Concepts and Major Debates, ed. George Ritzer and
Zeynep Atalay, 334–343. Oxford: Wiley-Blackwell, 2010.

———. "Situating Glocalization: A Relatively Autobiographical Intervention." In
*Global Themes and Local Variations in Organization and Management: Perspectives
on Glocalization*, ed. Gili S. Drori, Markus A. Hollerer, and Peter Walgenbach,
25–36. New York: Routledge, 2014.

Roudometof, Victor. "Glocalization, Space, and Modernity." *European Legacy* 8, no. 1 (2003): 37–60.

———. "Transnationalism, Cosmopolitanism and Glocalization." *Current Sociology* 53, no.1 (2005): 113–135.

Roy, Olivier. *The Failure of Political Islam.* Cambridge, Mass.: Harvard University Press, 1994.

———. *Globalized Islam: The Search for New Ummah.* New York: Columbia University Press, 2004.

———. "There Will Be No Islamist Revolution." *Journal of Democracy* 24, no. 1 (January 2013): 14–19.

Rubin, Barry, ed. *Islamic Political and Social Movements.* London: Routledge, 2013.

———. *The Muslim Brotherhood: The Organization and Policies of a Global Islamist Movement.* London: Palgrave Macmillan, 2010.

Ryan, Michael W. S. *Decoding Al-Qaeda's Strategy: The Deep Battle Against America.* New York: Columbia University Press, 2013.

Sachedina, Abdulaziz. "Political Islam and the Hegemony of Globalization: A Response to Peter Berger." *Hedgehog Review* 4, no. 2 (Summer 2002): 21–29.

Sageman, Marc. *Leaderless Jihad: Terror Networks in the Twenty-First Century.* Philadelphia: University of Pennsylvania Press, 2008.

Sassoon, Joseph. *Saddam Hussein's Ba'th Party: Inside an Authoritarian Regime.* Cambridge: Cambridge University Press, 2012.

Schimmel, Annemarie. *Mystical Dimensions of Islam.* Chapel Hill: University of North Carolina Press, 1975.

Scholte, Jan A. *Globalization: A Critical Introduction.* London: Macmillan, 2000.

Schwedler, Jillian. *Faith in Moderation: Islamist Parties in Jordan and Yemen.* New York: Cambridge University Press, 2007.

Seale, Patrick. *Asad of Syria: The Struggle for the Middle East.* Berkeley: University of California Press, 1988.

Shariati, Ali. *An Approach to the Understanding of Islam.* Houston: Free Islamic Literatures, 1980.

Silber, Mitchell D. *The Al Qaeda Factor: Plots Against the West.* Philadelphia: University of Pennsylvania Press, 2012.

Snow, David A. and Robert D. Benford. "Ideology, Frame Resonance, and Participant Mobilization." *International Social Movement Research* 1 (1988): 197–218.

———. "Master Frames and Cycles of Protest." In *Frontiers in Social Movement Theory,* ed. Aldon D. Morris and Carol McClurg Mueller, 133–155. New Haven, Conn.: Yale University Press, 1992.

Snow, David A., Sarah A. Soule, and Hanspeter Kriesi, eds. *The Blackwell Companion to Social Movements.* Oxford: Blackwell, 2004.

Soroush, Abdolkarim. *Reason, Freedom, and Democracy in Islam.* Oxford: Oxford University Press, 2000.

Starr, Stephen. *Revolt in Syria: Eye-witness to the Uprising.* London: Hurst, 2012.

Stern, Jessica and J. M. Berger. *ISIS: The State of Terror.* London: William Collins, 2015.

Sutton, Philip W. and Stephen Vertigans. "Islamic 'New Social Movements'? Radical Islam, Al-Qaeda and Social Movement Theory." *Mobilization: An International Journal* 11 (2006): 101–115.

Swietochowski, Tadeusz. *Russian Azerbaijan, 1905–1920: The Shaping of a National Identity in a Muslim Community.* Cambridge: Cambridge University Press, 2004.

Tadros, Mariz. *The Muslim Brotherhood in Contemporary Egypt: Democracy Redefined or Confined?* London: Routledge, 2012.

Taji-Farouki, Suha. *A Fundamental Quest: Hizb ut-Tahrir and the Search for the Islamic Caliphate.* London: Grey Seal, 1996.

Tarrow, Sidney. *Power in Movement: Social Movements and Contentious Politics.* Cambridge: Cambridge University Press, 1998.

Thornton, William H. "Mapping the 'Glocal' Village: The Political Limits of Glocalization." *Continuum: Journal of Media and Cultural Studies* 14, no. 1 (2000): 79–89.

Tibi, Bassam. *Political Islam, World Politics and Europe: From Jihadist to Institutional Islamism.* London: Routledge, 2014.

Tilly, Charles. *Social Movements, 1768–2004.* London: Paradigm, 2004.

Tomlinson, John. *Globalization and Culture.* Cambridge: Polity Press, 2000.

Tomsen, Peter. *The Wars of Afghanistan: Messianic Terrorism, Tribal Conflicts, and the Failures of Great Powers.* New York: Public Affairs, 2011.

Trimingham, Spencer J. *Islam in Ethiopia.* London: Routledge, 1965.

Unal, Ali, and Alphonse Williams, eds. *Fethullah Gülen: Advocate of Dialogue.* Fairfax, Va.: The Fountain, 2000.

Varisco, Daniel M. "Mitigating Misrepresentation." In *Islamism: Contested Perspectives on Political Islam*, ed. Richard C. Martin and Abbas Barzegar, 125–132. Stanford, Calif.: Stanford University Press, 2010.

Volpi, Frederic, ed. *Political Islam: A Critical Reader.* London: Routledge, 2011.

Wasserman, Herman and Rao Shakuntala. "The Glocalization of Journalism Ethics." *Journalism* 9, no. 2 (2008): 163–181.

Weiss, Michael and Hassan Hassan. *ISIS: Inside the Army of Terror.* New York: Regan Arts, 2015.

Wickham, Carrie Rosefsky. *Mobilizing Islam: Religion, Activism, and Political Change in Egypt.* New York: Columbia University Press, 2002.

———. *The Muslim Brotherhood: Evolution of an Islamist Movement.* Princeton, N.J.: Princeton University Press, 2013.

Wiktorowicz, Quintan, ed. *Islamic Activism: A Social Movement Theory Approach.* Bloomington: Indiana University Press, 2004.

Williams, Brian Glyn. "On the Trail of the 'Lions of Islam': Foreign Fighters in Afghanistan and Pakistan 1980–2010." *Orbis* 55, no. 2 (Spring 2011): 216–239.

Willis, Michael. *The Islamist Challenge in Algeria: A Political History.* New York: New York University Press, 1999.

Yavuz, Hakan, *Islamic Political Identity in Turkey.* New York: Oxford University Press, 2003.

———. *Toward an Islamic Enlightenment: The Gülen Movement.* New York: Oxford University Press, 2013.

Zachs, Fruma. "Cross-Glocalization: Syrian Women Immigrants and the Founding of Women's Magazines in Egypt." *Middle Eastern Studies* 50, no. 3 (2014): 353–369.

Zahab, Mariam Abou and Olivier Roy. *Islamist Networks: The Afghan-Pakistan Connection.* New York: Columbia University Press, 2006.

Index

Acknowledgments

This project has evolved over a long period of time. My job in the Department of Defence Studies at King's College London has allowed me to travel around the Middle East. Thus, some of the research and writing took place in Doha, Manama, and Abu Dhabi. Also, my research was greatly facilitated by hospitality provided by the London School of Economics' European Institute, the Department of Political Science of Luiss Guido Carli University, Moscow State Institute of International Relations, the University of Maryland's START Center, the University of Macedonia's Department of Balkan, Slavic and Oriental Studies at Thessaloniki, and the University of Cyprus's Department of Social Sciences and Political Sciences.

I am indebted to many colleagues and friends who helped me to write this book. First, I wish to thank Clark McCauley and Don Ellis for their helpful comments on parts and drafts of the manuscript. I am particularly appreciative of extended discussions that I had with Carool Kersten, Jonathan Hill and Rod Thornton. Many other colleagues who shared their critical insights with me deserve special thanks, including Madawi al-Rasheed, Abdullah Baabood, Costas M. Constantinou, Donatella Della Porta, Rohan Gunaratna, Asteris Huliaras, Efraim Karsh, Gary LaFree, Raffaele Marchetti, Mohamed Nawab Mohamed Osman, Louis A. Ruprecht, Ibrahim Sharqieh, Panayiotis Tsakonas, Lorenzo Vidino and Sheikh Musa Admani. Additionally, I have benefited from many long conversations with convert-activists, members of Hizb ut-Tahrir, Salafi scholars and officials of the Muslim Brotherhood. I am grateful to my anonymous reviewers for their feedback, which helped improved the manuscript considerably. Also, I would like to thank my editor at the University of Pennsylvania Press, Peter Agree, for his constant support and encouragement for the project. The entire team at Penn Press has been most helpful. Besides, I would like to thank my undergraduate and postgraduate students in all countries and places I have taught over the years. Their feedback and criticism have helped me shape my views on political Islam.

I am grateful for the critical discussion of a previous version of Chapter 4 that was presented at the British Association of Islamic Studies on April 14, 2014, in London. I would like to thank the publishers for granting me permission to include parts of the article "European Converts to Islam: Mechanisms of Radicalization," *Politics, Religion and Ideology* 13, no. 1 (2012), in Chapter 1.

Thanks, as always, go to my parents, Chrysa Afedaki and Stelios Karagiannis, for their love and support. Their encouragement has been an asset throughout my life. Finally, I would like to make a special note of thanks to the inhabitants of Nea Smyrni (a suburb of South Athens established during the 1920s by Greek refugees from Izmir), where I was raised. I learned from them to be proud of my cultural heritage, but also to be tolerant and respectful of other faiths. Their democratic ethos and openness have inspired me both as a citizen and a scholar. Being a descendant of Istanbul Greeks, an ethnoreligious minority that was heavily persecuted, I have always felt the need to understand the Muslim Other. This book is my intellectual journey toward trying to comprehend and learn the complexities of political Islam that has been misunderstood as being a monolithic and unchanging movement.